D1139590

DEVELOPMENTAL PSYCHOLOGY
THE INFANT AND YOUNG CHILD

THE DORSEY SERIES IN PSYCHOLOGY

Consulting Editor   *Gerald C. Davison*
State University of New York
at Stony Brook

DEVELOPMENTAL PSYCHOLOGY

THE INFANT AND YOUNG CHILD

Hiram E. Fitzgerald
Ellen A. Strommen
John Paul McKinney
all of the
Department of Psychology
Michigan State University

1977

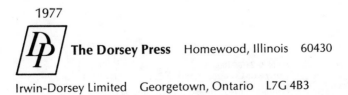 **The Dorsey Press**   Homewood, Illinois   60430

Irwin-Dorsey Limited   Georgetown, Ontario   L7G 4B3

© THE DORSEY PRESS, 1977

All rights reserved. No part of this publication may be
reproduced, stored in a retrieval system, or transmitted,
in any form or by any means, electronic, mechanical,
photocopying, recording, or otherwise, without the prior
written permission of the publisher.

First Printing, February 1977

ISBN 0-256-01888-X
Library of Congress Catalog Card No. 76–22254
Printed in the United States of America

PREFACE TO DEVELOPMENTAL PSYCHOLOGY

During the past several years the amount of research being devoted to issues of human development has hit an all time high. Several new journals have been founded, new centers for research have been established, and the percentage of psychologists devoting their energies to developmental research has increased. With this in mind the authors of this three-volume series have felt that a new sort of text could better serve the needs of the beginning student who is interested in human development but overwhelmed with the sheer volume of data and the requirement to sift the wheat from the chaff.

Thus the three volume format. The first volume covers infancy and early childhood; the second deals with middle childhood, and the third with adolescence and young adulthood. We have tried to be selective in our coverage of each area, and to include the best of the recent work without ignoring earlier research which has now become classic. However, careful selection always implies a compromise. In that sense, these volumes constitute more an introduction to the literature than an exhaustive treatment. We hope the beginning student will find here a challenging overview and an invitation to pursue an area that the three of us have found exciting and rewarding. The advanced student will, we hope, be able to use this series as a guide to a reading of the original studies in each area, an absolute necessity for the serious student who wants to understand children and their development.

Finally, and most importantly, our major emphasis has been on the child. We hope that the reader who shares that orientation will find these volumes informative and useful.

January 1977

Hiram E. Fitzgerald
Ellen A. Strommen
John Paul McKinney

PREFACE TO
THE INFANT AND YOUNG CHILD

Infancy and early childhood is a time of rapid change. They are truly the formative years as so often described in popular literature. For example, contrast the newborn infant, so limited in its abilities, with the active, inquisitive, exploring four-year old. And yet, today we know that even the newborn infant has abilities that far exceed our previous notions of what the newborn was able to do. For many children, infancy and early childhood is a time when a trusting relationship is developed with loving caregivers. For others, it is a time when events seriously interfere with the opportunity to develop a feeling of security and competence to deal effectively with the world. But infancy and early childhood is not just a time of change for the young child. It is also a time of change for parents and other family members. Indeed, adding a baby to the family unit brings parents perhaps the greatest set of responsibilities they may encounter in their lifetimes.

Some contemporary writers have concluded that personality development, for all practical matters, is essentially completed by age three. While we believe that the events of the first three years of life provide a foundation for subsequent development, we do not share the view that infancy and early childhood determines all subsequent development. Much happens to the individual during middle childhood, adolescence, adulthood, and aging, and the events during each of these periods can have dramatic consequences for the individual.

We have attempted in this volume to introduce the events that shape the foundation upon which subsequent development is built, the changes that occur in the infant and young child, the changes that occur in caregivers, and the ways in which children and caregivers influence one another during early socialization. We hope that you will share just a bit of our excitement and awe for these first few remarkable years of human life. We also hope that you will gain a deeper appreciation for the responsibilities that accrue to anyone who wishes to provide an optimal environment for the growth and development of infants and young children.

And now some personal notes. Yvonne Brackbill introduced me to the topic of infancy and early childhood during my graduate years at the University of Denver. Her committment to the scientific study of human development has been a constant exemplary model. Many students have offered their thoughtful criticisms of my views concerning the events of infancy and early childhood. I look forward to continued discussions with each of them. Carolyn Kent Rovee, Paul Spear, Thomas Achenbach, and Eric Gelber provided superb critiques of previous drafts of the manuscript. I am indebted to each of them. Somehow, Nora Menard and Sherry Lott kept their typewriters from overheating through the many drafts of the text. Veronica Wauby conscientiously assisted with library research, as did Dolores Fitzgerald and Katherine Hildebrandt with proof reading.

Writing a book is not an easy task and it requires sacrifice both from the writer and from those close to him personally. To my wife Dolores and to our children, Steven, Stephanie, and Katherine, whom we have seen graduate from infancy and early childhood: *Hvala za vaše strpljenje razumevanje.*

January 1977   **Hiram E. Fitzgerald**

CONTENTS

PART FOUR   THE ORGANIZATION OF SOCIAL BEHAVIOR

PART ONE

Historical introduction

BOX 1–1
Study questions

What is developmental psychology, and who is considered to be its founder?

What does the developmental psychologist mean by the terms *system, organization,* and *adaptation?*

What were some important historical influences on the emergence of developmental psychology as a formal subdiscipline of psychology?

What is meant by "the epigenetic concept of development"?

How do developmental psychologists view the relative influences of biology and environment on the developing individual?

What is meant by the phrase "the active infant"?

What is a "critical period" of development?

What are the differences between longitudinal and cross-sectional research designs?

What are normative, correlational, and experimental research methods?

What special problems are associated with observational research methods?

What special problems are associated with infant research?

1

DEVELOPMENTAL PSYCHOLOGY

Historically, psychology was first defined as the study of the *soul,* then as the study of the *mind,* or consciousness, and finally as the study of *behavior.* Today, most definitions of psychology refer either to behavior or mental processes, or perhaps to both. Most students of the history of psychology point to 1879 as the "birth date" of modern psychology, for in that year Wilhelm Wundt established the first laboratory for psychological research at the University of Leipzig, in Germany. The first "psychologists," including Wundt, were not trained in academic psychology but in philosophy, physiology, biology, astronomy, mathematics, medicine, and theology. Psychology drew content, method, and theory from each of these disciplines, but it was especially the cohesion of elements within philosophy, physics, and physiology that gave substance to psychology as a distinct formal discipline.

While psychology was establishing roots as a formal discipline, areas of specialization within psychology were also taking root. One of these areas, first known as *genetic psychology,* was the immediate forerunner of contemporary developmental psychology. Most of the first developmental psychologists crossed Wundt's path at one time or another and were trained in scientific psychology. But it was the revolutionary event in biology, the theory of evolution, which more directly set the stage for the emergence of developmental psychology.

What is contemporary developmental psychology? It is a specialization within general psychology concerned with *changes in the organization of behavior* throughout the life span. To better understand what this definition implies, it is useful to consider three historical-contemporary characteristics of developmental psychology. These characteristics involve the relationships between developmental psychology and biology, theory, and scientific methodology. We will consider each of these relationships in sequence.

DEVELOPMENTAL PSYCHOLOGY AND BIOLOGY

System and organization

A baby is a system; an adult is a system. In fact, in a very real sense, both the adult and the baby are supersystems, composed of many interrelated systems. At the very least, the human being is a composite of anatomical, biochemical, neurophysiological, motor, perceptual, cognitive, learning, linguistic, and social systems.

A system is a whole, a complete thing. A system is made up of parts which are related to one another as well as to the whole. A system is a whole that functions as a whole because of the interdependence of its parts. Moreover, the whole is not reducible to its parts. This does not mean that study of the parts is fruitless. Nothing could be further from the truth. Holism only asserts that the parts cannot be added together to equal the whole. The very process of integration gives the whole properties which are generated by the integrated or organized system itself.

Systems become organized. *Organization* refers to the degree to which the parts of a system are interdependent. Organization implies a hierarchy or orderliness of development. Thus, we may speak of levels of organization whereby higher levels can control lower levels, which in turn can influence higher levels only in the sense of providing the underlying substrate necessary for higher-level organization (Scott, Stewart, & De Ghett, 1974). For example, socialization can control the organization of growth processes, whereas growth influences socialization only in providing the organism with the basic capabilities for the organization of social relations.

How do systems become organized? They are created from originally unorganized material as the organism adapts to its environment. As a system becomes more highly organized it becomes more stable and predictable. But the environment is neither always predictable nor always stable. Thus, adaptation demands both flexibility and a changing or active environment. Thus, systemic organization requires a concept of development that is constructive—that emphasizes the active nature of organism and environment.

Concepts of development

Nearly all concepts of development have originated in the biological sciences. One concept, *preformation* (advanced by Leibniz, 1646–1716) asserted that development was merely the unfolding of an already formed organism—often called a *homunculus*. The *ovulists* (for example, Schwammerdam, 1637–1723) thought that the homunculus was inside the ovum, that the sperm only initiated the unfolding process. The *animal cultists* (for example, van Leeuwenhoek, 1632–1723) placed the homunculus inside the sperm and thought that the ovum provided nourishment for the developing organism.

In 1758, a German zoologist, Wolff (1733–94), suggested an alternative explanation of development derived from his studies of the embryological development of chicks. Wolff argued against the idea that an organism is generated through the development of an already completed whole. He demonstrated that development was a process of continued new formation from originally unorganized material, through the differentiation of parts. Modifications in embryonic structure were caused by environmental events and by interactions among the parts of the differentiating organism. In effect, Wolff proposed that development was a process wherein each new level of organization was a reorganization of prior levels, not an additive sum of prior levels. This concept of development is known as *epigenesis*.

Psychobiology

Psychobiology is a way of thinking about organisms as both biological and psychological. To be sure, the task of analyzing the interaction of behavioral and biological functions is not an easy one. At each level of development the organism's behavioral capabilities expand and the organism engages the environment in progressively more complex ways. In turn, environmental events exert an increasing influence on the developing organism as it becomes increasingly capable of moving about freely in its environment.

Thus, a goal of developmental psychology stemming from the psychobiological point of view is to understand how behavioral and biological systems become organized during the process of adaptation to the environment. If one thinks of development as the emergence of a variety of interdependent systems, all of which are simultaneously part of a complex, whole individual, then several questions assume paramount importance. How do individual systems develop? How do they become interdependent? How does organization or disorganization of one system affect organization or disorganization of other systems or of the whole? How do organisms adapt to their environments? What processes regulate the organization of behavior?

Critical periods Are there particular times during the life span when conditions are more or less ideal for the organization of a behavioral system? Although the evidence is not complete, it suggests that such periods do exist. Periods when the organization of behavior is most easily affected by environmental events are generally called *critical periods* (and are sometimes referred to as *sensitive* or *optimal periods*) (Scott et al., 1974).

Some examples of critical periods are well known. During the first trimester of pregnancy, when the physical growth of the fetus is rapid, the fetus is highly susceptible to damage from a number of environmental events, such as maternal disease, drugs, and radiation. Human brain growth is most rapid from the third trimester of pregnancy to the second postnatal year. Malnutrition during this period can seriously impair the organization of behavior. Moreover, there appear to be critical periods for the organization of infant social attachments, certain cognitive and emotional behaviors, and language skills. The critical period for language is roughly the first 13 years of life (until puberty). If organization is interfered with past this age, as for example, in the disorder aphasia, rehabilitation is extremely difficult. If aphasia occurs prior to age 13, however, rehabilitation is comparatively easy to accomplish.

At least three kinds of critical periods are defined by the rate of organization of a particular process (Scott et al., 1974). When a behavior system is organized completely in a relatively short period of time, the critical period has rather precisely defined onset and offset values. In human beings, few, if any, organizational processes occur so quickly. For other critical periods the rate of organization builds up, peaks, and then gradually levels off. An example would be the organization of the social attachment between infant and caregiver. Finally, organization may be intermittent, with alternate periods of slow and rapid change, as, for example, is characteristic of learning processes. In other words, there may be times during which some things are learned more readily than others. Stage theories of development also fit this model of critical periods. For example, each of Erikson's stages of psychosocial development presents a conflict which must be resolved before the next stage can be successfully organized. Thus, each stage is of critical importance to the organization of the personality.

As we shall see in the chapters to come, the study of infants and young children has suggested much of the evidence for critical periods in human development. We have yet to determine, however, the boundaries of human critical periods or the extent to which interference with behavioral organization during a critical period has long-term effects on the developing organism.

DEVELOPMENTAL PSYCHOLOGY AND THEORY

Genetic psychology

G. Stanley Hall (1844–1924) deserves the title "father of developmental psychology." Hall founded the first scientific journal in developmental psychology, *Pedagogical Seminary* (1893), later renamed *The Journal of Genetic Psychology* (1927). He brought the questionnaire method to American psychology and with his students developed over a hundred questionnaires covering a wide range of topics on childhood and old age. Prominent students of Hall included H. H. Goddard (work with retardates), L. M. Terman (intelligence testing), and Arnold Gesell (motor and mental development).

In his most important work, *Adolescence: Its Psychology, and Its Relations to Physiology, Anthropology, Sociology, Sex, Crime, Religion, and Education* (1904), Hall advanced the theory that "ontogeny recapitulates phylogeny." In other words, Hall suggested that the development of the

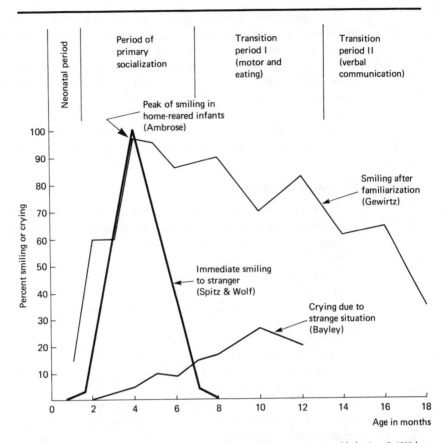

Source: Reprinted from J. P. Scott, *Early experience and the organization of behavior.* © 1968 by the Wadsworth Publishing Company, Inc. Reprinted with permission of the author and Brooks/Cole Publishing Co. (Monterey, Calif.: 1968).

FIGURE 1–1 Smiling and crying in human infants in relation to periods of development. The peak of the smiling response to a strange face occurs at about four months and is characteristic of the period of primary socialization, during which the first social attachments are formed.

individual (ontogenesis) repeated the various phases in the evolution of the species (phylogenesis). He thought that the prenatal period reflected the aquatic phase of human evolution. Infancy (0–4 years) recapitulated the animal phase. Hall likened the newborn's involuntary grasp reflex to that of the nonhuman primate. Childhood (4–8 years) reflected humankind's hunting and fishing cultures. Youth (8–12 years) repeated the savage or primitive periods in cultural development, and Hall thought that at that age children were especially sensitive to drill, discipline, and training. Adolescence (12–25 years) repeated the 18th century's idealism, revolt against the old, passion and emotionality, and commitment to goals. In late adolescence, the individual repeated the beginnings of present-day civilization.

Hall's recapitulation theory went beyond the implications of evolutionary theory in its view of adaptation as more or less completely governed by internal organismic factors rather than as a process involving organism-environment interaction. In any event, his theory resulted in a strong maturational orientation among early developmental psychologists and some contemporary developmental psychologists. Hall's advice to parents also strongly reflected the maturation view. He advised parents to tolerate their children's socially unacceptable behavior, for, after all, these children were merely repeating the various stages of the species' evolutionary development.

Psychoanalytic theory

The first systematic theory of personality was advanced by Sigmund Freud (1856–1939). The impact of Freudian theory on Western culture has been so great that few people are unfamiliar with Freud's name. Freud was a physician and neurologist by training, and it was his work in neurology that drew him closer and closer to the formulation of psychoanalysis as a therapeutic method. The psychoanalytic theory of personality development, in turn, was a direct outgrowth of the application of psychoanalytic therapy.

Freud's theory stimulated considerable controversy over such topics as the role of instincts in human behavior, the structure of the mind, the function of conscious and unconscious processes, the stage sequencing of personality, and the various intricate relationships between parent and child that Freud thought determined the individual's personality. Freud's theory of personality development is a stage-sequence theory. Within each stage the individual must resolve a developmental conflict. If the conflict is not resolved, the individual can become *fixated* at a particular stage. Freud believed that certain adult personality types reflected such fixations.

Psychosexual stages Psychoanalytic theory divides the *oral stage* (roughly 0–2 years) into two periods: *oral-passive* and *oral-sadistic*. During early infancy *libidinal energy* (an innate motive force) is directed to the infant's mouth and upper digestive system. Mother becomes the primary gratification object in that she provides nourishment through breast or bottle. When *weaning* to cup begins, the infant is faced with a conflict, in that the primary source of gratification must be given up. Fixation during the oral stage may produce the *oral-passive character*, a person who is dependent and demanding, or the *oral-sadistic character*, a person who is sarcastic, independent, aggressive, and hostile.

The *anal stage* corresponds roughly to the toddler years of development. At that stage libidinal energy is directed to the anal region, as the toddler begins to achieve self-control of bowel and bladder. Toilet training practices provide the basis of conflict. According to psychoanalytic theory, fixation at the anal stage produces either the *anal-retentive* or the *anal-aggressive character*. Anal-retentive personalities are overly concerned with orderliness, are suspicious and rigid, and engage in a variety of obsessive-compulsive patterns of behavior. Anal-aggressive personalities go the other way—messiness, indifference to routine, and personal sloppiness are their hallmarks.

The *phallic stage* roughly covers the years from three to five. During those years the source of libidinal energy shifts from the anal region to the genital region. The developmental conflict is one of making an identification with the appropriate same-sex adult. This conflict is often referred to as the *Oedipus complex* for boys and the *Electra complex* for girls. Initially, both boys and girls become attached to mother. However, this attachment places the young male in direct rivalry with his more powerful father for his mother's attention. The young male develops *castration anxiety,* or the fear that his father will injure his penis if active competition for his mother is pursued. The conflict is resolved when the young male represses (moves into the unconscious) his sexual feelings toward his mother and his feelings of rivalry toward his father. Simultaneously, he identifies with his father, internalizing his father's behaviors, attitudes, and values.

Since the young female obviously does not have a penis she cannot fear castration, but the very fact that she has no penis leads her to desire one. Since mother also has no penis, the young female becomes caught between her desire for her mother's love and her desire for her father's penis. In either case, for boys and for girls, resolution of the complex has two key results. First, it initiates and largely completes the process of identification with the same-sex parent. Second, it gives rise to the *superego,* which consists of the conscience and the ego ideal.

A major function of the superego, as a structure of the personality, is to restrict the free expression of id impulses. The *id,* present from birth, is the source of motivational energy. It operates according to the *pleasure principle,* seeking immediate gratification of needs. The third component structure of the personality, the *ego,* acts as a mediator between the id and the superego. The ego operates according to the *reality principle.* Following the phallic stage, a period of *latency* sets in, which, after puberty, is replaced by the *genital stage* of mature sexuality.

What did Freudian theory contribute to developmental psychology? It was the first systematic theory of personality development and the first major theory to attribute special importance to the early years of human development. Moreover, as we shall see, it stimulated a major effort to reconcile two opposing theoretical traditions, behaviorism and psychoanalytic theory. Perhaps the most serious weakness of Freudian theory is that it fails to embrace the *principle of refutation*—in other words, psychoanalytic theory is not sensitive to empirical data which may work against the basic assumptions of the theory or against predictions that can be derived from the theory. In addition, Freudian theory did not place adequate emphasis on ego functions or take adequate account of social and cultural influences on personality development. Efforts to blend the psychosexual stages of development into the social and cultural contexts are characteristic of contemporary psychoanalytic theorists, notably Erik Erikson.

Erik Erikson   Whereas Freud stressed the biological determinants of personality and the functions of id and superego, Erikson stresses personality development in light of the individual's historical and cultural past. Moreover, Erikson is primarily concerned with the development of ego functions.

For Erikson, personality is not fixed or final, it is constantly subject to change. Erikson uses the Freudian term *libidinal energy* to refer to the regulatory force which drives epigenetic development. He believes that personality organization occurs in a sequence of stages, his "eight stages of man." Each stage poses a conflict which must be resolved before one can advance to the next stage. Each stage is a turning point or choice point in the organization of personality. Central to infancy and early childhood is the infant's need to develop a sense of trust in its environment. This sense of trust prepares the individual to enter into autonomous and self-initiated behavior.

We will return to Erikson's theory in Chapter 10. For the moment, however, let us note that there are already signs that Erikson's "psychosocial" theory of personality is more easily tested by direct experimentation than Freud's theory has proven to be.

Functionalism

Wundt defined psychology as the study of conscious experience, and developed the method of *introspection* to investigate the elements of the mind. He believed that descriptions of immediate experience would provide data for the analysis of mental elements. From these elements the rules or laws which integrate the elements could be discovered. This approach in psychology came to be known as *structuralism*. Since each element introspected from any one experience was thought to be a sensation (redness, roundness, softness, emptiness, and so on), the structuralist was faced with the task of identifying a nearly infinite number of mental elements.

Functionalism was a direct reaction against the structuralist approach. In the United States, functionalism emerged largely through the efforts of William James (1842–1910) and John Dewey (1859–1952). The central theme of functionalism was that mental processes and behavior were mechanisms used by the organism to adapt to its environment. Some functionalists emphasized mental processes and behavior as inseparable aspects of adaptation, viewing both organism and environment as active. For these functionalists, adaptation was an active process, an active organism in interaction with an active environment. Other functionalists took a different view of adaptation. Led by John Watson, a radical functionalism emerged which rejected the study of consciousness and defined psychology exclusively as the science of behavior.

Behaviorism   Watson's behaviorism took stimulus-response associationism as its basic model and stressed the environmental determinants of behavior. Watson accepted Locke's empiricist dictum that at birth the mind is a tabula rasa (blank slate), entirely dependent upon the environment for its contents. In this view the organism was a passive object that was shaped more or less completely by the environment.

Watson went beyond his facts, especially in his rejection of the "mainstream" functionalist view that the organism is an active agent in the adaptation process. Distinctions are still made between active and passive views of behavioral organization. Those who stress the active nature of the organism are said to favor *organismic* interpretations of behavioral development, whereas those who stress the passive nature of the organism are said to favor *mechanistic* interpretations. It is possible that neither extreme position is absolutely correct. Rather than view active and passive as irreconcilable positions, perhaps we should apply them as explanatory models when suggested by the particular developmental phenomena being investigated.

BOX 1–2
Contrasting views of human nature or models of development

Mechanistic view	*Organismic view*
Passive organism	Active organism
Basic metaphor: machine	Basic metaphor: Living organism
Elementaristic: the whole is predictable from its parts	Holistic: Each part derives meaning from the whole
Mechanistic	Teleological (purposive)
Behavioral change: Determined by efficient and material causes	Behavioral change: Structures and functions change during development (epigenetic)
Antecedent-consequent: Cause and effect	Structure-function reciprocity
Continuous: Present behavior is predictable from earlier behavior in an additive sense	Discontinuous: Changes in the parts or in the organization of the parts result in a whole with new systemic properties; new properties are emergent in the sense that they cannot be predicted from the sum of the parts
Causation: Material, efficient	Causation: Material, efficient, final, formal
Unidirectional	Reciprocal, interactive

Source: Adapted from Reese and Overton (1970); Overton and Reese (1973), with permission of the authors and Academic Press, Inc., New York and London.

How did Watson influence developmental psychology? His book on the care of infants and children marked the first attempt to transpose the results of experimental research to child-rearing practices (Watson, 1928). In so doing, he stimulated the emerging belief that the behavior of children and their parents could be studied by experimental methods. The central theme of Watson's behaviorism—that behavior could be shaped by effective and efficient control of the environment—encouraged the view that child rearing was a unidirectional process, from parent to child. This view became a key assumption of social learning theory, which arose as an attempt to reconcile psychoanalytic theory with general learning theory.

Social learning theory   Social learning theory has had many spokesmen, including Bandura and Walters (1963), Bijou and Baer (1961), and Whiting and Child (1953). However, Robert Sears (e.g., Sears & Dollard, 1941; Sears, Maccoby, & Levin, 1957) deserves special mention for stimulating the empirical study of concepts taken from psychoanalytic theory. Social learning theory begins with the assumption that all behavior is learned. Behavior acquisition as viewed by social learning theory can be compared to a chain in which each new behavior is linked to an old behavior. Development is seen as a continuous process but also as an additive process, in which the whole equals the sum of its parts. Moreover, social learning theory sees early social behavior and personality as learned primarily through child-rearing practices. Working under the assumption that socialization of the child was primarily a one-way process from parent to child, social learning theory regarded the mother-child dyad as the primary unit of behavior to be studied. (Only recently has father's role in child rearing become an actively studied topic.)

Contiguity is seen as one important determinant of learning. Contiguity refers to a temporal relationship between stimulus events. When two different stimuli occur closely together in time, the response to one stimulus is gradually associated with the other stimulus. When the association is sufficiently strong, both stimuli are capable of producing the response. *Reinforcement* is seen as another important determinant of learning. Reinforcement refers to a change in the probability of a behavior's occurrence as a function of a stimulus event which follows that behavior. (See Chapter 6 for more discussion of these learning processes.)

However, social learning theory has not been just a theory of learning. It has been an explicit attempt to apply learning theory and experimental methods of research to the study of the social behaviors and personality characteristics that, according to psychoanalytic theory, arise from the parent-child relationship. Thus, social learning theorists set out to experimentally investigate such topics as the development of aggression; the effects of conflict, punishment, and other aspects of child-rearing practices on the child's social behavior and personality; and the specific child-rearing practices that were thought to be important in learning sex-role identification.

Social learning theorists insisted that psychoanalytic concepts be defined behaviorally. For example, these theorists defined *dependency* by a number of behaviors, including physical contact and seeking help, approval, or attention. They suggested that the child's psychological dependency on its mother arose from its initial biological dependency on her. Mother was seen as instrumental in reducing tension in the infant by providing *primary reinforcement* in the form of food, comfort, and protection from harm. In the process of fulfilling these needs, mother became associated—through contiguity—with primary reinforcers. In other words, she acquired *secondary reinforcement* value, so that her social behavior or her mere presence would reinforce and maintain the child's behavior. The strengthening or weakening of dependent behaviors could be examined by studying the methods used by parents to reinforce their children's behavior.

But social learning theory does not represent a simple extension of Watsonian behaviorism. In fact, almost from its beginning, social learning theory rejected Watson's extreme mechanistic view. This is perhaps best illustrated by the social learning approach to the study of identification. Identification with the appropriate sex-role model was not thought to come about by direct parental teaching. Rather, much of identification was learned vicariously by observing the behavior of others. Such learning requires an active organism, one capable of evaluating the behavior of others in reference to itself.

Social learning theory stimulated an intense study of child development and child-rearing practices. It encouraged the idea that parents could be taught to become more effective child-rearers and that knowledge of child development could be attained through rigorous methods of study. Perhaps its most serious error was in viewing socialization of the child as a one-way process, thereby neglecting the child's ability to elicit and maintain social behavior in adults. As we shall see in Chapters 9 and 10, many developmental theorists now view socialization as a reciprocal process in which parents and children influence one another, although not necessarily equally.

Genetic epistemology

Jean Piaget (1896–   ) has spent over 50 years studying the development of intelligence. Piaget often refers to his approach as *genetic epistemology*, which means the development of ways of knowing the external world. According to Piaget, two functions characterize all living organisms —*organization* and *adaptation*. Intellectual development consists of progressive, sequential changes in the structure of organization. Cognitive systems or structures change through adaptation. Adaptation is composed of two invariant processes—*assimilation* and *accommodation*. When the child applies existing cognitive structures to new information, the structures must change to accommodate the new information. At the same time, the new information is assimilated or incorporated into the existing cognitive structures. Assimilation and accommodation elicit changes in cognitive structures enabling the individual to cope better with its changing environment. Assimilation and accommodation underlie all adaptations of structure and maintain a state of *equilibrium*. Whenever a state of disequilibrium exists, intellectual growth takes place *if* the child is able to recognize the contradiction or discrepancy between what its cognitive structures are able to handle and what the new situation demands.

Piaget believes that changes in intelligence occur in sequence. Each period depends on the previous period, so that the development of intelligence is characterized by an invariant sequence. Thus, Piaget is interested in a description of mental development, a natural history of when the child is capable of performing certain cognitive operations. The periods are: *sensorimotor* (birth to 18–24 months); *preoperational* (2 to 5–7 years); *concrete operations* (6 to 11–12 years); and *formal operations* (from 12–13 years on). Piaget also proposes various *stage-sequences* which characterize cognitive development within the major periods. One such stage-sequence describes the development of *causality,* or the ability to reconstruct a cause given knowledge of the effect (see Table 1–1).

TABLE 1–1

Piaget's stage-sequence describing the origins of causality during the sensorimotor period of intelligence

Stage one: Global causality. From the first few weeks of life to around four months of age, the infant interprets the world egocentrically. It makes no distinction between self and nonself, and does not recognize that objects out of sight have permanent existence.

Stage two: Feelings of efficacy. From about five to seven months of age, the infant develops simple reflex habits in which images and sounds are associated, as in feeding. But it does not yet anticipate one stimulus from the presence of another. It functions entirely in terms of immediately present stimulation. None other exists for it. The infant's sense of causality is one of diffuse feelings of efficacy when some effort is accidentally perceived to bring about some desired effect.

Stage three: Magico-phenomenalistic causality. At around eight or nine months of age, the infant begins to externalize and spatialize causality, but always in terms of self-action. The infant discovers that one may intend to bring about an effect, but fails to grasp that physical or spatial contact between the cause and the effect are necessary. Thus, the infant operates magically on the surroundings to bring about phenomenal or naively perceived effects that happen to be contiguously connected to self-effort.

Stage four: Elementary externalization and objectification of causality. Roughly extending in time from 9 to 11 months of age, the fourth period sees the infant distinguishing between self and nonself obstacles to perception. The infant brushes aside the hand of another person who holds a desired object, thus evidencing comprehension of external causality. The infant's egocentricism is diminished.

Stage five: Real objectification and spatialization of causes. The toddler perceives that he or she is only one object in a world of objects, and that causes directly operate on objects to bring about effects. In this fifth stage, extending from approximately 12 to 15 months of age, the child perceives the external causation of effects correctly but does not know how to evoke them at will.

Stage six: Representative causality. At approximately 18 months to two years of age, the child is able to abstract reality. The child can reconstruct a cause from the presence of its effect. The use of language has developed, allowing the child to take into account stimuli that are not immediately present. Past experiences are now meaningful.

Source: Adapted and reprinted from C. F. Monte, *Psychology's scientific endeavor* (New York: Praeger, 1975), p. 27. With permission of Christopher F. Monte, © 1975 and Praeger Publishers, Inc.

What has Piaget's theory contributed to developmental psychology? Certainly, his theory of cognitive development stands out, both as an intriguing theory in itself and as a stimulant for an extraordinary amount of research. But perhaps more important Piaget has forced a reconceptualization of the process of development. His theory is functional in its emphasis on adaptation, structural in its emphasis on the organization of cognitive systems, and content-oriented in that it takes behavior as its basic data.

However, Piaget's theory is not complete. For example, it directs little attention to individual differences in cognitive development, especially to the different rates at which children progress through the various periods of cognitive development.

RESEARCH METHODS IN DEVELOPMENTAL PSYCHOLOGY

The developmental psychologist is interested both in events which have immediate consequences for the individual and in events which have long-term consequences. To meet these interests, developmental psychologists use a variety of research methods. Before a specific method is selected, however, the investigator must decide whether to focus on behaviors which accompany age changes within the same individuals over time or on behaviors which reflect age differences among individuals at given points in time. When the object of the study is to describe behavioral changes within the same individuals, the study is said to be *longitudinal*. When behavioral differences within a specific age group are being investigated, the study is said to be *cross-sectional*. Each of these approaches has advantages and disadvantages. Recently, methodologists have advocated a third approach, *modified longitudinal*, to deal with disadvantages inherent in the other two.

Longitudinal studies

Longitudinal studies have provided developmental psychology with some of the best information yet obtained regarding the stability or instability of intellectual skills, personality traits, skeletal growth, physical development, and language development.

The major advantage of the longitudinal approach is that it enables one to study changes in an individual's behavior over time, thereby gaining valuable information regarding the stability or instability of behavior. For example, do children who score high on intelligence tests during the preschool years also score high during late childhood and adolescence? Do children who show early language proficiency continue to show high competence in linguistic skills in later years? Do newborn infants who are highly active motorically become hyperactive preschoolers? Longitudinal designs are also best for evaluating the effects of early experience. Do different child-rearing environments have different long-term influences on behavior? Are different socio-economic levels related to different developmental histories?

Longitudinal studies involving long time periods, especially those covering several generations, have several disadvantages. They are expensive, both in economic terms and in terms of the time needed to find answers to problems which require more immediate solutions. Consider, for example, the current demand for day care for infants and toddlers. Although longitudinal studies of the effects of early group care of infants and toddlers are necessary, the demand for day care is now. Day-care staff must have curriculum programs, and parents of children in day care must be given some indication of the consequences of this particular type of supplemental child care.

Another disadvantage of the longitudinal approach is that frequent changeover in staff requires retraining and may produce a loss of valuable time for research or introduce discontinuity in data collection. Longitudinal studies must also grapple with the problem of repeated testing. Children given tests at three- or six-month intervals over a period of five or six years are more than likely to acquire the knack of test taking. This may result in improved performance as a result of test sophistication rather than of changes in the processes being tested. Finally, long-term longitudinal studies suffer from the loss of subjects through death, moving away from the locale of the study, or simple withdrawal from the study.

Cross-sectional studies

Most of the research literature generated by developmental psychologists is cross-sectional in design. Cross-sectional studies require less time and money than do longitudinal studies, and they produce information more or less immediately. Which of several educational programs best facilitates the development of reading skills in kindergarten children? How does infant day care affect the social-emotional attachment between parent and child? How do punishment and reasoning compare as techniques for eliminating temper tantrums? What is the best way to quiet a fussy baby? These are all questions that require more or less immediate answers, and the cross-sectional design is well suited for this purpose.

Although cross-sectional designs may give quicker answers to problems and be less costly in time and money than longitudinal studies, they have some disadvantages. For example, cross-sectional designs do not allow us to study behavioral changes in particular individuals, only behavioral differences among individuals. Suppose we were interested in the relationship between activity level and performance. Suppose, in addition, that one group of subjects were composed of newborns and another group were composed of seven-month-olds. If we found that activity level was correlated with performance in newborns but not in seven-month-olds we could draw appropriate conclusions concerning age differences in the behaviors studied. We could not, however, infer that there are changes in the relationship between activity level and performance during the first seven months of life for any individual infant. Why not? Because we have not studied the same infants at each age level. It just may be that when the newborns we have studied reach seven months of age, they will continue to show the relationship observed during the newborn period. Of course, they may not show such stable behavior. The point is that the cross-sectional design cannot give us information one way or the other about behavior change in a particular individual.

Modified longitudinal studies

In response to the disadvantages of both longitudinal and cross-sectional designs, developmental psychologists have turned to a design which incorporates features of both methods. In the example noted above, the newborn and seven-month-old infants represented groups of babies born at different times. One of these groups represented a sample of a larger population of all newborns, the other a sample of all seven-month-olds. Of course, this assumes that the babies were chosen randomly from the larger population. Each sample is called a *cohort*. Different cohorts, then, are groups born at different times. People born in 1940 might be different from those born in 1970 because the socio-cultural environments they were born into were different. Similarly, babies born in December might react differently to a given experimental task than might babies who were born in July.

One modified longitudinal method, called the *trifactorial model* (Schaie, 1965), allows the investigator to analyze behavior for changes in individuals over time, for differences between groups of individuals at the same age level, and for the time of testing. Using different cohorts and overlapping age levels greatly reduces the time required to gain information about the stability of individual behavior while simultaneously providing useful information regarding behavioral differences at different ages and within a given age.

As a scientific discipline, developmental psychology strives to accumulate a systematic and organized body of knowledge regarding behavior. To achieve this goal, developmental psychologists attempt (1) to establish appropriate developmental norms for assessing individual deviations from the "average" expected at any age level, (2) to study the relationships among a variety of behavior traits, and (3) to study the antecedent or causal conditions that give rise to behavior. These research approaches are called *normative, correlational,* and *experimental,* respectively. Each of these approaches must meet a minimum set of standards so that the knowledge gained by its application can be accepted with confidence.

Normative research methods

Normative studies provide rich and useful information concerning the sequence and "average" age of appearance of many behaviors. By means of such studies, investigators have established norms for gross-motor development, fine motor skills, language development, and social-personal behaviors. The important questions asked through normative studies are not the *how* or *why* of development but rather the *when* and *how much*.

When does a given behavior typically appear during development? How much of a given behavior occurs in a given population? Thus, through normative research we know that the "average" baby sits at six months, walks unassisted at about 11–12 months, and is somewhere between 30 and 38 inches tall by age two. We also know that extensive individual differences are associated with each normative behavior, that the "average" baby is to a large extent a statistical baby.

Correlational research methods

Correlational research methods are used to examine the relationships among a variety of behaviors or events. The behaviors or events may be highly positively related, highly negatively related, or unrelated. When two things are highly positively related they have a correlation approaching 1.00. If a measure of maternal rejection is related .85 with aggression toward others in preschool-age children, we can infer a strong positive relationship between high maternal rejection and high aggression toward others. When the behaviors are unrelated, their correlation approaches 0.00. If maternal rejection is correlated .16 with children's aggression, we can infer that the behaviors are unrelated. When behaviors are highly negatively related, their correlation approaches −1.00. If maternal rejection correlates −.78 with children's aggression, we should expect to find highly rejecting mothers to have children who are low in aggression toward others. Correlational methods have been used to study the relationships among such variables as intelligence and creativity, body build and personality traits, test scores and academic performance, parental acceptance-rejection and the dependency needs of children, and the value orientations of parents and children.

Correlations point out relationships but do not provide direct tests of cause-effect relationships. A may be highly related to B because of their shared relationship to C, but not, perhaps, because of a causal relationship between A and B. Correlational techniques do, however, allow the investigator to test hypotheses, to use sophisticated statistical techniques for data analysis, and to select and partially control for the variables to be used in a study.

Experimental research methods

In experimental designs the experimenter selects, manipulates, and exercises control over the variables being studied. The variables to be controlled are called *independent* and *dependent* variables. Independent variables are the stimuli which the investigator has selected in order to assess their effects on the dependent variables. Experimental methods are generally (but not always) used in research laboratories rather than in more naturalistic settings. As a result, the experimenter tends to have more or less precise control of the independent variables. Sometimes the experimenter may fail to consider a variable which may influence the behavior being measured, or may wish to systematically control the influence of a particular variable. In such cases, the variable is called an *extraneous* one. Failure to recognize the influence of extraneous variables or to control them systematically may cause the experimenter to draw false conclusions regarding the effect of the independent variable on the behavior being measured.

Dependent variables are the behaviors which the investigator has selected for study. That is, dependent variables are the behaviors observed in relation to the independent variables. Experimental methods are generally used to investigate the question "What would happen if . . . ?" Because so many aspects of the experimental method are under the control of the experimenter, this method enhances the *replicability* of any particular study. Replicability refers to the possibility of repeating an experiment by using exactly the same procedures that were used before. Replication is one of the most important ways that research findings can be confirmed and accepted with confidence.

In any well-designed experiment, changes in the dependent variable can be attributed to the independent variable. When this proves to be the case, the experiment is said to have *internal validity*. In any experiment, however, it is possible that sources of invalidity are present. If an extraneous variable can cause the changes in the dependent variables, the experiment is said to be *confounded,* or subject to invalidity (Campbell & Stanley, 1963; Crano & Brewer, 1973).

Observational research methods

One of the problems facing developmental psychology is the fact that surprisingly little is known about the natural settings in which children are reared. Such information is crucial for a complete science of behavior. Thus, there is a new concern among many developmental psychologists that data collected under rigid laboratory procedures may not accurately portray the intricacies of the child's real world. The revival of observational or naturalistic studies of behavior reflects this concern.

Observational research methods are neither new nor restricted to the study of infants and young children. From early baby biographies to studies of motor development, play, language behavior, and cognitive behavior, observational methods have contributed important information to developmental psychology. The general problems associated with observational methods are well known. Briefly, the observer must be able to record or rate the behavior of interest reliably, objectively, and immediately. For infants who are prelocomotor and preverbal, the observer has the additional problem of being compelled to rely primarily on spontaneous behavior, reflexes, or conditioned responses as behavior indices.

Although, by definition, any analysis of behavior requires observation, the term *observational method* is used to characterize specific procedures of data collection. Nevertheless, it is difficult to arrive at a comprehensive definition of observational method because of the wide variability among investigators in their choice of the operations to be emphasized. Crano and Brewer (1973) propose three dimensions of observational methodology that provide a basis for comparing the various operational procedures used in the study of behavior. These are the participant-nonparticipant, structured-nonstructured, and response-restriction dimensions.

The *participant-nonparticipant* dimension refers to whether or not the observer is a member of the group which is being observed and to the method the observer uses to gain entry into the observational setting. The participant observer is an observer who has been accepted by the observees as a bona fide member of the observational setting. The nonparticipant observer is an observer who either forces his or her way into the observational setting (is not accepted as a "natural" participant) or is completely isolated from the setting (for example, an observer seated behind a one-way viewing screen watches mother and child interacting). The participant-nonparticipant dimension must be considered in studies of mother-child interaction in the home, in the preschool, or in any other setting in which the observer is known to be observing by those being observed. When parents and children are being observed in the home setting, it is often necessary for the observer to visit the home several times before conducting the actual study, so that parents and children feel comfortable in his or her presence.

The *structured-nonstructured* dimension refers to the specific techniques used to record and code the behaviors being observed. The structured coding scheme focuses the observer's attention on specific and predetermined aspects of behavior—often at the expense of losing valuable information for which no coding category has been devised. The more nonstructured the observational method becomes, the more freedom the observer has to record all aspects of behavior in the observational setting. A difficulty with the completely nonstructured method is that the observer can become overwhelmed by the mass of information inherent in any social behavior setting.

The *response-restriction* dimension refers to the constraints that the observer and the observational setting place on the behavior of the person or persons being observed. Thus, studying mother-infant interaction in the home setting may lead to quite different maternal behaviors than may be observed in the university laboratory setting. In line with recent admonitions against the relative neglect of observational research in favor of highly controlled laboratory research, many contemporary developmental psychologists are attempting to bridge the gap between the laboratory and more naturalistic research settings. This might be done, for example, by observing dependency behavior in the natural situation and then studying the behaviors of high- and low-dependent children in more highly controlled settings.

ETHICAL CONSIDERATIONS

Developmental psychologists engaged in the study of children have always been especially aware of the ethics of research, perhaps because of the tender ages of their research participants. Guidelines for the ethics of research with human beings have been developed by the American Psychological Association (1974), by that association's Division on Developmental Psychology, and by the Society for Research in Child Development. In general, these guidelines provide for the anonymity of individual subjects, the protection of subjects from physical and psychological harm, and the consent of children, parents, guardians, or those acting *in loco parentis* (teachers, school principals, and so on) to research participation, based on their informed opinion regarding the research. At the heart of all the specific ethical guidelines are the ideas that the research participant's rights supersede those of the experimenter, that the research participant must be protected from invasion of privacy, and that the experimenter is first and foremost responsible for the ethical conduct of the study.

SUMMARY

Almost from its beginning, developmental psychology was a multidisciplinary approach to the study of the developing organism. Theories and methods drawn from general psychology, biology, and medicine were combined to give substance to developmental psychology as a unique discipline. Toward the end of the 19th century and early in the 20th century, developmental psychologists emphasized the biological aspects of development, especially those aspects that seemed in line with evolutionary theory. From 1920 to 1960, developmental psychology gradually yielded to the influences of behavioristic and social learning theory, and emphasized the environmental determinants of behavior. Today, developmental psychology emphasizes the study of behavior, although contemporary developmental psychologists exercise great freedom in drawing inferences about the underlying structural properties of the mind.

Contemporary developmental psychology emphasizes the psychological-biological-sociological unity of the developing organism. It accepts the epigenetic concept of development and views the organism as both active and reactive. It emphasizes the interaction between structure and function as a major determinant of the organism's adaptation to the environment.

To study the psychobiological organization of behavior, developmental psychologists use research methods common to many scientific disciplines. They apply normative, correlational, and experimental methods, for example, to questions regarding behavioral stability in individuals, age differences in behavior, and differences in behavior within an age group.

The study of infants and young children is not new to developmental psychology. The study of infant behavior has at least an 85-year history, with perhaps the greatest period of research productivity having occurred between 1925 and 1935. Following a decline in research that began just prior to World War II and continued into the mid-1950s, there was a revival of interest in the early years of development and especially in the period of infancy. In the chapters that follow, we will consider much of our current knowledge of the first few years of human life. The most logical starting point for this review is the beginning, and so we now turn to conception and the prenatal period of development.

SUGGESTED ADDITIONAL READING

Bertalanffy, L. von.   *General systems theory.* New York: Braziller, 1968.
Harris, D. B. (Ed.).   *The concept of development.* Minneapolis: University of Minnesota Press, 1957.
Maier, H. W.   *Three theories of child development.* New York: Harper & Row, 1965.
Monte, C. F.   *Psychology's scientific endeavor.* New York: Praeger, 1975.

PART TWO

The development of early organism-environment interaction

BOX 2–1
Study questions

What are the differences between mitotic and meiotic cell division?

What accounts for the genetic uniqueness of the individual?

How are sperm and ova produced?

Who determines the sex of the new individual?

What is implied by the statement "Phenotype equals genotype in interaction with the environment"?

If mother has blue eyes, and father has brown, how is it possible for baby to have gray?

Biologically speaking, which is the "weaker sex"?

On what basis could one say that conception is possible even though intercourse took place before ovulation?

What are the distinguishing features of the three stages of prenatal development?

What factors can degrade the prenatal environment and thereby interfere with the fetus's opportunity for normal development?

What is an accurate definition of prematurity?

THE PRENATAL PERIOD

It is well known that fertilization occurs when an egg (ovum) and a sperm combine. It is less well known that our knowledge of the mechanisms of conception is relatively recent. The ancient Greeks were well aware that intercourse was related to the production of offspring, but were unaware of the existence of ova or sperm. The male was thought to implant the "seed of life" into the female, who served only as a reservoir of nourishment for the growing organism. In the 17th century a Dutch scientist, Regnier De Graaf, discovered that the female produced an ovum. Shortly thereafter, another Dutch scientist, van Leeuwenhoek, discovered the sperm cell. Despite the discovery of the two human germ cells, or gametes, the theory of fertilization continued to differ very little from that of the Greeks. Not until the 19th century was it finally determined that union of the ovum and the sperm was essential for the creation of the new individual.

BIOLOGY OF REPRODUCTION

Mitotic and meiotic cell division

All cells of the body develop from the united sperm and ovum (the zygote) by a process of cell division called *mitosis*. Each zygote contains *chromosomes.* These, in turn, are made up of *genes,* which are the genetic material passed on from generation to generation. In mitotic cell division, an identical copy of the original zygote is produced. This occurs in a series of stages:

1.   The chromosomes duplicate, forming "double chromosomes" or a "matched set" of chromosomes.

2.   The double chromosomes line up horizontally along the midline of the cell.

3.   Members of each matched set separate and move away from the midline and toward the opposite ends of the cell.

4.   The cell starts pinching apart into two cells near the midline.

5.   The nuclear membrane draws around and encloses the two cells, now fully separated, such that each "new" cell now contains an identical set of chromosomes.

Genes consist of deoxyribonucleic acid (DNA), ribonucleic acid (RNA), and protein. DNA, found in the nucleus of the cell, is the central control mechanism regulating the production of protein. One of its jobs is to produce RNA in the cell nucleus. Two forms of RNA are produced: *messenger* RNA and *transfer* RNA. The messenger RNA leaves the nucleus and goes to a *ribosome* located in the cytoplasm surrounding the nucleus. The message carried contains the proper timetable for amino acids to convene and produce protein. Transfer RNA has the job of getting the amino acids to the message. Each transfer RNA has only one specific amino acid to take to the message. When an amino acid–transfer RNA meets with a ribosome–messenger RNA, protein production begins. Keep in mind that DNA serves as a regulator whereby amino acids link to produce protein. Since these substances and their activity derive from the chromosomes, it can be seen that the individual's genetic code is intimately involved with the DNA, RNA, and protein composition of the chromosomes.

In the normal human being, each cell is *diploid,* which means that it contains pairs of chromosomes—23 pairs, or a total of 46 chromosomes. One of the pairs determines the sex of the offspring, while the other 22 pairs serve functions other than sex determination. Each parent contributes one half of the chromosome complement to the new organism. But how is this possible? It was seen that in mitotic cell division the zygote divides, creating two "daughter" cells, each containing the full complement of chromosomes. Clearly, another type of cell division is required to produce cells containing a *haploid,* or half-number of chromosomes.

This type of cell division is called *meiosis.* In meiotic cell division the chromosomes pair and come together at a point called the *synapsis.* Each gene on one chromosome pairs with its corresponding gene on the other chromosome. During meiosis two phenomena occur which effectively guarantee that the new individual will be genetically unique. One of the phenomena, *crossing-over,* occurs when the chromosomes pair up. The other, *segregation,* occurs when the chromosomes begin to separate. In crossing-over, parts of the genes strung together on one chromosome exchange with genes strung together on another chromosome (see Figure 2–1). In segregation, the chromosomes separate, one half moving toward one or the other pole of the cell. Segregation refers to the fact that the movement to the poles is random. Thus, at least three factors assure genetic individuality: (1) the unique genetic code on the chromosomes selected from some part of the parental genetic material; (2) crossing-over, by which genetic material on the chromosomes rearranges itself; and (3) segregation, by which chromosomes randomly move from one polar area of the dividing cell to another.

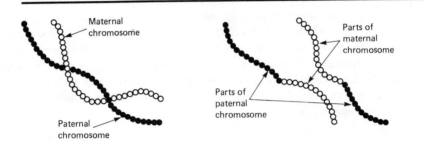

FIGURE 2–1 "Crossing-over." During the formation of male and female gametes, chromosomes may become intertwined. When the chromosomes break loose, sections of the two chromosomes may be exchanged. Crossing-over is one factor which assures genotypic uniqueness for all indviduals, with the exception of identical twins.

The process by which the sperm and ova are formed is referred to as *gametogenesis.* Gametogenesis of the sperm is referred to as **spermatogenesis,** while that of the ova is referred to as **oogenesis.** During mitotic cell division in the testes, certain cells (spermatogonia) are set aside. Spermatogenesis refers to the process of cell division whereby spermatogonia are changed into spermatozoa, or *sperm,* a process that requires approximately 2.5 months to complete. The **primary spermatocyte** still contains the diploid number of chromosomes. Further meiotic cell division produces two **secondary spermatocytes,** each with a haploid number of chromosomes; that is, each contains 22 autosomes (non-sex determining chromosomes) plus one X or Y sex-determining chromosome.

Oogenesis occurs in the ovary. Beginning approximately at the sixth prenatal week in a female fetus, small groups of cells **(primary follicles)** are formed through mitotic cell division. The primary follicles contain the female gamete, or **oogonia.** During the remainder of prenatal development, oogenesis proceeds only to the formation of **oocytes.** Meiotic cell division then stops, only to resume again when ovulation occurs at puberty. Just before ovulation the primary oocyte completes its division, producing two daughter cells, the **secondary oocyte** and the **polar body.** At this point in particular, oogenesis differs from spermatogenesis. Whereas each secondary spermatocyte eventually produces two sperm cells, each secondary oocyte produces only one ovum. The polar bodies disintegrate along the way. The secondary oocyte continues its meiotic cell division until, just prior to fertilization, the ovum is complete. It is in this way that a haploid ovum meets a haploid sperm and a new diploid individual is created.

The sex of the individual is determined by the chromosome tagging along with the 22 autosomes. The maternal diploid sex determining chromosomes are identical (XX), while the paternal diploid sex-determining chromosomes are different (XY). The letters *X* and *Y* are standard designations for sex-determining chromosomes because they do in fact resemble the appearance of the chromosomes themselves. (The X chromosome actually bears a resemblance to the letter *X;* the Y chromosome, however, looks more like a *V* than a *Y.*) The X or Y male spermatozoa remaining after meiotic cell division eventually determine the sex of the new offspring; that is, the baby's sex is determined by its father. An X from the father and an X from the mother makes a female baby, whereas a Y from the father an an X from the mother makes a male baby.

Phenotype and genotype

The chromosomes contain the genetic units of heredity. These structures are the genes, which exist in two forms, or *alleles*. The genes determine the *genotype,* or the inferred genetic makeup of the individual. The genotype is inferred because it is not observable. On the other hand, the genotype does contribute to the *phenotype,* or the observable characteristics of the organism. A fundamental principle of behavior genetics is that all individuals are unique organisms, with the exception of identical twins. Recall that this uniqueness is assured through such processes as crossing-over and segregation. Phenotypes result from the interaction of the genotype with the organism's environment. In other words, heredity and environment interact to produce the observable characteristics of the organism, including behavior.

In some cases the phenotype reflects *dominant* characteristics, while in other cases it reflects *recessive* characteristics. The concepts dominant and recessive derive from the action of the alleles. If *D* represents one allele of a gene and *r* another allele of the same gene, we would have four possible combinations of the two gene alleles: *DD, Dr, rD,* and *rr.* Whichever combination results, remember that one allele comes from the (haploid) sperm and one from the (haploid) ovum, so that the final pair of alleles received from the two parents contains one of the four possible combinations, depending on which was received from each parent. If the individual's phenotype *Dr* or *rD* is the same as *DD,* the *D* trait is said to be dominant. If the individual's phenotype expresses *rr,* the trait is said to be recessive. Eye color provides a clear example of dominant and recessive characteristics. Brown eyes are dominant, blue eyes are recessive. Thus, when *B* (brown eyes) and *b* (blue eyes) combine (*BB, Bb, bB, bb*), the *Bb* and *bB* combinations resemble *BB,* not *bb.* That is, three out of four children will be expected to be brown-eyed. Anytime, a *B* (dominant) is present, its characteristic will be manifested in the phenotype. If both parents phenotypically reflect recessive characteristics (that is, both are blue-eyed), all offspring would be expected to be blue-eyed. If one parent is blue-eyed (*bb*) and the other brown-eyed (*Bb*), two of the children would be expected to be blue-eyed, and two brown-eyed. Note that we have referred to the expectancies for certain eye colors. We did this because each child's probability of having a particular eye color is independent of another child's probability of having the same eye color. Therefore, we cannot say for certain that three out of four children *will* have a certain eye color, but only that they can be *expected* to have a certain eye color. Actually, because of genetic variability, some of the children may even be green-eyed or gray-eyed.

Biological vulnerability

For some reason yet unexplained, more male than female babies are conceived (Rhodes, 1965): approximately 120–150 males for every 100 females. One speculation is that Y sperm are lighter and faster than X sperm, thereby increasing the probability that Y sperm will reach the ovum first. By the end of the prenatal period, however, the ratio reduces to approximately 105 to 100. Moreover, mortality statistics show that more males than females die at every age that has been studied through the first 20 years of life. Clearly males are biologically more vulnerable than females.

Biological vulnerability refers to the degree of mortality or morbidity associated with an organism's tolerance for biological or environmental stress. Higher mortality and/or morbidity in males has been associated with many factors, including susceptibility to infectious diseases; cardiovascular, renal, and gastrointestinal infections; congenital malformations; chromosomal abnormalities; blood incompatibility; and toxemia of pregnancy (Allen & Diamond, 1954; Rhodes, 1965).

Sex-linked chromosomal anomalies   In many cases a defect may be due to defective genes in the sex-determining chromosomes. Common examples of this type of chromosomal defects are *color blindness* and *hemophilia.*

Recall that the normal chromosome complements for males and females are XY and XX, respectively. Occasionally, additions or subtractions occur. In *Turner's syndrome* the female has only 45 chromosomes (she lacks one X). Persons afflicted with this disorder phenotypically lack secondary sex characteristics, are short, and have underdeveloped ovaries. *Klinefelter's syndrome* characterizes phenotypic males (XXY). These persons have underdeveloped male or female sex glands, enlarged breasts, and are often mentally retarded.

Autosomal anomalies   Not all chromosomal anomalies involve the sex-determining chromosomes. In PKU the individual lacks an enzyme necessary to convert phenylalanine (a protein found in milk) to phenylpyruvic acid.

A toxic substance is formed from incomplete metabolism in the blood, and mental retardation is the inevitable outcome unless the disorder is treated. Newborns are now routinely tested for PKU either by analysis of blood samples or by a litmus paper test of the urine. Treatment involves placing the infant on a special diet. Such treatment provides an excellent example of how an environmental intervention can negate a genetically programmed defect.

One of the most frequently occurring anomalies is *Down's syndrome,* one form of which is known as *trisomy 21* (the layman's term for this anomaly is *mongolism*). The Down's baby has 47 chromosomes (the extra one added to the 21st pair, hence *trisomy* 21), is typically mentally retarded, and is identifiable phenotypically by the unusual appearance of the skull, face, tongue, eyes, hands, feet, and neck.

When fewer than 44 autosomes appear in the zygote, the condition is known as *monosomy,* a disorder that is always fatal.

Chromosomal anomalies have several causes, including nondisjunction, translocation, deletion, and inversion. *Nondisjunction* results when the chromosomes fail to separate during meiotic cell division. Consequently, one gamete has both chromosomes, while the other has none. In *translocation,* part of one chromosome becomes attached to another chromosome. It is thought that Down's syndrome is caused by either nondisjunction or translocation. In the latter case, chromosome 21 gets "hooked" onto or rides piggyback on chromosome 15 in a carrier. The carrier has the normal 23 pairs, but they are misarranged. If the member of pair 15 (with 21 hooked) and the remaining free 21 are given to a mate who also provides a 21, then offspring will have three number 21 chromosomes instead of the normal two. Sometimes part of a chromosome is *deleted* during cell division, while occasionally *inversion* of the parts of a chromosome occurs.

One of the more interesting aspects of human sexuality is the extent to which "nature" has worked to provide optimal conditions for the union of the sperm and the ovum. For example, ovulation (release of the ovum from the ovary into the Fallopian tube) occurs at relatively predictable times during the course of each menstrual cycle. The time between release of the ovum and its descent into the Fallopian tube is roughly six hours. Sperm can live from 12 to 36 hours. Thus, impregnation could occur even if intercourse precedes ovulation. Moreover, nature has provided nearly insurmountable odds again the ovum's chances of escaping fertilization.

The ovum is one of the largest cells in the human body, roughly 1/175 inch in diameter (Corner, 1944). To seek out this target, from 200 million to 500 million sperm are released with any one ejaculation of seminal fluid. The number of sperm cells released is a function of the amount of seminal fluid released. This amount ranges from 2.5 to 5.0 cubic centimeters, with approximately 100 million sperm per cubic centimeter. Several thousand of these sperm will eventually cross the cervical barrier and literally seek out the ovum. Only one of this abundance of sperm must penetrate the ovum in order to complete fertilization. If fertilization does occur, the ovum continues its three-to-four-day journey down the Fallopian tube, eventually becoming embedded in the uterine lining. If fertilization does not occur, most of the uterine lining is discharged along with blood during menstruation.

STAGES OF PRENATAL DEVELOPMENT

The nine calendar months of normal gestation are typically divided into three stages: the period of the ovum, the period of the embryo, and the period of the fetus.

The period of the ovum (conception to second prenatal week)

During the period of the ovum the fertilized zygote makes its three-to-four-day descent down the Fallopian tube and enters the uterus. Now the zygote exists as a freely roaming *blastocyst*. Mitotic cell division begins, and the chromosomes duplicate and separate, over and over again. The major developmental task of this period is implantation of the blastocyst into the uterine wall, an event which occurs approximately 24–36 hours after entrance into the uterus. When implanted in the uterine lining, the blastocyst is surrounded by maternal blood. The *trophoblast,* or outer covering of the blastocyst, forms two parts. One part will become nutrient material for the embryo, while the other will become the placenta and the umbilicus. Having become embedded in the lining of the uterus, the organism is now relatively secure in the uterine environment, and the conditions for placental growth and umbilical attachment are now met.

The period of the embryo (second to eighth prenatal week)

The period of the embryo is characterized by the continued differentiation of the zygote into three layers: the *ectoderm,* the *mesoderm,* and the *endoderm.* From the ectoderm will eventually emerge the nervous system, skin and skin glands, hair, and nails. From the mesoderm come the musculature, skeleton, and circulatory and excretory systems, as well as some portions of the reproductive system. From the endoderm emerge the lining of the gastrointestinal tract, the Eustachian tubes, trachia, bronchia, vital organs, and glands, as well as other portions of the reproductive system. In addition to marking the differentiation of the layers, the period of the embryo marks the time when the placenta develops and the 10–20-inch umbilical attachment between the placenta and the embryo is formed. By approximately the 18th–21st day the heart begins to form, and by the end of the third prenatal week a faint heartbeat might be detected. The organism is now surrounded by the *amniotic sac* and the *amniotic fluid,* which provide protection from physical injury. The critical feature of this period is *histogenesis,* or the differentiation of parts. It is during the period of the embryo that environmental intrusions into the developmental process can produce particularly severe and permanent damage to the organism.

The period of the fetus (two months to term)

The period of the fetus is marked by the continued development and growth of the basic systems and the replacement of cartilage by bone cells. The major developmental feature is *morphogenesis,* or the organization of the developing structures. The period comprises a critical juncture in pre-natal development: the *point of viability.* This refers to the time, generally assumed to be 26 weeks of gestation, after which the fetus has a reasonable chance to survive if born. Although generally defined by weeks of gestation (which even today are difficult to determine precisely), the point of viability can be predicted more precisely by taking into account such factors as the birth weight and the length of the fetus. On the basis of studies of thousands of babies born in the Moscow Lying-in Hospital, Makeyeva (1959) suggests 1,000 grams birth weight and at least 35 centimeters birth length as lower limits on the likelihood that a prematurely born infant will survive. In any event, by the 26th week all of the major systems have developed, and the remaining months are devoted to the continued growth and strength-ening of the fetus in preparation for its entrance into an environment that is decidedly different from the prenatal one.

FACTORS DEGRADING THE PRENATAL ENVIRONMENT

We have seen how various chromosomal anomalies affect the developing organism. In addition to chromosomal anomalies, a variety of environmental factors can degrade the prenatal organism so as to thwart its opportunities for normal development. It is often difficult to isolate the specific causative agent that insults the prenatal environment. One reason for this is the degree of interaction that exists between the fetus and the mother. Nevertheless, a vast literature points with various degrees of certainty to several significant categories of insult that degrade the fetal environment. Some of these will be considered below.

Malnutrition

Nearly all of us are aware of the importance of nutrition in our own lives. In addition, we have probably all seen examples of children, whether in Biafra, rural or inner-city America, or in countless other parts of the world, who suffer appallingly from severe lack of food. Indeed, some "experts" believe that malnutrition may be the most important of all the environmental factors that detrimentally influence prenatal development.

What is meant by malnutrition? Some investigators draw a distinction between two kinds of malnutrition (Hurlock, 1964). One of these, *qualita-*

tive hunger, refers to inadequate supplies of the necessary vitamins, amino acids, and so on, essential for normal growth and development. The other, quantitative hunger, refers to insufficient quantities of food, but with minimal vitamin and nutritional requirements met. Other investigations distinguish among three levels or degrees of malnutrition (Gomez et al., 1956). First-degree malnutrition refers to body weights between 76 percent and 90 percent of the average weight of a normal infant. Second- and third-degree malnutrition refer to body weights from 62–75 percent and below 61 percent, respectively, of established norms. Naeye (1970) supports the suggestion that not all malnutrition is directly related to the amount of food consumed. For example, clinical disorders related to malnutrition include placental and uterine disorders, multiple births, and inadequate diets that result from poverty.

Qualitative malnutrition has been found to be associated with premature birth, subnormal length and weight of the newborn, and fetal malnutrition resulting in babies who are small for their gestational age (Antonov, 1947; Gruenwald, 1970). A slow rate of intrauterine growth has also been linked to higher mortality and greater susceptibility to morbidity (Drillien, 1970).

In general, severe malnutrition appears to have direct degrading effects on the developing brain and nervous system. In a series of experiments with malnourished African children, evidence indicated that malnutrition suffered during the first two years of life resulted in a smaller head circumference, a reduction in brain size, abnormalities in brain wave activity, and impairment of the visual system (Stoch & Smythe, 1968). Studying the effects of malnutrition on the developing brains of nine Chilean infants who had died of starvation, Winick and Rosso (1969) found reduced brain weight as well as abnormalities in the brain's protein, RNA, and DNA composition. One hypothesis is that malnutrition has its greatest degrading influence on the organism in the last trimester of pregnancy and the first few postnatal years (Dobbing, 1970), when the brain is in its period of most rapid growth.

In general, nutritional deficiencies have been associated with mental deficiency, nervous instability, cerebral palsy, lower birth weight, decreased birth length, rickets, general physical weakness, and death.

Infectious disease

Infectious diseases are potentially damaging to the developing fetus. This is particularly true during the first trimester of prenatal development. We have all very likely heard that "German" measles (rubella) can be dangerous during the first few prenatal months. Such information is not to be taken lightly. It has been estimated that hundreds of infants born in Michigan during the 1964–65 rubella epidemic were severely affected by prenatal insult. For example, one of the highest incidences of hydrocephalism was recorded during that outbreak. Other infectious diseases known to produce degrading effects include the venereal diseases—syphilis and gonorrhea—and poliomyelitis. Infectious diseases have been associated with a high incidence of stillbirths, miscarriages, blindness, mental deficiency, deafness, microcephaly, and deaf-mutism.

Blood incompatibility

There are sound reasons for requiring that prospective couples receive blood tests prior to marriage. Protecting one's future offspring by uncovering and curing a venereal infection is far more important than any temporary embarrassment one may suffer. In addition to identifying the presence of venereal and other infections, blood tests can alert parents and obstetricians to potential blood disorders that might subsequently require special prenatal and postnatal care.

One of these disorders, *erythroblastosis fetalis,* is caused by the Rh factor, so named after the Rhesus monkeys used in research that isolated the blood incompatibility. Persons are either Rh-positive or Rh-negative: approximately 85 percent of Caucasians, 93 percent of Negroes, and nearly all Oriental peoples are Rh-positive. Thus, these persons have a genetically determined red blood cell antigen (the Rh antigen, or rhesus factor) which, when compatible with the fetus, produces no difficulty. When the fetal Rh factor and the maternal Rh factor differ, however, difficulties arise. The Rh antigen is really a group of six antigens—C, D, E, c, d, e—and it is the D factor which leads to the classification of Rh+ or Rh−. If the allele combination contains a *D,* the Rh designation will be positive, but if the allele combination contains a *d,* the Rh designation will be negative. When an Rh-negative mother has an Rh-positive fetus, mixes in the blood streams produce antibodies that pass through the placental sieve and cause destruction of red blood cells in the fetus. In contrast, fetal blood mixed with the mother's will cause antigen sensitization in her blood system. If uncorrected, this condition will lead to even greater problems with the next pregnancy. Fortunately, Rh incompatibility can be treated. For infants, exchange transfusions can be done in utero, thereby removing the incompatibility between the fetal and maternal Rh factors. For mothers, immunization with Rh immunoglobulin within several days after delivery will prevent the formation of the Rh-antibodies. Once immunized, the maternal blood no longer presents a problem for the next pregnancy. If the condition is not corrected, however, the fetus may abort, be miscarried, or be stillborn (Stevenson, 1973).

Drugs

With the increasing use of drugs in our culture, attention should be paid to the potentially harmful effects of drugs on the developing organism. The thalidomide tragedy of the early 1960s is a painful example of the wrong way to discover the harmful effects of drugs. Many pregnant women, notably in Germany, who were taking this tranquilizer gave birth to offspring afflicted with a variety of physical deformities (for example, incomplete development of the arms, the legs, or both). The physical and emotional distress caused by this particular tranquilizer makes it seem well worthwhile to advise caution in combining drugs with pregnancy.

Narcotics have been found to cross the placenta readily. Taussig (1962) found barbiturates to be associated with fetal distress. The newborn organism is certainly unprepared to combat the distress of withdrawal from heroin addiction acquired in utero. A variety of agents used as anesthetics and analgesics have been found to cross the placenta and enter the fetal bloodstream. Although there is some evidence that LSD may cause structural alteration of the white blood cells, studies of the effects on the fetus of heroin and derivative drugs are currently inconclusive.

It should not be surprising to find that nicotine, an extremely toxic drug, may be detrimental to the fetus. As long ago as 1938, it was reported that smoking was associated with an increase in the fetal heart rate (Sontag & Richards, 1938). In one study, heavy smokers were deprived of cigarettes for a 24-hour period. The pregnant women were then offered a cigarette. Even before a pregnant woman was able to light the cigarette, the fetal heart rate accelerated, suggesting that the woman's conditioned emotional-hormonal response influenced the fetus (Lieberman, 1963). Prematurity has been linked to the degree of smoking during pregnancy, the heaviest smokers having the highest incidence of prematurely born or lightweight infants (Simpson, 1949).

Studies have shown that pregnant women ingest anywhere from three to ten different drugs during the course of pregnancy, including such apparently harmless drugs as aspirin (Bowes, 1970). Unfortunately, pregnant women ingest many drugs whose possible effects on the fetus have never been studied. The safest approach would be to exercise extreme caution in taking such drugs during pregnancy.

Radiation

Several studies conducted in the cities of Hiroshima and Nagasaki have disclosed the horrendous effects of extreme atomic radiation. In Hiroshima, radiation was associated with stillbirth, abortion, malformation, and low birth weight (Neel, 1953). In Nagasaki, pregnant women who were within 2,000 meters of the hypocenter of the blast had higher fetal, neonatal, and infant death rates. Among infants who survived the blast, mental retardation and growth retardation were characteristic effects of radiation (Yamazaki, Wright, & Wright, 1954).

An atomic blast is not the only means by which radiation adversely affecting the fetus is received. In many instances, women with cancer or pelvic tumors require radium therapy. Small amounts of such radiation treatment have not been directly associated with fetal insult, but large dosages should be avoided. Unfortunately, there is no clear definition of what might be an excessive dose for any one individual. In general, the earlier in pregnancy that radiation is experienced, the greater is the potential harm to the fetus.

Maternal age

It has been suggested that the optimal age range for childbearing is from approximately 20 to 29 years of age (Scott, 1968). The largest percentage of fetal difficulties as a function of mother's age is associated with women over 40 years of age. For example, incidence of Down's syndrome is highest among babies born of women over 40. If there is any relationship between maternal age and the declining adequacy of the female reproductive system, one might expect to find higher instances of fetal distress as a result of old eggs. Recall that all of the ova are formed before birth and that only the final stages of meiotic cell division occur at ovulation. Thus, 40-year-old women have 40-year-old eggs. One might speculate that some similar process occurs in the male's reproductive system, although in this case it would not involve the age of sperm. Whatever the reason, it is clear that women maximize their chances of having a healthy baby if they bear their children during their twenties.

A note of caution applies here, as well as to most of our discussion of factors degrading the prenatal environment. This cautionary note concerns the use of expressions like "higher incidence." In fact, most babies at *all* maternal age levels are perfectly normal. "High incidence" refers to the likelihood of an event at one age period compared to its likelihood at some reference age (say, 20–29, years). However, although the factors discussed may affect only a small percentage of fetuses, they are quite important. Five percent of all the babies born each year in the United States is a lot of babies!

Maternal emotional state

Since there are no direct neural connections between mother and fetus, it may seem unlikely that the mother's emotional state can affect the fetus. The belief that maternal thoughts can directly influence the fetus is responsible for all sorts of cultural taboos regarding the pregnant woman. For example, in some cultures pregnant women are not permitted to handle knives for fear that this will cause severing of the umbilicus, while in many parts of the United States there are taboos against eating certain foods lest birthmarks shaped like those foods appear on the newborn. Such beliefs have no basis in fact. Nevertheless, the mother's emotional state has been linked to both fetal and postnatal behavior.

Rabin (1965) suggests that motivation for parenthood may set the tone for future parent-child relations long before the child is even conceived. Other investigators have found that women who are dissatisfied with their social status or emotionally unstable are less happy with their pregnancies and more anxious and emotionally maladjusted during pregnancy (Davids & Rosengren, 1962). The effects of prolonged chronic anxiety, upset, and unhappiness with pregnancy have been linked with hyperactivity, irritability, crying, feeding difficulties, and sleeping problems in offspring (Sontag, 1957). Moreover, at least one investigator reports that mothers of colicky infants are more tense and anxious during their pregnancies than are mothers of noncolicky infants (Lakin, 1957). Mothers of colicky infants also reported feeling inadequate about their ability to care for the coming baby.

Since there are no direct neural connections between mother and fetus how might the maternal emotional state exert its influence on the fetus? The influence could not be a direct effect of the nervous system but would have to be an indirect effect in which the hypothalamus is stimulated to produce substances that cause the eventual release of hormones into the blood. Hormones carried in the maternal blood readily cross the placenta —even though the maternal blood itself does not—and enter the fetal bloodstream. The hormonal imbalance that may result is more than likely to affect both the structural and the functional development of fetal organ systems.

It is obvious that an extraordinary number of events can markedly affect the course of development during the prenatal months. Malnutrition, disease, blood incompatibility, drugs, maternal age, and emotional state have all been found to disrupt normal prenatal development (Barnes, 1968; Ferreira, 1969; Stevenson, 1973).

PREMATURITY

Of all the topics associated with prenatal development, premature birth probably receives the least attention in the introductory course in human development. The implications of premature birth for later development demand more extensive consideration.

The typical notion of prematurity is that the infant is born sometime before nine months' gestation. Though correct in part, this definition does not account for the discouraging prognosis for prematurely born infants. The World Health Organization, recognizing that length of gestation was an inadequate single index of prematurity, established a definition based on low birth weight (WHO, 1961). A premature infant was defined as one whose birth weight was less than 2,500 grams (5.5 lbs). By this definition of prematurity, approximately 8 percent of all births are premature. This means that in the United States approximately 300,000 babies a year are born prematurely. These babies account for nearly one half of all neonatal deaths, and those surviving have the highest rates of physical and psychological handicaps.

It was once thought that birth weight and gestation length would provide sufficiently accurate measurements for reasonably successful diagnosis and prognosis of the prematurely born. Although this is generally true, other factors are also important. For example, Drillien (1964) suggests that birth weight and gestation length fail to take into account such interacting factors as geographic and sexual differences, birth order, social status, the mother's age, multiple births, and the adequacy of prenatal care.

In general, prematurity as defined by short gestation and low birth weight has been found to be associated with intellectual deficiencies, perceptual-motor dysfunction, brain injury, immature speech, cerebral palsy, visual defects, and difficulty with abstract reasoning. Moreover, these effects hold up even when investigators control for the effects of race, maternal attitudes, maternal rearing practices, and social class (Wiener, Rider, Oppel, Fischer, & Harper, 1965).

Drillien's (1964) study utilized a longitudinal procedure, used in many studies of prematurity. With this method the investigator chooses a sample of infants who are characterized by the specific condition which is the subject of the study. Then an appropriate matched control group is selected, presumably devoid of the condition of interest. Both groups are then followed longitudinally to assess the incidence of the condition of interest. Thus, if premature birth is the condition of interest, one would select a group of prematurely born infants and match them with a group of full-term infants. During the longitudinal study one could administer a variety of tests and examinations to determine the presence of differences between the groups.

The most reasonable course of action for resolving the problems of prematurity is prevention. Makeyeva (1959) emphasizes the prophylactic techniques used extensively in obstetric practice in the Soviet Union to minimize prematurity. These procedures include: avoiding excessive intake of liquids and food, limiting salt intake, restricting manual and mental work, getting fresh air and lots of sleep, and wearing loose-fitting and comfortable clothing! However, even if these procedures were followed rigidly, many babies still would be born prematurely. Prevention then takes on another meaning: mothers need assistance to avoid what Lindemann (1965) has called *anticipatory grief.*

Anticipatory grief refers to the fact that prematurity is difficult not only for the baby but also for the mother. Premature birth means that mother and baby are going to be separated for some period of time. In some instances this period could extend to months. Because the baby is at such high risk, many parents prepare themselves for the worst; that is, they anticipate the baby's death. If the baby survives, it is often difficult for parents to reestablish positive feelings toward it. They seem almost to have "forgotten" that they had a baby. At home, the prematurely born baby may not help parents to develop positive feelings since the baby tends to be difficult to care for, having more feeding, sleeping, and temperament problems than the full-gestation baby. To counter the phenomenon of anticipatory grief and the subsequent estrangement between parents and baby, many hospitals require the mother (but unfortunately, not the father) to make daily visits to the hospital to participate actively in the care and management of the baby.

Obviously, not all prematurely born infants are subjected to the devastating conditions described here. Nevertheless, the incidence of infants who do suffer untoward effects because they were born too soon or with extremely low birth weights is sufficiently great to warrant continued research on adequate preventive and prophylactic techniques for assisting the premature infant to normal development.

SUMMARY

The prenatal period covers the span of human life from conception to birth. Conception occurs when the sex gametes (sperm and ovum) unite. This union sets into motion the growth and development of the new organism, initially through a process of cell division called mitosis. Each normal new cell contains 23 pairs of chromosomes, one of which is responsible for determining the sex of the organism. The sex gametes undergo an additional, special division called meiosis. After meiotic cell division each sperm or ovum contains only 22 single chromosomes (autosomes) and one sex-determining chromosome. When sperm and ovum unite, the new organism again has the full complement of 46 chromosomes.

Genes exist in two forms called alleles and are located on the chromosomes. Alleles can be either dominant or recessive. Genes are responsible for regulating the genetic program of the individual, but this program is not fixed and invariant. At all stages of development the environment contributes to the content of the program. In most cases we can only infer the genetic makeup, or genotype, of the organism by noting the observable characteristics, or phenotype.

Biological vulnerability refers to the degree of morbidity or mortality associated with the organism's tolerance for stress. Chromosomal anomalies interfere with the organism's chances for normal development. In addition, various environmental factors can degrade the prenatal environment and threaten the very survival of the fetus.

The prenatal period is divided into three subperiods: the period of the ovum, the period of the embryo, and the period of the fetus. Although most fetuses take 270–280 days to develop, some infants are born considerably earlier. We generally refer to such babies as premature. However, a definition of prematurity based solely on length of gestation has proven to be inadequate. At the very least, one must also consider the birth weight and birth length. Despite modern prenatal care and hospital facilities, prematurity continues to be a threat to the organism. In fact, even special hospital care may actually result in some degree of sensory or social deprivation or departure from the normal stimulation of the environment. Nevertheless, the prospective parent must keep in mind that most babies, whatever the possible difficulties, arrive in the world in perfectly good shape. How they arrive and what happens to them during the first month of life is the topic of the next chapter.

SUGGESTED ADDITIONAL READING

Birch, H. G., & Gussow, J. D.   *Disadvantaged children: Health, nutrition, and school failure.* New York: Harcourt, Brace & World, 1970.

Ferreira, A. J.   *Prenatal environment.* Springfield, Ill.: Charles C Thomas, 1969.

Vandenburg, S. G. (Ed.).   *Methods and goals of human behavior genetics.* New York: Academic Press, 1965.

BOX 3–1
Study questions

What are the three phases of the birth process and the phenomena associated with each phase?

What are birth malpresentations, and how do they differ from the normal birth presentation?

What influences do maternal delivery medications have on the newborn's behavior and subsequent development?

What factors must be considered when determining whether or not a newborn baby is at risk?

What are some behavioral characteristics of the newborn?

How does state, or level of arousal, affect the newborn's responsivity to environmental stimulation?

How may a baby be pacified?

What significance do biological rhythms have for the organization of caregiver-infant interaction?

What are the advantages and disadvantages of breast feeding for the organization of caregiver-infant interaction?

Should infants be fed on schedule or on demand?

3

BIRTH AND THE NEWBORN PERIOD

The period of development emphasized in the preceding chapter covered a time span of approximately nine months. In this chapter our goal is less ambitious. Now we will focus on a time span of roughly 30 days, including both the birth process and the newborn period of development. Occasionally we will stray to the end of the first year of life, as the continuity of the topic demands. Today, the newborn period covers the time of the hospital stay, usually about five days. However, some infants stay in the hospital for longer or shorter periods. Consequently, we will not adhere to the five-day definition.

PARTURITION (LABOR AND DELIVERY)

On the average, 270–280 days after conception, the birth process, or *parturition*, begins. Fetal movements decrease and become more variable about one month before parturition. The lower segment of the uterus "drops," and the fetus orients its head into a presentation position. For multiparous women (those who have given birth previously), the drop in the uterus and fetal positioning are often rapidly followed by the onset of labor.

About one week before labor, many pregnant women experience symptoms suggesting the onset of labor. This *false labor* differs from true labor in several ways. During false labor, the pains are irregular and seldom change in intensity, the cervix does not dilate, and there is rarely any spotting or discharge of blood. The beginning of true labor is marked by all or various combinations of the following: dilation of the cervix, contractions of the upper portion of the uterus, abdominal pains (muscle contractions), and backaches. Early contractions may be so "painless" that many women do not associate them with labor. In fact, since the severity of contractions during labor is to some extent determined by the amount of oxygen supplied to the muscles, teaching women to breathe properly and to relax may eliminate much of the "pain" of labor.

Parturition is generally divided into three phases. The first phase covers the period of time from the onset of labor to full dilation of the cervix. During this phase the amniotic sac may rupture as it is pushed toward the cervix. While this is sometimes uncomfortable and embarrassing for the mother, it is perfectly normal and a sign that labor is underway. If the obstetrician has not yet been reached, he should be reached immediately, for there is considerable variation in the length of time between the breaking of the "water bag" or "sac" and the final phases of parturition. Some women experience a gush of water and deliver within hours, others may drip for as long as a full day, or in rare cases, for as long as a week before reaching the final stage of labor. In the last situation, infection may occur, and the obstetrician should be informed daily of the maternal condition.

The second phase of parturition covers the period of time between full dilation of the cervix and the birth of the baby. During this phase the lower segment of the uterus expands and becomes continuous with the fully dilated cervix and vagina, to form the birth canal. The upper segment of the uterus continues to contract, thus providing assistance to the fetus as it moves through the canal. This phase ends when the baby is born.

The third phase of parturition covers the period from birth to expulsion of the placenta and membranes, or *afterbirth*. Following delivery of her baby, the mother is given a brief respite from the uterine contractions. Soon, however, the contractions begin anew, stimulating the passage of the after- birth. After the third phase ends, the mother leaves the delivery room.

Birth presentations

Presentation refers to the position of the fetus during parturition and to the part of the fetus's body that first emerges from the birth canal. Most infants are presented in the *vertex position,* which means that they move through the birth canal headfirst, the upper and back parts of the head leading the way.

Approximately 5 percent of all births deviate from the vertex position. These *malpresentations* may be caused by a variety of factors, including (1) maternal pelvic difficulties, (2) placental difficulties, (3) multiple preg- nancies, and (4) stillbirth. Malpresentations include:

Breech: Any part of the pelvic extremity leads. In a *full breech* the buttocks emerge first; in a *half breech* one leg emerges first.

Brow: Although the head emerges first, as in the vertex position, the upper front (brow) of the face leads.

Face: This is a headfirst position in which the whole frontal face leads.

Transverse: Here the shoulder or upper extremity leads. The fetus lies across the uterus. Delay in the emergence of the head makes the transversely presented fetus especially susceptible to anoxia (oxygen deficit) and/or damage to the head.

Compound: Two body parts emerge simultaneously, as, for example, the head and a hand.

The presentations thus far discussed involve the transport of the fetus through the birth canal, sometimes with the assistance of an *episiotomy*— a surgical incision of the vulva designed to widen the passage for the fetus. However, for some babies delivery through the birth canal is either impossible or inadvisable. Some babies are simply too large for the available opening, while others may be in danger of infection as they pass through the birth canal. When it is dangerous for the baby to be delivered through the birth canal, delivery can be accomplished by *cesarean section*. This involves the surgical removal of the fetus by incising the abdominal and uterine walls. The condition known as *placenta praevia*—in which the placenta is implanted over the cervical opening—also suggests delivery by caesarean section. In placenta praevia, if the baby is born through the birth canal, the placenta would have to be delivered first. This would seriously endanger the fetal oxygen supply.

Birth complications

Most babies survive the prenatal period and the events of birth with few, if any, complications. Some do not. In the previous chapter we reviewed many factors that can thwart normal development by affecting the organism during prenatal development. However, arriving at parturition unscathed does not assure the fetus protection from other possible insults. In some instances it may be misleading to designate these complications as parturitional. Some complications seen at birth originate earlier in the prenatal period. In addition, many complications arise as a direct result of insult incurred during the birth process.

Jaundice is one of the most frequent problems of parturition. It has been estimated that nearly 50 percent of all full-gestation babies and nearly 80 percent of premature infants become jaundiced. Bilirubin, a red bile pigment found in the body as sodium bilirubinate, is formed from hemoglobin during the destruction of red blood cells. Through action of the enzyme glucuronyl transferase, the liver is responsible for conjugating bilirubin, that is, for changing it into an acceptable biochemical (bilirubin glucuronide). If the enzyme system and/or the liver is immature, bilirubin remains unconjugated and poses a danger to the infant. Jaundice occurs when unconjugated bilirubin overloads the baby's bloodstream and is deposited in the skin. The skin takes on an orangish or yellowish appearance that becomes readily noticeable around the third or fourth postnatal day. If the condi-

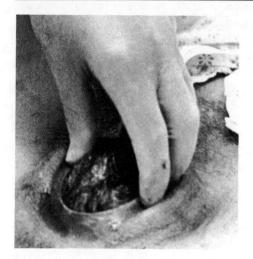

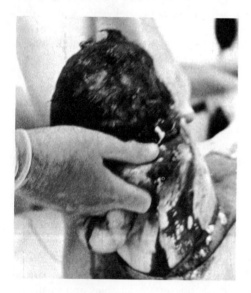

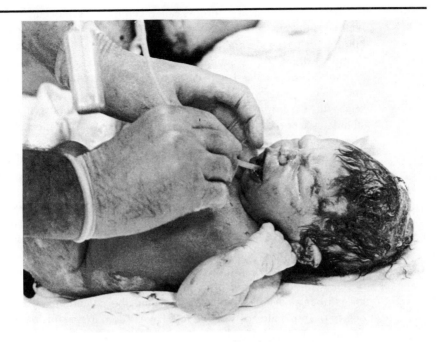

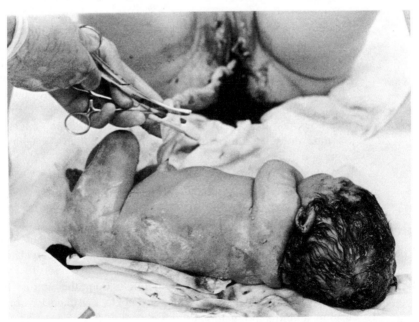

Photograph courtesy of H. Vermeulen

FIGURE 3–1a, b, c. Normal presentation of the baby during delivery. 3–1d. Following delivery, the residual fluids are cleared from the nose and mouth. 3–1e. The cord is cut, and the baby is left to its own resources for the first time in its life.

tion persists, the clinical syndrome called *kernicterus* can occur, with mental retardation almost the inevitable result. This is because the unconjugated bilirubin damages the brain.

In its extreme forms, jaundice may require blood exchange transfusion. A more recent practice has been to treat jaundice with phototherapy. The unclothed newborn, its eyes carefully protected, is placed under warm, bright fluorescent lights and "baked" for as long as 24 hours. Phototherapy stimulates action of the enzyme responsible for the conjugation of bilirubin, thereby eliminating the jaundice.

Respiratory complications   All babies experience a brief period of oxygen deficit and carbon dioxide retention during parturition. Barring other complications, most babies tolerate these short respiratory pauses with little difficulty. Prolonged respiratory pauses, however, have more disastrous effects. *Newborn apnea,* the absence of breathing for periods exceeding about 20–30 seconds, is accompanied by a lowered heart rate and cyanosis (lack of oxygen, retention of carbon dioxide, skin color from blue to purple). One type of respiratory complication, *anoxia* (lack of oxygen), is the leading cause of death during the birth process. One unfortunate aspect of respiratory forms of fetal distress is that by the time the condition is detected, the degree of anoxia already suffered may have caused irreparable damage to the organism, such as brain damage.

Diarrhea   Diarrhea caused by the bacterial infection *salmonellosis* is the scourge of the newborn nursery. It can spread rapidly throughout the nursery if careful hygienic procedures are not followed. Husbands whose wives have elected to room in with their baby, or who have chosen lying-in (baby spends the day with mother and the night in the nursery), quickly become familiar with these hygienic procedures when they visit the hospital. Scrubbing hands and arms, wearing a gown, and leaving the younger children in the waiting room are all practices designed to minimize the spread of infectious diarrhea as well as other bacterial or viral infections. Since diarrhea prevents sufficient retention of body fluids, dehydration poses a grave danger to the newborn.

Maternal complications   Abnormalities of the mother pose additional dangers to the fetus during parturition. Two possible complications are toxemia of pregnancy and placenta abruptico. *Toxemia of pregnancy* refers to a condition in which poisons (toxins) circulate through the bloodstream. The toxic substance may be linked to functionally inadequate kidneys, high blood pressure, and so on. The condition can lead to fetal convulsions (eclampsia), anoxia, and mortality. *Placenta abruptico* refers to a condition in which the placenta separates prematurely from the uterus. Intrauterine bleeding occurs, often without being detected. Marked loss of blood can lead to stillbirth and maternal shock.

The developmental consequences of such complications have prompted some physicians to recommend more extensive use of incubator care for all newborns suspected to be at risk.

Obstetric medications: Analgesics and anesthetics   The drugs used during labor and delivery are referred to as analgesics and anesthetics. Although distinctions between the two terms have been suggested (analgesics are supposed not to interfere with consciousness, whereas anesthetics often do), such distinctions are mainly of heuristic value. Both categories of obstetric medication cause an overall depression of newborn responsivity, either temporarily or well into the first year of life.

Although commonplace in American culture, the use of analgesics and anesthetics during labor and delivery is the exception rather than the rule in other cultures. Despite the heavy use of these chemical agents, little attention has been paid to their possible influence on the developing organism. The few studies that have addressed the problem report response depression during the first few days of life (Kron, Stein, & Goddard, 1966; Stechler, 1964).

Nearly all anesthetics and analgesics used as medications during parturition rapidly cross the placenta and enter the fetal bloodstream. This can occur as rapidly as 60 seconds after the mother has been given such drugs (Bowes, 1970). Thus, it is not uncommon to find tranquil newborns in the nursery or newborns so sedated that even the most primitive reflexes are depressed. Given this state of affairs, it is indeed surprising that so little research has been directed to the study of the potential effects of these drugs on behavioral development.

Preliminary results of a longitudinal study of the effects of obstetric medications on behavior development add empirical support to the growing public aversion to the use of such medications during parturition. Infants exposed to delivery medications were compared with infants born without medication on several measures, including the Graham Scales of Neonatal Development and the Bayley Scales of Infant Development (Conway & Brackbill, 1970). At 2, 5, and 30 days of age, the development of infants born with delivery medication was significantly poorer than that of the nonmedicated infants. In addition, infants receiving direct delivery medication required more trials to extinguish the orienting response (see Chapter 5) to an auditory stimulus for as long as five months after birth. All in all, a wiser policy for the administration of delivery medications seems advisable. At the very least, minimal use of drugs that depress responsivity would seem in order.

ASSESSMENT OF THE NEWBORN

How does one determine the biobehavioral status of the newborn infant? What factors must be considered in any evaluation of the newborn? These are questions of assessment. Although we will deal with developmental assessment again in Chapter 4, several aspects of assessment are specific to the newborn. Assessment of the newborn is important for at least two reasons: first, it establishes the newborn's current level of functioning; second, it provides a base for predicting the likelihood of subsequent abnormalities in development (see Chapter 4).

Accurate evaluation of the current level of functioning relative to any prediction of future functioning is dependent upon the determination of the newborn's gestational age (GA). Accurate determination of GA is important because it helps to establish whether the newborn is a small-for-date, large-for-date, short-gestation, or a long-gestation infant. The correct GA is, then, a necessary prerequisite for reliably interpreting the significance of the newborn's present condition. Recall from the previous chapter the dissatisfaction with older definitions of prematurity which were based exclusively on the number of weeks the infant was in utero. Thus, a 34-week-gestation baby weighing 6 pounds 5 ounces would have been classified as premature according to the weeks-in-utero criterion. Clearly, however, the baby would not be premature according to a birth weight criterion.

Methods for assessing GA typically involve a comparison of the newborn's level of functioning with some established norm. The electrical activity of the newborn's brain may be compared with normative data to evaluate the newborn's status with respect to brain development (Dreyfus-Brisac, 1966). Physical characteristics of the newborn may be compared with prenatal growth norms, or the reflexive repertoire of the newborn may be compared with developmental norms for the appearance of reflexes.

One method for assessing GA combines the use of neurological signs (posture, head lag, arm and leg movements) with a variety of phenotypic criteria (skin texture, nipple formation, breast size, ear form). This combination of neurological and phenotypic criteria has shown much promise as an accurate method of assessing GA (Dubowitz, Dubowitz, & Goldberg, 1970).

In addition to assessing GA, the obstetric staff must evaluate the immediate viability of the newborn. Does the newborn show signs of respiratory distress? Does the newborn appear to be at risk? The most widely used assessment technique employed in the delivery room is that developed by Virginia Apgar. The subsequently labeled *Apgar* test is administered one minute and/or five minutes following full delivery of the baby. Evaluation on five criteria is performed, with a maximum score of ten indicating that baby survived the prenatal period and parturition in the best possible condition. Of the five signs described in Table 3–1, appearance is the least meaningful.

TABLE 3–1
Apgar scoring chart

Category	Rating		
	0	1	2
Activity (muscle tone)	Flaccid	Some flexion in extremities	Active motion
Pulse (heart rate)	None	Slow (below 100 beats per minute)	Over 100 beats per minute
Grimace (reflex irritability) .	No response	Grimace	Strong cry
Appearance (color)	Blue, pale	Body pink; extremities blue	Completely pink
Respiration (respiratory effort)	Absent	Slow	Good, crying

Source. Adapted from V. Apgar, "A proposal for a new method of evaluation of the newborn infant," *Current Research in Anesthesia and Analgesia,* 1953, *32,* 260–267.

Many perfectly normal newborns are cyanotic, or exhibit bluish extremities, shortly after birth, when the Apgar is administered. In most babies the condition is quickly corrected as oxygen intake and carbon dioxide outflow become stable.

In general, the objectivity and thus the reliability of the Apgar evaluation is greater when the anesthesiologist or the obstetric nurse rather than the delivering obstetrician conducts the assessment. The obstetrician's familiarity with the mother, both parents, or the whole family would probably interfere with objective judgment. There is nothing unique to this type of evaluation setting that would automatically eliminate "experimenter or observer bias."

BEHAVIOR OF THE NEWBORN

Four prominent characteristics of the newborn are its appearance, dependency, individuality, and competence. The *appearance* of the typical newborn includes (a) bluish-gray eyes, which may remain the same color or darken to a deep brown; (b) inactive tear glands; (c) a short neck, if any; (d) light to heavy growth of fine-textured hair over the body surface; (e) a bulging abdomen; (f) a broad, flat face; (g) disproportionately small arms, legs, and trunk and a disproportionately large head; (h) soft, flexible bones; (i) soft skin frequently speckled with blotches; (j) eyes which do not move conjugately; and (k) perhaps a misshapen head.

Of all young organisms, the human newborn is by far the most *dependent* upon its caregivers for its survival. Compared to the human adult, the newborn has a more rapid heartbeat, more rapid and irregular respiration, higher and more variable body temperature, shorter and less stable waking periods, a greater need to eliminate body wastes, and an inability to search for its own food. The newborn must be repeatedly cleansed, fed, pacified, and in general protected from potential insults to its integrity. Moreover, these caregiving needs must be met for a longer period of time than that required by the young of any other species.

The human being's psychobiological *individuality* was discussed in the previous chapters. As a reminder, recall that with the exception of identical twins, each human organism has its own unique combination of genotypic and phenotypic characteristics. Thus, some babies are boys, some are girls; some are black, some are white; some are active, and some are passive; some are at risk, and some are not.

Contrary to the historical notion that the newborn is a passive, unresponsive organism, contemporary theory and research suggest that in many respects the neonate is quite *competent*. As every parent can attest, the newborn can sneeze, wheeze, hiccup, spit up, cry, raise its head, suckle, and so on. Although much of the newborn's motor activity is random and not subject to voluntary control, a rich repertoire of organized reflexes gives the newborn a more highly organized behavior repertoire than it initially seems to have. One of the first and still among the most exacting descriptions of the newborn's behavior was provided by Dennis (1934). His description included specific ocular, facial and oral, throat, head, head and arm, trunk, reproductive organ, and foot and leg behaviors, as well as coordinate behaviors of many body parts.

BOX 3–2
Behavior repertoire of the newborn: Coordinate behavior of many body parts

Resting or sleeping posture—legs flexed, fists closed, upper arms out straight from shoulders, forearms flexed at right angles so that they lie close to head.

Opisthotonic position—strong flexion (backward arch) from head to heels, especially noticeable when the infant is held upside down.

Backbone reflex—concave bending of a side that is stroked or tickled.

Lifting head and rear—typically appears in older infants, sometimes seen in neonate.

"Fencing position"—when the neonate's head is rotated, the arm toward which the face is rotated extends and the other flexes, and the legs do likewise (tonic-neck reflex).

"Springing position"—when the infant is held upright and tilted forward, the arms extend forward and the legs are brought up.

Stretching, shivering, and trembling—slight shivers often occur during micturition, as in adults.

Startle response (often called the Moro reflex)—consists of throwing the arms apart, spreading the fingers, extending the legs, and throwing back the head; elicited by loud noises, falling, and extreme thermal stimuli but may also occur spontaneously.

Crying and unrest—mass activity.

Creeping movements—when the newborn in the prone position, with legs and arms drawn under the body and head is lifted, each pair of extremities alternates in movement.

Extremities extended to the side—when the neonate is held upright and rotated around the vertical axis, arms and legs are extended in the direction of rotation.

Bodily jerk—in response to loud noises, arms and legs flex strongly and jerk upward.

Source: Adapted from W. Dennis, "A description and classification of the responses of the newborn infant," *Psychological Bulletin*, 1934, *31*, 5–22, with permission of the American Psychological Association, Inc.

At one moment the baby may be crying and thrashing about, and in a few more moments it may drop into a deep sleep. Or a sleeping baby may literally jump to a screaming rage, only to be sound asleep again by the time mother arrives on the scene. Such rapid changes in behavior are referred to as *state* changes, or changes in the level of arousal. For the developmental psychologist, the study of arousal level is important because the state of the baby regulates its responsivity to environmental stimulation. Indeed, arousal

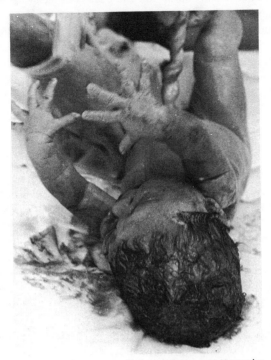

Photograph courtesy H. Vermeulen

FIGURE 3–2   The Moro reflex, or startle response, is among the first to be observed in newborns. In normal infants the reflex disappears from the behavior repertoire by four–six months of age. Its absence during the first few months, or its persistence past six months, suggests dysfunction of the central nervous system.

level, or state, is important for all aspects of behavior throughout the life span.

State

The level of arousal, or state, refers to the organism's overall level of functioning at any given moment in time, on a continuum ranging from deep sleep, through various levels of alertness, to screaming rage (Brackbill & Fitzgerald, 1969).

State is typically assessed behaviorally or physiologically, or by some combination of the two. Behavioral assessment of state usually involves observing the baby's overt behavior and rating that behavior on some predetermined scale. Simultaneous recording of physiological and behavioral responses is desirable, for often one category of responses will reflect state changes while the other will not. For example, in a study that compared prone (on the stomach) and supine (on the back) resting postures in new-borns, it was found that although physiological measures of state (heart rate, respiratory pattern) revealed no differences between the two postures, be-havioral ratings did. Newborns placed in the prone position moved about less and spent more time sleeping than did those placed in the supine posi-tion. When placed in the supine position, on the other hand, babies spent more time in drowsy sleep and considerably more time crying than when placed in the prone position (Brackbill, Douthitt, & West, 1973).

Pacification

One arousal level of particular interest to parents is the state called "cry-ing awake." In every household with a young infant this question is raised sooner or later: What can we do to quiet the baby? (Often the wording and phrasing are somewhat different!) Many parents use a rubber pacifier for this purpose. Others handle the baby and attempt to soothe it by back rub-bing, lullaby singing, and any other thing that comes to mind. However, some parents do not like to use pacifiers to quiet their babies, and parents often do not have the time or energy to use physical contact techniques. Are there any other ways to quiet baby? Is the parent a necessary component of the pacifying experience? The answer to the first question is apparently yes, but the answer to the second question is no.

The Salk imprinting hypothesis   Lee Salk has advanced an interesting hy-pothesis that during the prenatal period the fetus becomes imprinted, or fixed, on the sound of its mother's heartbeat (Salk, 1973). From this hypothe-sis, Salk predicted that during the postnatal months auditory stimulation of a type approximating the maternal heartbeat should serve to soothe the baby. Previous investigators had already demonstrated that continuous auditory stimulation reduced gross motor activity and led to more regular respiration rates in newborns (Warner, 1887; Canestrini, 1913; Irwin, 1941).

Working in a hospital nursery, Salk presented newborns with the sound of a tape-recorded normal heartbeat, at 72 beats per minute. The dependent variables in the study were the amount of weight gained, the amount of food consumed, and the amount of crying that occurred from the first to the fourth day of life. These same measures were recorded for another group of newborns who did not experience the tape-recorded sounds. Surprisingly, newborns exposed to the tape-recorded sounds gained more weight than did the no-sound group, even though the two groups consumed the same quantity of food. Moreover, the sound group spent considerably less time crying than did the no-sound group. Salk concluded that the greater crying of the no-sound group required a greater consumption of the available energy (food), thus leading to less weight gain.

In another study Salk compared the pacifying effectiveness of the heart-beat sound with that of a metronome beating at the same rate and with the sound of recorded lullabies. This time the children ranged from 16 to 37 months of age and were all residents of the New York Foundling Hospital. In this study the heartbeat sound was found to significantly reduce the time required for children to fall asleep when compared with all other sound conditions. The metronome, lullabies, and no-sound conditions did not differ from one another in effectiveness.

These studies by Salk stimulated many investigators to consider just what mechanisms are responsible for pacifying babies. Does the infant imprint prenatally to its mother's heartbeat? Is some other feature of the heartbeat sound—for example, its continuous and monotonous character—responsible for the pacification effect? Is sound the only or merely the best sensory experience that can be used to pacify a baby?

Pacification and the continuous stimulation effect   When mother picks up her baby in an effort to pacify it, the baby receives a virtual onslaught of stimulation. The handled infant receives tactile-kinesthetic, auditory, visual, thermal, olfactory, and gustatory stimulation singly, simultaneously, or in various combinations. Some authors have argued that babies have a need for tactile-kinesthetic stimulation, and that receiving such stimulation reduces their level of arousal (Kulka, Fry, & Goldstein, 1960). Casler (1965) suggested that extra tactile stimulation (handling) is beneficial to infants who are deprived of normal handling. Institutionalized infants given daily extra handling performed better on several measures of infant development than did infants who received only the normal amount of handling.

One quite effective method for pacifying baby is *swaddling*. This form of tactile-kinesthetic stimulation has been used for thousands of years. It involves wrapping the baby tightly from neck to toe with long, narrow strips of light cloth. Laboratory studies of swaddling have done little more than confirm the effectiveness of this age-old pacifying practice (Brackbill & Fitzgerald, 1969).

The most common American swaddling method is to wrap the baby in a receiving blanket, a method that works well for the newborn but enables an older infant to readily kick its way out. Interestingly enough, poorly swaddled babies are more irritable than are babies who are well swaddled or are not swaddled at all (Wolff, 1966).

A more common pacifying practice in the United States is to set the baby in motion, that is, to apply *vestibular stimulation*. Historically, vestibular, or motion, stimulation was applied by rocking the baby in a cradle. Now that cradles are out of style, this form of rocking has been replaced by jiggling cribs, walking the baby to and fro in a carriage, or rocking the baby in a rocking chair. Laboratory studies of vestibular pacification again support popular parental techniques for quieting babies. In a series of experiments, vigorous rocking was found to be a very effective inhibitor of distress: more babies slept and fewer cried when rocked (Pederson & Vrugt, 1973). It has been suggested that the pacifying properties of rocking or walking may be related to the similarity between their rhythms (back and forth, back and forth) and the rhythmicity of other biological activity (Kessen & Mandler, 1961), perhaps of a type experienced in utero.

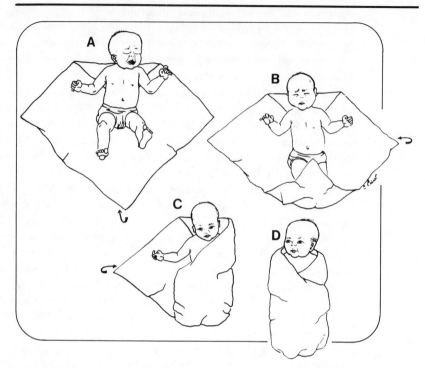

Drawings by Catherine T. Best

FIGURE 3–3 A cozy wrap for a fussy baby: swaddling, American style. **3–3a.** Fold corner of receiving blanket over and lay baby on blanket tummy-side up. **3–3b.** Fold lower corner of blanket over baby's legs, keeping baby's arms at sides. **3–3c.** Pull right side of blanket over baby and tuck snuggly underneath. **3–3d.** Pull left side of blanket over baby and tuck under. Now lay baby on tummy for a nice, restful nap.

Although the pacifying properties of swaddling and rocking do not provide a direct test of Salk's imprinting hypothesis, they at least demonstrate that applying auditory stimulation is not the only way to quiet the young infant. More direct evaluation of the Salk hypothesis has been provided by Brackbill and her associates. In one study, each newborn was presented with four different auditory conditions: a tape-recorded heartbeat, a metronome, recorded lullabies, and no sound. Measures of gross motor activity, heart rate, respiration, and crying were taken. Contrary to Salk's results, the tape-recorded heartbeat did not prove to be any more effective than the other two sounds. All sounds were better pacifiers than the no-sound condition. Similar results were obtained with three-year-old children (Brackbill, Adams, Crowell, & Gray, 1966).

If the pacifying effects of auditory stimulation are not specific to heartbeat sounds, what quality of the auditory stimulation is responsible for the pacifying effect? In one study, the arousal level of newborns exposed to continuous auditory stimulation was compared with the arousal level of newborns exposed to intermittent stimulation. Continuous stimulation decreased the arousal level, whereas intermittent stimulation increased it (Brackbill, 1970). It seems that the continuous, monotonous quality of stimulation is responsible for pacification, and that it makes little difference whether the stimulation is tactile-kinesthetic, vestibular, or auditory. Thus, one key to pacification is the *continuous stimulation effect* (Brackbill, 1975) of external stimulation. Moreover, the effect is greater when the stimulus intensity is moderate to slightly strong, at least for auditory stimulation (Brackbill, 1975).

As noted, mothers generally provide a multimodal repertoire of stimulation when they pacify their babies. Does this pacify baby any more effectively than stimulation from only one sensory modality? Newborn babies were exposed to four different pacifying conditions: visual, auditory, tactile, or thermal stimulation only; combinations of two and three of these conditions; and all four conditions in combination. The results of the experiment indicated that the pacification effects of continuous sensory stimulation are additive: a combination of visual, auditory, tactile, and thermal stimulation was more effective than combinations of two or three of these conditions (Brackbill, 1971).

Since most of the above studies were concerned with the infant's initial response to pacifying stimulation (usually involving about 20-minute periods of stimulation), one remaining question concerns the prolonged effects of continuous stimulation. Newborns were exposed to the four types of stimuli used in the study of additive effects cited above for a two-hour period. The initial pacification effects were again observed, and, quite important, it was found that they remained relatively unchanged over time (Brackbill, 1973).

The advantages of using continuous stimulation when infants are irritable or ill have been detailed (Brackbill & Fitzgerald, 1969). In such conditions, the baby may be driven by such a demand for exogenous stimulation (stimulation arising outside the baby) that, failing to receive it, the baby generates excessive endogenous stimulation (stimulation arising within the baby). The excessive crying and thrashing which result not only upset parents but prevent the baby from obtaining vitally needed rest. If upset and anxious parents knew that continuous stimulation can pacify a baby, much child abuse might be prevented. Indeed, "the most frequently reported precipitating cause [of child abuse] is the child's prolonged crying, which parents are at a loss to deal with and can tolerate no longer" (Brackbill, 1969, p. 374).

In light of this rather one-sided presentation of the pacifying effects of continuous stimulation, an important note of caution must be sounded. Despite the impressive pacifying effects of continuous sensory stimulation, it is not advocated that these techniques be employed as the sole means of quieting the baby. There have been no studies of the long-term effects of continuous stimulation.

BOX 3–3
Lullaby from the womb

When a baby comes home from the hospital, his parents quickly discover that the predictable bouts of howling are not always due to hunger, fatigue, colic or a wet diaper—and when no obvious cause can be found for the infant's distress, he is usually left to cry himself to sleep. But now, an obstetrician at Tokyo's Nippon Medical College has suggested that crying babies may sometimes just be homesick for the familiar prenatal environment of their mothers' wombs.

Dr. Hajime Murooka came to this conclusion during an attempt to find a "natural" way of calming babies so that he could examine them with delicate instruments, such as an electroencephalograph, which records brain waves. To provide a comforting substitute for the womb's security, Murooka placed a tiny microphone inside the uterus of several pregnant women and recorded their internal body sounds. When he played back the amplified sounds to groups of screaming infants, almost every single one stopped crying—frequently in less than a minute—and many of them dropped off to sleep. This pacifying effect, says Murooka, is most dramatic in babies less than a month old, whose memory of the womb is still fresh.

Rhythm: Murooka's discovery has resulted in the production of a popular record and cassette version of the original womb sounds, put out by the Toshiba-EMI company. Titled "Lullaby Inside Mum," the unaccompanied body sounds produced by blood pulsing through various maternal blood vessels actually constitute only a small portion of the commercial record. In other selections, the womb sounds are used as a sort of rhythmic back-up section for a variety of classical pieces by Schumann, Tchaikovsky, Bach, Massenet and others. For Toshiba, "Lullaby" has become something of a hit, with about 8,000 copies sold to anxious new parents since January. Mr. and Mrs. Motoo Ota have been using the cassette to soothe their new baby daughter for two months. "The baby falls asleep," says Mrs. Ota, "as soon as we turn it on."

Source: *Newsweek*, March 31, 1975, pp. 71–72. Reprinted with permission, copyright 1975 by Newsweek, Inc. All rights reserved.

BIOLOGICAL RHYTHMS

Biological rhythms are any regular, repeating pattern of activity, ranging from such obvious patterns as the menstrual cycle to more subtle rhythms, such as the release of adrenocorticosteroids into the bloodstream. The most general classification of biological rhythms divides them into *exogenous* and *endogenous rhythms*. The maintenance of exogenous rhythms is dependent upon factors external to the organism. Placing an organism into an environment devoid of all possible external cues (for example, without variations in light and temperature) will lead to a breakdown in the rhythmicity of exogenous rhythms. The maintenance of endogenous rhythms, on the other hand, is relatively, if not completely, independent of environmental influences. Endogenous rhythms have been defined as self-sustaining rhythms that have a limited range of potential environmental determinants (Aschoff, 1965).

.A more specific classification of biorhythms is based on the length of time required for the rhythms to complete a full cycle of activity. *Circadian rhythms* complete a full cycle in about 24 hours; *ultradian rhythms* complete a cycle—sometimes measured in seconds—in less than 24 hours; and *infradian rhythms* complete a cycle—sometimes measured in years—in more than 24 hours.

The development of biorhythms

Biological rhythms make their appearance during prenatal life. Figure 3–4 illustrates the rhythmic activity of the fetus during the last 130 days of prenatal life. Note especially the marked reduction in variance and "quieting" that occurs shortly before parturition. The activity curves for other fetuses tend to follow the same general pattern.

Postnatally, such rhythmic activities as the daily heart rate, body temperature, the gross body activity associated with feeding, urinary excretion, digestion, and activity-quiescence attain regularity at different times and do not

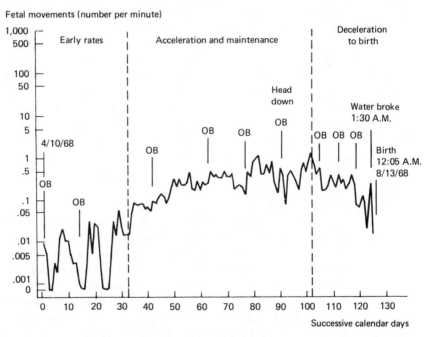

Source: D. D. Edwards and J. S. Edwards, "Fetal movement: Development and time course," *Science*, 1970, *169*, 95–97. With permission of the authors and the American Association for the Advancement of Science.

FIGURE 3–4 Graphic presentation of the time course of fetal movements during prenatal development.

begin to synchronize (occur together) until the infant is approximately four months of age. On the basis of the collective research on the ontogeny of biological rhythms, the following listing gives the ages at which specific rhythms make their appearance during infancy.

Age of appearance	Rhythm
Prenatal	Fetal activity
First postnatal week	Skin resistance
2d–3d postnatal week	Urine excretion; REM-NREM sleep
3d–6th postnatal week	Sleep-wake cycle
4th–9th postnatal week	Body temperature
6th–18th postnatal week	Daily heart rate
2d postnatal month	Sodium and potassium content of urine
8th postnatal month	Adult rhythm of REM-NREM sleep

Note that each of the above rhythmic phenomena is associated with rather long periods of time, some in fact representing circadian rhythms (heart rate, body temperature, skin resistance, sleep-wake). However, there are rhythms of much shorter duration that have consequences for the regulation and organization of behavior.

Biorhythms: REM-NREM

REM-NREM refers to rapid eye movement sleep and non–rapid eye movement sleep. Several stages of sleep have both behavioral and physiological characteristics. Electrophysiological tracings of brain wave activity can be used to differentiate the various sleep stages (see Figure 3–5).

In stage 1 sleep, the body relaxes, the heart rate slows down, and brain wave activity becomes irregular, desynchronized, and variable. In stage 2 sleep, there is a further reduction in physiological activity, and quick bursts of electrical activity (spindles) appear in the brain wave tracings. In stage 3 sleep, large, slow brain waves appear, the muscles become quite relaxed, respiration is regular, and the heart rate, blood pressure, and temperature continue to decline. In the deepest stage of sleep, stage 4, the muscles are very relaxed, and the brain waves are slow and of high amplitude. When in this stage, the sleeper can be awakened only with extreme difficulty.

About 60 minutes after the human adult falls asleep, the electrical activity of the brain indicates that the sleeper is moving from deep sleep (stage 4) to lighter stages of sleep (stage 1). About 30 minutes later, the brain wave activity appears to be that of stage 1 sleep. There is, however, one important difference—the sleeper's eyes begin to move. These rapid eye movements (REMs) indicate that the sleeper has begun to dream. One of the more mysterious aspects of REM sleep as compared with NREM sleep is that the younger the human being, the more sleep time is spent in REM sleep. For example, the newborn spends approximately 50 percent of sleep time in REM sleep.

One cannot help wondering what the newborn is dreaming about. No one really knows. One suggestion (Berger, 1969) is that the high percentage of REM sleep reflects the immaturity of the oculomotor system and serves to strengthen the neural pathways that mediate consensual eye movements (movements of both eyes in the same direction). Another suggestion is that the amount of time spent in REM sleep is related to the amount of external stimulation processed by the organism: the less waking time spent taking in external stimulation, the more sleep time spent in REM or endogenously produced stimulation states (Roffwarg, Muzio, & Dement, 1966). As the baby spends proportionately more time awake, there is a corresponding decrease in the proportion of REM sleep relative to total sleep time. Thus, one might expect that if the neonate were overstimulated, or perhaps stressed, there would be a reduction in the amount of time spent in REM sleep. This suggestion finds some support in a study of the effects of circumcision on newborn REM-NREM sleep (Emde, Harmon, Metcalf, Koenig, & Wagonfeld, 1971). Circumcised newborns spent more time in NREM sleep on the night following the circumcision than did noncircumcised comparison newborns. It appears that stress or environmental overstimulation may actually suppress REM sleep by reducing the requirements for endogenously produced stimulation.

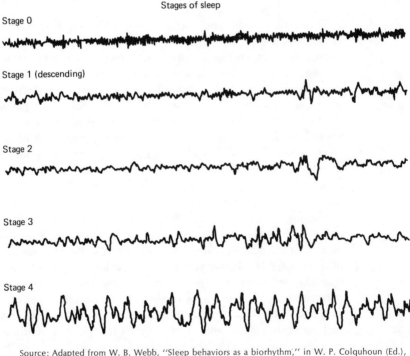

Source: Adapted from W. B. Webb, "Sleep behaviors as a biorhythm," in W. P. Colquhoun (Ed.), *Biological rhythms and human performance* (London and New York: Academic Press, 1971), pp. 149–177. Reprinted with permission of the author and Academic Press, Inc.

FIGURE 3–5 Electroencephalogram (EEG) stages of sleep

Biorhythms: Crying and sucking

Crying   The newborn's cry is undifferentiated, eliciting general and prompt caregiving (Bell & Ainsworth, 1972). Later in the newborn period, the cry becomes differentiated into the hunger, or *basic*, cry, the *anger* cry, and the *pain* cry (Wasz-Hoskert et al., 1964). What features of the cry change, and what components of the cry differentially signal caregivers to respond to the infant's needs?

Wolff (1967) suggests that the significant changes occur in the temporal characteristics of the cry. Analyzing cries by means of a sound spectrograph (a device that makes "pictures" of sounds), Wolff found rather precise temporal differences among basic, anger, and pain cries. The first part of the cry is expiratory; this is followed, in sequence, by a rest period (baby cannot cry and breathe simultaneously), an inspiratory "whistle," and another rest period. The pattern then repeats itself.

For the basic and anger cries, respectively, the mean duration of the inspiratory cry was 0.62 and 0.69 seconds; of the rest period, 0.085 and 0.20 seconds; of the expiratory whistle, 0.195 and 0.11 seconds. The pain cry, however, differed sharply from the other two cries. Here the duration of the inspiratory cry was five times longer, while the rest period lasted for as much as seven seconds.

Given these basic data, Wolff conducted a very interesting experiment. He played tape recordings of different cries and noted mothers' reactions to the cries. Mothers listening to the tape-recorded pain cries were described as being anxious and very concerned about the baby's welfare. Then Wolff spliced the pain cry tapes so that the rest interval approximated that of the basic and anger cries. No other aspect of the pain cry tapes was altered. Mothers exposed to the altered tapes responded as if the cries were basic or anger cries rather than pain cries. Although a great deal of additional research must be done to specify the ability of precise components of different cries to differentially cue caregiver behavior, Wolff's observations suggest that the rhythmic features of cries provide one important cue—informing parents of the infant's needs.

Sucking   Sucking is a behavior of obvious psychobiological importance to the infant, since it is the primary means of obtaining food for quite a few months of life. Some sucking behavior occurs in the absence of food or any other specifiable eliciting stimulus. This sucking involves movement of the lips, jaw, and tongue; often occurs with the mouth closed; and is readily observed in the lighter stages of sleep. Observing this type of nonnutritive sucking, Wolff (1967) found that the number of sucking movements per sucking burst ranged from 4 to 12, with rest periods of from two to ten seconds between bursts. The number of sucks per burst and the interburst rest intervals were extremely consistent for the same baby.

Wolff then noted sucking behavior when the baby was given a pacifier. During quiet sleep the number of sucks per second ranged from 1.9 to 2.3. This rhythmic rate is amazingly consistent with the rhythmic rate of response stereotypies (motor movements) found in various abnormalities. For example, children with Down's syndrome; autistic, schizophrenic, and blind children; and children with psychomotor retardation all show the same rhythmic rates when rocking on hands and knees or while sitting and when repetitively nodding their heads (Wolff, 1968). However, whether the same endogenous clocking mechanism regulates normal nonnutritive sucking and abnormal response stereotypies has yet to be determined.

Biorhythms: Caregiver-infant organization

The study of REM-NREM sleep, crying, and sucking raises exciting questions concerning the role that rhythms may play in the early organization of the infant's behavior. Is it possible that rhythmic phenomena play an equally important role in the organization of caregiver-infant interaction? Direct evidence of rhythmicity in caregiver-infant interaction is being gathered in a longitudinal study being conducted in Boston (Sander, 1969).

In one part of the study, babies awaiting adoption roomed in with a nurse. Some babies roomed in exclusively with one nurse for a 10- or 18-day period. Other babies were cared for by one nurse during the first 10 days, then were cared for by a different nurse during days 11 through 28. Nursery babies were fed at scheduled 4-hour intervals and experienced three changes in the caregiver staff during each 24-hour period.

One obvious difference between the two groups was the markedly greater activity and crying in the nursery babies. Perhaps less obvious was the change in circadian rhythmicity that occurred over the ten days. Crying and activity in the one-day-old nursery babies was distributed irregularly throughout the 24-hour period, with a slight concentration during the nighttime. However, by the tenth day most activity and crying shifted to the nighttime hours. In contrast, the activity of the room-in babies was more regularly distributed throughout the first 24-hour period. By the tenth day, crying and activity were clearly shifting toward the daytime hours. Moreover, the caregiver's activity (frequency, promptness, and duration of intervention) matched that of the baby in both the onset and the duration of the activity. The interaction pattern for the nursery infants and their caregivers showed little evidence of a similar match-up of infant and caregiver behavior.

Comparisons of caregiver behavior were made between the two room-in nurses, who were designated Nurse A and Nurse B. When babies were switched after ten days from Nurse A to Nurse B, they showed an abrupt decrease in crying, suggesting that Nurse B was giving more attention to her caregiving assignment. A similar decrement did not occur for the infants switched from Nurse B to Nurse A. Interestingly enough, inspection of the caregiving records revealed that Nurse A responded to the infant's cry more rapidly and intervened more frequently than did Nurse B. On the other hand, when Nurse B did provide caregiving she spent longer periods of time with the baby than did Nurse A.

This is a good illustration of the importance of both quantity and quality in caregiving behavior: quantity, in terms of the frequency and speed of interventions; quality, in terms of the length of time spent with baby when intervention is called for. While the work of Sander and his associates has yet to bear the bountiful fruits of long-term longitudinal study, the data we have summarized suggest that the quality of early infant-caregiver interaction will reflect the degree to which caregiver and infant activity rhythms become synchronized. Indeed, Sander (1969) argues that *regulation* may be the basic element in the infant's developing interactions with caregivers and with the environment in general.

FEEDING STYLES AND SCHEDULES

Of all the possible interactions between the caregiver and the newborn, none has attracted more attention or generated more controversy than feeding. Both mother and infant are biologically prepared for this interaction. On the infant side are the rooting and sucking reflexes, which serve to orient the baby toward the breast or bottle. On the maternal side are lactation and the ejection reflex, which prepare the mother to supply the nourishment sought. Lactation refers to the production of milk, while the ejection reflex initiates milk flow and is, not so incidentally, highly susceptible to the influence of maternal emotional states, such as pain, fear, or embarrassment (Newton, 1971).

Breast feeding versus bottle feeding

During the first third of this century breast feeding was clearly the preferred feeding method in practice and in the professional literature. Around the time of World War II, public opinion shifted drastically, and professionals began to question the theoretical basis for recommending breast feeding, a position usually traced to the Freudian theory of orality (Levine, 1951). Indeed, by the 1960s pediatric texts were openly acknowledging not only that the mother's feeding-style preference was an important predictor of success at breast feeding, but were also providing illustrations of babies for whom breast feeding was not advisable. For example, difficulties with the ejection reflex may result in engorgement of the breasts, interfering with the infant's ability to properly grasp the nipple and causing great discomfort to the mother.

There are biological advantages to human milk. Studies comparing the nutritive qualities and the biochemical composition of human milk with cow's milk clearly indicate that each species is provided with the milk that is most appropriate for its own offspring (Ziai, Janeway, & Cooke, 1969). One investigator suggests that the excessively high sodium content of commercial infant formulas is partly responsible for the marked increase in high blood pressure (hypertension) since World War II (Guthrie, 1968). The sodium content of human breast milk is considerably lower than that found in cow's milk or in commercial infant formulas. Nevertheless, the evidence for the biological advantage of human milk over cow's milk must be viewed in total perspective. Several studies of the content of human breast milk have identified disturbingly high levels of various drugs (for example, analgesics and anesthetics) that no parent would willingly administer to an infant. Well over a hundred different drugs have been isolated in samples of human breast milk (see Catz & Giacorca, 1972).

Often-cited advantages of breast feeding include (1) its ready availability, correct temperature, and lack of "preparation time"; (2) its promotion of maternal uterine contraction, delay in ovulation, and the prevention of menstrual cramping and mood states; and (3) its possible role as an inhibitor of breast cancer (Harfouche, 1970; Newton, 1971). Breast milk also helps the infant to resist infections and gastrointestinal disorders. Nowhere is this better illustrated than in underdeveloped countries, such as Guatemala, where weanling diarrhea is always a threat when babies are finally weaned from the breast (Mata, Fernandez, & Urrntia, 1967). Finally, compared to bottle-fed babies, breast-fed babies have been reported to be held, touched, and talked to more during the feeding interaction (Richards & Bernal, 1971).

One might expect the incidence of breast feeding to be high in underdeveloped countries, where alternative commercial formulas are not readily available. The relatively long periods of time that infants are breast-fed in such countries seems to support this view (Barry & Paxson, 1971). In these countries, the important factors influencing the incidence of breast feeding appear to be (1) the availability of adequate nutritional substitutes, (2) the overall hygienic conditions of the culture, and (3) the overall economic conditions of the culture.

When cultural conditions permit viable alternatives to breast feeding, its incidence of occurrence seems to be regulated by other factors, such as social class, educational level, and current social fads. All in all, we know less about the consequences of feeding methods than might be expected, given the significance of the feeding experience during early development. Evidence that the quality of the caregiver-infant interaction differs as a function of feeding style as early as the first ten days of life (Richards & Bernal, 1971) suggests the need for the intensive study of the developmental ramifications of breast and bottle feeding. For example, it may be that the physical contact (handling) the infant receives during feeding may be of greater developmental significance than the particular feeding method used. If this is so, then father with bottle can certainly accomplish as much as mother with breast or bottle so far as the infant is concerned.

Scheduled feeding versus demand feeding

Another important dimension of feeding is when to do it. Over the years child-rearing "experts" have variously recommended feeding babies at precise intervals (on schedule) or feeding them when they are hungry (on demand). Biologically, the newborn appears to be prepared for scheduled feeding. During the first several days of life there is little correspondence between the newborn's behavior and the hospital nursery routine. By the fourth day, however, the newborn's activity and crying show evidence of becoming time-locked to the hospital feeding routine (Campbell, 1968).

The baby's ability to adapt rapidly to scheduled feeds is nicely illustrated by two studies that investigated the effects of changing newborns from one schedule to another. In the first study, newborns were placed on a three-hour feeding schedule. About 15–20 minutes before feeding time, the babies showed an increase in gross motor activity. Then the babies were switched to a four-hour schedule. For a day or two following the switch, the babies continued to act as if they were on a three-hour schedule. Gradually, however, they adapted to the four-hour schedule, so that an increase in gross motor activity again occurred 15–20 minutes prior to schedule time (Marquis, 1941). Krachkovskaia (1959) obtained similar results, using changes in the white blood cell count, rather than motor activity, as the dependent variable. Newborns previously on a three-hour schedule were switched to a four-hour schedule. Within several days the rise in the white blood cell count that had preceded a scheduled three-hour feed by about 15 minutes had shifted so that it now preceded the four-hour feed.

Recall Sander's suggestion that rhythms may be the fundamental regulators of behavioral organization. In this light, perhaps the newborn's rapid adaptation to a regular feeding schedule represents the initial organizer of caregiver-infant interaction; that is, it may be the initial means by which baby and mother organize their daily interactions. However, before deciding to plop the nipple into baby's mouth every four hours on the dot, let us consider this topic in more detail.

Unfortunately for those who desire simple solutions, the clear-cut dichotomy of scheduled versus demand feeding does not accurately reflect the complex realities of the real world. For example, Ainsworth and Bell (1969) identified nine different patterns of caregiver-infant interactions that were relevant to the question of when to feed the baby. The nine patterns were:

1. *Demand: thoroughgoing and consistent*—mother was keenly aware of and responded to the infant's signals of hunger.
2. *Schedule: flexible*—mother was highly sensitive to the infant's signals of hunger but attempted to place the infant on a mutually satisfactory schedule. Feeding was also a social occasion for mothers using this method.
3. *Demand: overfeeding to gratify the baby*—mother tended to generalize the infant's signals of hunger to too many behaviors and continued the feeding, sometimes in an on and off fashion until all the food prepared was consumed.
4. *Schedule: overfeeding to gratify the baby*—mother interpreted nearly all mouthing movements as signs of hunger; feeding was fast in contrast to the previous method, where feeding was nicely paced.
5. *Schedule: too much staving off*—mother made the baby wait for un-

necessarily long periods of time before feeding, failing to interpret hunger cues when given.

6. *Pseudodemand: mother impatient*—feedings were disorganized mainly due to mother's failure to satisfy the baby; the holes in the bottle nipples were so large that food was expelled more rapidly than baby could swallow it.

7. *Pseudodemand: overfeeding to make the baby sleep*—mother willfully stuffed the baby so that it would sleep for long periods of time; even when the baby attempted to avoid eating, mother stuffed the food down.

8. *Schedule: rigid*—mother fed the baby strictly according to the clock, with no regard to signals from the baby.

9. *Arbitrary*—mother showed no consistency in organizing feeding.

Babies in feeding patterns 1 and 2 cried least prior to and during feeding. Overall, the first four patterns reflected a general sensitivity to the baby's rhythmic behavior, a tendency to respond promptly to signals for caregiving intervention, a desire to gratify the baby, and a tendency to provide physical contact exceeding that required merely to feed the baby. When feeding patterns 5 through 9 were used, there was much greater disorganization in caregiver-infant interaction, and the mother was obviously the dominant member of the dyad.

Clearly, recommendations advanced in the popular child-rearing literature to schedule- or demand-feed are oversimplifications of what is required. The newborn seems biologically primed for scheduled feeding. However, the quality of the caregiver-infant interaction overrides somewhat the nature of the feeding pattern used. When the mother is sensitive to her infant's needs and consistently responds to those needs, regulation of the mother's routine and the infant's routine is facilitated. Note that consistency itself implies an orderliness, regularity, or routine to caregiving.

SUMMARY

The newborn period of development covers the events of birth and, liberally defined, the first few weeks of postnatal life. Parturition is divided into three phases: from labor to dilation of the cervix, from full dilation of the cervix to birth of the baby, and from birth to expulsion of the afterbirth. Babies are presented in a variety of positions which are distinguished by the position of the body and the part of the body to emerge first.

Complications that may arise during parturition include jaundice and anoxia. While these disorders can be treated with few apparent long-term effects, untreated jaundice or prolonged anoxia can result in severe damage to the organism. Maternal complications, such as toxemia of pregnancy and placenta abruptico, also spell potential danger for the fetus.

Recently, great interest and concern have been directed toward the effects of obstetric medications on the fetus and the newborn. Preliminary evidence suggests that these obstetric medications may depress responsivity for as long as five months after birth. Obviously, many situations demand the use of anesthetics. Nonetheless, greater care should be used when administering these drugs during parturition.

The newborn is characterized by its appearance, dependency, individuality, and competence. Behaviorally, the newborn is not the passive organism it was once believed to be. The reflexive and behavioral repertoire of the newborn represents the basic ingredients from which all higher levels of organized behavior emerge. One of the most striking aspects of behavior during this period of development is the rapidity with which the newborn changes from one behavioral state to another. One end of the state continuum, screaming rage, is of continual concern to parents. Studies of pacification techniques tend to support the age-old practices for quieting infants. Moreover, these studies suggest that the critical aspect of pacification is the continuous, monotonous character of sensory stimulation, whatever type of stimulation is given. While the TV set, vacuum cleaner, or swaddling can effectively pacify baby, the most desirable pacifying agent is a loving and compassionate caregiver. When patience wears thin, however, it is good to know that other means are available to pacify baby humanely.

Also of recent interest among infant researchers is the role of biological rhythms in regulating initial caregiving-infant interaction. To date, the most extensively investigated rhythms have been those associated with sleep. However, the rhythmic features of crying and sucking suggest that the patterning of these behaviors is an important dimension in early caregiver-infant interaction. What little evidence currently exists suggests that the organization of caregiver-infant interaction is facilitated when caregiver and infant have fairly similar daily routines. The best feeding schedules seem to be those that reflect the mother's awareness of the infant's hunger cues, are not overly rigid, and provide opportunities for caregiver and infant to interact socially.

There are advantages and disadvantages to both breast and bottle feeding. For the human species the most important dimension of the feeding method used may be the physical contact that the infant receives when being held during feeding. The most important aspect of feeding for caregiver and infant is for both to be relaxed so that both may enjoy this special time together. One distinct advantage of bottle feeding is that it enables father to participate in this important aspect of caregiving.

SUGGESTED ADDITIONAL READING

Luce, G. G.   *Body time.* New York: Pantheon Books, 1971.

Newton, N.   Psychological differences between breast and bottle feeding. *American Journal of Clinical Nutrition,* 1971, *29,* 993–1004.

Salk, L.   Thoughts on the concept of imprinting and its place in early human development. *Canadian Psychiatric Association Journal,* 1966, *11,* 295–305.

BOX 4–1
Study questions

Does growth occur in a linear fashion, in spurts, or in "cycles"?

When does handedness develop?

Should parents or educators encourage the acceleration of developmental processes in young infants? What might be some advantages and disadvantages of such acceleration?

What is meant by "levels of organization"?

Briefly describe the general changes that take place in the central nervous system during early development. How are these changes related to behavior?

What are the differences and similarities between neurological and developmental examinations of the infant?

What does "regression to the mean" predict about the expected height of one's children?

What does a body temperature of 99.0 degrees Fahrenheit imply for a one-year-old baby?

Describe the development of posture, locomotion, and prehension.

What are some valuable suggestions for beginning bowel and bladder training and seeing it through to completion?

Describe the development of the ability to draw.

4

PHYSICAL GROWTH AND
MOTOR DEVELOPMENT

Infancy and early childhood is a time of rapid growth and development. Changes occur so rapidly, in fact, that many parents are often left wondering whether their rambunctious four-year-old really ever was as small and dependent as that tiny baby in the hospital newborn photograph. Although growth normally follows an orderly pattern toward increasingly mature physique and behavior, it does not proceed in a strictly linear fashion. From time to time there are periods when growth levels off or when there is even regression to less mature forms. For example, many babies insist on crawling even though they have mastered upright locomotion. After a time, however, upright locomotion becomes their predominant posture for getting around in the world.

PRINCIPLES OF MORPHOLOGICAL DEVELOPMENT

Arnold Gesell was one of the foremost investigators of physical growth. He compared developmental processes to a spiral in order to conceptualize the fluctuating nature of development and to illustrate the ever-higher levels of organization achieved at each point along the life span. Gesell drew a parallel between the development of the embryo and the postnatal development of the organism. He applied certain principles of embryological development to all postnatal developmental processes. Those principles, known as the *principles of morphological development,* were: (1) the principle of individuating maturation, (2) the principle of developmental direction, (3)

71

the principle of reciprocal interweaving, (4) the principle of self-regulating fluctuation, and (5) the principle of functional asymmetry (Gesell, 1954).

Gesell's basic maturational stance was expressed in the *principle of individuating maturation*. He saw growth as controlled by endogenous factors rather than by exogenous factors. Development unfolded in an orderly fashion regardless of the environment. Gesell recognized that development was unique for each individual, but his emphasis was solely on the structural growth of the organism, whereas the point of view expressed in this text is that of structure-function interaction. The *principle of developmental direction* specifies the course of structural differentiation. *Cephalocaudal* development refers to differentiation occurring in order from head to foot. *Proximo-distal* development refers to differentiation occurring first at the center and last at the peripheral extremes of the body. The idea of spirallike growth is the thrust of the *principle of reciprocal interweaving*. Thus, the development of locomotion and fine motor skills requires the coordination of paired or opposed motor systems. Flexion of the limb is opposed to extension of the limb, and both must become coordinated if walking is to develop properly. The opposition of forefinger and thumb must become coordinated if the child is to develop the ability to pick up an object using only these two fingers.

The oscillatory or fluctuating nature of development and the endogenous organizers of growth are recognized in the *principle of self-regulating fluctuation*. Examples of this principle include biological rhythms, such as the sleep-wake cycle and the feeding rhythms discussed in the previous chapter. The central theme of this principle is that the organism moves from instability to stability during development but at the same time retains the flexibility to adapt to its environment. Finally, the emergence of laterality or cerebral dominance is the basis for the *principle of functional asymmetry*. The most obvious example of this principle is, of course, the emergence of handedness.

Laterality

During the development of the brain, the cerebral cortex becomes differentiated into two structural units, or *hemispheres,* which "communicate" with each other by means of a mass of interconnecting nerve fibers called the *corpus callosum*. The two hemispheres have different functional properties. The hemisphere on the left controls the right side of the body, and the hemisphere on the right controls the left side of the body. The processing of speech sounds occurs in the left hemisphere, whereas the processing of visual-spatial information occurs in the right hemisphere.

There is evidence to suggest that the right hemisphere is dominant during the developmental period prior to the emergence of speech (Harris, 1973). Electroencephalographic (EEG) recordings of brain wave activity in newborns presented with repetitive flashing lights show responsivity only in the right hemisphere or the visual-spatial cortex (Crowell, Jones, Kapuniai, & Nakagawa, 1973). When similar stimulation is presented to adults, they also show dominance in the right hemisphere, but there is in addition a spillover of brain activity into the left hemisphere through the corpus callosum. Crowell and his associates found little evidence for this spillover in newborns, suggesting that the corpus callosum is functionally incapable of providing communication between the hemispheres during the first few days of life.

The direct recording of brain activity will no doubt ultimately give important answers to questions concerning the development of the cortical hemispheres. However, thus far most evidence for the development of laterality has been based on functional data. For example, the tonic-neck reflex is most often oriented toward the right (Gesell & Amatruda, 1945; Turkewitz, Gordon, & Birch, 1965). Further, this directional posture seems to persist, although not as a reflex, throughout the first year of life. The preference for head-to-right posture may reflect the dominance of the right hemisphere during infancy (Harris, 1973). That is, the baby lying on its back keeps its left ear up to better detect exogenous auditory stimulation. On the other hand, there is some evidence to suggest that for some behaviors the left hemisphere may be dominant. When newborn babies are either asleep or awake, fisting of the right hand occurs more often than does fisting of the left hand (Cobb, Goodwin, & Saelens, 1966). Since the connections from the hemispheres to the body are crossed, right dominance would have predicted greater fisting in the left hand. Thus, it may be that behaviors are hemisphere-specific in the newborn in order to provide optimal conditions for the organization of specific behavioral systems. The point at which the two hemispheres begin to communicate via the corpus callosum may also be the point at which integration among behavioral systems begins.

Handedness   It goes without saying that we live in a right-handed world: most people are right-handed, and this majority has neatly organized the environment for its own convenience. It has often been thought that forcing a child to be right-handed leads to developmental problems, such as stuttering and reading and writing handicaps. Although the evidence does not support such a simple relationship, extreme caution should be exercised when encouraging right-handedness if the child seems to be showing an inclination for left-handedness.

Although the world may be right-handed, the individual entering it for the first time is not unilaterally handed. Clear evidence of handedness does not appear until sometime between 48 weeks and four years of age. In one study comparing the unilateral handedness of infants with the handedness of their mothers, no evidence was found that would link the eight-month-old's handedness with maternal handedness. The babies of the right-handed mothers (89 percent of the sample) were just as likely to show no handedness at all as they were to show unilateral handedness. Moreover, fewer than half of the babies of right-handed mothers showed a preference for the right hand at eight months of age (Cohen, 1966). The same study found evidence suggesting that the early establishment of handedness is related to the eight-months-old's performance on infant developmental examinations. Over

90 percent of the babies who scored above their expected age norm showed unilateral hand preferences, while only 42 percent of those at the mean for their age and 40 percent of those below the mean showed such preferences.

BOX 4–2
Schematic sequence of major forms of handedness

16–20 weeks: Contact unilateral and generally tends to be with left hand.

24 weeks: A definite shift to bilaterality.

28 weeks: a shift to unilaterality, most often to the right hand.

32 weeks: A shift back to bilaterality.

36 weeks: Bilaterality dropping out and unilaterality coming in. Behavior is usually characterized as "right" or "left," and the left predominates in the majority.

40–44 weeks: Same type of behavior, unilateral, "right or left," but now the right predominates in the majority.

48 weeks: In some a temporary shift, and in many a last shift, to use of the left hand—as well as use of the right hand—either used unilaterally.

52–56 weeks: A shift to clear unilateral dominance of the right hand.

80 weeks: A shift from rather clear-cut unilateral behavior to a marked interchangeable condition. Much bilaterality and use of the nondominant hand.

2 years: Relatively clear-cut unilateral use of the right hand.

2.5–3.5 years: A marked shift to bilaterality.

4 years: Predominant unilateral, right-handed behavior.

Source: A. Gesell and L. B. Ames, "The development of handedness," *Journal of Genetic Psychology,* 1947, *70,* 155–175. Reprinted with permission of L. B. Ames and The Journal Press.

Evidence for laterality other than handedness is very skimpy. Anecdotal evidence suggests laterality for "eyedness," "footedness," "earedness," and "sidedness." The scanty research data that are available tend to support such anecdotal observations.

ORGANIZATION OF GROWTH PROCESSES

Gesell's approach to growth recognized structure-function interaction although he emphasized the biological or maturational control of growth and development. An equally intense student of motor development, Myrtle McGraw (1946), was one of the first developmental psychologists to point out that structural development itself was influenced by function. Her studies of motor development suggested that it reflected the emerging organization of the nervous system.

Specifically at issue was the development of cortical control over behavior. Initially, behavior is regulated by subcortical mechanisms; that is, the newborn's behavior is largely reflexive or random. As the cortex develops it acquires the function of inhibition. In consequence, it commands the function of the subcortical centers, and more and more behavior becomes voluntary.

Changing reflexes to voluntary behavior   One intriguing question related to the shift from subcortical to cortical control of behavior concerns the reflexes which appear in early infancy, become disorganized and disappear, only to reappear later in infancy as voluntary behavior. Examples include the swimming and stepping reflexes, both of which disappear by the third or fourth month of life. Could one take a disappearing reflex, strengthen it by systematic practice, and thereby minimize the disorganization phase? The effect would be to demonstrate a smooth transition from reflexive control to voluntary control and, more than likely, to accelerate the appearance of voluntary control.

Zelazo, Zelazo, and Kolb (1972) studied this problem, using four groups of one-week-old male infants. Infants in the *active exercise* group received daily strengthening of the walking and placing reflexes from the second postnatal week through the eighth week. Those in the *passive exercise* group received an equal amount of daily contact, but received no strengthening of the reflexes in question. Infants in the *no exercise* group received no special training or handling, while infants in the *control group* were merely tested when they were eight months old to assess the effects of repeated testing per se. At the end of the training program, infants in the active exercise condition showed substantial increases in the number of walking responses elicited during testing as compared with their scores at two weeks of age, and as compared with the infants in the other groups. In fact, babies in the passive exercise and no exercise groups showed a decrease in the number of responses to a level comparable to that of babies in the control condition.

In a follow-up study of maternal reports of the age at which unassisted walking began, walking occurred earliest for infants previously in the active exercise group, and occurred latest for infants in the eight-week control condition. Zelazo et al. suggest that earlier walking may facilitate the development of a sense of competence in the infant. Is it possible, on the other hand, that such early training interferes with other organizational processes? We will return to this point shortly.

In the first chapter we introduced the psychobiological point of view and noted that it assumes a reciprocal structure-function interaction during development. Moreover, we introduced the concept of levels of organization, noting that the developmental psychologist looks at levels of behavioral organization in much the same way that the biologist looks at levels of the organization of matter.

The Zelazo et al. study raises interesting and controversial questions regarding any program that attempts to accelerate development. (We are

distinguishing here programs that attempt to remedy developmental deficiencies from those that attempt to accelerate development in children who
otherwise have every opportunity for normal development.) Consider this
question: Will forceful intervention to accelerate the organization of behavior interfere with the organization process itself? Or, more specifically,
what effect will acceleration of motor competence have on the organization process *if* the baby is not also cognitively or emotionally prepared
for enhanced motor competence? What effect will acceleration of motor
competence have on the brain structures which themselves are undergoing
organization?

Cratty's model of behavioral organization

Let us consider each major aspect of development as a system. At the very
least, we would have a cognitive system, a sensory-perceptual system, a
motor system, and a verbal system. The notion of organizational levels implies that each system moves developmentally toward order and non-
randomness, as does integration among the systems. Although we can study
the development of each of these systems independently, such studies
would be somewhat deficient since the systems are not independent. As a
result of interaction among the systems, factors influencing one system also
influence the other systems.

Cratty (1970) has captured the flavor of this organizational process with
his conceptual model of behavioral organization. He has proposed a number of axioms and postulates in an effort to provide a theoretical framework
from which hypotheses can be generated and applied to the study of organization. Some of his axioms are compatible with the concepts of differentiation and of levels of hierarchical organization. It is important to bear
in mind, however, that each successive level of organization represents
more than just the additive complexities of all lower levels of organization.
That is, each higher level of organization is greater than the sum of its parts.

> *Axiom 3, Postulate 3:* Not only does there seem to be an optimum time for
> the insertion of educational experiences to elicit the most improvement in
> an attribute or group of attributes, but the reverse also seems to be true.
> (p. 282)

> *Postulate 4:* An overexercise of a group of attributes may tend either to blunt
> the emergence of ability traits within another classification or to delay their
> appearance to some degree. (p. 282)

Cratty's axioms and postulates can be applied to the questions regarding acceleration of the organizational process that were raised by the Zelazo
et al. study. In some instances "blunting" may represent the normal fluctuations in intrasystem development occasioned by interference from the
simultaneous development of other systems. For example, in a study of the
development of bladder control and vocabulary size in a female baby, Clark
Hull and Bertha Hull (1919) reported what may be an example of the in-

hibitory influence one system may have on another (see Figure 4–1). This example also illustrates the principles of reciprocal interweaving and self-regulatory fluctuation. Voluntary control of the bladder showed steady improvement until about the 18th postnatal month, when the curve plateaued, with no appreciable improvement until about the 27th month. On the other hand, vocabulary growth accelerated markedly from the 18th through the 27th month. The suggestion, of course, is that the child cannot master bladder control and vocabulary growth simultaneously. Other investigators have reported similar interaction effects between gross motor development and language skill development (see Shirley, 1931).

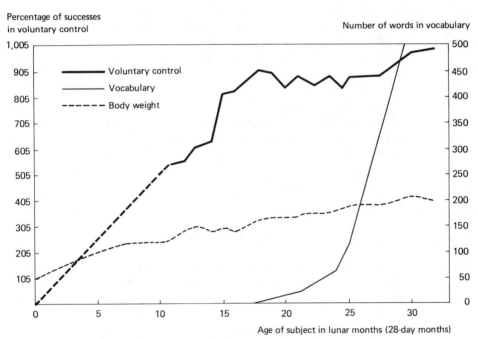

Source: C. L. Hull and B. I. Hull, "Parallel learning curves of an infant in vocabulary and in voluntary control of the bladder," *Pedagogical Seminary*, 1919, 26, 272–283. With permission of The Journal Press.

FIGURE 4–1 The development of voluntary bladder control, vocabulary, and body weight over the first 31 months of life.

The interactions we have just considered occur during normal development, with no systematic attempt on the part of the investigators (or, so far as we know, the parents) to accelerate one process or the other. It may be argued that the disappearing reflexes are holdovers from Homo sapiens' evolutionary past and no longer serve an adaptive function. They do indeed drop out of the behavior repertoire. But, more important they are followed by a period of disorganization, which in turn is followed by the appearance of learned skills or voluntary behavior. Moreover, it can be assumed that the behavioral sequence during development reflects similar changes in the developing nervous system. Unfortunately, we have no way of knowing to what extent interference with this normal sequence of events will interfere with the organizational process.

The Zelazo et al. experiment suggests that strengthening the walking and placing reflexes speeds up the subsequent acquisition of voluntary walking. What we cannot tell from their experiment is the effect that the acceleration of walking will have on other systems undergoing organization. Cratty's model predicts (1) that changes in one system affect changes in other systems through bonding; (2) that there are critical periods when the organism is optimally prepared to respond to exogeneous stimulation, and (3) that strengthening an attribute when the organism is not "psychobiologically prepared" for such strengthening may interfere with the organizational process. Thus, the possibility exists that acceleration training of the sort studied by Zelazo et al. may actually interfere with organization in other attribute categories, such as cognitive, emotional, language, or perceptual abilities.

At this stage of our understanding of the development of human behavior it would seem to be most judicious to exercise extreme caution in attempting to accelerate development which is proceeding normally. Obviously, however, enrichment should be used to counter conditions that breed developmental lag. Here, however, our goal is to restore the conditions which typically engender normal development rather than to create "super babies."

THE DEVELOPMENT OF THE NERVOUS SYSTEM

The development of the nervous system can be considered in light of two more specialized aspects of development: *morphogenesis,* or the development of gross structures, and *histogenesis,* or the development of fine structures. Because extensive discussion of neural development is beyond the scope of this text, only a brief overview of morphogenesis and histogenesis will be given. In our discussion we will adhere to the traditional subdivisions of the nervous system: the central nervous system (CNS), consisting of the brain and spinal cord; the peripheral nervous system (PNS), consisting of the cranial and spinal nerves; and the autonomic nervous system (ANS), consisting of the sympathetic and parasympathetic branches (Ranson & Clark, 1959).

The central nervous system

The structural differences between the newborn's brain and the mature brain are roughly comparable to the functional differences between newborns and adults. In the newborn the subcortical structures of the brain are more highly developed than the cortical structures. Therefore, the newborn infant functions primarily, although not exclusively, at the subcortical level.

Attempts have been made to describe the functional organization of the brain, the usual plan being to arrange functional levels into hierarchies in the nervous system. Drawing upon six such hierarchies (see Altman, 1966; Bronson, 1965; Denny-Brown, 1960; Doman et al., 1960; Herrick, 1956; Himwich, 1951), we can construct a composite picture of the hierarchical organization of brain function from the highest level to the lowest level: cortex, subcortex (thalamus, pyramidal tract, hypothalamus, limbic system), midbrain, cerebellum, pons, reticular formation, medulla, primary sensory and motor centers in the brain stem and the spinal cord, and sensory and motor end organs at the periphery. One important point to remember is that few behaviors or mental activities of the organism, whether they involve the cortex directly or not, are independent of the influence of the CNS.

One of the most important CNS structures is a mass of cells and neural pathways located in the brain stem but with connections from the spinal cord to the midbrain. This mass of cells and nerve fibers, called the *reticular formation,* is thought to function as a master control center for the CNS. Thus, it is thought to be involved in all excitatory, inhibitory, and integrative functions of the nervous system. These functions include arousal, wakefulness, muscular control, stimulus reception, nerve conduction, and the selective integration of sensory stimulation. The reticular formation is also thought to play an important role in orientation, attention, perception, learning, and cognition (topics discussed in later chapters).

Brain growth

At birth, the human brain weighs about 350 grams, and all the major segments (lobes) of the brain are differentiated, though they are by no means fully developed. Structurally, the lobes have not yet assumed the proportionate sizes characteristic of the mature brain. The frontal and temporal lobes are less well developed than the occipital and parietal lobes, reflecting their slower rate of development during the prenatal period. In general, the development of the back part (posterior) of the brain is more advanced than that of the front part (anterior).

By the third postnatal month the brain convolutions have increased, as have the lengths of the frontal and temporal lobes. From the sixth to the ninth postnatal month, the color of the cerebral cortex changes from pinkish gray to gray, and by one year of age the gray matter of the brain has become clearly distinguishable from the white matter. Sometime during the latter part of the second year of life, the comparative proportions of the lobes are essentially those of the mature brain. By the end of the second year, the brain weighs approximately 1,050 grams. From the third trimester of pregnancy to the end of the second year of life, the brain undergoes its period of most rapid growth. By the fifth or sixth year of life, the size of the child's brain is nearly that of an adult's.

Myelinization

A nerve is a bundle of fibers, each of which is functionally independent of the others. Structurally, one can distinguish nerves on the basis of whether or not they are myelinated and whether or not they are covered by neurilemma. *Myelin* is a white, protein-fat substance that covers (myelinates) the nerve. Nerves may also be covered by a thin membranous substance called *neurilemma*. In general, unmyelinated nerve fibers are the gray matter of the nervous system.

Every so often along the myelinated nerve, the neurilemma touches the nerve fiber itself, at points called the nodes of Ranvier. During neural transmission, nervous impulses literally hop from node to node, speeding up transmission of the impulses. Interestingly enough, the number of myelinated nerves increases as one goes up the phylogenetic scale. Consequently, there are more myelinated nerves in the human species than in any other. Although function is not dependent upon the presence of myelin, the development of a functional system closely approximates the development of that system's myelinization. By way of example, let us consider the development of vision.

Myelinization of the optic nerve begins slightly before birth. By three months of age the optic nerve is well myelinated, and by six months it is nearly fully myelinated. Rapid improvements in the functional abilities of the visual system also occur during the first six months of life, corresponding to the rapid myelinization of the optic nerve and the optic tract. However, despite the lack of myelin around the human newborn's optic nerve, the newborn possesses rather sophisticated visual abilities, including the ability to discriminate visual patterns (see Chapters 5 and 7).

The myelinization process provides an excellent illustration of structure-function interaction. Structurally, myelinization can occur independent of function. However, function not only stimulates but can actually speed up the process (Sperry, 1951). Perhaps this accounts in part for the strengthening effects reported by Zelazo et al. Myelinization begins sometime around the fifth prenatal month, when it is especially noticeable in the auditory nerve. Recent evidence suggests that complete myelinization is not achieved until sometime during late adolescence.

The peripheral nervous system

Functionally, nerves can be categorized in several ways. For example, there are *sensory nerves,* which respond to endogenous and exogenous stimulation; *motor nerves,* which stimulate muscles and glands; and *association nerves,* which provide interconnections between sensory and motor nerves. The nerves making up the PNS likewise serve an association function. These nerves interface the CNS with all parts of the body. Two categories of nerves make up the PNS: spinal nerves and cranial nerves (Ranson & Clark, 1959).

The autonomic nervous system

The ANS derives its name from the Greek word meaning self-regulating. However, the ANS is linked to the CNS. In fact, one way to conceptualize the ANS is to think of it as the principal means by which the CNS influences glands and the muscles of the heart and other vital organs.

The ANS is divisible into two systems or branches: the *sympathetic* branch and the *parasympathetic* branch. Each of these branches is controlled by a different part of the hypothalamus, which is probably the structure most directly responsible for the regulation of autonomic activity. The anterior portion of the hypothalamus is associated with parasympathetic activity, the posterior portion with sympathetic activity. The two branches of the ANS are also referred to as the *cholinergic* (parasympathetic) and the *adrenergic* (sympathetic) systems, after the types of chemicals secreted by structures (postganglionic neurons) within the system.

Sometimes the parasympathetic and sympathetic systems excite the organism, sometimes they inhibit it. Sometimes the systems seem to be antagonistic (sympathetic stimulation dilates the pupil of the eye, parasympathetic stimulation constricts it), while at other times they work together, as, for example, in sexual excitation.

NEUROLOGICAL-DEVELOPMENTAL ASSESSMENT

There are two basic approaches to assessing the functional integrity of the nervous system—the neurological approach and the developmental approach.

The *neurological examination* makes extensive use of reflexes to assess the structural-functional integrity of the CNS and the PNS and to identify possible abnormalities. The lingering presence of reflexes which normally disappear from the behavioral repertoire may indicate neurological damage. For example, when a young baby is lying on its back, an examiner can elicit the tonic-neck reflex by turning the baby's head. The persistence of this reflex beyond the time when it usually disappears (about the seventh postnatal month) may be associated with neurological damage, such as cerebral palsy. The afflicted individual would lack the ability to inhibit the tonic-neck reflex. This deficit has an especially disruptive effect on walking. On the other hand, the persistence of the reflex may fall within the scope of normal variation. From this example it is clear that a variety of indices should be used in the course of assessment.

The *developmental examination* also provides a measure of the infant's maturational status. This examination incorporates a more complete assessment of the infant's behavior, including fine and gross motor skills and adaptive, personal-social, cognitive, perceptual, expressive, and receptive language behavior. The developmental quotient (DQ)—the score derived from the developmental examination—is often used as an index of accelerated or retarded development.

The neurological and developmental examinations have many similarities. They share the goals of assessing the organism's current level of functioning, the maturational stage of development, and emerging adaptive capabilities. The most distinctive difference between the two examinations is the greater extent to which the neurological examination makes use of reflexology (Taft & Cohen, 1967) or muscle tone (Andre-Thomas, Chesni, & St. Anne-Dargassies, 1960). When damage to the CNS is suspected, the pediatric neurologist may rely primarily on reflexes which strongly predict clinical damage in diagnosing the source of the trauma.

Both organismic and environmental factors may confound the assessment of current functioning. Organismic factors include the infant's nutritional status and level of arousal and the extent of CNS damage. Significant environmental factors include the physical characteristics and strangeness of the testing room, and the personality and testing expertise of the examiner. Although a great deal is known about the influence of organismic and environmental factors on the test performance of children and adults, little systematic research has directly investigated the extent to which such factors bias assessment of the infant. What evidence does exist suggests that even with the youngest infants care should be taken to avoid such confounding.

One can use several techniques to minimize the extent to which organismic and environmental factors may bias assessment. For example, one can rely exclusively on highly trained testers, in the hope that their expertise will increase the accuracy of the assessment. Or one can use several testers and then check for consistency among their independently derived evaluations. Still another technique is to increase the number of items assessed. This technique is based on the tenuous premise that the more information one has, the more accurate is one's assessment. It also suffers from the limitation that increasing the number of items increases the duration of the test and adds to the possibility that organismic factors will interfere with the assessment. All in all, what we can say with certainty is that assessment of the infant requires, at the least, a very skilled tester. The more inexperienced the tester, the greater is the likelihood that organismic or environmental factors will bias the results of the test.

Suppose that we have just completed an examination of the infant. The most logical next question is, What does our assessment say about the infant's future behavior and development? Or, put otherwise, what is the predictive value of infant assessment?

The predictive significance of infant assessment   The value of any test rests on its significance for assessing current behavior and for accurately predicting future behavior. In fact, we might well argue that if a particular test gives us no reliable information about future behavior, the test has no merit.

Many questions have been raised in studies of the predictive significance of early assessment. Can one predict potential CNS impairment in high-risk infants? Can one predict later behavioral ability on the basis of the DQ score? The most frequently investigated question, however, has been: Does performance on developmental examinations predict subsequent performance on intelligence tests?

The research on the predictive significance of both the developmental and the neurological examination generally suggests poor predictive power. This has been due in part to the differences between what is being assessed in the developmental (and the neurological) examinations and what is being assessed in the intelligence test. The overall intelligence test places considerable emphasis on the verbal skills of the young child, whereas the developmental examination measures primarily the sensorimotor and perceptual development of the infant. Historically, the two tests have measured different things, and the poor correlation between them results from the fact that they are measurements of qualitatively different phenomena.

Even professionals in research and clinical settings who use infant and preschool "intelligence tests," sometimes on a daily basis, do so in the knowledge that such tests have serious limitations. In fact, one survey disclosed the following list of complaints regarding early assessment instruments: "Poor validity, manuals inadequate or difficult to use, limited norms, poor predictability, insufficient diagnostic precision, culturally outdated, inadequate picture of child's functioning, too subjective, and lack of theoretical rationale for dimensions measured" (Stott & Ball, 1969, p. 73).

Nevertheless, research designed to enhance the predictive significance of infant assessment continues. Honzik and her associates asked pediatricians to rate newborns as "definitely suspect," "suspect," "possibly suspect," and "nonsuspect." Eight months later the mental and motor performance of the infants was tested by psychologists unfamiliar with the pediatric diagnoses. While exceptions did occur, the general results showed a fairly strong relationship between the pediatric and the psychological assessments (Honzik, Hutchings, & Burnip, 1965). In another study various measures of infant behavior at age 20 months were compared with subsequent levels of school achievement and intelligence test performance at age ten years, again with encouragingly high predictive significance (Werner, Honzik, & Smith, 1968). These studies notwithstanding, the overall predictive power of infant tests remains depressingly low (see Chapter 7).

PHYSICAL GROWTH

Physical growth progresses in a fairly orderly fashion, and for any individual child the growth rate is quite stable. Most infants show the same sequence of behaviors as they gradually gain the ability to walk upright. Moreover, there are rather stable changes in height, weight, and body proportions. For example, in our culture most babies show increments of two pounds per month during the first six postnatal months, and increments of one pound per month during the remainder of the first year.

The major determinants of growth are genetic. Thus, tall parents are likely to have tall children, and short parents are likely to have short children. However, the children of tall parents are likely to be shorter than their parents, whereas the children of short parents are likely to be taller than their parents. This is due to the operation of the principle of *regression to the mean.*

Consider two samples drawn from the same population. The mean (average) height of sample A is 6 feet 2 inches. The mean height of sample B is 5 feet 6 inches. In general, children born of sample A parents will be taller than children born of sample B parents. However, when we consider an individual child within either sample, regression to the mean operates so that that child is likely to move toward the mean height of the sample. For example, if both sample A parents are taller than the mean height of the sample, regression to the mean predicts that their children will be shorter than they are (not necessarily shorter than the sample mean, however). If both sample A parents are shorter than the mean height of the sample, their children are likely to be taller than they are (again, not necessarily taller than the sample mean). Regression to the mean is best demonstrated at the group level. With individual parent-child comparisons, the amount of variation implicit in individual differences may mask any regression effect—as you probably realize if you are shorter or taller than your parents than would be predicted by regression.

Physical growth is influenced not only by genetic determinants but also by many environmental factors. Among the most important environmental factors are nutrition, prenatal and postnatal care, and social-emotional deprivation. The extent to which these factors may counter or disrupt physical growth has not yet been established. Evidence from studies of nutritional intervention in undernourished populations as well as clinical reports of the failure of children to thrive point to environmental factors as influential determinants of physical growth.

Weight and height

It is a nearly universal finding that boys are slightly heavier than girls at birth and, in general, throughout the life span. In our culture, the average birth weight of Caucasian male babies is slightly greater than 7.5 pounds, while that of Caucasian females babies is slightly less than 7.5 pounds. For American Negroes the sex differences are in the same direction, but the group mean weight is less, closer to 7.0 pounds. The weight of the average newborn American Indian is slightly greater, exceeding 7.5 pounds.

Table 4–1 summarizes the range in average birth weights for various peoples throughout the world. These data were compiled by Howard Meredith, an investigator who has devoted a major portion of his professional career to the compilation of world wide growth norms. As indicated in Table 4–1, the variation in live birth weights is nearly as great within a geographic region as it is among geographic regions.

TABLE 4–1

Average birth weight of liveborn infants of selected peoples of the world

Under 2,900 grams (under 6.38 lbs)
Africa: Bambuti Pygmies, Quiocos, Congo Negroes, Ghana Negroes
Asia: Burmese, Timor Islanders, Ryukyu Islanders, Indians
Australia: Pitjantjatjatjava aborigines
Oceania: New Guinea Euga and Papura, New Ireland natives
North America: Caucasians (altitudes above 10,000 feet)

2,900 to 3,200 grams (6.38 lbs–7.05 lbs)
Africa: Baganda, Baluba, Chope, Mandinka, Ronga, Yoruba
Asia: Malayans, Chinese, Japanese, Lebanese, Thai
North America: Mexicans, United States Negroes
South America: Bush Negroes
Europe: South Italians

3,200 to 4,300 grams (7.05 lbs–7.49 lbs)
Africa:Kuo
Asia: South Koreans, Singapore Caucasians
Oceania: New Guinea Dutch
Europe: Romanians, North Italians, West Germans, East Germans, Swiss, French,
    Russians, Poles, Czechs, British, Slovaks, Belgians
South America: Chileans, Uruguay Caucasians, Guinea Negroes
North America: United States Caucasians

Over 3,400 grams (over 7.49 lbs)
Asia: Iraqi
Australia: Australian Caucasians
North America: Assiniboine, Cherokee, Creek, Paiute, Papago, Sioux, Cheyenne,
    Chippewa, Choctaw, Kiowa

Source: Adapted from H. V. Meredith, "Body weight at birth of viable human infants: A worldwide comparative treatise," *Human Biology*, 1970, *42*, 217–264. With permission of the author and the Wayne State University Press.

In our culture we classify newborns weighing less than 2,500 grams (5.5 pounds) as premature. This is based on the premise that newborns weighing under 2,500 grams are less viable than are newborns weighing over 2,500 grams (see Chapter 2). Although this criterion is generally true, it is also relative to our culture (and many others). In many other cultures the *average* birth weight is not much greater than 2,500 grams. A birth weight of 2,500 grams for a Timor Islander would not be unusual, whereas the same birth weight for a Cherokee baby would be considerably below the average Cherokee baby's birth weight. This illustrates the point made in Chapter 2 that birth weight as a definition of prematurity must be considered relative to the population of babies being considered. Obviously, not all Timor Islander babies are premature. Moreover, the relationship between birth weight and viability shows great cultural variability (Meredith, 1970). Such variability cannot be accounted for simply by variations in the standards of living among cultures. For example, the death rate of babies born in the United States is higher than that of babies born in many other countries. Indeed, the death rate for nonwhite American babies is alarming, considering the overall level of economic development that has been achieved in the United States.

Not only are boys heavier than girls, but they are also taller. The average girl is shorter than the average boy until about age 11. For the next two years or so she may well be slightly taller than her 12- and 13-year-old male peers. Around age 14 the average male is once again taller than the average female. This illustrates a much more general phenomenon than simple changes in height: girls mature at a faster rate than boys and thus reach their adolescent growth spurt earlier.

Body proportions also change with age. The head of the newborn accounts for 25 percent of its total body length. In contrast, the size of the adult head is only about 12 percent of the total body length. Changes in the relative proportions of head, neck, trunk, arms, and legs continue until age 25, when body proportions stabilize.

Dentition

In rare instances a newborn baby may have one or two teeth. The normal variation for first dentition, however, ranges from six months to two years of age. On the average, the eight upper and lower front teeth erupt sometime during the 5th to the 12th month of life. During the next 18 months the remaining 12 "baby teeth" erupt, bringing to 20 the total number of teeth acquired during first dentition. The shedding of the first teeth usually begins at about age six and continues through the elementary years. The eruption of permanent teeth, or second dentition, begins sometime between five and seven years of age and continues through the teen years. The so-called wisdom teeth are the last to erupt and in some cases do not do so until the late twenties.

While many pediatricians deny any relationship between teething and anal-genital rash, runny nose, slight fever, or "heavy" urine, caregivers often observe these "nonsignificant" coincidences. The relationship between irritability and tooth eruption is equally well known to caregivers, especially when the peak rhythm of teething pain occurs between midnight and six A.M. Except for various concoctions that can be rubbed on the gums in an effort to alleviate pain, parents are generally helpless when dealing with a teething baby. Perhaps the most important caregiving that the parents can provide is the comfort and security engendered by their presence.

Body temperature

The clinical sign of illness that parents use most often is probably body temperature. A hot baby generally implies a sick baby. In fact, babies are warm, about 0.8 degrees Fahrenheit warmer than the somewhat mythical 98.6 degrees Fahrenheit adult body temperature. For that matter, if our standard of reference is the average adult body temperature, the 13-year-old is slightly cold. Average body temperature during the years of puberty tends to be lower than the adult average. Actually, even among adults there are rather wide individual differences in basal body temperature.

Although babies tend to have higher body temperatures than do adults, body temperatures exceeding 100 degrees Fahrenheit should be carefully monitored, and if they persist, the pediatrician should be consulted. In this regard it is well to remember that body temperature shows normal variation during each 24-hour period. Since body temperature drops during the nighttime, a high temperature at night conveys a different meaning than does the same temperature recorded during the day. Moreover, since the adult's body temperature also varies during each circadian cycle, the touch method for detecting fever—feeling the forehead, face, or neck—is very inaccurate. When fever is suspected, its existence should always be confirmed with a good thermometer.

THE DEVELOPMENT OF GROSS AND FINE MOTOR SKILLS

The active four-year-old is a running, jumping, falling, throwing, skipping, tumbling, tricycle- or bicycle riding bundle of energy. These large muscle behaviors do not suddenly appear in the four-year-old but are the end products of the interaction between neuromuscular development and experience. On the other hand, there are many times when the four-year-old can be seen sitting quietly playing with puzzles, clay, dolls, crayons, scissors, or glue. The former behaviors involve the use of relatively large muscle masses—they are the *gross motor skills.* The latter behaviors are the *fine motor skills,* so designated primarily because they require rather good prehension and eye-hand coordination.

Gross motor skills

Posture and locomotion   From birth to three months, the infant shows a gradual reduction in head lag when pulled to a sitting position, and a gradual increase in head control and midline positioning. Toward the end of this period the baby can roll from side to back, hold its head high when lying in a prone position, and sit briefly with support.

From three to six months, the baby makes its initial attempts at locomotion. These early crawling movements consist of "dragging" itself along the floor with the hands and arms, the legs providing little if any assistance. Sitting alone for brief periods is possible, although the sitting posture is quite unstable.

From six months to 12 months, the baby acquires the ability to sit alone, stand alone, roll from back to stomach, creep, and walk. Indeed, tremendous growth in postural control and locomotion occurs during the second half of the first year, all of which has important implications for caregiving. Baby is no longer content to sit all day in the playpen.

TABLE 4–2

Developmental progression of motor behavior when proscribed testing procedures are followed.

Motor behavior	Average age achieved (in months)	Expected normal variation (in months)
Lifts head when held at shoulder	0.1	—
Lateral head movements	0.1	—
Crawling movements	0.4	0.1–3
Arm and leg thrusts	0.8	0.3–2
Head erect and steady	1.6	0.7–4
Turns from side to back	1.8	0.7–5
Elevates self by arms	2.1	0.7–5
Sits with support	2.3	1–5
Turns from back to side	4.4	2–7
Makes effort to sit	4.8	3–8
Pulls to sitting position	5.3	4–8
Sits alone momentarily	5.3	4–8
Rolls from back to stomach	6.4	4–10
Sits alone, steadily	6.6	5–9
Early stepping movements	7.4	5–11
Pulls to standing position	8.1	5–12
Raises self to sitting posture	8.3	6–11
Stands up by furniture	8.6	6–12
Stepping movements	8.8	6–12
Walks with help	9.6	7–12
Sits down	9.6	7–14
Stands alone	11.0	9–16
Walks alone	11.7	9–17
Walks sideways	14.1	10–20
Walks backward	14.6	11–20
Stands left foot alone	22.7	15–30+
Jumps off floor, both feet	23.4	17–30+
Stands right foot alone	23.5	16–30+
Jumps from bottom step	24.8	19–30+
Walks upstairs alone: both feet on each step	25.1	18–30+
Walks downstairs alone: both feet on each step	25.8	19–30+
Walks on tiptoe, ten feet	30+	20–30+
Distance jump: 14–24 inches	30+	25–30+
Hops on one foot, two or more hops	30+	30+

Adapted from the Bayley Scales of Infant Development and reprinted with permission of the author and of The Psychological Corporation. © 1969. New York, N.Y. All rights reserved.

During the next several years the ability to walk forward and backward, climb stairs, jump, hop, and skip develops in just that sequence. An interesting experiment by Shipiro (1962) suggests that each of the component behaviors in locomotion is acquired in a burst rather than in a steady, day-by-day fashion. Studying the development of walking in a single female baby, Shipiro found that 25 days elapsed between the time of unassisted standing and the first unassisted steps. By the 28th day after unassisted standing the baby was able to complete 4 steps before falling; by the 35th day, 30 steps; by the 45th day, 240 steps in sequence; and by the 59th day, 1,250 steps in uninterrupted sequence.

Bowel and bladder control The child's mastery of bowel and bladder control is of great concern to most parents. Indeed, interest in toilet training has been just as high among professionals, whether they are psychoanalytic theorists expounding on the anal period of development or learning theorists expounding on effective methods for training bowel control.

In the newborn, wetting occurs about 18–20 times daily, and bowel movements occur from 3–5 times daily. By six months bowel movements are most likely to occur during feedings, or after naps, and there is a substantial decrease in the number of wettings per day. By the 12th month, fairly regular bowel movement patterns have been established, and the periods of dryness have lengthened. Many parents begin potty-training their children sometime from the 9th month to the 12th month, although there is evidence to suggest that this may be a waste of energy. When bowel and bladder training is delayed until 18 months to two years, children seem to achieve mastery in a much shorter period of time and with less fuss than those who are started prior to the 12th month. In general, boys achieve control later than do girls. This may well reflect the fact that girls are further along in general development than are boys of an equivalent chronological age.

There are startling cultural differences as to when potty training is begun. For example, in 1958 over 60 percent of English and Welsh mothers started to potty-train their babies within the first two postnatal *weeks,* and over 84 percent initiated training by the sixth month (Douglas & Bloomfield, 1958). In contrast, in 1957 the average age for initiating potty training in the United States was seven months (Sears, Maccoby, & Levin, 1957). Equally interesting is the fact that in the English sample older mothers initiated potty training earlier than did younger mothers.

Expecting a baby to achieve mastery of bowel or bladder control prior to six months is expecting the impossible. Myelinization of the nerves controlling the sphincter muscles is not complete until around the sixth month. Moreover, some evidence suggests that voluntary control of the sphincter muscles is not possible until approximately 18 months of age. Although, as we have noted, myelinization and function are not necessarily related, they are not completely independent either.

The process of independent toileting involves a number of skills, many of which adults take for granted. For example, the infant must learn to put the seat up or down, pull pants down, get on the toilet seat, wipe, and flush. Each of these behaviors can be trained separately and rewarded. If dirty diapers are not particularly upsetting to caregivers, it would seem advisable to delay potty training until sometime around the child's second birthday, and to provide the child with natural modeling experiences. Changing baby's diaper as soon as possible after wetting or voiding is advisable so that the baby comes to prefer "dryness." Moreover, infants should be rewarded positively for successes rather than punished for failures.

Fine motor skills

Prehension The newborn's grasp is a reflex of unusual strength, and since it is involuntary the newborn will let go only with considerable difficulty. During the first six months the baby will acquire rather good control of eye-hand coordination. Although thumb-sucking has been observed in the fetus by the use of fetal photography, it is not a coordinated behavior during the first postnatal trimester. Very young infants do suck their thumbs, fingers, or hands, especially when drowsy or sleeping. Initially, however, hand-to-mouth contact occurs as a result of random movements of the arm and head.

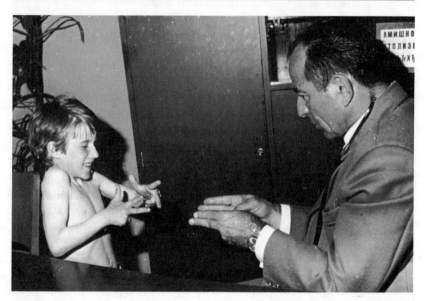

Photograph courtesy Hiram E. Fitzgerald

FIGURE 4–2 Dr. Cvjetko Brajovic, director of the Institute for Psychophysiological and Speech Disorders, Belgrade, Yugoslavia, is administering part of the initial screening test given to children referred to his clinic. The child's task is to imitate a series of finger movements. The child's performance on this and other tasks gives the examiner information concerning the nerves which regulate motor behavior.

Compared to the newborn, the six-month-old has rather good voluntary control of the arms. The reflex grasp has been replaced by a voluntary one. The six-month-old can pick up and drop objects as well as throw them. Integration of the visual system and prehension can be observed as the baby lies in its crib or playpen, staring at the opening and closing of its hands. From six to nine months the baby obtains objects by raking them in, the palm playing an important role in picking up objects. Now the baby has good voluntary control of the grasp and for the first time will be able to transfer an object from one hand to another. From 9 to 12 months the baby moves from an inferior pincer grasp (finger pad to thumb pad) to closer approximations of fingertip-to-thumbtip grasp. Early in the period the baby approaches objects with the index finger extended; later it can pick up objects with finger and thumb in opposition. This is an especially good time to give baby plenty of finger foods—breakfast cereals, for example —providing good practice for picking up small objects.

By 18 months the toddler can hold crayons and similar objects and is capable of playing with toys that require objects to be placed in holes or slots. Often, to mother's consternation, the toddler has no difficulty opening drawers or doors, especially those that guard the kitchen pots and pans. But this also means that the toddler is able to open the kitchen cabinets that contain household poisons, cleansers, and other toxic substances. Such potential hazards should have been removed many months before the toddler was able to crawl about and open doors.

Drawing   The young child has been described as a "linguistic genius" because of the novelty and creativity of early language behavior (Chukovsky, 1963). This same creativity can be seen in the preschooler's drawings: the three- and four-year-old is in every respect an "artistic genius." With rare exceptions this art for art's sake will never again flow so spontaneously and so naturally.

Levels of organization have been identified in the child's increasing ability to represent reality and fantasy through "artistic genius." The following developmental progression is a composite based on Biber's (1934) analysis of 7,000 drawings, Kellogg and O'Dell's (1969) analysis of 1 million drawings, and Cratty's (1970) analysis of the construction of geometric forms.

Six stages in hand-eye control underlying the ability to draw have been identified. Around the middle of the second year of life the toddler shows an increasing interest in *scribbling*. Initially, the toddler's scribbles are not much more than haphazardly distributed random marks. Around the second birthday one can see evidence of visually directed movements as the child makes initial efforts at *enclosing space*. Toward the end of this stage the child will be able to complete a circle, the first geometric form to appear developmentally. During the third and fourth year the child will add other *diagrams* (shapes), especially the cross and square. The triangle and diamond are not accurately reproduced until the sixth and seventh year, respectively.

In the fourth stage, patterns are formed by *combining* several figures; for example, a circle and cross may be combined to represent mommy or daddy. In the fifth stage, *aggregates* of more than two figures in combination will be formed, and in the final, *pictorial* stage the child will begin labeling the objects depicted in drawings. What distinguishes labeling at this stage from earlier labeling is that the objects and labels begin to bear some resemblance to reality. Thus, suns begin to look like suns, houses like houses, animals like animals. Obviously, these stages overlap. The five-year-old who can draw a house will also scribble a lot. The six-year-old who can construct complex aggregates will also draw many simple geometric forms.

Drawing of the human form begins around age four and follows a sequence that closely mirrors the above stages (Cratty, 1970). First the preschooler draws circles as faces, with random marks for facial features. Parts of the face, facial expressions, fingers, and feet are added later, and finally the limbs and torso are given width.

Printing The child's ability to print also follows a developmental progression. As was the case for the development of drawing, the age at which various skills will be accomplished varies for each child, and we are citing only the normative ages for skill accomplishment. Attempts to begin printing letters and numbers occur just prior to and during the kindergarten period. Initially, letters and numbers are scattered all over the paper, and reversals of letters (*b* for *d*, and vice versa) are common. Some four- or five-year-olds will be able to print the alphabet and their first and last names. Others will not. By seven years of age, reversals in letters and numbers should have declined markedly, although occasional reversals still occur. The development of the child's ability to draw and print provides an excellent example of the organizational bonding implicit in Cratty's model for the organization of behavior. The ability to print a letter or draw a triangle is dependent upon organization of the visual system and the motor system, as well as integration between the systems. For this reason, drawing and printing are usually referred to as sensorimotor or perceptual-motor skills.

SUMMARY

Physical and motor development reflect the oscillatory or fluctuating nature of development, with constant movement toward higher and higher levels of behavioral organization. The organization of behavior tends to reflect the gradual transition from subcortical control to cortical control. Attempts to strengthen early reflexive behavior suggest that extra practice may accelerate physical and motor development. It is not clear, however, what effect the acceleration of motor competence has on the organization of behavior in general.

It is important to understand the development of the neural systems that underlie behavioral development. Indeed, no behavior occurs without involving some aspect of the central, peripheral, and/or autonomic nervous systems. These systems are not mutually exclusive: feedback mechanisms provide for constant "communication" among them. In infancy and early childhood, the integrity of the neural systems as well as normal behavioral development is assessed by neurological and/or developmental examinations. In general, scores obtained from these examinations have poor predictive significance for subsequent intellectual functioning.

In our culture the average newborn male weighs slightly more than the newborn female, and throughout the remainder of development males tend to be heavier as well as taller than females. On the other hand, the average birth weights of newborns vary considerably among cultures and within cultures.

The four-year-old is a running, jumping, falling, throwing, skipping, tumbling bundle of energy. Although gross motor activities occupy much of the young child's playtime, there are also "quiet times." In the quiet times, preschool children will approach crayoning and painting with as much enthusiasm and persistence as they invest in more active play. The keen observer of young children will be struck by two seemingly contradictory aspects of early childhood. There are both marked differences and striking similarities among children. Thus, while this one-year-old may be using a spoon to self-feed and that one-year-old may not, the processes governing the ability of both one-year-olds to use such implements are more or less the same, and eventually both will be more or less equally skilled. What varies greatly are the ages at which different children acquire particular perceptual and motor skills. This is well illustrated by the various ages at which children achieve voluntary control of bowel and bladder.

SUGGESTED ADDITIONAL READING

Cratty, B. J. *Perceptual and motor development in infants and children.* New York: Macmillan, 1970.

Douglas, J. W. B., & Bloomfield, J. M. *Children under five.* London: George Allen & Unwin, 1958.

Kinsbourne, M., & Warrington, E. K. Developmental factors in reading and writing backwards. *British Journal of Psychology,* 1963, *54,* 145–156.

Ranson, S. W., & Clark, S. L. *The anatomy of the nervous system: Its development and function.* Philadelphia: Saunders, 1959.

PART THREE

The development of
information processing skills

BOX 5–1
Study questions

What is a perceptual system?

What is the function of the orienting reflex?

What factors regulate the infant's preferences for visual stimuli?

Do young children prefer simple forms or complex ones?

What is the "discrepancy hypothesis"?

How are orienting, perception, and attention related?

When do babies perceive depth?

What are the functions of the auditory system?

When can infants localize sound sources?

How do caregivers influence the organization of perceptual systems?

Can infants discriminate among various tastes or smells?

What functions do touch and temperature regulation serve for the developing child?

5

DEVELOPMENT OF THE
PERCEPTUAL SYSTEMS

If asked to describe the perceptual world of the newborn infant, most people would probably use terms similar to those offered by William James around the turn of the century. James saw the newborn's world as a "vast, blooming, buzzing confusion." To the extent that the newborn is a relatively immature organism, James was correct. Consider, for example, the visual abilities of the newborn as compared to those of older organisms. *Visual acuity* ranges from 20/150 to 20/400 in the newborn and does not approach the 20/20 acuity of the mature eye until the child is about age four. The human eye is *hyperopic* (farsighted) until about middle childhood, when it becomes *myopic* (nearsighted). The ability to accurately adjust the eye for the perception of objects at a distance (accommodation) is present from about the fourth month but does not approach the functional level of the mature eye until about the second or third year of life. The newborn can fixate a target at a distance of approximately 3 to 30 inches, but by the end of the first month objects three feet away can be fixated.

Nevertheless, James was for the most part incorrect in his evaluation of the perceptual abilities of the newborn. However, 75 years ago empirical studies of the human infant were practically nonexistent. Unlike James, we now possess substantive empirical evidence regarding visual perception in the young child. One of the frequently recurring themes of today's literature concerning early development is that the physical and social environments of the infant are anything but confusing to it. In fact, more often than not, the infant's physical and social world tends to be structured, orderly, and even potentially predictable. Objects continue to exist even when removed from view or when presented from a different spatial orientation. Objects at a distance appear to be moving slower and to be less clear than do objects moving at the same rate at closer range. Temporal sequences of common events are repeated frequently, often with the same outcomes. Language is orderly and grammatical in its construction and in its utterance. To a considerable extent, family units tend to be stable, and the members of the family tend to be consistent in their interactions with infants and young children.

Stability, however, should not be regarded as indicating simplicity. Infant researchers have many more unsolved than solved problems. One basic problem facing infant researchers is to determine how the infant becomes attuned to the regularities in its environment. In other words, how is it that the infant selectively acquires information embedded in a global mass of available stimulation, and how does the infant effectively and competently adapt to the demands of a changing environment? We have sampled some possible answers to these questions in previous chapters, and we will sample others in the chapters to come. In this chapter we will consider some of the basic processes which form the substrate for all behavior. We will be concerned with the development of sensory and perceptual systems. We will emphasize the orienting, visual, and auditory systems for two reasons: first, because infant researchers have favored their study; second, because over the entire life span they remain the primary sensory systems involved in human information processing. Nevertheless, as we shall see, these systems are not independent of other important modes of sensory experience.

PERCEPTUAL SYSTEMS

Most contemporary theorists agree that infants and young children actively extract from the available environmental stimulation that which has immediate relevance for the organism (J. Gibson, 1966; Piaget, 1969; Zaporozhets, 1965). The alternative view, that infants and young children are passive recipients of externally imposed stimulation, has not proven to be a useful model for explaining how sensory experiences are integrated into more highly organized perceptions or behaviors.

The distinction between active and passive sensory experiences is an outgrowth of a historic problem in psychology: that of distinguishing between *sensation* and *perception*. One distinction assigns to sensation the qualitative sensory experiences (for example, hot, loud, red, bitter) that arise in direct response to the stimulus activating a specialized receptor mechanism (for example, eye, ear, skin), while assigning to perception the function of preparing the organism to respond (Hebb, 1966). Theorists have also distinguished between *passive* sensory experiences resulting from receptor excitation and *active* perceptual systems that serve a stimulus detection function (Forgus, 1966) or an investigatory or information processing func-

reassessment of sensory and perceptual processes.

tion (J. Gibson, 1966). Gibson's theory, in particular, calls for a significant

From stimulus to response   Let us digress for a moment, however, to consider just what happens when an organism responds to a stimulus. First, the stimulus must be received by the appropriate receptor, converted into energy form, and conducted to the higher neural centers where a linkage between sensory process and motor mechanism occurs. The appropriate effector mechanisms then carry out the executive orders of the central nervous system, and a response takes place. But this is not the end of the story. The response, in turn, gives rise to afferent impulses through a process called *reafference* or *feedback*. Feedback instructs the organism to either terminate or continue ongoing stimulus-oriented behavior. It is through the feedback process that a behavior system becomes self-regulatory.

The organism comes into contact with external stimulation in two ways. First, at any given moment, available environmental stimulation imposes itself on the organism's sense receptors. The organism is a passive recipient of this kind of stimulation. One really cannot control the function of the ear. If the environment contains music above the auditory threshold, the ear "hears" it. However, the organism may or may not "listen" to it. The music is available, but it is not necessarily an effective stimulus.

Second, the organism actively seeks out stimulation. Available stimuli are not necessarily effective stimuli, and effective stimuli are not always immediately available. The organism must seek them out, must select from the available stimulation that which will be effective. The toddler may choose to play with a dollhouse rather than with blocks, to play in the sandbox rather than splash in the wading pool. In each case, the toddler is actively selecting from the available sources of stimulation a particular sort that will provide a particular sensory experience and a particular kind of feedback. However, as used by Gibson the term *active* does not necessarily imply intention or volition. "Active" search for stimulation can be mediated by a regulatory mechanism that assists the child in *selectively attending* to the immediately crucial and adaptive aspects of the available stimulation. As we shall see shortly, the orienting reflex plays an important role in this regulatory process.

Gibson's theory of the senses as perceptual systems rejects the historic notion of a set number of sensory modalities because such schemes fail to account for proprioceptive experiences (feedback) and for the diversity of experience obtained when the senses are active rather than passive. In place of the traditional list of sensory modalities, Gibson proposes modes of external attention—listening, touching, smelling, tasting, and looking—which are not to be confused with passive processes, that is, to hear, to feel touches, to smell, to taste, to see.

From these five modes of external attention Gibson develops five active, interrelated, self-regulatory perceptual systems: the *basic orienting system,* the *visual system,* the *auditory system,* the *taste-smell system,* and the *haptic system.*

THE BASIC ORIENTING SYSTEM

The basic orienting system is said to be operative when the infant turns its head to localize a sound source, when it centers its eyes to fixate a stimulus target, or when it searches for mother's breast or the bottle. The basic orienting system assists the organism to maintain body posture (that is, orientation to gravity) and balance. The basic orienting system also includes geographic orientation, for example, migration and homing behavior, which is most easily observed in nonhuman organisms.

During the 1930s a good deal of research with infants was devoted to the study of postural and locomotor orientation. More recently, study of the orienting reflex has come to the fore.

The orienting reflex

The *orienting reflex* (OR) is the organism's relatively brief, initial reaction to novel stimulation or to change in ongoing stimulation. If baby is lying quietly in its crib sucking on its bottle and father walks into the room and says "Nice baby," baby is very likely to stop sucking and visually attend to father. If we are recording the baby's heart rate activity as well, we are very likely to observe a slowing down (deceleration) of the heart rate shortly after father speaks. Thus, we would have observed a behavioral (cessation of sucking) and a physiological (heart rate deceleration) component of the baby's OR to the novel auditory and visual presence of father.

However, we would not necessarily observe both behavioral and physiological components of the OR. For example, it is very difficult to observe the heart rate deceleration component in the newborn infant (Graham & Jackson, 1970). Nevertheless, one can study newborn orienting, since other components of the OR are more easily elicited than heart rate deceleration during the newborn period (for example, sucking or eye-opening). Which components of the OR may be elicited seems to depend very much on the baby's state, or level of arousal.

Sokolov's contribution   Although the OR was first identified by the distinguished Soviet physiologist Ivan Pavlov (he called it the "investigatory" or "What is it?" reflex), Pavlov did not undertake a major systematic analysis of OR phenomena. However, another Soviet investigator, Ye. N. Sokolov, has spent the major portion of his scientific career investigating the parameters of the OR as well as its functional significance.

Sokolov (1963) distinguishes among three classes of basic reflexive behaviors: orientation reactions (ORs), defensive reactions (DRs), and adaptation reactions (ARs). DRs are elicited by very intense stimuli, and function to protect the organism from such aversive stimulation by impelling it either to remove the painful stimuli or to escape from them. ARs closely resemble what Western psychologists more commonly call homeostatic mechanisms. Thus, body temperature remains fairly constant even though the external temperature changes dramatically. A strong light causes the pupil of the eye to constrict, and it remains constricted as long as the illumination is present. However, as the eye adapts to the light source, the magnitude of the constriction may decrease somewhat.

Sokolov views the orienting system as a dynamic, regulatory, reflex loop or feedback system. What gets regulated is the information exchange between organism and environment. Functionally, the OR operates to enhance the organism's ability to process impinging sensory information. That is, the OR prepares the organism to selectively attend to external stimulation.

BOX 5–2
Similarities and differences among orientation reactions, defensive reactions, and adaptation reactions

Orientation reactions:

> Major neural involvement: Central—cortex, hippocampus, and reticular formation.
> Generality of reaction: General, analyzer nonspecific.
> Purpose: To bring organism into contact with the stimulus.
> Habituation: Readily habituate.

Defensive reactions:

> Major neural involvement: Peripheral—receptor organ; central—subcortical.
> Generality of reaction: General, analyzer nonspecific.
> Purpose: To break contact with the stimulus.
> Habituation: Habituate slowly if at all.

Adaptation reactions:

> Major neural involvement: Peripheral—at the receptor organ.
> Generality of reaction: Specific to the analyzer stimulated.
> Purpose: To maintain general homeostatic balance.
> Habituation: Do not habituate.

Attention *Attention* refers to the process that directs the organism toward aspects of environmental stimulation in order to handle the information contained in specific stimulus events or stimulus objects. Attention enables the organism to be selectively aware of environmental information.

Early in the first year of life, attention is primarily an elicited reaction that is closely linked to the OR and perhaps synonymous with it. Nearly any change in the stimulus environment will elicit the OR if the stimulus change is moderately intense. For example, an auditory stimulus will cause the one-month-old baby to stop sucking on its bottle. But this cessation is momentary; very soon baby will resume sucking. During the next two or three months, the orientation system and attention show rapid differentiation, due primarily to an increase in the duration of attention. Thus, the three-month-old lying in its crib can stare for a relatively long time at its hands or at a mobile hanging over the crib. The two-year-old can be absolutely transfixed by a 30-second television commercial or a two-minute cartoon. When one tries to get the two-year-old to sit patiently through an entire reading of "Sleeping Beauty," quite a different level of attention results. After the first page or two the toddler may find practically any other activity more interesting than the story. However, the four- or five-year-old may not only sustain attention through "Sleeping Beauty" but may request another story as well.

What factors account for differences in the attention span of the same child from one situation to another and for changes in the child's attention span over time? At one level of analysis these questions could be answered by discussing the structural and functional development of the reticular formation and the cerebral cortex, neurological structures important in the regulation of attention. However vital this level of explanation may be for a total understanding of the attentional process, it goes beyond our present purposes. A second level of analysis would be in terms of the characteristics of the external stimulus environment and of the inferred mental operations performed by the child. As we will see in Chapter 7, an example of this type of explanation has been termed the *discrepancy hypothesis.* For the present, our main interest is in the preparatory response to attention, the OR. For the infant researcher, one of the most interesting aspects of the OR is that it habituates upon repeated presentations of the same stimulus.

Habituation

Presented with a change in ongoing stimulation, the alert infant or young child responds to that change. We say that the infant orients to the perceived change in ongoing stimulation. Upon repeated experiences with the same stimulus, however, the child will gradually stop responding or will gradually reduce the magnitude of the OR. When this occurs, we say that habituation of the OR has occurred. Thus, *habituation* refers to the gradual response decrement that occurs when an organism receives repeated presentations of the same stimulus. Habituation has been demonstrated at all age levels, from infant to adult, and to all sorts of stimuli, including auditory, visual, olfactory, tactile, and gustatory stimuli. (The experimental procedures for demonstrating habituation are summarized in Table 5–1.)

Habituation and adaptation   Let us suppose that during the habituation phase we are presenting a 1,000-hertz square wave auditory signal and that the OR component being measured is heart rate deceleration. On the initial trials (presentations of the auditory stimulus) we could expect to observe decelerations of large magnitude. Gradually, however, the decelerations would become smaller and smaller.

TABLE 5–1
Procedures for demonstrating habituation

Procedures	Example*
Phase 1: Habituation	
Procedure: Repeated presentations of stimulus A	Stimulus: 750-hertz pure tone—90 decibels
Observations:	Response: Heart rate deceleration
Initial trials: OR elicitation	
Later trials: Response decrement	
Phase 2: Dishabituation	
Procedure: Repeated presentations of stimulus B	Stimulus: 400-hertz pure tone—90 decibels
Observations:	
Initial trials: OR elicitation	Response: Heart rate deceleration
Later trials: Response decrement	
Phase 3: Rehabituation	
Procedure: Repeated presentations of stimulus A	Stimulus: 750-hertz pure tone—90 decibels
Observations:	Response: Heart rate deceleration
Initial trials: OR elicitation	
Later trials: Response decrement	

* From B. M. Lester, "The consequences of infantile malnutrition," in H. E. Fitzgerald and J. P. McKinney (Eds.), *Developmental psychology: Studies in human development*, rev. ed. (Homewood, Ill.: Dorsey Press, 1977).

At this point it would be impossible for us to tell whether the response decrement was due to an active cortical inhibition of the response (habituation) or to a passive fatiguing of the peripheral receptor organ (adaptation). The question is whether habituation and adaptation are the same process or different processes. Habituation theory suggests that the organism actively constructs a neurological model of the effective stimulus input during each successive presentation of the stimulus. When the model of the stimulus is well formed, central neural mechanisms inhibit the organism's response to the stimulus, resulting in habituation. In contrast, when repeated stimulation results in receptor fatigue, *adaptation* is said to occur. Thus, repeatedly presenting a stimulus that is passively sensed by the organism leads to adaptation, whereas repeatedly presenting a stimulus that is actively perceived leads to habituation.

If the response decrement reflected receptor fatigue, the introduction of a new auditory stimulus should produce little, if any, change in the heart rate response. At least, it should not elicit an OR. If, however, the response decrement reflected cortical inhibition, then the introduction of a novel stimulus should elicit an OR, and heart rate deceleration would again occur.

The distinction between habituation and adaptation is important since the major theoretical model used in infant habituation research assumes an active, cortical process. Sokolov (1963) has theorized that a central neural process mediates habituation and dishabituation of the OR. According to his theory, incoming stimuli leave traces of their characteristics (neural models) primarily in the cortex. Excitation arising from an incoming stimulus is transmitted to the cortex, which in turn acts as an analyzing center that compares the incoming stimulus with the established neural model. If the incoming stimulus matches an existing model, the cortex directs impulses to the reticular formation to inhibit or block the organism's OR to the incoming stimulus. On the other hand, if the incoming stimulus does not match the neural model, the cortex is assumed to direct impulses to the reticular formation to elicit an OR. The rate of habituation is thought to reflect the rate of model formation.

Thus, a rigorous test of habituation must permit analysis of both response decrement (habituation) and response recovery (dishabituation). The dishabituation procedures depicted in Table 5–1 permit just such an analysis. On the initial dishabituation trials a cortical mediation hypothesis can be supported only by a reelicitation of the OR. The most conservative assessment of dishabituation is provided by choosing a stimulus from the same sensory modality as the habituating stimulus. Care must be taken, however, to select a stimulus that is sufficiently different from the original stimulus to minimize the possibility of a mismatch.

The third phase of the habituation procedure, rehabituation, involves the re-presentation of the original stimulus. Rehabituation allows one to study memory processes in young infants. Thus, if the magnitude of the OR on the first rehabituation trial is less than the magnitude of the OR on the original habituation trial, we can assume that the infant "remembers" something about the original stimulus. We can make the same assumption if the rate of habituation is faster during rehabituation than it was during habituation.

Habituation: Orienting and the cortex We have seen that Sokolov's theory predicts that a neural model of the stimulus is built up at the level of the cortex, and that our ability to stop responding to repetitive stimulation is a function of cortical inhibition. Note that this process is entirely different from pacification, which also refers to a shutting down of the infant's behavior. In habituation, the process is one of active cortical inhibition based on the organism's ability to cortically match impinging stimuli with a neural model. In pacification, the process is one of passive reaction to stimulation that, most likely, is neurally mediated at the lower brain stem, or at least subcortically. Apart from Sokolov's theory, what evidence do we have that the cortex is indeed the structural mediator of habituation?

One way to assess the role of the cortex in response inhibition is to study organisms which one suspects have suffered cortical injury. One early study compared infants who had suffered birth trauma with nontraumatized infants. Assessment of the habituation of sucking to an auditory stimulus indicated that significantly more traumatized than nontraumatized infants failed to habituate (Bronshtein, Antonova, Kamenetskaya, Luppova, & Sytova, 1958). Eisenberg, Coursin, and Rupp (1966) obtained essentially the same results in their study of normal, suspect, and high-risk infants: the greater the degree of suspected trauma, the more resistant to habituation were the infants.

The most direct investigation of the role of the cortex in inhibiting the OR, however, is Brackbill's (1971) study of an anencephalic infant. An anencephalic infant has suffered marked damage to the brain together with damage to the skull bones. An autopsy performed after this infant's death indicated an intact cerebellum and lower brain stem, but no telencephalon (which means that the structural damage to the cortex and olfactory bulbs was so great that function was impossible). Whereas most anencephalic infants survive only a few days, this infant lived for about 5½ months (see Figure 5–1).

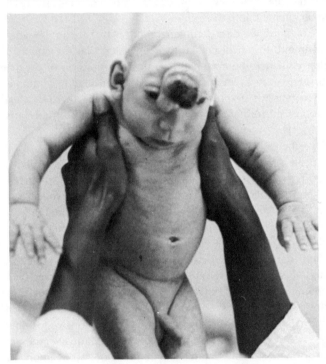

Source: Reprinted with the permission of the author and the American Psychological Association, Inc., from Y. Brackbill, "The role of the cortex in orienting: Orienting reflex in an anencephalic human infant," *Developmental Psychology*, 1971, *5*, 195–201.

FIGURE 5–1 Frontal view of an anencephalic infant. The infant's brain damage extended to the whole of the frontal cortex and the olfactory bulb but not to the cerebellum or brain stem.

In studying the anencephalic infant's auditory habituation, Brackbill failed to obtain evidence indicating that it was able to inhibit the startle response, even after 560 applications of an 80-decibel tone. In contrast, normal infants tested as controls at age 28 days required only 22 applications of the stimulus to meet the habituation criterion. Brackbill's study is important for at least two reasons. First, it demonstrated that the cortex is not essential for OR elicitation—the anencephalic infant *did* respond on most trials. Second, it would appear from the study that the cortex is absolutely essential for inhi-

bition of the OR (habituation) to occur. Moreover, since the responses of
the normal infant tended to be weaker than those of the anencephalic infant, the cortex appears to serve the additional function of suppressing the
amplitude of the responses that do occur.

Habituation: Orienting and malnutrition   The study of brain-damaged
infants enables us to make direct inferences as to which part or parts of the
nervous system mediate orienting and habituation. But what about possible
neural damage that may be much less apparent than, for example, that of
the anencephalic infant?

In Chapter 2 we discussed general hazards that can degrade the prenatal
environment. In our discussion we suggested that the effects of nutritional
insult are likely to be maximal from the last trimester of pregnancy through
the first few years of life: that is, during the period of maximum brain growth.
Extensive studies of preschool- and school-age children clearly establish
the poorer performance of malnourished children on all sorts of psychological tests.

Nevertheless, relatively few attempts have been made to directly assess
the effects of malnutrition during infancy. What studies have been conducted reflect the same general finding—poorer performance for the malnourished infants. Unfortunately, the studies which have focused on infancy have been concerned with reporting gross differences in behavior,
particularly as measured by standard infant developmental scales (Chase &
Martin, 1970; Cravioto & Robles, 1965). While infant developmental scales
are useful as descriptors of overall psychomotor function, they do not specify
the underlying psychological processes that may be affected by malnutrition.

On the other hand, specific psychological deficits are a characteristic
feature of the clinical syndrome of malnutrition. The infant suffering from
nutritional insult is universally found to be unresponsive to stimulus changes
in the environment. The exploratory behavior, curiosity, and activity typical
of the normal infant are dramatically reduced or absent among malnourished
infants. In fact, so marked is this condition that one of the hallmarks of recovery from malnutrition is the reappearance of the smile (Clark, 1951).

Recently, Lester (1975) took a significant step toward specifying what may
be the fundamental process responsible for the poor performance of malnourished infants on psychological-developmental tests: namely, a deficit in
their initial response to stimulation. In this experiment the subjects were
lower-class, one-year-old male infants residing in Guatemala City, Guatemala. Half of the infants were well nourished, and half suffered from either
second- or third-degree malnutrition. That is, the mean weight of the malnourished infants was only 75 percent of what one would expect for a
one-year-old according to norms developed by Gomez et al. (1956) in
Mexico City.

Lester's study was designed to provide an experimental test of the hypothesis that the infant's ability to respond appropriately to impinging environmental stimulation is affected by nutritional insult. The major dependent
variable was heart rate deceleration. The well-nourished infants showed

rather marked heart rate deceleration on the initial trials of each phase of the experiment. That is, well-nourished infants responded to a novel stimulus with a strong and well-pronounced OR. Moreover, with repeated presentations of the same stimulus in each phase of the experiment, habituation of the OR was demonstrated.

However, there was no evidence to suggest that malnourished infants even responded to the presentations of the tone. If anything, there was a slight acceleration at the beginning of each phase. Since heart rate acceleration is a component of the DR, perhaps the 90-decibel intensity of the stimulus was actually an aversive stimulus for the malnourished infants.

In any event, the results of Lester's study reveal a clear nutritional effect on the infant's ability to respond to and process impinging novel auditory stimulation. Infants suffering from malnutrition were found to evidence either a depressed OR or no OR at all. These results support the clinical observation that stimulus receptivity is adversely affected by nutritional insult and further suggest that this loss of receptivity is due to the absence of OR elicitation. Presumably, if infants cannot orient to a stimulus they will not be able to process the relevant information contained in the stimulus environment.

THE VISUAL SYSTEM

Many people equate the workings of the human eye with those of the camera. Gibson believes this to be a poor analogy since the eyes serve primarily as instruments of detection of selected features of the environment, and only secondarily, and perhaps incidentally, as instruments for the reflection of visual experience.

Among the perceptual systems, the visual system of infants and young children has been the most intensely studied. These studies indicate that very young children organize visual information in much the same way that adults do. Indeed, we now know that James's opinion of the visual world of the infant was considerably off the mark. The evidence justifying the contemporary view of the infant's visual competence is the product of some fascinating recent research. This research addresses three general aspects of visual perception: form perception and visual attention, the acquisition of perceptual constancies, and the perception of spatio-temporal relationships.

Form perception and visual attention

The study of the development of form perception received its contemporary impetus from the work of Robert Fantz. Early in the 1960s Fantz launched an intensive investigation of the development of visual perception. His studies were based on the premise that the amount of time an infant spends looking at an object or a picture will give an accurate measure of the infant's relative preference or of the picture's relative attractiveness for the infant. Typically, the infant lies on its back or is seated in a reclining chair. Overhead are one or two panels upon which one can place (or project) visual stimuli. These stimuli can be presented singly (successively) or in pairs (simultaneously). If an infant spends more time looking at one stimulus than at another, the assumption is that the stimuli are recognized as different and that one is preferred to the other.

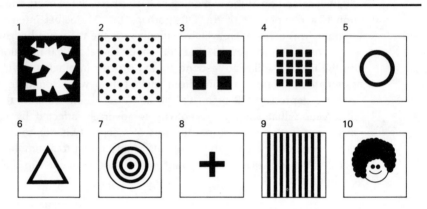

FIGURE 5–2 Examples of the stimuli used in the study of visual perception during infancy.

In most studies of form perception, stimuli such as those illustrated in Figure 5–2 are presented in pairs. For example, the infant may see a red circle on the left and a bull's-eye pattern on the right. Because infants have side preferences, it is necessary to vary the right-left positions of the stimuli from trial to trial. While the infant is looking at the stimuli, the experimenter records one of several aspects of the infant's looking behavior (called *visual fixation*). The experimenter could record how much time goes by before the infant first looks at one of the stimuli (response latency), or the total amount of time the infant looks at the stimulus (duration, or total fixation time), or the number of times the infant looks at the stimulus and then looks away (number of fixations). The experimenter is hidden from the infant's view and makes fixation time observations by peering through a small hole located in the stimulus panel between the two targets. The target is judged to be fixated when it is reflected on the cornea of the eye and located over the pupil. This simple method has proven highly reliable. By means of the fixation techniques, infants have been found to have visual preferences for (a) social patterns over nonsocial patterns (for example, human faces versus geometric designs), (b) complex targets over simple targets (for example, checkerboard patterns versus triangles), and (c) geometric patterns over solid color surfaces (for example a checkerboard pattern versus a red nonpatterned surface).

The fixation method is not without problems, however. One problem is that an infant "looking" at a stimulus might not be actively attending to it. The idea is that the infant may have been "captured" by the physical properties of the stimulus, that it may be *stimulus-bound*. Paradoxically, being captured by a stimulus may interfere with the ability to actively attend to the information contained in the stimulus. On the other hand, visual fixation may fail to accurately reflect the attentional process of an infant who is attending to a stimulus. To compensate for such possibilities, investigators have adopted a research strategy involving the use of several dependent variables. Typically, these variables include the directional heart rate response, arm movements, vocalizations, and smiles. This strategy does not represent a fail-safe solution, however, since quite often the different measures of attention correlate poorly.

When the specific attributes of patterned stimuli are considered, developmental trends in form perception and attentional preferences become difficult to interpret. For example, many investigators emphasize the *complexity* of the visual targets. Typically, complexity is defined by the number of elements or contours in the stimulus or by the degree of organization among the elements contained in the stimulus pattern. By definition, then, the target in Figure 5–2 which contains 16 squares is more complex than the one containing only 4 squares. Similarly, stimulus 1 in Figure 5–2 is more complex than stimulus 3 since it has more contours (or points of transition between black and white) and greater disorganization or randomness.

Hershenson (1964) found that infants were most responsive to the *least* complex of the stimulus targets presented, whereas Spears (1964) observed that infants were most attracted to the *most* complex stimuli. Initially, these results were considered contradictory. Then it was pointed out that one of the important differences between the two sets of data involved the age of the infants used in the studies. Subsequently, Brennan, Ames, and Moore (1966) demonstrated an age-by-complexity interaction. Three-week-old infants preferred the least complex stimulus, whereas 14-week-old infants preferred the most complex stimulus. An intermediate level of complexity was preferred by infants who were eight weeks old.

Differential responsiveness to complexity reflects the fact that there are qualitative differences between the perceptual organization of the 14-week-old and that of the newborn. One such difference—unrelated to the effects of the complexity dimension—can be seen in the directional patterns infants show when *scanning* a visual stimulus (Salapatek, 1969). Very young infants display what has been called an "addiction to contour" (Kagan, 1970), concentrating their attention on the vertices or boundaries of patterned forms. Hence, it seems unlikely that these infants respond to stimulus targets as a gestalt, or whole; instead, they probably select distinctive features of targets in order to detect differences among them. Older infants and young children are responsive to more global attributes of stimulus targets. The complexity dimension may account more adequately for their response patterns than for those of younger infants.

It is not clear whether children respond to an object as a whole or perceive specific elements of the object and then integrate the elements into an organized whole. To some extent this depends on the nature of the object being perceived. In general, if the object is complex, young children tend to turn to the elements or parts. If the object is simple, young children seem to respond to the object as a whole. In any event, young children have difficulty with both part and whole perceptions.

Another determinant of attention is the relative *novelty* or meaningfulness of a stimulus. The logic underlying the investigation of stimulus novelty as a determinant of visual attention is related to habituation and to the theory of neural model formation. Greenberg (1971) found that infants preferred to look at stimuli slightly more novel than those that had been repeatedly presented earlier. Saayman, Ames, and Moffett (1964) observed that 12–15-week-old infants consistently preferred a novel visual stimulus over one which they had previously seen for a period of 4½ minutes. They also noted that visual exploration of a stimulus decreased with increased exposure to it. As a result of these experiments, visual preference measures following stimulus familiarization were applied to the study of infant memory processes in particular and cognitive processes in general.

The perception of facial features   A particularly interesting outgrowth of research in infant visual perception was the demonstration that stimulus features as meaningful as those contained in the human face evoke optimal attention from infants. Initially, at about four months and perhaps earlier, the eyes are a particularly salient feature for the infant. The eyes consistently elicit more visual attention and smiling than do the nose and mouth. Around the fourth month, infants begin to respond to the two eyes as a structured unit (Caron, Caron, Caldwell, & Weiss, 1973) but have not yet organized a concept of the invariant configuration of the eyes, ears, nose, and mouth. For example, when Caron et al. presented four-month-old infants with distorted facial stimuli, the less facelike a distortion was, the more attention the stimulus received. By five months of age, similar procedures indicated that the mouth had become as salient a feature as the eyes, and that the configuration of the face was viewed as a distinct visual entity.

Studies such as that conducted by Caron et al. increase our understanding of just what physical attributes of the human face infants find compelling. But faces have qualities other than those specifiable in physical dimensions. For example, faces are also social stimuli. In fact, when we study infant preferences for particular faces, the results are not always what we might expect. For example, Carpenter, Teece, Stechler, and Friedman (1970) found that one- to eight-week-old infants spent more time looking at a store manikin's head or at a three dimensional abstract face than at their mother's face. Given the choice between looking at a female stranger's face and that of their mother, infants not only spent less time looking at their mother's face but became distressed when it was presented.

Carpenter suggests that infants reacted negatively in this situation because mother was a familiar visual stimulus behaving in an unfamiliar way in an unfamiliar setting. Older infants attempted to elicit responses from mother by smiling, cooing, and even crying, but mother did not react. One assumes that mother would react to her infant's signals outside the confines of the laboratory. Thus, what an infant might have learned to expect from mother at home was discrepant with her behavior during the experiment. The infant may have looked more at the stranger because of her novelty and looked less at mother because her behavior was discrepant with what the infant had come to expect in eight short weeks.

Spatiotemporal perception   The infant's ability to perceive and respond to objects as they are displaced through space and time is as important as its ability to perceive and integrate the perceptual information contained in stationary two- and three-dimensional social and nonsocial forms. Absence of the ability to judge correctly the distance, velocity, and direction of moving objects severely restricts the infant's mobility. The toddler's inability to respond accurately to the spatiotemporal information provided by an onrushing automobile attests to the relative immaturity of this perceptual system during early development. On the other hand, the eight-month-old's quick mustering of his or her motoric and vocal responses when approached by a stranger indicates that the ability to detect the movement of objects through space and time is certainly not absent in infancy.

Ball and Tronick (1971) have presented evidence indicating that as early as two weeks of age the infant is capable of detecting such spatiotemporal qualities as direction, impending collision, and the rate of approach of both real objects and their optical equivalents (that is, shadows). The infant's response to approaching or *looming* objects is a complex of motoric actions. These include averted gaze, head turning, and increased muscle tonus. Moreover, it seems that learning plays a relatively minor role in the infant's initial reaction to looming objects because the reaction appears so early in development and because no age differences have been found in the ability of infants to detect such objects.

Perceptual constancies and depth perception

From the infant's impoverished two-dimensional retinal world, perceptions are somehow made up of complex spatiotemporal relationships in the three-dimensional world. Quite clever research has been conducted recently which suggests some of the ways in which this perceptual translation process is organized.

Do infants organize such spatial relationships as distance simply on the basis of the size of the retinal image produced? Or do they apply a complex perception, such as size constancy, when organizing spatial relations? In adults, *size constancy* is indicated by the realization that objects remain the same in size but only appear smaller when they are seen from a distance. Moreover, changes in the angle of perception as well as changes in distance do not change an adult's perception of an object. In other words, the perceived size of an object remains constant even though the retinal image varies. You perceive your tall friend as tall, whether he or she is standing next to you or is two blocks away. But do infants behave similarly?

Perceptual constancies   T. G. R. Bower (1966) applied the principle of generalization from learning research in an effort to determine how six- to eight-week-old infants perceive objects. Simply put, the principle of *generalization* states that stimuli perceived as similar to other previously experienced stimuli will evoke the same response as those stimuli in direct proportion to the degree of perceived similarity. The utility of this principle becomes clearer within the context of Bower's experiment.

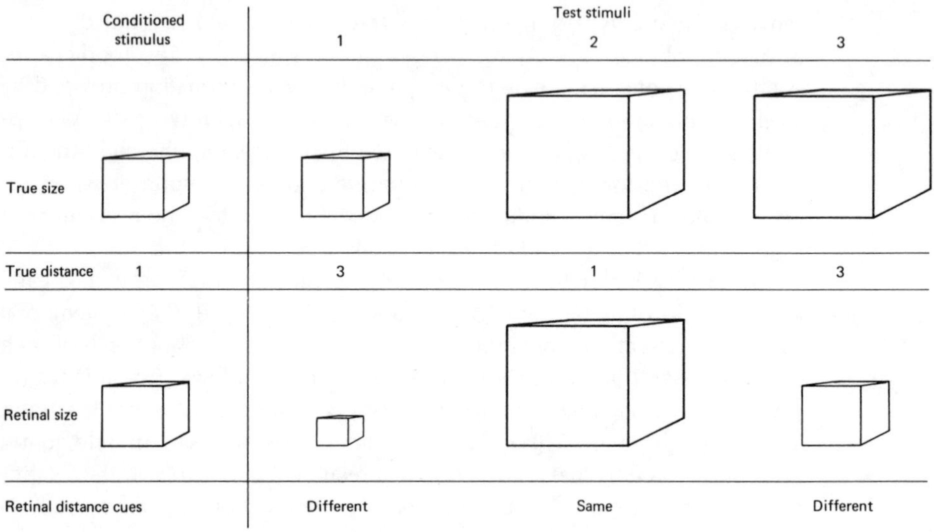

Source: Reprinted with permission from the author and Copyright © 1966 by Scientific American, Inc. from T. G. R. Bower, "The visual world of infants." *Scientific American*, 1966, *215*, 80–92. All rights reserved.

FIGURE 5–3   Size constancy was investigated by using cubes of different sizes placed at different distances from the infants. The conditioned stimulus was 30 centimeters on a side and one meter away, the test stimuli were 30 or 90 centimeters on a side and one or three meters away. The chart shows how the test stimuli were related to the conditioned stimulus in various respects.

During an initial training session, infants learned to turn their heads to press a panel in the presence of a 30-centimeter white cube located one meter from them. The panel press response was reinforced by the experimenter who would jump up in front of an infant and play peekaboo for a few seconds. When the infant learned to press the panel only in the presence of the test cube, the generalization tasks began. Generalization was assessed by presenting three different cubes in sequence (see Figure 5–3). The first test stimulus was the same in size as the training cube, but it was placed three meters away from the infant. The second and third stimuli were 90-centimeter cubes placed either one meter or three meters away. The results of the experiment indicated that responses to the generalization cubes were regulated by the real size of the cubes and their distance from the infant, and not by retinal size or distance cues. In other words, more responses occurred to stimulus 1 than to stimulus 2 and more to stimulus 2 than to stimulus 3, suggesting that the image on the retina played an inconsequential role in the infant's reaction to the cubes. But if the retinal image does not determine responsivity, what does?

Studies of human adults have shown that *retinal disparity* and *motion parallax* are important cues in depth or distance perception. So Bower's next step was to design a series of tasks that would enable him to evaluate which of these cues was most influential in determining the infant's perception of distance.

Three groups of infants were trained to respond to the same cube used in the first experiment. However, restrictions were placed on the cues that would be available during the learning task. Infants in one group (Monocular) wore a patch over one eye to remove *retinal disparity* as a potential cue. Infants in a second group (Binocular–slides) were shown slides of the cubes rather than the real cubes. Although monocular cues, such as perspective, shading, and texture, were available, retinal disparity and *motion parallax* were unavailable to these infants. The third group of infants (Binocular–stereoscopic) viewed stereograms of the cubes through special stereoscopic goggles. The goggles removed motion parallax as a potential cue but permitted all other cues to be used.

Infants in the Monocular group responded in the same way as did the Binocular infants in the first experiment. Consequently, it appears that motion parallax is the most crucial cue to depth. The behavior of the infants in the group viewing slides of the cubes suggested that the size of the retinal image alone was detected. From this it appears that young infants cannot use pictorial cues to organize their visual experiences. That retinal disparity provides some useful information is indicated by the performance of the group viewing stereograms. The combined results of Bower's work indicate that quite young infants have size constancy. Bower has argued that the appearance of this perceptual phenomenon so early in life supports the contention that perceptual organizers are biologically based and relatively independent of learning, although, of course, not independent of experience.

Using a similar procedure, Bower also studied *shape constancy* and *object orientation*. Figures were presented which preserved the real shape, the spatial orientation, or the retinal shape of the training stimulus. The general pattern of responses indicated that infants are able to maintain shape constancy despite changes in spatial orientation or retinal image projection. However, they are not able to discriminate among objects in situations which require that they maintain shape constancy and spatial orientation at the same time.

The visual cliff   Much of our knowledge concerning the development of depth perception has been obtained in studies using an apparatus called the "visual cliff" (Gibson & Walk, 1960). In these studies infants were placed on a board in the center of a glass-topped table. Under one half of the table was a checkered cloth in contact with the glass surface (the "shallow" side). Under the other half was an identical checkered cloth, placed at a distance of about four feet from the glass surface, thereby simulating a drop-off or cliff. Gibson and Walk wanted to see whether infants could be coaxed to leave the center board on the table and crawl out over the "visual cliff." With remarkable consistency, infants approximately 6 to 14 months old refused to leave the center board even when their mothers tried to get them to do so. However, these infants quickly responded when their mothers coaxed them to crawl out over the shallow side of the apparatus. It is clear that infants are able to perceive depth at least as early as the time that they are capable of self-locomotion.

Color, form, and illusion   Questions involving the perception of colors, color-form preferences, and the perception of illusions have also been subjected to intensive research. In general, preschool-age children tend to make brightness discriminations more easily than they make color discriminations. Developmentally, children move toward preferences for blue, red, or yellow—for primary colors rather than secondary colors—and seem to be less sensitive to colors than are adults. Changes also occur in the characteristics of objects that influence children's preferences. Initially, size of object is more predictive of preference than is color or form, and color is preferred over form. By the end of early childhood, however, form seems to be preferred over color. There are also developmental changes in children's susceptibility to illusions. However, these changes depend to a great extent upon the illusion in question. Susceptibility to some illusions increases with age, whereas susceptibility to other illusions decreases with age.

THE AUDITORY SYSTEM

According to Gibson, the auditory system serves three primary functions: (1) it provides the sensory apparatus that is essential for hearing sound; (2) it provides information concerning the nature of the sound source; and (3) it provides information concerning the direction of the sound source. The first of these functions refers to the sensory experience of the passive organism, that is, to the receptor mechanism which determines the range of vibration to which the organism is sensitive. In the normal human adult this range is generally stated to be from 20 to 20,000 hertz (cycles per second). The range of maximum acuity is from 1,000 to 4,000 hertz.

The newborn infant can hear, but it hears best when sounds are moderately loud. The residual fluid from the amniotic sac temporarily blocks the normal vibration of the ossicles of the middle ear. Moreover, the ossicles of the middle ear are not fully functional at birth because of the presence of connective tissue which restricts ossicle movement. Within a few months, however, the ossicles are fully functional. Auditory sensitivity is sufficiently well developed in the newborn to permit tests for deafness. These tests usually involve presentation of a loud sound and observation of behavioral orienting or startle responses. Although the tests are not fail-safe—they identify *false positives* (infants who are judged to be deaf but are not) as well as *false negatives* (infants who are deaf but are judged not to be)—the number of infants they correctly identify as deaf is sufficiently large to more than justify testing.

Over the first two years of life there is a gradual reduction in the intensity of an auditory stimulus required to elicit a response from the young child. This developmental change is probably related both to changes in the functioning of the ear and to changes in attentional processes.

The second and third functions of the auditory system refer to overt and covert listening, which are the auditory system's modes of attention. In *overt listening*, the organism makes postural adjustments in order to localize the sound source and to enhance the quality of the information that can be extracted from the impinging sound. In *covert listening*, information extraction occurs at neural centers. In both modes of attention, the adjustments made by the organism modify the nature of the impinging stimulus as well as the feedback to the organism.

Sound localization

The development of the ability to localize sound sources serves as an excellent example of the active nature of the auditory system and of its interdependence with other perceptual systems. The ability to localize sounds is particularly dependent upon the integration of the auditory system with the basic orienting system and the visual system. For example, sound localization in human adults is impaired when the head is held in a fixed position (Bartley, 1969), thus eliminating feedback to the organism from the postural adjustments that usually accompany attempts to localize sounds.

Just as there are cues which aid the infant to organize visual perception, there are cues which facilitate its organization of auditory perception. Particularly helpful in sound localization are three *binaural cues: time difference* (the difference in the time at which sound reaches one ear and then the other), *intensity difference* (the weaker intensity of sound at the ear opposite from the sound source), and *phase difference* (the difference in sound pressure waves between the two ears).

When can an infant localize a sound? Using somatic components of the orienting reflex as the dependent variable, Chun, Pawsat, and Forster (1960) found that the ability to localize sound was poor prior to about the fourth to the sixth month. Apparently, normal infants can localize sounds well when they are about six months old, and orienting behavior can be used to assess this capability. The possibility exists, however, that a different component of orienting might reveal successful localization at an even earlier age. To date, however, suggestions that newborns can localize sounds

(Wertheimer, 1961) seem premature. The Chun et al. results suggest that the infant must achieve some minimal level of organization before feedback from the basic orienting system can supplement feedback from the auditory system, enabling the infant to localize a sound. However, the ability to localize a sound source in space is also related to visual feedback.

Marshall Haith and his associates have been studying visual scanning patterns in newborn infants. A preliminary report from their studies suggests that when newborns are visually scanning mother's motionless face, the scanning pattern moves more or less randomly over the entire face. However, when mother begins to speak, her infant's scanning pattern becomes localized to one of her eyes (Bergman, Haith, & Mann, 1971). Perhaps the early organization of sound localization is facilitated by talking caregivers who maintain eye-to-eye contact with their infants.

A most interesting experiment by Aronson and Rosenbloom (1971) suggests that infants become quite upset when auditory-visual spatial localization is violated. In this experiment infants were placed in front of a window through which they could see their mothers. The mother's voice was transmitted to the infant through two speakers located in the same room as the infant. Initially, the mother's voice was broadcast with the stereo amplification system in balance so that her voice appeared to be coming from her position in the center of the viewing window. Then the stereo system was altered so that her voice would appear to come from 90 degrees to the right of her position or 90 degrees to the left of her position. When the mother's voice and position were coordinated, infants remained visually alert, calm, and relaxed. However, when the mother's voice was displaced, infants rapidly became distressed, as indicated by struggling movements of the arms, legs, and torso; vigorous mouthing of the tongue; and crying and fussing. This study suggests that infants' perception of auditory and visual information is best when the stimulus sources are coordinated in space. Analogous phenomena can be observed in older children and adults. For example, when a young child is speaking to a caregiver who happens not to be looking at the child, the caregiver is likely to have little hands grab his or her face and turn it so that eye-to-eye contact can be maintained during the conversation. For adults, gaze aversion is often interpreted as a lack of interest in a conversation.

Signal value of adult speech

Infants appear to be biologically primed to perceive and respond to certain characteristics of human speech. Sometime during the first three months, infants can discriminate such phonemes as /ba/ and /ga/ (Moffitt, 1971) and /ba/ and /pa/ (Eimas, Siqueland, Jusczyk, & Vigorito, 1971). Moreover, it appears that the active perception of speech is facilitated by rhythmic body movements. Condon and Ogston (1966) observed a remarkable synchrony between the micro-units of body movements in adults and the natural rhythmicity of speech. Changes in the configuration of body parts occurred simultaneously with changes in the articulation of speech sounds. Thus it might be said that, in a sense, the body "dances" to a rhythm established by the structure or organization of speech, with the speaker raising an eyebrow or crooking an elbow in time with a phonetic sequence. Interestingly enough, this pattern is reproduced in the behavior of individuals listening to the speech. This is not to say that the precise components of the movements of speaker and listener are identical, only that the rhythmic patterns of those movements are similar. Taken by itself, this observation supports the view that perception, in this case listening, is an active process.

Extending this procedure to newborn infants (12 hours to 14 days old), Condon and Sander (1974) found high correspondence between the adult speech pattern and the pattern of the newborn's movements. Furthermore, it made no difference whether the adult speaker was present physically or was talking via a tape recorder. Nor did it matter whether the language being spoken was English (American version) or Chinese—synchrony occurred in both cases. On the other hand, tapping sequences and disconnected vowels that lacked the natural rhythm of speech elicited no motor movement–speech unit coordination.

Since this line of research is itself in its infancy stage, it remains to be demonstrated whether such coordination between the punctuation of speech patterns and of motor movements facilitates the acquisition of language. Some conclusions are suggested, however. First, newborns are able to respond in an organized manner to human speech sounds. Second, their response to speech differs from their response to other sounds (though non-speech rhythms, such as music, have not yet been investigated in this context). Third, coordinated motor movements are elicited regardless of the language spoken. Newborns respond in an equally well-organized fashion to any language.

THE TASTE-SMELL SYSTEM

The typical definition of a sense advanced by physiologists refers exclusively to the receptor mechanism that gives rise to the impulses conducted to higher neural centers. The chemoreceptors and mechanoreceptors for *gustation* and *olfaction* are located in the oral and nasal cavities, respectively. Since the taste sensation is highly dependent upon the particular odorous characteristic of the nutritive substance, taste has traditionally been viewed as a relatively "minor" sensation. This view has been buttressed by the fact that taste is an unreliable measure of the lethal nature of substances. Gibson's view of taste as part of a perceptual system stands in marked contrast to this traditional view. According to Gibson, taste assists in the selection of substances capable of being ingested by providing information about their temperature, texture, and consistency. Through its interaction with the haptic action of the mouth, taste provides information concerning the size, shape, specific gravity, and granularity of substances.

Since the human newborn appears to have an ample supply of taste buds, it might be expected that the gustatory capabilities of the infant and young child have been well established. That this is not the case is illustrated by Spears and Hohle's (1967) thorough review of sensory and perceptual processes in infancy, which required only two pages to review the literature on gustation (and part of that was devoted to the structural basis of the sensation). This paucity of literature may be attributed to two major factors. The first factor is that taste has been viewed as a relatively unimportant sensory experience that is dependent upon olfaction. The second factor is that it has been difficult to develop reliable measures of gustation suitable for use in infant research.

Using facial movements as the major dependent variable, Pratt, Nelson, and Sun (1930) were unable to demonstrate evidence of taste discrimination in newborns. On the other hand, using the newborn's sucking behavior, Jensen (1932) successfully demonstrated discrimination of milk and saline solutions. In Jensen's study, facial expressions proved to be a poor measure of taste discrimination. When compared to polygraphically recorded sucking responses, facial expressions were found to be associated with only a very few of the discriminative sucking responses. Very recent research tends to support Jensen's conclusion that newborns can discriminate among tastes.

Although toddlers and young children can discriminate among tastes, there is little consistency in their preferences among various tastes. One toddler may show no signs of dislike for beer, while another may quickly purse its lips, spit, and utter "Yuck, I no like!" Not only are there differences among children in food preferences, but differences in food preferences occur in the same child over time. The extent to which taste preferences contribute to food likes and dislikes in young children has not been investigated adequately.

Early studies of infant *olfaction* were troubled by several methodological problems, not all of which have been resolved. Despite these problems, investigators have made some progress in assessing the infant's olfactory abilities. For example, in one experiment the newborn's response to tincture asafetida was compared with its response to diethyl phthalate (Lipsitt, Engen, & Kaye, 1963). The dependent variables—respiration and leg thrust—were recorded polygraphically. Not only did the investigators find that newborns do respond to odors, but even more important they demonstrated that with careful methodological control it is possible to study more intricate questions regarding infant olfaction. For example, they found that olfactory thresholds decrease systematically over the first few days of life. This means that progressively weaker odors are required to elicit responses in newborns.

It seems clear that the infant can detect odors at a very early age, but can the infant also detect differences among odors? Rovee (1969) studied newborns' responsiveness to five odorous aliphatic alcohols—propanol, pentanol, hexanol, actanol, and decanol—which differ in the number of carbons in the alcohol molecule (three, five, six, eight, and ten, respectively). The dependent variable was gross motor activity. Rovee found that the response magnitude and the rate of adaptation decreased as the number of carbons in the alcohol molecule increased. Moreover, the response threshold decreased as the length of the carbon chain increased. This study suggests that newborns can detect minute differences among odorous substances and can respond differentially to them as a function of the information contained in their odors.

In subsequent studies, Rovee and her associates (Rovee, 1972; Rovee, Cohen, & Shlapack, 1975) have found little variation in odor sensitivity throughout the life span. This suggests that olfaction is a very primitive sensory process. Olfaction is one of the phylogenetically oldest sensory systems (audition and vision being phylogenetically newer sensory systems). Moreover, it seems to be the most highly developed sensory ability of the newborn as well as one of the last sensory abilities to become impaired in old age.

THE HAPTIC SYSTEM

Gibson classifies the receptors serving the haptic system as mechanoreceptors because they are responsive to mechanical energy. The pitfalls of this seemingly innocuous judgment must be carefully noted: by attributing the perception of action-produced haptic stimulation to mechanoreceptors, Gibson minimizes the importance of chemoreceptors and photoreceptors in haptic perception. (He withholds judgment as to whether thermoreceptors are involved in haptic perception.)

The specific mechanoreceptors—free nerve endings, encapsulated nerve endings, and hair cells—are distributed throughout the body, but are associated especially with the skin, joints and ligaments, muscles and tendons, the outer surface of the blood vessels, and the semicircular canals, vestibule, and cochlea of the inner ear. Since the entire surface area of the body and most of its parts contain mechanoreceptors, we may infer, as does Gibson, that the haptic system interacts with all other perceptual systems.

The maintenance of *body temperature* is vital to the survival of the organism. For this reason alone we should expect to find that very young infants are sensitive to temperature changes, and in fact they are. Mestyan and Varga (1960) conducted an experiment studying thermoregulation in the newborn. Infants were placed in an air-sealed chamber which was then immersed in water. Changes in the water temperature raised or lowered the temperature inside the chamber. The investigators found evidence of a change in thermoregulation over the first six days of life. When placed in a cooled environment, infants over six days of age maintained constant body temperature, whereas those less than six days old did not. Mestyan and Varga made an important methodological contribution to the study of temperature sensitivity. Enclosing the baby in an air-sealed chamber and manipulating the temperature of the medium in which the chamber is immersed, severely restricts the influence of direct tactile stimulation. From the perceptual systems point of view, however, it is impossible to totally separate tactile from thermal stimulation because they are interrelated aspects of the haptic system. The surface of the chamber used by Mestyan and Varga does touch the infant's body surface, which, as we have noted, contains receptors sensitive to haptic stimulation. On the other hand, the air-sealed chamber provides distinct advantages over previous methods used to administer thermal stimulation. Its major disadvantage is that it cannot be used to present thermal stimuli to specific parts of the body surface.

Research conducted in the 1930s clearly demonstrated the young infant's sensitivity to *tactile* stimulation. In addition, research with such non-human organisms as rhesus monkeys has alerted all developmentalists to the importance of tactile stimulation in early life (see Harlow, 1971). The infant's earliest active exploration, in addition to visual scanning of the environment, is accomplished primarily through touch, including oral and prehensile exploration.

The study of tactile sensitivity in the newborn suggests that sensitivity to touch is regulated by many factors. Bell and Costello (1964) compared three methods for evaluating tactile sensitivity: blanket removal, air jet stimulation to the abdomen, and stimulation with an esthesiometer. They found that tactile sensitivity was correlated with such variables as the type of feeding, body build, state, maternal parity, and the method of assessing sensitivity. We shall have occasion throughout the remainder of this volume to point out the importance of tactile stimulation for early development, especially in our discussion of the development of social behavior (Chapter 9).

SUMMARY

The historic view that the infant and young child are passive recipients of sensory stimulation has been replaced by the view that receiving external stimulation involves both active and passive processes. Passive contact with stimulation occurs at the receptor level and involves central neural processes minimally at most. Active contact with stimulation, on the other hand, involves much central neural mediation. Adaptation procedures are used to study passive contact with stimulation, whereas the active processing of stimulus information is investigated by means of orienting and habituation procedures. The latter procedures are thought to provide important information concerning the infant's ability to selectively attend to relevant stimulus information.

James Gibson has suggested that attention and perception are complexly related processes which can be studied most meaningfully when the senses are conceptualized as perceptual systems. He suggests that there are five active, interrelated, self-regulatory perceptual systems: the basic orienting, visual, auditory, taste-smell, and haptic systems. This innovative theory of the senses as perceptual systems provides the basis for an important re-analysis of the organism's role in information processing. Gibson's theory is not restricted to the perceptual systems in infancy and early childhood; it applies throughout the life span. Nevertheless, the infant and young child are ideal subjects for empirical tests of the theory, since during the early years of development one has the opportunity to study both the emergence of independent perceptual systems and the development of integration among the systems. Finally, the concept of reafference or feedback is consistent with the contemporary developmental view that the infant is actively engaged in determining the course of its behavior and development.

SUGGESTED ADDITIONAL READING

Bower, T. G. R.   *Development in infancy*. San Francisco: Freeman, 1974.

Cohen, L. B., & Salapatek, P. (Eds.).   *Infant perception: From sensation to cognition*. Vol 1: *Basic visual processes*. New York: Academic Press, 1975.

Cohen, L. B., & Salapatek, P. (Eds.).   *Infant perception: From sensation to cognition*. Vol. 2: *Perception of space, speech, and sound*. New York: Academic Press, 1975.

Fantz, R. L.   The origin of form perception. *Scientific American*, 1961, *204*, 66–72.

BOX 6–1
Study questions

What is the organizational relationship between the nervous system and learned behavior?

What is the most complex type of learning that has thus far been demonstrated in the human infant?

How does the baby begin to form associations among the stimulus events in its environment?

In classical conditioning, what are the important constraints influencing the baby's ability to associate stimulus events?

What evidence suggests that the ability to learn increases as the baby grows older?

How has the learning psychologist approached the question of individual differences in behavior?

How does instrumental conditioning differ from classical conditioning?

What must one consider before attempting to study the modification of operant behavior in infants?

How do the learning processes of the infant differ from those of the preschooler?

What is the best reinforcer one can use to strengthen operant behavior?

What are the stages in the development of discrimination learning during infancy and early childhood?

6

THE DEVELOPMENT OF LEARNING

It would take a most uninterested observer to be unaware of or unimpressed by the tremendous changes that occur in the ability to learn over the first years of life. Broadly defined, *learning* refers to changes in behavior that occur as a result of experience. Often, learning is placed in opposition to *maturation,* which refers to changes in behavior that occur regardless of experience. Actually, neither definition is completely correct, because learning and maturation are not independent processes. Much of what can be learned depends upon the organism's readiness, or preparedness, for learning. In turn, learning may alter or restructure the rate of maturational change. In other words, learning and maturation are interdependent processes. Although maturation of the structures of the nervous system provides the necessary conditions for learning to occur, learning itself is a significant determinant of structural organization (Rosenzweig, 1971).

We have stressed repeatedly that all behavior—from the simplest to the most complex—is organized developmentally, and learning is no exception. Phylogenetically, the human species has reached a higher level of behavioral organization than any other species. Although organisms from the lowly planaria to the chimpanzee are known to be capable of rather sophisticated learning, it is generally accepted that the learned behavior of human beings achieves the highest level of complexity. And yet human beings do not begin life with the ability for complex learning. They acquire this ability as a result of interaction between the organism and the environment. In this sense, one can argue that the ability to learn is itself a product of adaptation. The organism's ability to learn is constrained by its underlying structural preparedness for learning. What, specifically, is learned, however, depends upon the individual's particular environmental experiences.

CLASSICAL CONDITIONING

The ability to inhibit responding to a repeatedly presented stimulus is the most elementary type of learning. Put somewhat differently, habituation demonstrates the gradual loss of the elicitation properties of a stimulus due to cortical inhibition. Classical conditioning, on the other hand, demonstrates how a stimulus gains elicitation properties due to cortical excitation. Simple classical conditioning procedures are used to investigate this question: How does the organism learn to associate a stimulus which initially has a low probability of eliciting a specified response with a stimulus which has a high probability of eliciting a specified response, such that the former stimulus acquires the elicitation properties of the latter?

Two points about our question must be expanded. The first point concerns what we mean when we say that a stimulus has elicitation properties. Recall from the previous chapter that responding to a stimulus requires afferent, central, and efferent neural involvement, as well as feedback. The afferent receptors are specialized in that they are uniquely sensitive to specific types of physical energy. The central neural processes have the job of selecting from the available stimulation impinging upon the receptors that which is effective for the organism. Thus, the elicitation potential of a stimulus is a product of both passive afferent-receptor processes and active central processes.

The second point concerns the specification of the response. Since all stimuli have potential as eliciting stimuli, why do we assign high and low probability values to different classes of stimuli? Well, the fact is that all stimuli do not have elicitation properties for all responses. In other words, there is stimulus-response specificity just as there is receptor specificity. Thus, there are both organismic and environmental factors that interfere with the ability to learn. Collectively, these factors are referred to as *constraints* on the learning process.

Simple classical conditioning

In classical conditioning, the *conditional stimulus* (CS) must have an initial low probability of eliciting the response of interest, whereas the *unconditional stimulus* (UCS) must have an initial high probability of eliciting the response. Thus, an increase in illumination (UCS) elicits pupillary reflex constriction, whereas a tickle on the abdomen does not. A puff of air blown near the eye elicits a blink, a moderately intense sound does not. When an abdominal tickle does elicit pupillary constriction or a moderate sound does elicit a blink, each stimulus has become a CS. Each stimulus has changed from one having a low probability of eliciting a specified response to one having a higher probability of eliciting that response.

The UCS elicits a known and specifiable response called the *unconditional response* (UCR). For example, a puff of air elicits a blink (UCR). When the CS acquires elicitation properties similar to those of the UCS, the response it elicits is called the *conditional response* (CR). Thus, the presence of the CR is the measure of whether or not learning has occurred. Several characteristics of the CR are measurable, including its magnitude and its latency. Although the CR and the UCR are essentially the same response, they do differ. For example, since the UCS is usually a stronger stimulus than the CS, the magnitude of the UCR will be greater than that of the CR, or the latency of the UCR will be shorter than that of the CR (that is, the UCR will occur more rapidly following UCS presentation than will the CR following CS presentation).

The most famous example of classical conditioning is Pavlov's original demonstration of conditional salivation in dogs. Pavlov was interested in the signal value of stimuli. He proposed one of the first learning hierarchies when he described the first and second signal systems (Pavlov, 1927). The *first signal system* included learning of the simple associations between signal stimuli (CSs) and reinforcing stimuli (UCSs). The *second signal system* represented more complex learning and came into play when words acquired signal value. Now words rather than nonverbal sensory stimuli could signal and regulate behavior.

Simple conditioning procedures   The CS is conditional because it acquires its elicitation properties via a set of conditions, one of the most important being its temporal closeness to the UCS. In fact, the CS-UCS relationship determines to a great extent the different types of classical conditioning procedures (see Figure 6–1). In *simultaneous conditioning,* the onset and offset of the CS and the UCS occur at the same time. In *delayed conditioning,* CS onset occurs prior to UCS onset, but UCS onset occurs prior to CS offset. Thus, although CS and UCS have different onset times in delayed conditioning, for some brief period of time CS and UCS occur together. When CS and UCS are completely separated in time, the procedure is called *trace conditioning,* presumably to reflect the idea that some neurally stored aspect of the CS holds over in time and is subsequently reinforced by the UCS. In infant conditioning research the simultaneous and delayed procedures have generally been preferred over the trace procedure.

In delayed conditioning the time between onset of the CS and onset of the UCS is called the *interstimulus interval* (ISI), and the time between offset of the UCS and onset of the next CS is the *intertrial interval* (ITI). In trace conditioning the ISI is the time between CS offset and UCS onset, while the ITI is the same as in delayed conditioning, UCS offset to onset of the next CS. In *temporal conditioning,* the last of the simple conditioning procedures illustrated in Figure 6–1, there is no specified CS. Only the time intervening between UCS presentations is known. Thus, temporal condi-

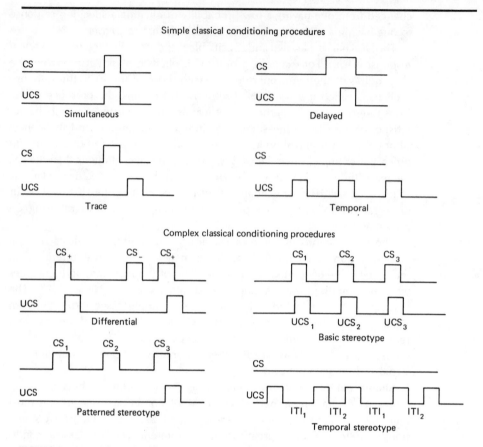

FIGURE 6-1 Simple and complex classical conditioning procedures. An upswing of the bar represents stimulus onset, a downswing represents stimulus offset.

tioning is defined by the presentation of the UCS at fixed, unvarying intervals, for example, the presentation of an air puff every 20th second.

Complex classical conditioning

Simple classical conditioning procedures are used to study the very basic associations which the baby forms among stimuli. Thus, the "sound of footsteps" becomes associated with mother's coming into the room; the routine of bedtime (putting on pajamas, turning on the music box, a kiss on the forehead) becomes associated with "time to sleep." But, very early in life the baby obviously learns much more complex relationships among stimuli than those implied by simple conditional response formation. For example, it learns to respond to some stimuli and not to others. In the laboratory this type of learning is explored by the procedure of differential conditioning.

Complex conditioning procedures In *differential* (discrimination) conditioning there are two CSs, only one of which (CS+) is associated with the UCS. The CS− is never paired with the UCS. Learning occurs when the organism responds to the CS+ and inhibits response to the CS−. The strongest demonstration of differential conditioning is made when the organism is also required to reverse the discrimination.

The final procedure depicted in Figure 6–1 has been applied only recently to the study of learning during infancy. *Stereotype conditioning* is the procedure for investigating sequential behavior and is defined operationally by the presentation of a series of CSs which are always in the same order. An ordered system of CSs requires that the organism learn not only each CS-UCS association, but also the pattern or order of occurrence. Thus, the organism must become as responsive to the position of stimulus elements in the pattern as to the quality and intensity of each element (Brackbill & Fitzgerald, 1972).

The importance of control groups

In classical conditioning, as in other experimental methods, control groups must be used to assess the effects of the independent variable on the experimental group. Specifically, in classical conditioning we must be certain that the increased power of the CS to elicit the UCS represents the results of a true association between the CS and the UCS rather than an apparent learning effect due to pseudoconditioning. *Pseudoconditioning* refers to "conditioning" which is caused by procedural errors rather than a true association between the CS and the UCS. Thus it is necessary to compare the performance of experimental subjects with that of subjects who receive one or more control procedures. The detailed discussion of these procedures is beyond the scope of this text. Suffice it to say, however, that they test for the effects of the CS alone, of the UCS alone, and of the CS-UCS pairing. If any control procedure produces an apparent learning effect, this is sufficient reason to suspect the results produced in the experimental group.

Instrumentation

The infant is a nonverbal and for some time a nonlocomotive organism. Consequently, we must rely on rather sophisticated instrumentation in order to study many of the infant's behavioral capabilities. That instrumentation may be divided into two broad categories: (1) instrumentation dealing with stimulus presentation—that is, controlling the environment by presenting specific stimulus contingencies and by minimizing unpredictable stimulus changes; and (2) instrumentation dealing with the responses of the infant by sensing, recording, and processing those responses. Generally speaking, in laboratory studies of infants the measurement of dependent variables requires rather sophisticated instrumentation specifically designed for monitoring and recording responses, whereas stimulus presentation and control can be accomplished with instrumentation less specifically designed for infants. In naturalistic observational studies of infants, less sophisticated in-strumentation is needed for stimulus presentation or response recording.

Instrumented psychological research has never been without its critics, many of whom view with great disdain the laboratory control of indepen-dent and dependent variables via instrumentation. This concern over "brass instrument" psychology has some merit. A case in point is provided by psy-chophysiological research, where typically several dependent variables are simultaneously detected by sensors, converted from one energy form to another by transducers, amplified, transmitted to a recording instrument, and finally analyzed by computers. At minimum, the responses in such re-search are highly dependent upon the various instruments employed, from initial presentation of the stimuli to eventual analysis of the responses. Thus,

Photograph courtesy Paul Rochlen

FIGURE 6–2 The polygraph is an instrument that has broadened the range of de-pendent variables available to the infant researcher. It can be used to record activity of the heart, brain, muscle, sweat gland, eye, or retina.

to a considerable extent instrumentation determines the responses to be measured, the errors that may influence the responses, and the interpretations that may be accorded the responses.

For infant research the advantages of instrumentation outweigh the disadvantages. Instrumentation has been responsible for many of the advances made over the past 20 years in our knowledge of the sensory, perceptual, cognitive, and learning processes of infants because it has expanded the range of dependent variables available to the researcher. This has been especially true in the study of early learning.

THE DEVELOPMENT OF CONDITIONAL RESPONSES

Conditioning and the CS

The first systematic theory of conditional response formation relevant to infancy and early childhood was offered by N. I. Kasatkin (see Brackbill, 1962). According to Kasatkin, there is an unvarying developmental order for CS effectiveness during the first six months of life (Kasatkin, 1972). The order is the same as that in which the sensory modalities are thought to become functional during the same time span (see Table 6–1). Kasatkin also argues that the CS is a more important determinant of conditioning than either the UCS or the UCR.

TABLE 6–1
Kasatkin's developmental sequence of conditionability as a function of the conditional stimulus

Class of conditional stimuli	First appearance (days)	Conditional responding	
		Semistable response (days)	Stable response (days)
Vestibular	8	15	30
Auditory	15–24	40	35–60
Tactile	28	45	60
Olfactory	28	45	60
Gustatory	35	45	75
Visual	40	60	90

Source: Adapted from Y. Brackbill, "Research and Clinical Work with Children," in R. A. Bauer (Ed.), *Some views of Soviet psychology* (Washington, D.C.: American Psychological Association, 1962), pp. 99–164. With permission of the author and The American Psychological Association © 1962.

In general, classical infant conditioning research does not support Kasatkin's views (Brackbill & Fitzgerald, 1969; Fitzgerald & Porges, 1971). Summarizing a number of studies designed to test Kasatkin's theory, Fitzgerald and Brackbill (1974) suggest that although their studies "do not allow one to summarily reject the possibility that there may be an orderly developmental pattern to postnatal neuro-behavioral organization, they do argue against the primacy of the CS and the immutability of CS effectiveness during early conditional reflex formation." For Fitzgerald and Brackbill the UCS and the UCR are at least equally important determinants.

Conditioning and the UCS

A comparison of two studies which attempted to condition eye blink provides some evidence of the importance of the strength and duration of the UCS for infant conditioning. In the first study, conditional blinking was successfully demonstrated in infants who were 33 to 133 days old. These infants were subjected to an auditory CS and to a two pound per square inch, 200-millisecond air puff as UCS (Lintz, Fitzgerald, & Brackbill, 1967). Naito and Lipsitt (1969) also demonstrated successful conditional blinking in infants, although their infants did not reach the higher criterion level employed by Lintz et al. In the Naito and Lipsitt study, the UCS was also an air puff; however, its strength was one pound per square inch and its duration was 50 milliseconds. The differences in the degree of conditionability demonstrated in these two studies cannot be attributed solely to the differences in the UCSs employed. There were also procedural differences as well as differences in the CS intensity and in the ISI and ITI values.

Since no studies have as yet directly investigated the effects of UCS intensity or duration on infant conditionability, at present we must rely on comparisons of research conducted in different laboratories for our conclusions. This was the case for the two blink studies noted above. Thus, while it appears that UCS strength and/or duration affect infant conditionability, only systematic study of the properties of the UCS will provide direct evidence on this question.

Conditioning and the ISI

We have already noted that classical conditioning demands that the individual learn a relationship between two stimuli, the CS and the UCS. Moreover, the CS-UCS relationship largely determines the different types of conditioning procedures. For many years investigators have searched for the temporal interval between CS and UCS that will produce optimal learning. For a long time these studies were restricted primarily to nonhuman subjects. The optimal ISI that emerged from the studies with nonhumans was approximately 500 milliseconds.

When conditional response formation began to be studied systematically with human adults, a very different picture of the optimal ISI emerged. Studies with somatically mediated responses, such as blinking and finger withdrawal, tended to support the 500-millisecond ISI value. However, when such autonomically mediated responses as heart rate, GSR, or pupillary reflex activity were used, intervals longer than 500 milliseconds produced better conditioning results.

Only a few infant studies have directly assessed the effects of the ISI on conditionability. One of the studies compared ISI values ranging from 0 to 9,000 milliseconds in an attempt to condition pupillary reflex activity to an auditory CS. No evidence of conditioning occurred at any ISI value (Brackbill, Fitzgerald, & Lintz, 1967). On the other hand, ISI values of 5,500 and 7,500 milliseconds produced successful conditioning of the autonomic skin-potential response. Intervals of 1,500 and 3,500 milliseconds did not produce successful conditioning (cited in Fitzgerald & Brackbill, 1976).

A study of the somatically mediated blink response compared 500, 1,000, 1,500, and 3,000 millisecond ISIs. Here only the 1,500 millisecond ISI was found to produce conditioning (Little, 1971). Undoubtedly, the length of the ISI will prove to be an important determinant of success or failure in the infant's ability to link one stimulus with another. Since neural conductance speeds up with myelinization, it would seem reasonable to predict that developmentally the ISI for conditioning would become increasingly shorter until its "optimal value" is reached.

Conditioning and the UCR

All this emphasis on the CS and UCS may cloud the fact that a response is involved in classical conditioning. Although conditional response formation is regulated by stimulus-stimulus learning and not stimulus-response learning, it is nonetheless the case that a response system is essential to the learning process. Thus, while the infant may be learning an association between two stimulus events, the key to conditioning is whether the CS can reliably elicit the UCR. In this regard it has been suggested that early conditioning is an interactive function of the sensory modality giving rise to the CS and the neurological system mediating the response (Fitzgerald & Brackbill, 1974). This stimulus-response specificity has been cited as one of the important constraints on infant learning (Fitzgerald & Brackbill, 1976). The basic point is that the parameters responsible for early conditioning (CS, UCS, ISI, and so on) may be different for autonomically mediated responses than for somatically mediated responses.

Conditioning and orienting

The relationship between orienting and conditionability has been studied in two ways. First, there has been an attempt to test Sokolov's hypothesis that OR elicitation facilitates the acquisition of conditional responding. In fact, Sokolov's theory predicts that if the CS does not elicit an OR, it will be difficult to establish conditioning. Early in conditioning, the OR stabilizes as the CS acquires signal value. Later in conditioning, the OR habituates. The idea is that the OR facilitates the development of an expectancy that the CS will be followed by the UCS.

Research with human adults tends to support Sokolov's prediction. Research with infants seems to be heading in the same direction. Ingram and Fitzgerald (1974) attempted auditory differential conditioning and reversal with three-month-old infants. Each infant received one habituation session, two differential conditioning sessions, and two reversal sessions. The CSs were a 1,000-hertz tone and a 500-hertz tone; the UCS was an air puff delivered to the infant's cheek; and the UCR was a measure of electrodermal activity of the skin recorded from the baby's foot.

Now, what the baby must do in this situation is learn to respond to the CS+ (for example, a 1,000-hertz tone) and not to respond to the CS− (for example, a 500-hertz tone). Some babies were able to learn the discrimination, and some were not. The individual differences in conditionability were related to individual differences in orienting. The babies were divided into two groups on the basis of the magnitude of the OR elicited by the very first stimulus presented in the experimental setting. Figure 6–3 summarizes the relationship found between orienting and conditionability. High-magnitude orienters tended to learn the discrimination, whereas low-magnitude orienters did not.

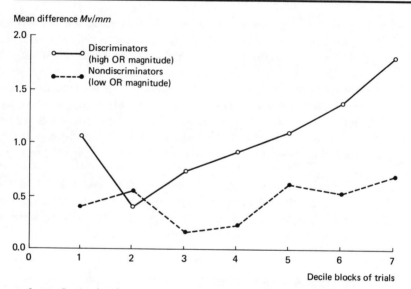

Source: Reprinted with permission from John Wiley & Sons, Inc., from E. Ingram and H. E. Fitzgerald, "Individual differences in infant orienting and autonomic conditioning," *Developmental Psychobiology*, 1974, 7, 359–367.

FIGURE 6–3 The relationship between discrimination conditioning and orienting response magnitude in three-month-old infants.

The second way that the orienting-conditionability relationship has been studied involves attempts to directly condition the OR itself. This has been primarily the work of Jaroslav Koch at the Institute for the Care of Mother and Child in Prague, Czechoslovakia. In Koch's studies, a conditional head rotation (turning the head to the right or the left in order to receive the UCS) is first established. Then different UCSs are compared as to their effectiveness for maintaining the conditional head rotation. In one study, the babies ranged in age from two months to five months (Koch, 1968a). The different UCSs employed were: (a) the face and voice of the mother; (b) the face and voice of a stranger; (c) noisemaking toys that changed on each UCS trial; and (d) a noisemaking toy that remained the same on each UCS trial. At each age level, different groups of babies received different UCS conditions. The results indicated that the older the infants, the higher was the percentage of correct responses early in conditioning, the faster was the conditioning that occurred, and the faster was the extinction of the OR. At all age levels the toys that changed on each UCS presentation produced the best conditioning. Koch's studies suggest that a novel, constantly changing stimulus is a potent reinforcer for maintaining conditional orienting in young infants.

Conditioning and individual differences

Chronological age Koch's finding that older infants acquire conditional responding more rapidly reflects a frequent result of Soviet and Czech research. Few Western researchers have reported the phenomenon. This has been due in part to the fact that few Western researchers have concentrated on individual differences in infant learning. Nevertheless, infant studies that have been analyzed for individual differences in conditionability have clearly revealed the presence of such differences (Brackbill & Fitzgerald, 1972). Perhaps the most crucial factor producing discrepancies between Soviet-Czech and Western research in the correlation of conditionability with age has been a procedural one. Soviet studies of infant conditioning tend to be longitudinal, whereas Western infant conditioning studies tend to be cross-sectional. Longitudinal studies involving daily conditioning sessions provide optimal conditions for the development of learning sets (see below). In such longitudinal studies, babies may be learning how to learn, and this learning may result in progressively faster acquisition of conditional responses. Babies in a cross-sectional study usually receive only one session (or at most several); thus, their performance is not aided by their learning how to learn. If age is related to conditionability, this is probably only as a by-product of the underlying changes in neurological development (Fitzgerald & Brackbill, 1976).

Arousal level State, or level of arousal, is another individual difference that influences learning. Obviously, it would be difficult to condition head turning in an infant screaming with rage or in a toddler lying on the floor, kicking and howling through a tantrum. The toddler has not yet acquired the ability to cortically inhibit such reactions. Extreme levels of arousal are not the only deterrents to conditioning. Even during a single conditioning session, rapid transitions from one state to another may influence conditionability. Certainly, the elicitation power of the UCS and the signal value of the CS differ for the individual infant if on trial 1 he is in a quiet, alert state and on trial 2 he is fast asleep.

The rhythmic sleep-wake and digestion patterns have also been found to influence conditionability. In an interesting experiment, Koch (1968b) first established conditional head rotations to an auditory CS in four-month-old infants. The infants were fed at seven different intervals after awaking or after falling asleep. The sleep-wake cycle was maintained at 2½ hours awake and 1½ hours asleep during the day time portion of the cycle. Manipulation of the two cycles was found to influence conditionability. The latency of head rotation was shortest—and therefore learning was best—when the two cycles peaked but did not overlap during the waking state. Apparently, babies are similar to children and adults; they learn best when awake and alert.

INSTRUMENTAL CONDITIONING

In conditional reflex formation, the response is initially dependent upon the elicitation properties of the UCS. Later, the response is brought under the control of the CS. Much of the behavior of the infant and young child is elicited behavior. However, much is not. A good deal of the young child's behavior is *emitted,* and emitted behavior often has no readily identifiable eliciting stimulus. Such *operant behavior* is modified by instrumental conditioning.

Some theorists argue that classical conditioning applies only to involuntary behavior, especially that which is mediated by the autonomic nervous system. On the other hand, instrumental conditioning is thought to apply only to voluntary somatically mediated behavior. Although this distinction holds for many responses, it is an oversimplification of a much more complex relationship between learning processes and the neural mediation of behavior.

MODIFICATION OF OPERANT BEHAVIOR

In instrumental conditioning, a change in operant behavior is dependent upon reinforcement that follows the behavior. Receiving reinforcement is contingent upon first emitting the operant behavior. In classical conditioning, one elicits the response of interest; for example, a nipple is presented to elicit sucking. But in instrumental conditioning, one increases a response that already exists; for example, one reinforces the infant to increase the rate of sucking. The effect of reinforcement is to strengthen operant behavior. Thus, in studies of operant behavior it is always important to have a measure of the baseline rate at which an operant behavior occurs in order to assess changes due to reinforcement against spontaneous fluctuations in the baseline rate. Most of the procedures of operant learning were first detailed by B. F. Skinner (1938).

Classes of operant behavior

Two classes of operant behavior have been studied in infants and young children. The first class includes operants that are "intrinsically" interesting, such as sucking, looking, vocalization, and smiling. The second class includes operants that occur at a high level or are easy to observe, record, and relate to stimulus operations. This class includes bar pressing, head rotation, knob pulling, window pressing, and box opening.

The operant responses selected for study typically follow the cephalo-caudal development of operant behavior. Studies with younger infants have used such operants as smiles, vocalizations, eye movements, and head movements. Studies with older infants and young children have used manipulative behaviors.

Categories of instrumental conditioning

The two basic types of instrumental conditioning are the discrete trial and free operant procedures. In the *discrete trial* procedure the experimenter presents a stimulus, following which the subject has a set period of time to respond. The trial ends either when the response occurs or if no response occurs during the time period set. For example, one could sound a bell or buzzer and then give a baby ten seconds to turn its head to the left and receive milk reinforcement. (In this example, the bell would also be a discriminative stimulus signaling the beginning of a trial.) If head rotation does not occur within the specified time, the trial would end. This proce-dure, which closely resembles classical conditioning, was applied by Hanus Papousek (1961) to the study of learning processes in the newborn. Papou-sek's use of the technique was similar to classical conditioning in that the newborn received milk reinforcement on each trial whether or not volun-tary head turning occurred. It was similar to operant conditioning in that the reinforcement (milk) was contingent upon the response (head rotation).

The second type of instrumental conditioning permits the subject to respond as often as possible. This is the *free operant* method. To continue our example, if the head turning study had been conducted under a free operant procedure, the response would have been reinforced every time the baby turned its head in the appropriate direction. The response would not necessarily signal the end of a trial (that is, the opportunity to respond).

Types of reinforcers

In instrumental conditioning, the reinforcement delivered is the key to the successful modification of operant behavior. Reinforcers are classified in a number of ways. One classification distinguishes between positive and negative reinforcement. *Positive reinforcers* increase the strength of the operants they follow. That is, when an emitted operant is followed by a posi-tive reinforcer, the strength of the operant is increased. *Negative reinforcers* increase the strength of the operants which remove them. That is, when an emitted operant signals the removal of a negative reinforcer, the strength of the operant increases. Another reinforcement condition, *punishment,* de-creases the strength of the operants it follows. (Actually, punishment could be the occasion for administering a negative reinforcer, as in spanking, or it could be the occasion for removing a positive reinforcer, as in not being allowed to have dessert unless all the peas are eaten.)

Another classification distinguishes between primary and secondary reinforcers. *Primary reinforcers* are analogous to the UCS in classical conditioning. For example, milk is a primary reinforcer for a hungry baby; bits of cookies are primary reinforcers for a hungry preschooler. *Secondary reinforcers* gain their reinforcing properties through associations built out of the organism's previous experience; in this sense, they are acquired reinforcers. For example, a parent's approving smile or words of praise can gain reinforcing properties for modifying operant behavior.

In instrumental conditioning, the symbol S^R is used to represent a primary reinforcer, while the symbol S^r represents an acquired reinforcer. Other symbols used as abbreviations for types of reinforcers include S^P for a primary negative reinforcer, and S^p, for secondary negative reinforcers. (P stands for punishment.)

Whenever operant behavior is different in the presence of one stimulus than in the presence of another stimulus, we have evidence of differential instrumental conditioning (discrimination). Recall that in classical differential conditioning the CS+ is followed by the UCS, while the CS− is never paired with the UCS. CS+ and CS− therefore have different elicitation properties associated with them. In instrumental differential conditioning the operant is reinforced in the presence of a discriminative stimulus (S^D), but not reinforced in the presence of another stimulus (S^Δ). S^D and S^Δ are therefore the instrumental analogs of the classical CS+ and CS−. Obviously, much of the behavior of the toddler and young child is learned via instrumental discrimination procedures. For example, the operantly emitted "dada" is reinforced ("Nice, baby") in the presence of the adult male member of the family (S^D), but it is not reinforced in the presence of the adult female member of the family (S^Δ). Actually this is a bit of an oversimplification because early in discrimination learning mother is also likely to reinforce "dada" by saying something like "No, I'm not daddy" or "Yes, dada." The effect is to slow down the acquisition of the discrimination while simultaneously increasing the operant level of responding. That is, baby may not say "dada" to the appropriate figure exclusively, but baby will surely say "dada" more frequently than he or she did in the past. Later on, baby will acquire the discrimination and associate the correct operant to the correct discriminative stimulus.

At least four important questions can be asked about the presentation of the reinforcing stimulus: How often should the operant be reinforced? When should the operant be reinforced? Where should the reinforcing stimulus be located? What kind of reinforcer should be used? Let us consider each of these questions in turn.

Schedules of reinforcement

In instrumental conditioning, the question of how often the operant should be reinforced is answered by the study of schedules of reinforcement.

Now there are really only two general answers to the question. We can reinforce the operant all of the time, or we can reinforce it some of the time. (Obviously, we could also *never* reinforce it, as in the procedure called **extinction.** However, since we are here concerned with the acquisition of behavior, not its disappearance, never reinforcing the operant cannot be one of our options.)

When we reinforce an operant each time it occurs, we are using a schedule of *continuous reinforcement* (CRF). For example, each time our preschooler asks for a cookie, we give him one. As you might suspect, the preschooler quickly learns that asking for a cookie gains a cookie. When we reinforce an operant some of the time we are using a *partial reinforcement* (PRF), or intermittent, schedule. In this case, we might honor every other request (on the average) that our preschooler makes. Modification of operant behavior tends to occur more slowly with PRF schedules than with CRF schedules, but eventually higher acquisition performance levels are attained with PRF schedules. Moreover, extinction of the operant behavior requires more time when the behavior is learned under PRF. The learning theorist would say that PRF schedules lead to greater resistance to extinction than do CRF schedules.

Why would this be the case? One explanation suggests that it is because PRF schedules provide the organism with experiences that are similar to extinction, whereas CRF schedules do not. For example, if daddy says yes every time Katherine asks for a cookie, Katherine will quickly learn to expect a cookie every time she asks for one. On the other hand, if daddy sometimes says yes and sometimes says no, Katherine should have a more difficult time learning that the way to get a cookie is to ask for it. What if daddy decides that Katherine is never again to have a cookie, that the operant verbal request will never again be reinforced? If Katherine learned under a CRF schedule, the first trial in which daddy says no is markedly different from any previous trial. If daddy continues to say no, Katherine will quickly learn that what used to be is no more. However, if Katherine learned under a PRF schedule, daddy's first no during extinction is no different from any previous no delivered during acquisition. Thus, it should take Katherine longer to realize that daddy is no longer going to deliver a cookie. While CRF schedules may lead to rapid learning, PRF schedules appear to be the best way to maintain learning.

Many PRF schedules have been studied in the laboratory setting, and it is quite likely that many more occur in nonlaboratory settings, such as the home or school. Whether PRF schedules are those carefully controlled in the laboratory or those that occur randomly in the home, their nature is determined by one of three dimensions: time interval, number, or rate. Most salaried employees are familiar with PRF schedules based on time: payday is the 1st and 15th of each month; that is, a certain time must go by before the operant is reinforced. A production worker who receives a bonus for every 50th unit produced is familiar with PRF schedules based on number; that is, a certain number of units must be produced before reinforcement is delivered. The baby who is able to maintain the presence of a desired caregiver by maintaining a high rate of vocalization is familiar with PRF schedules based on rate.

Most instrumental learning theorists consider all PRF schedules ultimately to reduce to one of four basic schedules: fixed ratio (FR), fixed interval (FI), variable ratio (VR), and variable interval (VI). With an FR schedule, every nth response is reinforced. For example, every fourth smile emitted by the baby is reinforced. If we allow a specific interval of time to lapse before delivering the reinforcer, then we are using an FI schedule. Thus, we would reinforce the first smile to occur after, say, 15 seconds lapsed. The VR schedule differs from the FR schedule in that on the average it reinforces every nth response. Thus, on the average we would reinforce every fourth smile. Sometimes, however, we might require only two smiles, six smiles, three smiles, or eight smiles for reinforcement. But across all trials we would achieve an average of four smiles for each reinforcement. There is a similar difference between the FI and VI schedules. With an FI:30, we would reinforce a smile that occurred after, say, 30 seconds had lapsed. With a VI:30, we would reinforce the first smile to occur after a time interval had lapsed, except that from trial to trial the length of the interval would differ. Over all trials, however, the average length of the interval would be 30 seconds.

Weisberg and Fink (1966) investigated FR and extinction performance of toddlers who were trained to press a lever in order to obtain snack reinforcers. Responding under FR:10 was established for four toddlers and under FR:15 for another toddler. In general, FR scheduling produced a high and constant rate of responding. Siqueland (1968) compared CRF and FR schedules in a study in which neonates were reinforced for ten-degree head rotation. The reinforcer was a five-second presentation of a nonnutritive nipple on which the newborn could suck. The FR group emitted a greater number of responses than did the CRF group.

In addition to the four basic schedules noted above, there are schedules which are used to reinforce either low rates of responding (DRL) or high rates of responding (DRH). In the laboratory, if we wished to increase the operant level of high-amplitude sucking, we would deliver reinforcement contingent upon high-amplitude sucking; low-amplitude sucking would not be reinforced. For practical purposes we might wish, for example, to increase the rate of high-amplitude sucking in high-risk infants, such as those prenatally addicted to heroin. Such infants evidence disorganization in sucking behavior and might benefit from direct operant modification of high-amplitude sucking.

In a DRL schedule, a timer is preset to some value. The subject must wait until the preset time lapses, and then the first response emitted is reinforced. Any responses emitted during the waiting time automatically reset the timer. This type of schedule produces a steady but low rate of responding. Using the DRL schedule, Weisberg and Tragakis (1967) demonstrated that low behavioral baselines can be produced in young children. DRL 10-second and DRL 18-second schedules of snack reinforcement generated and maintained low levels of responding.

Finally, instrumental learning theorists have identified a variety of *com-bination schedules*. However, combination schedules, like DRL and DRH schedules, have only begun to be used with infants and young children. We could start with a CRF schedule and then switch to an FR or FI schedule. Or, we could combine FR and FI schedules, FI and extinction, VI and FI, and so on. *Multiple, chain, pacing, tandem, mixed,* and *concurrent* are all terms that designate different combination schedules. For example, in a *multiple* FR:10 FI:30 schedule, the onset of each schedule would be signaled by a discriminative stimulus; perhaps a green light for FR:10 and a red light for FI:30. For FR:10 every tenth response might be reinforced; for FI:30 the first response after a lapse of 30 seconds might be reinforced. In *chain-ing,* a series of operants is joined by a stimulus that serves a dual function. First, the stimulus must serve as a reinforcing stimulus for the preceding operant. Second, it must serve as a discriminative stimulus to signal the ap-pearance of the next operant. Thus, in chaining each stimulus is both a reinforcing and a discriminative stimulus.

Extensive discussion of these schedules is beyond our purposes in this volume. In fact, very few attempts have been made to bring the operant behavior of infants and young children under the control of combination schedules.

Immediate versus delayed reinforcement

With few exceptions, the answer to the question of when reinforcement should be administered is the same for infants and young children as it is for nonhuman organisms and human adults: learning proceeds most effica-ciously when reinforcement is immediate rather than delayed. However, immediate reinforcement does not always lead to better retention. In fact, a series of discrimination experiments conducted by Brackbill and her asso-ciates with school-age children (for example, Brackbill & Kappy, 1962) indi-cated that delayed reinforcement (ten seconds) consistently led to better retention. In these experiments, acquisition of the discrimination was the same whether reinforcement was immediate or delayed.

In a series of experiments involving an operant manipulative task, Miller (1972) found that delays as short as one second were sufficient to affect acquisition. Some learning occurred under delays of one and two seconds, but three-second delays were clearly ineffective for learning. Miller sug-gests that the perception of stimulus events as contingent upon behavior may represent the first learned (cognitive) expectancies of infancy, whereas the perception of stimulus events as noncontingent upon behavior may interfere with the ability to acquire such expectancies. Similarly, Watson (1967) argues that *contingency awareness* (cognitive awareness of the con-tingent relationship between behavior and reinforcement) develops when the individual realizes that reinforcing stimuli are contingent upon some behavior emitted by the individual. Moreover, he suggests that noncontingent reinforcement may actually interfere with the organization of contingency awareness.

The location of the reinforcer

Recent experiments conducted by Schaffer in Scotland call attention to an aspect of reinforcement that has seldom been considered in instrumental learning situations with infants, namely, where to locate the source of the reinforcing stimulus.

In the first experiment (Miller & Schaffer, 1972), 6-, 9-, and 12-month-old infants received contingent or noncontingent reinforcement under three conditions of spatial displacement of the reinforcer. The infant was free to touch a cylindrical aluminum canister from which both auditory and visual reinforcers were delivered; that is, the infant had to learn that reinforcement was contingent upon touching or moving the canister. The canister (manipulandum) was located directly in front of the baby (0-degree orientation). Two identical canisters were displaced 5 degrees and 60 degrees, respectively, from the 0-degree canister. Infants at all age levels learned the response-reinforcement contingency under the 0-degree and 5-degree displacement conditions. However, only 9- and 12-month-old infants learned the contingency under the 60-degree displacement condition. In the second experiment, only the visual reinforcer was delivered, and only the 60-degree displacement condition was employed. Nine-month-old infants learned the task; six-month-olds did not (Miller & Schaffer, in press). This study confirmed a hypothesis derived from the first experiment, namely, that the six-month-old is not yet capable of integrating "touching of the lever" with "attending to the displaced reinforcer." Nine-month-old infants were able to attend visually to the source of reinforcement while touching the canister. Note that infants at both age levels were able to touch the canister and orient to the location of the reinforcer. However, the younger infants were not able to integrate the two events.

These are very interesting results. Consider the following situation. Six-month-old Stephanie is trying to lift small blocks in her playpen. Mother, standing behind her, is observing her efforts to grasp and lift the blocks. Each time Stephanie raises a block mother says "Good baby." Miller and Schaffer's work suggests that Stephanie is not yet capable of integrating "Good baby" with grasp-and-lift-cube when the reinforcer is spatially displaced to the extent suggested in our example. But their studies also suggest that if mother and baby were face to face, baby could effectively integrate the operant behavior with the reinforcer.

The comparative effectiveness of reinforcers

The last question to be considered concerns the nature of the reinforcer selected to modify operant behavior. Many different reinforcers have been employed in efforts to demonstrate operant learning in infants and young children. Among these reinforcers have been chimes, buzzers, bells, tones, music, novel toys, slides of geometric forms, schematic faces, moving mobiles, pictures of spinning clowns, steady lights, flashing lights, snacks, and voices.

Koch's studies, reviewed previously, suggested that the nature of the reinforcer was an important aspect of learning. Brossard and Decarie (1968) compared the relative reinforcing effectiveness of tactile-kinesthetic, auditory, vestibular, and visual stimuli alone or in various combinations for modification of smiling. The only significant difference in reinforcing effectiveness was that between the least effective stimulus (tactile alone) and the most effective stimulus (smiling and picking up baby). Schwartz, Rosenberg, and Brackbill (1970) analyzed the components of social reinforcement used to study operant modification of infant vocalizations. Three reinforcing stimuli were used: an auditory stimulus (a tape-recorded female voice saying "nice baby"); a tactile stimulus (rubbing the baby's abdomen with the palm of the hand); and a visual stimulus (the experimenter's smiling, nodding head). Whether presented alone or in combinations, these reinforcers were found to be equally effective for conditioning vocal behavior.

Thus, the results of efforts to find the optimal reinforcer for the modi-

Photograph courtesy Suzanne Siemering; photograph by Paul Rochlen

FIGURE 6–4 Apparatus used to study discrimination learning and comparative reinforcer effectiveness in older infants.

fication of operant behavior have been equivocal. Few systematic studies have been done, and those have only scratched the surface of the problem. Finding optimal reinforcers is an important task. For, after all, the more desirable the reinforcer, the greater the effort that should be expended to achieve the reinforcer and the greater the likelihood that the strength of the operant behavior will increase.

DISCRIMINATION LEARNING

In discrimination learning, the child must choose a specific stimulus from a set of two or more stimuli. The stimuli may be presented one at a time *(successive presentation)* or in pairs, triplets, and so on *(simultaneous presentation)*. In either case only one stimulus is rewarded (correct). The child's task is to learn which stimulus is correct so that it can select that stimulus on every trial. Generally, simultaneous discrimination learning is easier than successive discrimination learning. One notable exception occurs when the stimulus and response dimensions are spatially separated. For example, preschoolers seem to perform best when the stimulus, response, and reward occur in close contiguity (Jeffrey & Cohen, 1964).

Young children are constantly confronted with discrimination learning tasks. They must learn to discriminate a red ball from a blue ball, a red block from a red ball, the letter *A* from the letter *C*, a dog from a cat, a collie from a terrier, familiar caregivers from strangers, acceptable social behavior at home from the behavior permitted away from home, and so on. This process begins by at least the first month. The ten-month-old can clearly discriminate liver from beef, peas from carrots, and sometimes it discriminates with enthusiasm. But very soon thereafter the child must make far more complex discriminations, especially those which involve words, where the words are representational symbols for objects. What variables influence discrimination learning? How does the child use information gained from one discrimination problem to solve other problems?

Early explanations of discrimination learning were based on stimulus-response (S-R) association theory. Accordingly, rewarding correct responses and not rewarding incorrect responses were thought to generate approach and avoidance reactions, respectively. It was believed that over trials the child would develop strong approach responses to the rewarded stimulus and strong inhibitory responses to the unrewarded stimulus. The S-R model explained the performance of nonverbal children. However, it could not easily account for the performance of verbal children. A case in point is provided by the transposition problem.

Transposition

In transposition the child is trained to respond to the larger of two stimuli. When the response level to the larger stimulus is strong, the smaller of the two stimuli is replaced by a stimulus which is larger than the remaining stimulus. We can call the first two stimuli A and B, with B the larger of the two. The transposition stimuli would be B and C, with C larger than B. In the original learning, responding to B is rewarded. Now, what might the child be learning while attempting to solve the A and B discrimination? Does the child learn that B is the correct stimulus because it is rewarded, or does the child learn that the larger stimulus is correct? If the child is only learning about the specific stimulus that is rewarded, the S-R model predicts that the child will continue to select B during the transposition task. In general, three- and four-year-old children fulfill this prediction. However, older children do not. They tend to choose C during transposition. Presumably, they have learned that "larger than" is the key to solving the problem and use this "rule" to guide their behavior during the transposition task. The S-R model is therefore inadequate for explaining the performance of older children in this task.

An alternative *S-R mediation* model was proposed by the Kendlers (Kendler & Kendler, 1970). The term *mediation* refers to the mental operations which the child imposes between stimulus and response. What these operations are is not entirely clear; however, it seems fairly clear that words are one important source of mediation.

The Kendlers proposed a three-stage sequence to explain the shift from S-R association learning to S-R mediation learning. During the *preverbal stage* the child has no appropriate words to use as mediators between S and R. Presumably, no mental operations available to the preverbal child can be used to learn such concepts as "larger than." Once the preverbal child learns that B is correct, it "concludes" that B must be correct even when it is paired with a new stimulus.

The *verbal deficiency stage* is a transitional stage between S-R association learning and S-R mediation learning. Now words are available, but the child does not seem to apply them during problem solving. Occasionally, a child will be able to verbalize the correct solution even while continuing to make incorrect choices between the two stimuli. In such instances, the child is said to have a *mediation deficiency*. If the child knows the correct words but simply does not produce them, there is a *production deficiency*.

Performance in the *verbal mediation stage* fits the S-R mediation model. Now discrimination learning is largely under linguistic control. Actually, considerable individual variation occurs. The child may perform according to the S-R association model in one situation and according to the S-R mediation model in another situation.

Although many hundreds of discrimination learning studies have failed to produce the strong general laws of learning hoped for, these studies do suggest some conclusions. Keep in mind, however, that each conclusion has its exceptions. First, the age range of five to seven years is thought to represent the transitional period between S-R association and S-R mediation modes of problem solving (White, 1965). During this period the child shows significant advancement in problem-solving skills. Second, three- and four-year-olds find color discriminations easiest to learn, followed, in increasing difficulty, by number, size, and form discriminations. Five- and six-year-olds perform differently. They find form discriminations easiest, followed by color, size, and number (Lee, 1965). Third, preschoolers tend to respond more to position cues than do older children and adults. Finally, nearly all investigators now recognize the importance of language for higher-level problem-solving behavior.

When the child must choose between two stimuli, the task is called a *two-choice discrimination problem*. One of the stimuli is always rewarded. The positions of the stimuli are varied from trial to trial to prevent the use of position cues. Several sets of stimulus pairs are used, with each set consti- tuting one discrimination problem. As the child works his way through the problems he comes to choose the correct stimulus more readily and more consistently. In fact, after a time he can solve the problem after one trial. This phenomenon is called "learning to learn," or *learning set*.

Learning set

The idea in learning set is that the child learns a rule which can be applied to similar but novel discrimination problems. Perhaps the rule is that red (color) is always correct or that square (form) is always correct. Thus, the child learns that there are relevant and irrelevant dimensions of the stimuli.

Apparently, learning sets are acquired slowly in preschool children and the aged as compared with elementary school and college students (Levin- son & Reese, 1967). Moreover, both preschoolers and the aged show strong position habits and an inability to inhibit incorrect responses. In Levinson and Reese's study, the occurrence of nonreward provided more information about the problem than did reward for all groups but the aged. Levinson and Reese did not study the effects of recency and summation of nonreward, although both of these factors have been shown to facilitate children's per- formance in an instrumental learning situation (Davidson & Fitzgerald, 1970). They proposed a two-phase acquisition process common to all age levels. During the first phase, performance is at chance level, with a slow increase in learning. The second phase is marked by rapid learning. The two-phase process bears a striking resemblance to the Zeaman and House (1963) analysis of discrimination learning.

According to Zeaman and House, discrimination learning is regulated by two processes, attention and instrumental learning. Initially, the child must learn to attend to and discriminate the relevant stimulus dimensions—that is, the characteristics of the stimulus that indicate which dimension (color, form, size) is important for solving the problem. Only after organizing the attention response can the child begin to master the instrumental task.

Several studies have suggested that differences in performance among various groups (retardates, slow learners, normals) are due to differences in the attention response rather than to the instrumental task itself. Once the attention response is acquired, slow learners seem to learn at the same *rate* as other children. For example, Staats, Brewer, and Gross (1970) studied the effects of systematic training on alphabet learning in preschool children. They used various combinations of successive and simultaneous discrimination procedures to try to teach preschoolers the letters of the alphabet. The experimenters first tried to elicit an imitative verbal response to the letter *A* from a child. Then the child was shown a picture of *A,* and picture labeling was trained. Prompted trials were interspersed among unprompted trials and were held to a minimum. After the child learned *A,* the letter was paired with *B.* The child continued to concentrate on *A.* When the response to *A* was strong, the experimenters concentrated on *B.* Then *C* was combined with *A* and *B.* The procedure for the remainder of the alphabet was the same. After uppercase letters were learned they were paired with their lowercase letters and the procedure was repeated. The rate of acquisition showed a strong learning set effect: Additional letters were acquired more rapidly than were the first letters.

Staats et al. also implicated the Zeaman-House theory as potentially accounting for their findings. They argued that the letter is a stimulus event which facilitates acquisition of a verbal label. The child's attention and verbal label are maintained and strengthened by reinforcement, and eventually the child gains the ability to label and discriminate all letters. When this occurs, Staats et al. argued, the child is ready to read.

Other complex discrimination tasks, such as reversal and nonreversal shifts and intradimensional and extradimensional shifts, have been developed to study the organization of problem solving skills (see Volume 2). The pattern of the results obtained is not clear; however, they are fairly consistent in showing a significant change in problem-solving skills. This occurs at approximately five years of age, thus giving support to White's suggestion that the period from age five to age seven marks the emergence of adult patterns for a wide variety of cognitive and problem-solving behaviors.

SUMMARY

In this chapter we reviewed some of the basic ways in which learning occurs in early human development: classical conditioning, operant (instrumental) conditioning, and discrimination learning. Classical conditioning procedures are used to study the formation of stimulus associations. In any experiment investigating these relationships, experimental groups are generally compared with one or several control groups to guard against "apparent" conditioning, or pseudoconditioning. Important factors that constrain the baby's ability to successfully form associations include the nature of the CS, UCS, CS-UCS, UCR, and OR, and various organismic factors, such as state, or level of arousal.

The learning processes involved in instrumental conditioning are not dependent upon temporary connections between stimulus events or between stimuli and responses. Rather, learning depends on the temporal contiguity between response and reinforcement. Reinforcing stimuli may be presented in a variety of ways or according to a variety of schedules. When a continuous reinforcement schedule is used, the acquisition of behavior is rapid, but maintenance of the behavior is difficult when reinforcement ceases. When partial reinforcement schedules are used, acquisition is initially slow, but ultimate acquisition performance levels are high. Moreover, maintenance of the learned behavior is easier. The learning theorist usually expresses this by saying that partial reinforcement leads to greater resistance to extinction.

At least four important considerations should be taken into account when modifying operant behavior: (1) How often should the operant be reinforced? (2) Where should the reinforcer be located? (3) When should the operant be reinforced? (4) What kind of reinforcer should be used? Instrumental conditioning has been demonstrated in the infant and toddler by means of a variety of schedules and reinforcers. The study of instrumental conditioning during early development may provide the key to understanding how the human organism develops from highly reflexive behavior to behavior which is predominantly instrumental.

Studies of the young child's ability to solve problems requiring the ability to discriminate between two or more stimuli suggest that infants and preverbal toddlers respond on the basis of which specific stimulus has been rewarded. They learn that a specific stimulus is correct. Older children learn a relationship between the stimuli which they then apply as a rule in efforts to solve new discrimination tasks. This performance has prompted learning theorists to propose mediation models which attempt to take into account the cognitive processes that the child uses in problem solving.

SUGGESTED ADDITIONAL READING

Brackbill, Y., & Koltsova, M. M.   Conditioning and learning. In Y. Brackbill (Ed.), *Infancy and early childhood.* New York: Free Press, 1967, 207–286.

Fitzgerald, H. E., & Brackbill, Y.   Classical conditioning during infancy: Development and constraints. *Psychological Bulletin,* 1976, *83,* 353–376.

Stevenson, H. W.   *Children's Learning.* New York: Appleton-Century-Crofts, 1972.

BOX 7–1
Study questions

Define *intelligence, intelligent behavior,* and *cognition.* How are your definitions similar, and how are they different?

In how many ways have developmental psychologists approached the study of intelligence and cognition?

What criteria must a test possess to be considered a good diagnostic instrument?

Why is the heredity-environment argument concerning the origins of intelligence a pseudoargument from the psychobiological perspective?

How does Piaget's cognitive theory of intelligence differ from intelligence as defined by psychometric tests?

How do children differ in the way they are able to use symbolic representations of reality?

What are modes of categorization, and how do they reflect differences in cognitive processes?

Do young infants have memories?

How do attention and cognition go together?

7

INTELLIGENCE AND COGNITION

In the previous chapter we considered several ways in which infants and young children learn. We saw that much of early learning involves stimulus-stimulus, stimulus-response, and response-stimulus relationships. Learning of the sort discussed in the previous chapter is not restricted to early development; it occurs throughout the life span. However, much of what the developing child learns cannot be explained solely by classical or instrumental conditioning. In this chapter we will explore higher levels of behavioral organization involving the intellectual and cognitive capabilities of the organism.

Intelligence means so many things to so many people that it defies consensus definition. One definition equates intelligence with what is measured by psychometric tests. An intelligence test score derived in this fashion differs little from an achievement test score. A second definition refers to genetic endowment or potential. Although it is obvious that there are genetic components to intelligence, it is less obvious just what these components are and how they are affected by environmental experiences. A third definition essentially equates intelligence with "cognition" and is in general what may be called a psychobiological definition. That is, this definition recognizes that biological and environmental factors interact reciprocally during development. Indeed, this is the essence of behavior organization.

Cognition refers generally to the acquisition, maintenance, and utilization of knowledge. Etymologically, cognition is derived from the Latin *cognoscere*, which means to know in the sense of being acquainted with. As a generic term, cognition embraces a variety of phenomena, including all

149

those "by which the sensory input is transformed, reduced, elaborated, stored, recovered, and used" (Neisser, 1967, p. 4). Cognitive processes are those by which "an organism attains an awareness of and knowledge about external objects, the self, and the salient self-object relationships" (Hooper, 1973, p. 229).

Our review of intelligence and cognition is organized into two main sections, following an organizational scheme suggested by Elkind (1967). The *mental test approach* derives primarily from the mechanistic tradition in psychology, whereas the *developmental approach* derives primarily from the organismic tradition (see Chapter 1).

The *mental test approach* (Elkind, 1967) seeks to determine how much individuals differ in their mental abilities and to quantify those differences. Investigators utilizing this approach seek to establish normative growth trends and to determine the predictive significance of psychological tests, the general and specific intellectual abilities that intelligence tests measure, and the environmental variables that correlate with mental abilities.

The *developmental approach* seeks to understand the dynamics of cognition and to determine how cognitive processes change with age. Although a number of theorists (for example, Bruner, 1964; Werner, 1948) can be identified with this approach, Piaget's (1970) structuralist or constructionist theory of genetic epistemology is outstanding in the worldwide impact it has had on developmental theory and research as well as on educational philosophy. In our discussion of Piaget's theory we will focus on the period of sensorimotor intelligence and on the transitional period of preoperational thought. (For discussion of subsequent periods the second and third volumes of this series should be consulted.)

Within the developmental tradition there also are researchers who are not solely Piagetian in their theoretical orientation. These researchers have sought largely to bridge the gap between the study of individual differences in mental development and the changes in cognitive processes associated with increasing age and cumulative experience. In studying infancy and early childhood, these investigators have focused on the relationship between attention and cognition and on the development of such phenomena as "memory" and "competence."

Throughout the discussion of each approach one must keep in mind that they are not mutually exclusive, that they represent different degrees of emphasis. Indeed, one meeting ground between the two approaches is the process of development itself. Although the mental test theorist and the cognitive theorist may differ in their approaches to and explanations of cognitive processes, they share the goal of understanding how these processes are acquired, maintained, and utilized.

THE MENTAL TEST APPROACH

Human beings seem to have a basic need to assess their performance. Tests have been devised for athletic skill, academic achievement, vocational interest, personality, and mental health. Elaborate "rites of passage" determine whether or not one will be admitted into social groups, academic societies, labor unions, and religious and fraternal organizations. Even the period of infancy provides no relief from this desire to assess ability and performance. However, as we noted in Chapter 4, our ability to predict the infant's future behavior on the basis of developmental examinations is not very good.

An intelligence test yields an overall score called an *Intelligence Quotient,* or *IQ.* This score is obtained by dividing the child's obtained age value, based on the number of test items passed (Mental Age, or MA), by the child's actual chronological age (CA), and then multiplying by 100. Developmental examinations yield similarly derived scores called *Developmenental Quotients,* or *DQ,* which technically are not the same as IQ scores but which are all too often conceptualized as equivalent. Intelligence described on the basis of IQ usually follows this scheme: Very Superior (over 140), Superior (120–139), Above Average (110–119), Average (90–109), Low Average (80–89), Borderline (70–79), Educable (50–70), Trainable (25–50), and Severe Retardation (0–25).

Although estimates of the extent of developmental disorders in the United States vary, the figures given are seldom smaller than 8 to 10 percent of the population. The classifications of developmental disorders also vary, but five of the most frequently cited types are mental retardation, behavior problems, brain damage, physical handicap or disability, and verbal language disorganization (Stott & Ball, 1965). No matter what the developmental difficulty, the earlier therapeutic intervention begins, the more likely it is that the individual can be helped. This is true, of course, within the constraints imposed by the severity of the damage underlying the disorder and by the effectiveness of the therapeutic intervention.

The utility of any test depends not only on its ability to predict whether or not an individual will develop a disorder, but also on its ability to reveal clear deficiencies in current functioning (Gallagher & Bradley, 1972). However, the problem of evaluating current functioning is complicated by the fact that development does not proceed in a nice, neat, linear fashion. Thus, one is always faced with substantial variation in a particular individual's rate of development. Indeed, this variation is greatest during the early years of behavior organization when all psychobiological systems are in their emergent stages. Thus a child may appear retarded at one testing session or one age level but behave quite normally at another testing session or another age level. This phenomenon leads to many false positive diagnoses, that is, to tests that indicate deficiencies when none exist. Conversely, tests may produce false negative diagnoses, in which the test score indicates no developmental deficiency when in fact there is one.

Many developmental difficulties are phenotypically obvious, many are not. Moreover, many disorders do not reveal their symptomatic characteristics during early infancy. Disturbances in language behavior, emotional life, and learning are especially difficult to identify during infancy (Gallagher

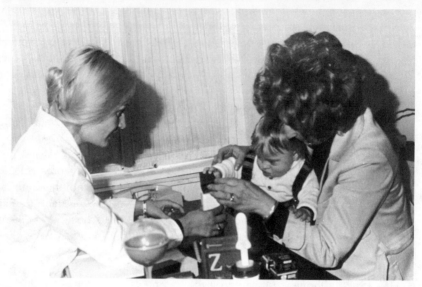

Photograph courtesy Hiram E. Fitzgerald

FIGURE 7–1   Jadranka Novak, psychologist at the Institute for Psychophysiological and Speech Disorders, Belgrade, Yugoslavia, administers a developmental examination in order to assess the degree of retardation in this Down's syndrome infant. The results of the examination are used as one basis for recommending various therapeutic programs for the infant.

& Bradley, 1972). For example, infant and preschool tests do not enable one to determine with confidence whether a child has normal but delayed language development or has language retardation that can be attributed to an underlying disorder.

Clearly, there are many difficulties yet to be resolved with infant and preschool testing instruments. One important unresolved difficulty is just what it is that infant and preschool tests measure, especially since it is often contended that differences in what is measured underlie the poor predictive relationship between infant-preschool tests and the intelligence tests used with older children and adults. Another problem is to isolate the factors which suppress achievement (as it is reflected, for example, in IQ scores). Recent studies point unmistakably to the effects of low familial-cultural socioeconomic status as one global dimension related to test performance.

Intelligence: Concrete skills or abstractions

Criticism leveled against the mental test approach often challenges the assumption that intelligence tests measure something other than achievement. Such criticism asserts that intelligence tests are no different from achievement tests (Weiner, 1973), and that the more skills or abilities one has learned, the better one's intelligence test performance will be. Accordingly, the IQ score is a measure of general intelligence, but of general intelligence that is "caused by" the specific skills the individual has learned. The more skills one attains, the more intelligent one becomes. This is the "concrete to abstract," or specific abilities to general intelligence, model of intellectual growth (see Crano, Kenny, & Campbell, 1972). But the model has problems. For one reason or another, many people are not able to learn certain skills. Conversely, many people who learn certain skills do not seem to be able to apply their knowledge in more general contexts. In other words, much of intelligence involves something other than specific learned skills. It involves abstractions, cognitive rules, and the ability to apply cognitive rules or structures in a variety of settings, some of which may be novel.

An alternative to the "concrete to abstract" order of intellectual development is an "abstract to concrete" model (Crano et al., 1972). According to this model, intelligence is defined as abstraction, cognitive structure, or rule, and it is this aspect of intelligence which is thought to "cause" or direct the acquisition of concrete skills. The "abstract to concrete" model implies that intelligence and achievement are not identical constructs, and that intelligence tests yield scores which represent something more than the sum of the relevant concrete skills implicit in the test items. We are left with another of psychology's "chicken and egg" problems. Does intelligence "cause" achievement (abstract to concrete), or does achievement "cause" intelligence (concrete to abstract). The answer, unfortunately, is not a simple one.

Crano et al. compared the intelligence test and achievement test scores of over 5,000 four-to-six-year-old children and found that in general the abstract to concrete model held. This was especially true for children from suburban schools. More specifically, however, there appeared to be a reciprocal relationship between skill acquisition and the development of cognitive abstraction. "Apparently, the integration of a number of such skills [concrete ones] is a necessary precondition to the generation of higher order abstract rules or schema. Such schema, in turn, operate as causal determinants in the acquisition of later concrete skills" (Crano et al., 1972, p. 272). This general pattern led the authors to conclude that, in general, intelligence causes achievement and that intelligence cannot be equated completely with achievement.

Data for children from inner-city schools did not correspond to the abstract to concrete model. In fact, it appeared that deficits in the early integration of concrete skills affected the organization of higher-order abstractions and inhibited the subsequent development of concrete skills. This reciprocity between specific abilities and higher-order abstractions suggests that there may be two (or more) fundamentally different (though interdependent) types of intelligence.

Fluid and crystallized intelligence

Investigators working within the mental test tradition have identified two types of intelligence. One type, fluid intelligence, is relatively uninfluenced by sociocultural educational experiences, while the other type, crystalized intelligence, is highly dependent upon such experiences (Horn, 1967, 1968). According to Horn's analysis, *fluid intelligence* provides the substrate for all intellectual abilities because it stems primarily from the *anlage,* or natural predisposition of the organism. Since fluid intelligence involves neural mechanisms directly related to such processes as perception and memory, it should be relatively independent of formal education and should show decline over the life span corresponding to whatever decline occurs in the physiological structures of the organism.

As the child acquires "aids" and "concepts," built onto the underlying anlage function, the second type of intelligence emerges. *Aids* are techniques acquired through experience which "compensate for limitations in anlage function." Examples would include such mnemonic devices as number groupings (for example, area codes for telephone numbers). *Concepts* are cognitive categories which the individual uses to classify experienced phenomena. According to Horn (1968), aids and concepts provide the structure of adult intelligence.

Since crystallized intelligence emerges directly from educational-cultural experience, abilities reflecting this type of intelligence should show steady growth over the life span. In fact, Horn (1967) presents evidence suggesting that fluid and crystallized intelligence follow the predicted developmental trends.

Horn's analysis of intellectual abilities follows a long tradition of using the statistical technique called factor analysis to determine what general and specific mental abilities are tapped by various test items. The most elaborate product of this approach is the "structure of the intellect" proposed by Guilford (1966). Guilford's model of intellectual abilities is composed of five operations, four contents, and six products, whose combinations yield 120 primary mental abilities (see Figure 7–2).

Guilford's model represents a conception of the structure of adult intelligence. Are the primary mental abilities of that model assessed by infant and preschool tests? Stott and Ball (1965) factor-analyzed five infant-preschool tests to determine whether any factors comparable to those in Guilford's model could be isolated. A surprising number of factors were identified. However, although all the infant-preschool tests contained some factors, none of them measured all the categories noted in Figure 7–2. For example, *divergent production* refers to thought processes that are flexible, searching, seeking alternative approaches (Guilford, 1966). *Convergent production* refers to thought processes that are on the straight and narrow path leading toward one solution. Stott and Ball found that the Merrill-Palmer Scale yielded no measure of divergent production, while the Stanford-Binet Test tapped neither divergent nor convergent production. On the other hand, divergent and convergent production were isolated in each of the tests administered at the youngest age levels. Although it is true that not all of the 120 primary mental abilities have been isolated in adult tests, it is also true that not all that have been isolated in those tests have been found in infant tests.

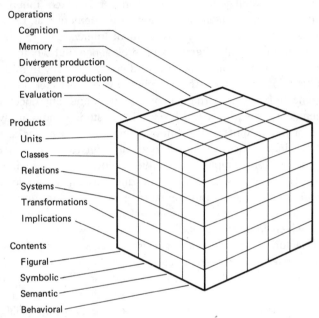

Operations
   Cognition
   Memory
   Divergent production
   Convergent production
   Evaluation

Products
   Units
   Classes
   Relations
   Systems
   Transformations
   Implications

Contents
   Figural
   Symbolic
   Semantic
   Behavioral

Source: From J. P. Guilford, "Intelligence: 1965 model," *American Psychologist*, 1966, *21*, 20–26. With permission of the author and the American Psychological Association, Inc., copyright, 1966.

FIGURE 7–2   The structure of the intellect.

The factor analytic method holds forth the possibility that the specific mental abilities measured by infant tests may be discovered as well as the possibility that tests may then be constructed to more accurately measure the equivalent abilities of infants and older children. On the other hand, it is possible that many specific mental abilities defy early measurement because they are emergent and thus quite variable. Under this condition, one might even expect to find large individual differences in the development of abilities reflecting both fluid and crystallized intelligence: fluid, because of differential rates of maturation of the nervous system; and crystallized, because of individual differences in environmental experience. Socioeconomic class is one environmental variable that has been cited increasingly as a major influence on the development of mental abilities.

Intelligence and socioeconomic class

The question of whether intelligence is primarily genetic or is determined primarily by environmental influences continues to occupy the attention of many researchers. From the perspective taken in this volume, the question is specious. All behavior, including whatever one defines as intelligent behavior, is a product of organism-environment interaction. Obviously, intelligence is genetic. But it is equally obvious that intelligence is also environmental. Intelligence does not derive from fixed, inherited, genetic structures, but from epigenetic development. It emerges and is constructed dynamically through organism-environment interaction.

There are individual differences in intelligence. But whether the intelligence of some groups of human beings differs genetically from that of other groups is another matter. The heredity-environment debate focusing on intelligence is based, in part, on a consistently found difference in IQ scores between American whites and blacks. These studies show an average difference of 15 IQ points, with whites scoring higher than blacks. Those who argue that intelligence is primarily genetic refer to these data to support their position (for example, Jensen, 1969). However, those who argue that intelligence is primarily genetic (1) deny any substantive significance to such determinants of behavior as maternal prenatal care, infant postnatal care, or the educational climate of the home, and (2) malign the concept of "heritability," which, interestingly enough, has been shown to reflect such environmental factors as socioeconomic class (Scarr-Salapatek, 1971) and may have little relevance to human genetics. On the other hand, it is a consistently documented fact that preschool children from low socioeconomic classes score lower on IQ tests than do preschool children from middle-class backgrounds and that these differences appear within racial and ethnic groups as well as between such groups. Moreover, these differences do not appear until about 15–24 months of age (King & Seegmiller, 1973; Bayley, 1965).

One study compared the intelligence test performance of black preschool children of four socioeconomic classes (Golden, Birns, Bridger, & Moss, 1971). The average Stanford-Binet IQ scores for each class were: middle class, 116; working class, 107; lower class without welfare, 100; lower class with welfare, 93. Since these differences did not appear until the third year of life, it seems that the detrimental influence of low social class on intellectual development begins when the child is actively engaged in language acquisition and the organization of symbolic representation (see below). However, the investigators had reason to suspect that social class in and of itself may not have been the critical dimension affecting test performance. Moreover, since infant developmental tests and intelligence tests do not measure the same things, it may be that infant developmental schedules are insensitive to the effects of social class, whereas intelligence tests are not.

Because the investigators had difficulty testing welfare children using the required standardized testing procedures, they questioned the validity of the welfare children's IQ scores. Consequently, in a subsequent study 18- to 24-month-old toddlers were tested under standardized and "optimal" conditions (Golden & Birns, 1971). It was predicted that if welfare children were given optimal conditions to perform, social class differences would be negated. Optimal conditions included the use of material rewards (candy) for motivation and allowing mothers to encourage children to respond. Scores on the standardized administration were black families on welfare, 94; black higher-education families, 99; white higher-education families, 100. However, under optimal conditions the scores were 106, 108, and 109, respectively. These data support the general finding that social class alone does not differentially affect test performance during the first one or two years of life. Motivational and test setting factors also seem to be important.

To the extent that we can consider the lower-class child at risk, a study by Willerman, Broman, and Fiedler (1970) has important implications. They argued that infants at risk may be more susceptible to poor socioeconomic conditions because of their depressed adaptability. Several thousand white infants from various socioeconomic levels were tested at eight months (Bayley Scales) and again at four years of age (Stanford-Binet). Consistent with previous findings, the infant scale performance did not reflect differences attributable to social class. On the other hand, infants who scored in the lowest motor quartile at age eight months obtained the lowest mean IQ at age four, and this group contained a disproportionately high percentage of lower-class children. Overall, the data of this study support the contention that retarded infant development predicts disproportionately poorer intellectual development, but only for lower-class children.

The poor performance of lower-class children on infant and preschool tests may in part be attributed to the test instruments themselves, or rather to the demanding requirements of standardized testing procedures. Few of the psychologists who construct such tests are members of the lower socioeconomic classes; fewer still belong to minority racial or ethnic groups. Nevertheless, even this would not account for the fact that infants at risk are further disadvantaged by lower-class conditions. But not all children from lower-class families score poorly, and not all children from middle-class families score well. In every culture many individuals have made valuable contributions to knowledge despite the poverty of their families. What factors within a social class may further specify environmental influences on the child's developing intellectual abilities? The most obvious factor, and one we have not yet considered, is the pattern of child rearing to which the child is exposed.

Intelligence and child-rearing practices

From the moment of conception on, parents play an obvious role in determining the intellectual capabilities of their children. Our concern here, however, is not with genetic determinants or prenatal influences, but rather with the postnatal relationship between parent and child. Longitudinal and cross-sectional studies have confirmed that maternal nurturance is one important correlate of the child's intellectual development. For example, Bayley and Schaefer (1964) reported maternal nurturance to correlate positively with the intellectual development of boys, while Kagan and Moss (1962) found that the daughters of restrictive mothers scored lower on the Stanford-Binet than did the daughters of nonrestrictive mothers.

Recently, Beckwith (1971) examined the relationship between maternal child-rearing attitudes and infant "IQ" scores. The infants had been adopted into middle-class homes when only five to ten days of age. Assessment included the administration of infant scales, observation of mother-infant interaction, and evaluation of maternal rearing attitudes. Beckwith found lower Cattell test scores among infants whose mothers restricted exploration of the home and who had relatively little verbal or physical contact with their infants. Mothers with high school education (compared to those with college education) were found to be particularly restrictive with their sons. Since education correlates with socioeconomic class and lower-class mothers are often found to be more restrictive than their middle-class counterparts, it seems plausible that maternal child-rearing attitudes may be one important dimension within social class that influences intellectual development. One must be cautious, however, about assuming that maternal restrictiveness necessarily implies low nurturance (Kagan, 1967). In any event, mother is only one member of the parental team. What about the role of fathers in the intellectual development of children?

Paternal influence   Two studies by Sutton-Smith, Rosenberg, and Landy (1968) studied the effects of father absence and father presence on one measure of achievement, the American College Entrance Examination (ACE). Father absence experienced during early childhood correlated significantly with poorer ACE performance. However, whether or not one had a sibling made a difference. Father absence had its greatest adverse effect on boys without brothers, only girls, and girls with young brothers. While most people would not consider night-shift work an instance of father absence, Landy, Rosenberg, and Sutton-Smith (1969) found this type of "father absence" experienced during early childhood to be associated with poorer performance for females on the ACE. In fact, the scores on the quantitative portion of the test were especially low under this "father absence" condition.

In a more direct study of paternal influences on intellectual development, Radin (1973) examined the relationship between father nurturance and the intellectual abilities of sons. Thirty white middle- and lower-class four-year-old boys were given the Stanford-Binet and Peabody Picture Vocabulary tests and were observed interacting with their fathers. In addition, the fathers were assessed on several measures of cognitive stimulation in the home. The study disclosed a strong positive relationship between father nurturance and the sons' intellectual performance among the middle-class father-son pairs. Moreover, the data indicated that fathers who frequently had academic interactions with their sons facilitated the development of their sons' intellectual skills. Radin suggested that the young boy may be more inclined toward academic skills when he perceives that his masculine model values such skills.

Because systematic study of the father's influence on his children's intellectual growth has just begin, one must be cautious about drawing broad conclusions. Only in the past few years have developmental psychologists seriously acknowledged that fathers are important influences on the developing child. As a result, depressingly little is known about paternal influences. Intensive study of paternal influences is currently under way, and we shall consider aspects of that research in subsequent chapters.

We are a long way from determining how environmental factors influence biological structure and function during early behavioral organization, too far away to draw careless conclusions regarding the precise determinants of behavior. Nevertheless, it does seem clear that the determinants of mental abilities are neither solely genetic nor solely environmental. Rather, mental abilities seem to flow from subtle and complex interactions between the organism and its environment.

THE DEVELOPMENTAL APPROACH

As we have implied throughout this volume, the concept of the "active, information-processing organism" has not been the historic view of the infant. Indeed, the infant has often been regarded as merely an incidental participant in development. The latter standpoint evolved from the empiricist influence on Western scientific psychology, which embellished the view of the infant as a passive organism and popularized the Aristotelian-Lockean concept of the tabula rasa as descriptive of the contents of the young infant's mind. Early American psychology, rejecting the nativistic and mentalistic tenets of rationalism and phenomenalism, adopted instead an environmentalism derived from the empiricist and associationist schools. Thus, functionalism and its brash child, behaviorism, emerged as the dominant theoretical base of American psychology, and the rat and pigeon ascended to favored positions for demonstrating the principles and laws of behavior. Growing disenchantment with simple associationist theories of behavior led many American psychologists to search both for alternative approaches to the study of behavior and for alternative theoretical systems to guide the empirical investigation of behavior. Cognitive theory has emerged as one of the major alternatives to classical behaviorism, with the Swiss psychologist Jean Piaget as one of its leading spokesmen.

The particular importance for a developmental psychology of cognition of this gradual weaning from behaviorism is that *mind* and *knowledge* have once again become legitimate words in the developmental psychologist's lexicon as well as legitimate topics for research. In its view of the organism as an acting, constructing, self-regulating being, Piaget's (1970) cognitive theory of genetic epistemology has clearly become a leading alternative to behavioristic explanations of cognitive development.

Piaget's theory   Piaget's theory of genetic epistemology—in every sense of the word a psychobiological theory—seeks to discover the "intimate relationships between the biological notions of interaction between endogenous factors and the environment, and epistemological notions of necessary interaction between subject and object" (Piaget, 1970, p. 731). According to Piaget (1967), cognitive development consists of actions which impel the organism toward a state of equilibrium, that is, toward a state of increasingly complex and stable organization. By *organization,* Piaget means the biological tendency to coordinate and integrate processes into systems or structures which are both biological and psychological. The organism is impelled to act when it is necessary to satisfy one or some combination of three sources of needs—physiological, affective, or intellectual. In fact, Piaget maintains that affectivity and intelligence are simultaneous aspects of every action. These actions give rise to structures—motoric, intellectual, affective—which become the organizational forms of mental activity.

In addition to the biological tendency for organization, the organism has a biological tendency to adapt to the environment. Cognitive adaptation is reflected in the equilibrium between the assimilation and accommodation processes (see Chapter 1), an equilibrium that does not achieve stability until about age seven or eight.

Assimilation and accommodation exert their complementary influences on organizational schemes. *Schemes* are actions or operations used to transform objects. They are the operational activities, or "operative" aspect, of cognition, and they provide organization and structure to action.

Let us reconstruct the general pattern of events. The infant enters the world with a reflexive repertoire of actions as well as the biological tendencies of organization and adaptation. As the infant interacts with the environment, the functional processes of assimilation and accommodation lead to the construction of increasingly complex and integrated schemes. For example, the neonate enters the world with the ability to suck. Yet it may take several days and many experiences before the infant is proficient in its ability to suck, and at first the action is directed to either breast or bottle. As the infant matures and reaches more masterful levels of development, it becomes capable of directing sucking behavior to a much broader range of objects. As the infant assimilates these objects into the sucking or mouthing scheme it simultaneously accommodates to the objects being mouthed. What was once a scheme for obtaining nourishment becomes a more complex scheme for exploring objects other than those associated with nourishment. Still later, the infant comes to suck its thumb as a result of integration, or generalizing assimilation, of eye-hand and mouthing schemes. Thus, the infant assimilates the various objects in the external environment into the sucking scheme, modifies or accommodates the scheme to the assimilated objects and thereby achieves a higher level of cognitive organization.

We previously defined cognition as the acquisition, maintenance, and utilization of knowledge. The definition of knowledge is the central problem of epistemology. Few cognitive psychologists have even attempted to take on this perplexing problem. It is to Piaget's credit that he has. To understand Piaget's definition of knowledge one has to start with his conception of the relationship between subject and object.

The development of the object concept According to Piaget (1970), knowledge is contained in the subject-object interaction. In his words, "In order to know objects, the subject must act upon them, and therefore transform them; he must displace, correct, combine, take apart, and reassemble them" (Piaget, 1970, p. 704). As the subject acts on objects, he simultaneously transforms the operative schemes of his actions. Thus, knowledge cannot be contained in the object itself, as the empiricists claimed, nor can knowledge be contained a priori in the subject, as Kant maintained. Knowledge for Piaget is always a product of the subject and object in interaction. Thus, Piaget proposes that the epistemological question be rephrased to ask "how he [the subject] becomes capable of objectivity," or in other words, how the subject comes to know the object.

TABLE 7–1
Piaget's periods of cognitive development and characteristic cognitive advances made at each level

Period 1: Sensorimotor organization (birth to age 2)
  1. Simple reflex schemes, such as rooting and sucking.
  2. Integration of reflexive schemes (for example, eye-hand coordination).
  3. Repetition of random movements to reproduce change. Initial differentiation of means-ends relationships.
  4. Intentional actions. Organization of object concept.
  5. Invention of alternative ways to achieve goals. Differentiation of self from environment (subject from object). Beginning of speech and language.

Period 2: Organization of concrete operations (2 years to 11 years)
  1. *Preoperational thought* (2 years to 6 years)
       Organization of speech and language and social behavior. Primarily egocentric reasoning. Acquisition of representational symbolism.
  2. *Concrete operations* (6 years to 11 years)
       Organization of flexible and systematic thought. Initial classification and grouping of objects. Development of conservation and the ability to reverse mental operations.

Period 3: Organization of formal operations (11 years +)
  Organization of abstract reasoning, formulation of hypotheses, engagement in deductive reasoning. Construction of propositional logic.

The *how* develops through a sequence of periods (see Table 7–1), during each of which major cognitive skills become organized. Since Piaget embraces the epigenetic view of development (see Chapter 1), he holds the progression through the periods to be invariant. During the period of sensorimotor organization, cognition proceeds from the reflex activity of the newborn organism to the considerably more coordinated and integrated schemes (actions, operations) of the two-year-old. At this stage the child acquires rudimentary knowledge of cause-effect and spatiotemporal relations. Compared to the seven-year-old, the three-year-old remains at a rather elementary level of cognitive functioning. Compared to the one-year-old, however, the preschool-aged child displays rather remarkable cognitive achievements.

Photograph courtesy Thomas Hagaman

FIGURE 7–3 Studying the development of object permanence. **7–3a.** The experimenter shows the baby an object and then hides it under a blanket. **7–3b.** A baby that has developed object permanence will search for the object, lift up the blanket, and get it. Younger infants react to this task as if the hidden object were "out of sight, out of mind."

One of the infant's major cognitive accomplishments in the sensorimotor period comes when it realizes that objects exist even when they are not immediately available to sense perception. This cognitive attainment has been called the development of the object concept, or *object permanence*. According to Piaget, objects exist independent of one's immediate sense perception of them. That is, even if objects are not immediately available to the senses, one *acts* in accordance with the "knowledge" that they continue to exist, that they have permanence. Thus, when you put this book down and leave the room, you "know" that the book remains on the desk. However, when a mother places her two-month-old in the crib and leaves the room, the mother is "out of sight, out of mind" so far as the infant is concerned.

During the first month of the period of sensorimotor organization an infant shows no evidence of object permanence. If a presented object is removed from its view, it makes no effort to search for the object. During the next two months the infant begins to display increased integration of auditory and visual schemes. Although there is still no evidence of active search for missing objects, the infant now displays spatial location of sounds and accommodation of the looking scheme to movement. Between four and ten months of age the infant begins to search for objects, utilizing looking and sucking schemes in particular. By the tenth month the infant can recognize an object when given partial information about it. For example, the infant may recognize a favorite teddy bear or dolly when only one leg protrudes from a covering blanket. According to Piaget, this represents the infant's ability to reconstruct wholes from parts. At approximately the ninth month the infant begins to search for missing objects. Sometime during the next nine months of life, the toddler will be able to follow an object through a sequence of hidden placements, thus achieving a fully elaborated object concept.

The object concept and social behavior. As we mentioned previously, Piaget considers every action to be simultaneously affective and cognitive, although in his research he has tended to emphasize the cognitive aspects. Schaffer (1958) has hypothesized a relationship between the object concept and aspects of affective development. During a study of the effects of institutionalization, he observed that fretting as a protest to separation did not occur in infants less than seven months of age. However, infants over seven months old did display a variety of negative responses to separation. Schaffer proposed that there was a direct relationship between the development of object permanence and the development of an affective attachment to specific caregivers (see Chapter 9). Only after the infant developed object permanence could it develop an attachment to a specific object, that is, to a specific caregiver.

In more recent studies Schaffer gains support for his hypothesis (Schaffer, 1971; Schaffer & Perry, 1969, 1970). In these studies infants were presented with visual stimulus targets differing in familiarity or novelty. In general, infants less than six months of age, although quite capable of perceptually discriminating the targets, appear to be incapable of utilizing centrally stored information. Infants from 8 to 13 months of age responded to stimuli on the basis of novelty rather than familiarity, while infants from 5 to 7 months of age were stimulus bound to the familiar targets. Schaffer (1971) suggests that infants less than six months of age are not capable of assimilating the new stimuli to the current schemata since they are not yet capable of actively comparing stimuli. He proposes an initial perceptual-learning mechanism and a subsequent response-learning mechanism to distinguish the two phases of cognitive development.

Freedman, Fox-Kolenda, Margileth, and Miller (1969) have reported a study that also bears on the relation between affectivity, cognition, and the development of the object concept. The standard procedure used to study the object concept requires the infant to act on objects presented visually. Comparatively little attention has been paid to the study of object permanence when the information contained in the object is presented in other sensory modalities. The emergence of the blind infant's ability to actively search for an object solely on the basis of the auditory stimulation produced by the object seems to follow exactly the same sequence and timing as the emergence of the visual object concept (Fraiberg, 1968). For example, as early as the tenth week of life, the blind infant can perceptually discriminate its mother's voice from those of others. However, as Freedman et al. (1969) point out, the blind infant cannot assimilate the stimulus to its current schemes until roughly the tenth month of life. Evidently, sighted infants do not differ developmentally from blind infants in their ability to search for an object presented in the auditory modality.

Summarizing to this point: Piaget has proposed a sequence characterizing the organization and development of intelligence. The periods are held to be invariant, which means that the individual moves through each period in succession and that cognitive operations in lower periods must be organized before the organization of later periods is possible. Two periods are of particular importance for infancy and early childhood—the sensorimotor period and the period of preoperational thought, which anticipates the organization of concrete operations. The emergence of the object concept is a major milestone of sensorimotor intelligence. The knowledge that objects exist even when "invisible" marks a significant turning point in the infant's construction of cognitive reality. Moreover, this turning point has both cognitive and affective implications. Other important cognitive events during the first two years of life are the development of cause-effect relationships and the separation of subject and object.

By now the reader should clearly understand that what Piaget means by intelligence is different from what is measured by an "intelligence" test. Within the mental test approach, Horn's concept of fluid intelligence best approximates aspects of Piaget's approach.

Preoperational thought   In the previous section on the mental test approach we cited evidence indicating that global aspects of the environment, such as socioeconomic class, play an important role in the organization of mental abilities. Moreover, we suggested that this influence is maximal during the end of the toddler period but extends through the preschool years. This corresponds to Piaget's period of preoperational thought.

The preoperational period marks the transition from the sensorimotor period to the period of concrete operations. Children's thinking during this period is fundamentally different from that of older children and adults. Preoperational children are *egocentric:* they cannot view problems or situations from another person's perspective. They cannot *reverse* cognitive operations. The concrete-operational child can understand that $3 + 5 = 8$, can reverse the operation ($8 - 5 = 3$), and can understand the equivalence involved. The preoperational child cannot. Preoperational children have difficulty taking in more than one aspect of a problem at a time *(centration),* and they have difficulty dealing with symbols, especially symbolic representations of objects. The two- or three-year-old child may find it difficult to understand that characters seen on the television screen are not really inside the television set, or that objects in pictures are intended to represent objects in reality. Symbolic thought is in its emergent phase. Preoperational children begin to transform the world into their own symbolic representations, largely through imitation of models, mental imagery, symbolic play, and language. However, their symbols are not subordinated to a system of logical operations. Consequently, they often "oversymbolize" and fail to distinguish between the imaginary and the real. For example, the three-year-old may have difficulty distinguishing between the possibility of imagining the existence of monsters and the possibility of the actual existence of monsters. As children emerge from the preoperational period, egocentrism and centration decrease, and reversibility, separation of subject from object, and the ability to subordinate symbols to logical operations increase.

Piaget (1970) maintains that each period and each transition from one period to the next develops at an optimal rate. This follows from the principle of epigenesis. Although attempts to accelerate the child's progression through the various periods may be successful (within limits), the implication is that parents and educators may do a great disservice to the child by attempting to formally teach information before the child has the cognitive capacity to understand the operations involved. Here one is reminded of Cratty's axiom (see Chapter 4) that interference in the organization of one psychobiological system may interfere with the organization of other systems as well. Piaget clearly objects to Bruner's (1960) modern-day restatement of Watson's view that one can teach anything to anybody at any time. Piaget asserts that "each time one prematurely teaches a child something he could discover for himself, that child is kept from inventing it and consequently from understanding it completely" (Piaget, 1970, p. 715). Thus, the instructional task becomes one of optimizing situations in which the child can make inventions. Obviously, Piaget's approach presents problems too. For example, how does one know whether an individual child will, in fact, reinvent knowledge, that self-discovery will occur? Modern education would probably do well to strike a compromise between the Bruner and Piaget positions until we are more certain of the processes involved.

In any event, the child's environmental situation has important consequences for the organization of intellectual abilities. Environmental factors which interfere with organization at one period may adversely affect organization at later periods. Thus, failure to develop an adequate object concept may prolong the child's *egocentric* view of reality and delay *decentering*. Recall Crano et al.'s hypothesis that lower-class children fail to develop an abstract-to-concrete organizational mode, thus interfering with their ability to master specific concrete skills. What is it about social class that would lead to differences in symbol formation, language behavior, and cognitive style? For some hypotheses concerning this question we can turn to Sigel's theory and research regarding a cognitive ability he calls *representational competence.*

Representational competence   Representational competence is an adaptive characteristic of the organism which is independent of cultural, ethnic, racial, or economic factors (Sigel, 1970, 1972). However, whereas the adaptive behavior applies to all persons equally, the *content* of the representation varies from one person to another as a function of individual experience. Social class is viewed as one major experiential variable which contributes to individual differences in representational thought. Thus, one may well expect to find social class differences in both the use of symbols and the ability to deal with and use abstractions. But if there are differences in representational competence that relate to social class how and when do these differences develop?

To study these questions, Sigel asks children to group three-dimensional real objects and two-dimensional photographic representations of objects. In an early experiment Sigel (1953) found that middle-class children used meaningfulness of the objects to form groups of related objects. Lower-class children performed quite differently. Their groupings of pictorial representations were formed with no apparent functional relationship among the items grouped. Following a suggestion made by one of the teachers in a lower-class school, Sigel compared the object groupings formed by middle- and lower-class preschool children. The groupings of three-dimensional objects by the middle- and lower-class children did not differ, indicating a common approach to the categorization of real objects. The middle-class children grouped three- and two-dimensional objects similarly, indicating their ability to shift concrete object classifications to representations of real things. However, the two-dimensional object groupings formed by the lower-class children differed markedly from their classifications of real objects. The teacher had suggested that perhaps her students did not understand that the pictures were intended to represent real objects. How can it be that lower-class preschoolers would not recognize pictures as symbolic representations of real objects?

Sigel suggests that differences in representational competence emerge from the different life-styles of middle-class and lower-class families, life-styles which underlie different orientations to the real world. The different orientations to real and symbolic objects were related to different child-rearing practices. For example, middle-class child rearing generally emphasizes orderliness and continuity in daily activities, a high use of abstract language referents and references to past, present, and future events, and the development of cognitive expectancies. Different life-styles, in turn, make for differences in the psychological *distance* between the individual and the environment, or, in Piaget's terms, between the self and the object. Thus, to increase the psychological distance between self and object, one has to use techniques which separate the child from a dependence upon the concreteness of the physical environment.

According to Sigel, language is the major mechanism for increasing distance and thereby the ability to deal with abstractions. Perhaps that is why such differences between social classes do not begin to appear until about two years of age. Sigel reasoned that when parental language is rich in abstract concepts referring to temporal events ("Remember what you did at the picnic last week?" "Would you like to see the Disney movie this Saturday?") and spatial symbolism ("Why don't you draw a picture of a beautiful red sunset?"), children learn to deal with abstract temporal and spatial phenomena. It is important to remember that language is itself a symbol system comprising both abstract words and words which are referents to concrete things.

One hypothesis advanced to account for the differences in performance between middle-class and lower-class children suggests that different cognitive styles are used to categorize objects. Three cognitive styles, or *modes of categorization,* have been identified (Sigel & McBane, 1967). Children who use *descriptive modes* categorize objects on the basis of some general, observable attribute common to the objects, such as color or form. Thus, a child may group all "squares" or all "red ones." This mode of categorizing generally increases with age. Children who use *relational-contextual modes* categorize objects on the basis of some functional relationship among them ("You use a *fork* to eat the *cake*") or of a theme which integrates them (woman-nurse-wheelchair-doctor-bed-baby). Relational-contextual modes tend to decrease with age. Finally, children who use *categorical-inferential modes* impose inferences on the objects they group. Young children seldom use these modes because they are just beginning to acquire class concepts and the ability to deal with symbols, including words.

Study of the categorization modes of middle-class and lower-class black children indicated that middle-class black children categorized two-dimensional and three-dimensional objects similarly, just as white middle-class children did. However, lower-class black children tended to use relational-contextual categorization modes and to be more variable in their categorizations of two- and three-dimensional stimuli. Sigel and McBane concluded that lower-class preschool children had greater difficulty in making the transition from sensorimotor to concrete-operational intelligence. Specifically, they seemed slower in developing a separation of self from object and in moving away from egocentric thought.

The message contained in the theory and research we have summarized seems quite clear. The environment must expose the child to abstract concepts, concepts which stimulate a detachment from a solitary dependence upon the concrete physical environment and which encourage the child to reconstruct or "reinvent" experiences. Such experiences should enhance the development of imagination and creativity and facilitate the child's ability to deal with abstractions. The net effect would be to increase the psychological distance between self and object and to enhance the development of representational competence.

Cognitive behaviorism

Thus far, we have considered cognitive development from two broad perspectives, which, following Elkind, we have labeled the mental test and the developmental approaches. The mental test approach focuses on normative growth trends, on individual differences in mental abilities, and on the implications of these differences for subsequent intellectual performance. Within the developmental approach, the Piagetian cognitive theory of development focuses on the child's construction of cognitive structures with relatively little concern for individual differences in cognitive functions. On the other hand, such neo-Piagetians as Schaffer and Sigel are very much concerned with individual differences and with the effects of environmental influences on the rate and form of cognitive development. However, not all investigators deservingly classified in the developmental approach are Piagetian in their approach to the study of cognitive processes. Some are more closely allied to general learning theory and represent what might be called cognitive behaviorism.

Broadly speaking, cognitive behaviorists are interested in the interdependence between cognitive processes and attentional, learning, and perceptual processes. Within this tradition, noteworthy advances have been made in our understanding of the relationship between cognitive development and attention, memory, contingency learning, and social behavior.

Attention and cognition   In Chapter 5 we implied that the discrepancy hypothesis had utility as an explanation for the regulation of attention and for its relation to cognition. The *discrepancy hypothesis* asserts that the amount of change between a familiar stimulus and a novel stimulus is a key determinant of attention. However, attention is regulated not only by the stimulus change dimension but also by the cognitive structures which the child uses to evaluate the degree of stimulus change and the relative importance of that change. At the very least, Kagan's (1970) version of the discrepancy hypothesis involves the integration of the orientation, attentional, perceptual, and cognitive systems.

According to Kagan, the child actively constructs cognitive representations of external events which preserve important features of those events. Two of the important features are the temporal and spatial characteristics of the events. The child's internal cognitive representation of a stimulus event is the *schema* for that event.

How are physical stimuli and cognitive schema related? The discrepancy hypothesis implies that "stimuli moderately discrepant from the schema elicit longer orientation than do either minimally discrepant (i.e., familiar) events or novel events that bear no relation to the schema" (Kagan, 1970, p. 828). In other words, a stimulus moderately different from the familiar stimulus will produce maximum attention. Herein lies an important mechanism which can account for the differentiation of orientation and attention. Any novel stimulus will elicit an orienting response. However, only those stimuli which are sufficiently discrepant from the schema but which also contain information common to that of the schema will elicit a strong attentional response. When a novel stimulus contains no information which the child can relate to his current cognitive structure, attention to that stimulus will be minimal.

Support for the discrepancy hypothesis has been obtained by many investigators. In one study, four-month-old infants were divided into three groups on the basis of their responses to visual stimuli during familiarization (McCall, 1971). The dependent variable was first visual fixation of the target. Infants in the group Short Lookers spent unusually short periods of time visually inspecting the stimulus target. The other two—Rapid Habituators and Slow Habituators—differed in the rate of habituation. Following the familiarization phase, the infants were presented with stimuli of varying degrees of discrepancy. Short Lookers responded to every discrepant stimulus. Rapid Habituators responded only to stimuli which were slightly discrepant from the familiar stimulus. These infants oriented, attended, and cognitively processed stimulus information during familiarization. Moreover, as predicted from the discrepancy hypothesis, they did not respond to discrepancies too far removed from the familiar stimulus.

Since Slow Habituators did not respond to any discrepant stimulus, it seems likely that they may have had orienting, attentional and/or cognitive deficits which prevented them from encoding meaningful stimulus information during familiarization. Lewis (1971) suggests that such reactions to discrepancy are due to the violation of the infant's *expectation* that current stimulation will be consistent with an established schema. That is to say, upon repeated presentations of a stimulus the infant not only encodes a neural model or schema of the stimulus but also develops cognitive expectations that the stimulus will recur. Thus, learning and memory are brought into the orientation, attention, and cognitive framework of the discrepancy hypothesis.

Memory   Do infants have memories? A clear-cut answer to this question would add considerably to our ability to judge the long-term consequences of early experience. In a sense, memory is the essence of learning. It does little good to acquire new information if none of that information enters into memory. In fact, we have already encountered instances suggestive of memory processes in young infants. Classical conditioning assumes that the organism can hold one stimulus (CS) in memory long enough for the stimulus trace to be associated with another stimulus (UCS). This is far from direct evidence of memory, implies only a short-term memory at best, and is perhaps better explained by attentional processes. Learning the signal significance of one's name or the familiar features of mother's face, however, implies a more active stimulus processing and a long-term memory store.

What does memory involve? At minimum, it requires an afferent perceptual input, information storage, active analysis of the stored information, and a decision-making process which regulates the organism's behavior. The study of memory suggests that there are two major types of storage—short-term and long-term. *Short-term memory* readily accepts information input but is also quick to let it go. *Long-term memory,* on the other hand, admits information more grudgingly, but once information is stored in long-term memory, it is more or less permanent and relatively easy to recall. Much of the substantive change in memory during development is associated with long-term memory. Memory improves during development, in part because the child is adding knowledge that provides a cognitive base in which new experiences can be embedded. Thus, knowledge or meaningfulness facilitates information storage and the improvement of memory. One investigator has suggested that memory change is a reflection of changes in the developing organism's ability to process perceptual features and changes in the decision rules which regulate cognitive activity (Olson, 1976).

The laboratory study of infant memory uses a procedure derived from habituation research. In the typical experiment two stimuli are selected, one of which is presented to the infant during a familiarization period. The familiarization technique may involve repeated presentations of the stimulus, or it may involve a single presentation of the stimulus for some predetermined interval (10, 20, or 30 seconds), timed from the moment that the infant first looks at the stimulus. Then the familiar stimulus is paired with a novel stimulus. If the infant looks more at the novel stimulus (infants seldom look at the familiar one), we infer that the stimuli have been discriminated *and* that the infant remembered something—just what is not known—about the old familiar stimulus. If the stimuli were equally novel, then the looking time would not be expected to differ.

Studies using this technique have provided solid evidence that from at least three months of life the infant's memory processes are reasonably well developed (Olson, 1976). Moreover, Olson and his associates have found that interference effects can be demonstrated in young infants. If infants are presented with a sequence of stimuli and then tested to see which stimulus in the sequence is remembered best, their performance suggests a *recency effect.* In other words, the last stimulus in the series is remembered best.

Social influences   Laboratory demonstrations indicate that habituation and familiarization procedures are useful tools for the study of cognitive processes in infants and young children. But little of the infant's everyday behavior occurs in nicely controlled laboratory environments. Most of the infant's waking hours are spent in contact with other human beings who respond to the infant's spontaneously produced behavior and who elicit behavioral reactions from the infant. That is, much of the infant's activity occurs in a social-emotional setting. The most common social-emotional settings are those involving parent-infant interactions. How do such interactions contribute to the stabilization of cognitive schema or to the development of cognitive expectancies? To answer this question it is necessary to draw upon several theories, including those of Sokolov, Piaget, and Rotter. Since we have considered Sokolov and Piaget already, we will turn to a brief overview of Rotter's social learning theory (Rotter, 1954, 1966).

For Rotter, the operational starting point for the study of behavior lies in the formula $BP = F (E \ \& \ RV)$—behavior potential is a function of expectancy and reinforcement value. Implicit in this formula is the assumption that the organism is an active rather than a passive agent in development. In this basic assumption Rotter's theory is consistent with the assumptions of cognitive theory. *Expectancy* is the perceived probability that one's behavior is causally linked to the desired reinforcement. The value of reinforcement refers to the degree of preference for a reinforcement when the possibilities for the occurrence of all reinforcements are equal.

Locus of control. The key to understanding the three primary constructs in Rotter's formula is the notion that behavior occurs in a situational framework. The psychological situation refers to what is experienced by the organism together with the *meaning* that the situation has for the organism. The situation is the meaningful environment in which behavior occurs. It is represented in the organism in terms of internal (personal) or external (nonpersonal) control over the consequences of behavior. *Internal control* refers to instrumental behavior that one believes is related causally to desired reinforcers. *External control* refers to reinforcement unrelated to one's behavior. The stronger the perceived expectancy that a particular reinforcement will be obtained, the greater the potential that behavior will be directed toward its attainment.

Several investigators have demonstrated that children with internal locus of control reach higher levels of academic achievement than do children with external locus of control. Rotter (1966) investigated the effects of generalized expectancy for internal versus external control of reinforcement and found that the effects of reinforcement for predicting behavior depend in part on whether the individual perceives reinforcement as contingent upon his or her own behavior or as independent of that behavior.

Locus of control has been difficult to assess during the preschool years primarily because tests used to measure it require language skills not yet available to preschool children. Efforts to assess it have been made, however. Stephen and Delys (1973) developed a test for preschoolers which assesses perceptual-cognitive style and shows promise of providing information about the early development of locus of control. But even their test goes beyond the competence level of infants and toddlers. Moreover, it does not provide a direct evaluation of parental influences. For this evaluation one must observe parents and infants interacting, particularly noting what effects contingent interactions have on the infants' behavior.

Lewis and Goldberg (1969) followed this research ploy in a study of mother-infant interaction. They found that habituation of the infant's behavior was related to the amount of contingent stimulation provided by its mother. In addition, the more immediate the mother's response to her infant's behavior, the more rapidly habituation occurred. Lewis and Goldberg concluded that, in general, habituation of the infant's spontaneously produced behavior is strongly related to maternal response to that behavior and to the contingent nature of maternal response. As they point out, historically, child psychology has emphasized the mother's role in the social-emotional development of her children. They suggest that reciprocal mother-infant interaction extends to all facets of development, including cognitive development. What do infants learn from contingent interactions with their mothers and with the environment in general? More and more, the evidence suggests that they learn a decision rule, an expectancy, or as J. S. Watson (1967) so aptly puts it, they learn *contingency awareness*.

Contingency learning The baby's initial contacts with the environment are random. Each of these random contacts provides feedback. Shaking a rattle provides movement-produced feedback, but equally important the baby sees, feels, and hears the rattle. Gradually, random contacts with the environment are replaced by self-initiated contacts. The infant smiles at its caregiver, who in turn smiles back or perhaps does not. In either case the infant receives feedback contingent on having first emitted a behavior. Although each of these interactions may increase or decrease the probability that the baby will emit another smile, something more than this seems to be learned. The baby seems to extract a more general principle, a more abstract rule regarding the relationship between its self-produced behavior and the probable consequences of that behavior. This cognitive structure may be called expectancy, contingency awareness, schema, or internal control. Each of these terms captures the flavor of the process.

When feedback confirms a baby's expectancy, that expectancy is strengthened. When feedback is discrepant with the baby's expectancy, the expectancy must change to assimilate the new information. If the novel event is too discrepant, the infant has difficulty assimilating the event into its schema (Piaget, 1952). However, contingent reinforcement of operant behavior is not the only learning process contributing to the infant's construction of higher-order cognitive expectancies. Learning to anticipate the consequences of signal stimuli is also important.

Action is the ingredient common to these two processes. Action means that the baby behaves, that the baby acts on the environment. The effects of action become the foundation for a generalized cognitive expectancy. But action also means that the baby must learn to associate signal stimuli with their consequences. The baby must learn to anticipate events given the occurrence of particular signal events. Hearing mother's footsteps signals her pending arrival. Seeing father put on his blue jeans may signal playtime or father's going to work. The child develops expectancies about the probable future consequences of the signal events in the environment.

Expectancies do not merely arise from action, however. They also regulate action. Presumably, expectancies enter long-term memory as decision rules or schemas. For example, the infant may recognize the object nature of a

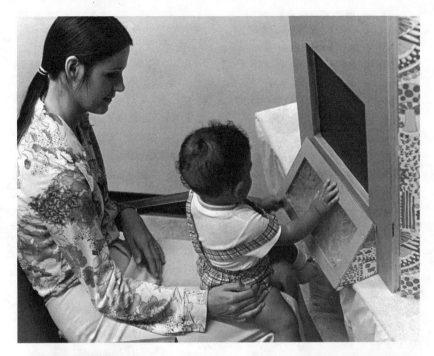

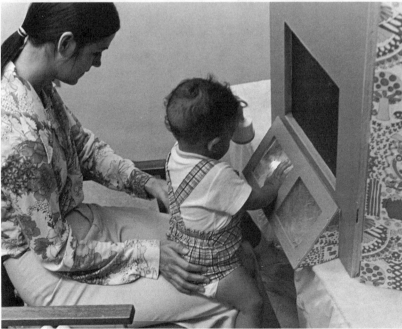

FIGURE 7–4 Apparatus used by Kodera (1975) to study the development of expectancies in older infants. **7–4a.** The infant is seated on its mother's lap in front of the apparatus. **7–4b.** The CS panel is illuminated, attracting an attending response and eliciting a touching response from the infant. **7–4c.** The door opens, contingent

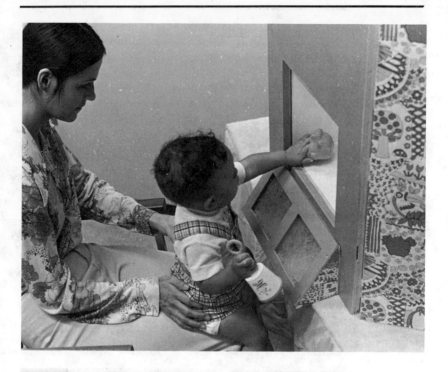

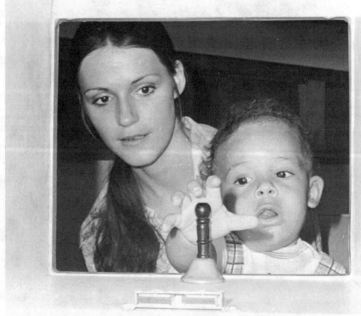

Photographs courtesy Thomas Hagaman

upon CS panel illumination, and reveals a novel toy. **7–4d.** The infant reaches for and obtains the toy.

toy by matching it with a class concept of "toy" objects. Reinstatement of these memories in the presence of a new toy allows the recognition of the toy and the class concept of toy events to occur simultaneously on the same cognitive level. In this illustration the new toy serves as a signal event (CS). In a recent study, Kodera (1975) reasoned that seeing the toy (CS) while simultaneously remembering previously experienced objects (UCS) and the motor behavior (UCR) associated with these objects, gives rise to an anticipation of a similar outcome (CR_1) from interacting with the new toy and approaching it (CR_2). To test his hypothesis, Kodera created a situation in which for some infants a light signaled the presentation of a novel toy (predictable situation), and for other infants the presentation of the light and the toy were completely random with respect to each other. The light illuminated a panel which could be pressed by the infant. However, in the predictable situation whether or not the infant pressed the panel, illumination of the panel was followed by the opening of a small door, revealing a novel toy. The infant could reach and secure the toy, thus ending one trial. Now, what could the infant learn? First, it could learn to anticipate the consequence of the illumination, that is, that CS occurrence reliably predicts toy presentation. If this expectancy has a directive function for the infant, one might expect it to make more and more frequent approach responses to the lighted panel. Thus, infants in the predictable situation are not only able to anticipate sequences of events but may also develop mistaken hypotheses concerning their own ability to control access to the toy. We say mistaken, because the toy will appear whether the infant touches the panel or not. Preliminary results of the experiment indicate that, over trials, infants in the predictable situation do, in fact, approach and press the panel following light illumination. Presumably, they are generalizing their expectancy rule to include the possibility that they are regulating the appearance of the toy. However, infants in the unpredictable situation gradually decrease their approaches to the panel. Since there is no contingent relationship between their behavior and either the occurrence of light or access to the toy, they have no reason to expect their behavior to be related to the events in the environment. It would seem, therefore, that both response-contingent reinforcement and expectancies associated with signal events provide important information which the child uses to construct more abstract cognitive rules.

SUMMARY

In this chapter we have reviewed two general approaches to the study of intelligence and cognition. The mental test approach emphasizes the psychometric evaluation of mental abilities. The developmental approach attempts to specify the mental structures and adaptive mechanisms which influence cognitive operations. Within the developmental approach, Piaget's theory of cognitive development stresses the importance of the differentiation of self from object during the early years of life. During the sensorimotor period, differentiation centers on the development of the object concept and object permanence. During the period of preoperational thought, the differentiation of self from object emerges, as does the development of representational competence. Neo-Piagetians have discovered that progress through the various periods of cognitive development is influenced by such global factors as child-rearing practices and social class. These factors seem to lead to different cognitive styles and to influence the content of representational thought.

Cognitive behaviorists also work within the developmental approach, but they are not committed to any one theory of cognitive development. They are particularly interested in how learning processes contribute to the development of higher-order cognitive processes. Thus far, research indicates that infants are attracted to novel events in the environment if the events are not too discrepant with the infant's current cognitive level of functioning. Moreover, events which are contingent upon the infant's behavior as well as events which have signal value for the infant seem to play an important role in facilitating the development of higher-order cognitive processes.

To be sure, neither the mental test approach nor the developmental approach can account for all the complexities of cognitive development. However, continued research and theoretical advances within each approach as well as efforts to integrate the approaches, will lead to a greater understanding of how infants and young children organize cognitive structures and how they apply them during the process of adapting to their environment.

SUGGESTED ADDITIONAL READING

Bruner, J. *The process of education.* Cambridge, Mass.: Harvard University Press, 1960.

Kagan, J. *Change and continuity during infancy.* New York: Wiley, 1971.

Piaget, J. *Origins of intelligence in children.* New York: International Universities Press, 1952.

PART FOUR

The organization of social behavior

BOX 8–1
Study questions

Is language unique to the human species?

Language development is an interactive process stemming from organismic and environmental factors. What are some of these?

How do caregivers influence early phonemic development?

How do mothers and fathers differ in their vocal interactions with infants?

When do children start to speak, what do they say, and how do they say it?

Do parents "teach" children language? Do children learn language from parents?

When do children acquire the ability to regulate their behavior through the use of language?

What factors interfere with normal language development?

What is the difference between expressive language and receptive language?

All language is communication, but not all communication is language. Is this statement correct?

8

THE DEVELOPMENT OF LANGUAGE AND COMMUNICATION

Language is one of the most interesting and most complex of human behaviors. Not only is language the dominant mode of human communication, but it is also intimately related to such processes as thought, cognition, learning and problem solving. The onset of language marks a point in the life span when significant reorganization of cognitive skills occurs (Bruner, 1964). It is not surprising, therefore, that so much energy has been invested in the effort to understand language development. Indeed, as one scholar put it, "Language ranks only slightly behind sex in the universal interest it inspires" (Roberts, 1967, p. xxix).

THE NATURE OF LANGUAGE

What is language? How does it differ from other forms of communication? Who has it, and who does not? When is language acquired? How is it acquired? The answers to these questions can be sought in many ways. One way is to refer to the descriptive features of language. These features include *phonemes* (the basic sounds of a language), *morphemes* (the smallest individually meaningful sounds), *syntax* (the rules for combining morphemes), and *semantics* (the meaningfulness of sounds).

The most common way to find the definition of a word is to consult the dictionary. Dictionary definitions of language generally begin by referring to words and the rules for combining them. This captures the flavor of what is meant by both language production and language competence. However, dictionary definitions also metaphorically attribute language behavior to

nonhuman organisms ("the language of the bees") as well as botanical species ("the language of the flowers"). But such metaphors do not reflect the
meaning of the term *language* as it is used in discussions of human language.
Dictionaries also define language very broadly as a form of communication,
but *communication* is in turn defined to include non-verbal modes of con-
veying information (for example, the wink of an eye or the stern look of a
parent).

Teaching language to animals

Hugh Lofting's imagination produced the most marvelous and famous of
all animal doctors, Dr. John Dolittle. Dr. Dolittle was unique among veteri-
narians because he was able to talk with the animals (and in their own
languages). Interest in animal communication has not been confined to
Lofting's literary imagination. Biologists and psychologists have also attempted to talk with the animals, or more specifically, they have attempted
to teach language to animals.

The procedure most commonly used to assess the continuity between
human language and the communicative behavior of nonhuman organisms
has been to study simians reared in human environments. Initially, such
studies yielded disappointing results. One chimpanzee, Viki, was reported
to be able to pronounce four "words" (Hayes & Hayes, 1952). Although
chimpanzees most certainly do vocalize, and there appear to be no substantive differences between the vocal behavior of chimpanzees reared in
the wild and those reared in captivity (Denny & Ratner, 1970), simians do
not have the essential structural mechanisms necessary for producing human
speech sounds (Lenneberg, 1969).

Notwithstanding their vocal behavior, the major portion of the chimpanzees' communication is composed of nonverbal signal stimuli. Indeed, Viki
learned to communicate by gesturing and demonstrated the ability to obey
spoken commands—an ability Viki had in common with both preverbal
human toddlers and other animal species. Human beings also communicate
by gesturing. The shrug of a shoulder, a pout, the upward thrust of the
arms, all convey a particular meaning related to the communicative situation. Moreover, in some cultures gestural communication may be as important as spoken communication. It was precisely this common ability of
humans and their primate "relatives" to communicate via gestures that
prompted investigators to study whether chimpanzees could learn a human
gesture language (Kellogg, 1968).

The Gardners set out to teach the chimpanzee Washoe the American
Sign Language of the deaf (Gardner & Gardner, 1969). American Sign Language consists of specific hand and arm movements which serve as substitutes for words, phrases, and sentences (Stokoe, Casterline, & Croneberg,
1965). Over a period of several years Washoe acquired a vocabulary of nearly
300 signs. The Gardners' study is impressive. They have demonstrated that
the chimpanzee (1) can learn gestures that represent a variety of word

classes, including nouns, pronouns, verbs, and adjectives, (2) can use signs and gestures spontaneously, and (3) shows some evidence of being able to combine signs into multisign sequences. Moreover, their research suggests that when one uses a communicative mode common to both chimpanzee and human (sign language), while avoiding uniquely human modes (speech), the chimpanzee can learn remarkably sophisticated communicative skills.

David Premack (1971) has taken a different approach to the study of language behavior in the chimpanzee. In contrast to the gestures that constitute Washoe's lexicon, Premack's chimpanzee, Sarah, must manipulate plastic objects that vary in size, shape, color, and/or texture. A square yellow object may represent "banana," a multisided blue object may represent "eat." To construct serially correct sequences of words, Sarah chooses the appropriate plastic objects and places them in vertical order on a form board ("Eat banana").

Can chimpanzees learn language? Certainly, Washoe and Sarah have done so well that they have challenged nearly every criterion historically advanced to define language as something uniquely human. Nevertheless, their language skills seem to be no more advanced than those of sensorimotor children (see Brown, 1973).

THE ORIGINS OF LANGUAGE

Although language specialists continue their efforts to specify the prerequisites of language, their efforts are not devoted exclusively to this problem. Indeed, this interest has prompted considerable theoretical controversy regarding the determinants of language. The debate has been between those who maintain that language is biologically determined and those who argue that language is environmentally determined. The universality with which the phases of prelinguistic vocalizations unfold, together with other linguistic universals (semantics, syntax), suggest a biological component of language. On the other hand, it is obvious that children learn the specific phonemes and inflections essential for speaking their native language. After all, French babies do turn into children who speak French, not Serbo-Croatian. Let us consider the evidence for biological and environmental influences on language development.

Biological influences on language

Advocates of the biological explanation of language behavior suggest the following points in support of this position (Lenneberg, 1967). First, there are anatomical, structural, and neurophysiological correlates of language (see Table 8–1). The key point is that clear relationships exist between the major stages of language development and the maturation of the nervous system. Note, for example, that at approximately 18–24 months of age a

TABLE 8–1
Structural and functional correlates of language

Age	Usual language development	Physical maturation of CNS	Lateralization of function	Explanation
0–3 months	Emergence of cooing.	About 60 to 70 percent of developmental course accomplished.	None: symptoms and prognosis identical for either hemisphere.	Neuroanatomical and physiological prerequisites become established.
4–20 months	From babbling to words.			
21–36 months	Acquisition of language.	Rate of maturation slowed down.	Hand preference emerges.	Language appears to involve entire brain. There is little cortical specialization with regard to language, though left hemisphere is beginning to become dominant toward end of this period.
3–10 years	Some grammatical refinement; expansion of vocabulary.	Very slow completion of maturational processes.	Cerebral dominance established between three to five years, but evidence that right hemisphere may often still be involved in speech and language functions. About one quarter of early childhood aphasias due to right-hemisphere lesions.	A process of physiological organizations takes place in which functional lateralization of language to left is prominent. "Physiological redundancy" is gradually reduced, and polarization of activities between right and left hemisphere is established. As long as maturational processes have not stopped, reorganization is still possible.
11–14 years	Foreign accents in newly learned languages.	Asymptote reached on almost all parameters.	Apparently firmly established, but definitive statistics not available.	Language is markedly lateralized, and internal organization is established irreversibly for life. Language-free parts of brain cannot take over except where lateralization had been blocked by pathology during childhood.
Mid-teens to senium	Acquisition of second language increasingly difficult.	None.	In about 97 percent of population, language definitely lateralized to the left.	

Source: Adapted from E. Lenneberg, "The natural history of language," in F. Smith and G. A. Miller (Eds.), *The genesis of language* (Cambridge, Mass: MIT Press, 1966), p. 248. Reprinted with permission of Elizabeth Lenneberg and the MIT Press.

marked shift from prelinguistic to linguistic vocalizations occurs at the same time that the brain is becoming lateralized.

Second, there is a universal developmental sequence of vocal behavior. Whether the child's native language is French, Spanish, Serbo-Croatian, Russian, or English, the ontogenetic sequence characteristic of vocal behavior is essentially the same (Brown, 1973).

Closely related to the universality of the sequence of language behavior is the evidence suggesting that language competence or knowledge of the rules of grammar is a universal characteristic of human beings (see Chomsky, 1965; McNeill, 1970). Because of its universality, some scholars believe that language competence comes to the child via innate cognitive or information processing mechanisms. The point here is not that all languages have the same structural rules of grammar or the same grammatical forms, for they do not. Rather, it is the capacity to "know" the rules of grammar that is thought to be biologically based. Indeed, every newborn has the capacity to master any of the world's languages. Once one language is encoded, however, it becomes increasingly difficult to master a second language. Thus, the young child learns the grammatical constructions of its first language with remarkably greater ease than the adult masters the grammatical constructions of a second language. Moreover, many children reared in bilingual homes learn two languages with greater ease than does the adult trying to learn a second language. Are we to assume that the young child is a "better" language learner than the adult? In a sense this may be true. Does the human organism have some biological capacity to process language structure that becomes an increasingly rigid cognitive capability as the nervous system becomes firmly organized? In fact, it is more likely that the

---

BOX 8–2
Developmental sequence of vocal behavior

Approximate beginning age	Vocal behavior
Day 1	Undifferentiated crying (general signaling)
1–2 months	Differentiated crying (specific signaling)
2 months	Cooing-babbling (phonemic expansion and contraction)
6 months	Lallation (self-imitation)
8 months	Echolalia (other-imitation)
9–15 months	One-word sentences (holophrastic speech)
15 months–3 years	Two-word sentences (telegraphic speech)
2–4 years	Multiword sentences
6 years	Mastery of syntax (rules of grammar)
8 years	Mastery of phonology

processes responsible for early language acquisition and those responsible for the adult's ability to learn a second language are completely different.

Further evidence of biological influences on language is provided by studies contrasting the phonemic vocalizations of deaf and hearing infants. One of these studies found that there were no differences in the vocalizations of deaf and hearing babies during the first few months of life (Lenneberg, Rebelsky, & Nichols, 1965). Thus, very early vocalizations do not seem to require either social reinforcement or contingent reinforcement for their appearance. By the second half of the first year of life, however, very clear differences between the vocalizations of deaf and hearing babies appear. This suggests that environmental factors become increasingly influential determinants of language behavior (especially phonology) as the infant approaches its first birthday. Moreover, it suggests that language development is a product of both the organism and the environment rather than the exclusive domain of one or the other.

Environmental influences on language

The infant's prelinguistic vocalizations clearly qualify as operants. Operant methodology, therefore, provides a useful laboratory tool for investigating how early vocalizations may be influenced by the environment.

In real life the infant seldom experiences opportunities to perceptually discriminate such precise speech sounds as /ba/ or /ga/ (see Chapter 5). It is much more likely that the infant's speech perception occurs in a complex social context ("Hello, pretty baby. Say dada"), and that the reinforcers delivered consist of complex social-sensory feedback. Thus, it is not surprising that researchers have favored the use of complex reinforcers in their search for the factors that modify early vocalizations.

The classic study conducted by Rheingold, Gewirtz, and Ross (1959) demonstrated that social reinforcement consisting of visual, tactile, and auditory components (a smiling face, light stroking of the baby's stomach, and "tsk" sounds) effectively increased the rate of vocalization. The effectiveness of such reinforcement was further specified by the demonstration of the importance of response-reinforcement contingency (Weisberg, 1963). Nonsocial reinforcement and noncontingent social reinforcement were unsuccessful in modifying vocal behavior. Only social reinforcement contingent upon the baby's vocal behavior was effective. Moreover, the contingent relationship must occur in a quite restricted time span. Even a three-second delay between vocalization and reinforcement may destroy the element of contingency (Ramey & Ourth, 1971).

Routh's experiment (1969) provided critical support for the importance of social reinforcement for modifying infant vocal behavior. There were three groups of infants, ranging in age from two months to seven months. One group received reinforcement for producing consonantlike sounds; one group was reinforced for producing vowellike sounds; and one group was reinforced for producing any kind of sound. In each instance the reinforcer was the complex one noted above. The results indicated that both the total vocal output (the all-sound group) and qualitatively specific vocalizations (the vowel and consonant groups) change as a function of complex social reinforcement. The successful demonstration of the acquisition, extinction, differentiation, and generalization of vocal behavior is persuasive evidence that learning plays an early role in at least the phonological aspects of vocal behavior.

On the basis of these experiments one might conclude that effective modification of infant vocal behavior depends upon the application of a precise, complex social reinforcer. Imagine parents smiling, nodding their heads, rubbing their baby's stomach, and repeating "tsk, tsk, tsk" each time their baby vocalizes. Obviously, the laboratory research thus far discussed does not give a totally accurate reflection of the real world—few parents consistently behave in this fashion, and yet their children do learn to speak.

Evidence obtained from laboratory and home settings indicates that the modification of the infant's vocal behavior is not dependent upon so complex a reinforcer. Laboratory evidence is provided by the systematic analysis of auditory, tactile, and visual components of social reinforcement (Schwartz, Rosenberg, & Brackbill, 1970). The three stimuli were a tape-recorded female voice saying "Nice baby," rubbing the infant's abdomen, and a smiling-nodding face. The stimuli were presented to independent groups singly, in pairs, and in the usual combination of all three. Schwartz et al. found that the three components of social reinforcement, whether presented singly, in pairs, or all together, were equally effective reinforcers for modifying vocalization rates in three-month-old infants.

This brief overview of laboratory studies clearly indicates that early vocal behavior is influenced by both organismic and environmental factors. On the organismic side may be listed the physical structures necessary to utter speech sounds, the neural structures which mediate verbal functions, the receptors which make possible the accurate perception of speech, and the cognitive structures which enable the child to understand and use grammatical rules. On the environmental side may be listed such factors as the agent of social reinforcement, the situational setting which determines the quality and quantity of reinforcement, and such things as the affective climate within which social reinforcement is delivered or withheld. In fact, one set of determinants cannot exist without the other and we must not think of "sides" as being independent determinants of language development.

PRELINGUISTIC VOCALIZATION

Like the chimpanzee, the human infant begins life as a vocal but nonverbal organism. Moreover, again like the chimpanzee, the human infant develops the ability to understand verbal commands when it is itself unable to speak. Unlike the chimpanzee, however, the human infant will in time develop spoken language. How does the infant develop from a vocal but nonverbal organism into a verbal one? To organize the study of this question it is convenient to consider two separate, although continuous and overlapping, periods of verbal behavior.

The *prelinguistic period* covers roughly the first year of life, from the newborn's first cry to the first words spoken with meaning. This period has been divided into five phases: undifferentiated crying, differentiated crying, babbling, lallation, and echolalia. The *linguistic period* covers the remaining years of language acquisition. It should be kept in mind that any ages associated with these phases are intended only as guidelines and that individual differences are the rule rather than the exception.

Undifferentiated crying

Beginning with the birth cry and extending to approximately the end of the first month of life, cry vocalizations are presumably undifferentiated. Are these cries of any social significance? One approach to this question has been to study "reflexive" crying in other babies. Early studies produced conflicting answers. Recent research, however, tends to support the general belief that reflexive crying is a real phenomenon. Moreover, it seems that the newborn's cry is more effective in eliciting reflexive crying than are other auditory signals.

Simner (1971) compared four groups of newborns who differed only in the cry-eliciting stimulus with which they were presented. One group (Newborn Cry) received the tape-recorded cry of a five-day-old female newborn recorded in the hospital nursery. Other groups received the tape-recorded cry of a 5½-month-old female infant recorded at home (Home Cry) or the "crying" produced by a computer synthesizer (Synthetic Cry). A Silent Control group was employed to establish baseline levels of crying associated with feeding and handling. Comparisons of crying behavior indicated that reflexive crying was related to the type of crying stimulus presented. The stimulus conditions that most closely reproduced the newborn's cry elicited more reflexive crying than did stimulus conditions more deviant from newborn crying.

In a second experiment, Simner exposed one group of newborns to the Newborn Cry condition and another group to feedback of their own cry. Although there were no statistically significant differences in reflexive crying between the two groups, there were trends toward greater heart rate acceleration and greater crying duration when newborns listened to feedback of their own cry. The general pattern of these results led Simner to conclude that crying is self-regulatory. That is, when the baby produces a cry (vocal stimulus), the cry in turn elicits additional crying (vocal response) and maintains the behavior. Perhaps this is one reason why exogenous stimulation of a constant rhythmic character is so effective in pacifying the infant. The endogenously produced rhythm (self-regulated crying) becomes disrupted by the application of exogenously produced stimulation (caregiver's handling, singing, rocking, and so on).

Differentiated crying

Another approach to the social significance of crying is to study the properties of the cry that elicit caregiving. Certainly, the very young infant has no better means than crying for summoning its caregiver. By one month of age, the infant's cry differentiates, and the basic and anger cries are clearly distinguishable. The adaptive function of undifferentiated crying is to elicit general and prompt caregiving, while that of differentiated crying is to signal more specific needs, such as hunger or distress. Caregivers do seem able to interpret just what their infants' cries are communicating. Recall our previous discussion of research which suggested that both promptness of response and the length of time spent with the newborn were important determinants of newborn crying and activity patterns and that the quality of the caregiver's interaction with the newborn was more important than promptness of response. Thus, newborns cried less and organized their day-night activity rhythm more rapidly for a nurse who responded more slowly to crying but who spent longer periods of time in each caregiving intervention. (Sander, 1969).

These results do not speak well for those child-rearing experts who advocate immediate response at all costs to baby's cry. But these results do not give a complete picture of the potential long-term effects of prompt caregiver intervention. For evidence bearing on this question, let us consider the results of a study conducted by Bell and Ainsworth (1972). Infants and mothers were observed in the home throughout the first year of life in an effort to determine the relationship between infant crying and maternal responsiveness to crying. The authors reported the surprising finding that infants cried as frequently during the fourth quarter of the first year of life as they did during the first quarter. However, older infants had shorter crying episodes than did younger infants. Mothers who ignored crying during the first few months of life (persistent staving off) tended to have babies who cried increasingly often over the remainder of the first year. Conversely, the most important factor related to reduced frequency and duration of crying proved to be the *promptness* with which mothers responded to crying. An even greater incentive for prompt caregiver response to the crying infant was the fact that the babies who cried least had the best communication skills at 8–12 months of age. In fact, prompt caregiving also has cognitive significance in that it provides early experience with contingent learning.

What do these findings suggest for parental child-rearing practices? They certainly indicate that crying babies should receive prompt caregiver attention. That is, child-rearing experts who advocate giving immediate response to the crying infant are correct. However, prompt responding is not enough. What the caregiver does during the intervention is also important. It is one thing to simply check baby's diaper or plop a nipple into its mouth, and quite another thing to provide baby with a rich social-affective encounter.

Babbling

Babbling may begin as early as the second month of life. It is generally thought to represent vocal play or active exercise of the vocal apparatus. McNeill (1970) suggests that babbling marks the end of reflexive prelinguistic vocalizations and the beginning of true phonemic development. According to one early investigator, babbling represents the period of time during which the infant acquires the phonemes of its native language (Latif, 1934). Sounds not used in the native language drop from the vocal repertoire *(phonemic contractions),* while sounds required for the native language are either refined or make their first appearance *(phonemic expansion).* Although investigators continue to debate the relationship of babbling to language, there is general agreement that phonemic development proceeds in an orderly fashion. Initially, back consonants and front vowels occur more frequently than do front consonants and back vowels, and vowel production exceeds consonant production.

Associated with the emergence of babbling is a steady increase in the amount of time that the infant is exposed to adult vocalizations. Sleep periods lengthen and become less frequent as the day-night rhythm stabilizes. Thus the infant gradually spends more and more of its waking hours with or near adults. The infant's ability to localize sounds shows marked improvement from the third month on, as does its attention span. Finally, one cannot help speculating that infants "tune in" human speech in much the same way that they seem to "tune in" the human face. This listening aspect of language development, called *receptive language,* is discussed in a later section of this chapter.

Lallation

Lallation, or the sequential utterances of the infant's own sounds, begins at around six months of age and lasts roughly through the ninth month. Sequences of intrinsic interest to parents are consonant-vowel (CV) combinations, such as *ma* and *da.* Although CV combinations are usually interpreted as baby's first words, they are typically meaningless. In addition to uttering CV combinations, the infant now responds to inflected voices, differentially attending to pleasant and unpleasant adult vocalizations. Attending to unpleasant vocalizations ("No!") usually takes the form of motor inhibition and visual orienting, which are of brief duration and rapidly habituate, much to the dismay of parents.

Echolalia

This last phase of the prelinguistic period begins at approximately nine months of age. Now the infant actively imitates ("echoes") adult speech sounds. There is some argument concerning the importance of imitation for language development. Those who emphasize the primacy of environmental determinants argue that imitation is of central importance. Those who emphasize the biological determinants of linguistic structure play down the importance of imitation. Although there has been much speculation regarding the role of imitation, few empirical studies have been reported.

These include a noteworthy two-year longitudinal study of vocal and gestural imitation (Uzgiris, 1972). Uzgiris defined imitation as the "immediate and fairly accurate reproduction of the act presented by the experimenter" (p. 467). The stimulus conditions for vocal imitation included cooing, babbling, novel sounds (sounds not found in the English language), familiar words (present in the infant's vocal repertoire), and new words (not present in the infant's spontaneous vocalizations). The stimulus conditions for gestural imitation included familiar actions (those already produced by the infant, such as banging hands on the table), complex actions (integrated motor actions not yet shown by the infant, such as "taking a block, putting it in a cup, and shaking the cup"), unfamiliar visible actions (motor actions that the infant could see but not perform, such as opening and closing a fist), and unfamiliar invisible actions (facial gestures, such as blinking).

The results suggested that imitation begins during the first year of life and that vocal imitation precedes gestural imitation. On the basis of these data, Uzgiris proposed a descriptive developmental sequence of imitative behavior. In the first few months the infant imitates only familiar behaviors which are emitted at a high operant rate. Since the infant is not able to imitate novel behaviors, imitation at this age level is more appropriately referred to as "pseudoimitation." In the second quarter year of life, infants use either a uniform response to any modeled behavior or make partial imitations. For example, some infants consistently vocalize in response to a modeled vocalization, but their vocalizations differ from those of the model. Toward the end of the first year of life, clear attempts to imitate are observed. Finally, by 18–24 months, accurate and immediate imitation of vocal and gestural behavior occur. This is also a time of rapid vocabulary growth.

Valuable information concerning language acquisition is provided by laboratory studies demonstrating the infant's remarkably accurate discrimination of phonemes as well as by studies indicating that infants will modify their vocal behavior in order to maintain the presence of social reinforcement. The infant's increasing competence in imitating adult vocalizations suggests that echolalia may be an important factor in guiding the organization of phonemic structure.

Although demonstrations of perceptual acuity, social reinforcement, and imitation are important, they provide only a small portion of the explanation of language acquisition. For example, they do not explain why the 16-month-old masters the word and concept mine (mine night-night, mine ball) when parents are referring to your blanket and your ball. If imitation were the primary process involved in language acquisition, one would expect the toddler to learn your first. Clearly, language learning involves cognitive processes far more complex than those accounted for by reinforcement theory alone.

LINGUISTIC VOCALIZATIONS

Toward the end of the first year of life, the infant utters its first meaningful word. Just what that word is and when it appears are matters for speculation. The following questions are useful guides for judging whether an utterance is a word: Is the sound used repetitively? Do appropriate gestures accompany the vocalization? Is the sound used with meaning? The consensus is that the first words with meaning are reduplicated syllables but that these are unlike the consonant-vowel reduplications uttered during the prelinguistic stage. There is quite a difference between the first word *mama* and the repetitive *ma-ma-ma-ma-ma* uttered during lallation.

Vocabulary growth

Sometime near its first birthday, baby utters its first meaningful word. Additional words are added gradually during the following six or eight months. As the child approaches its second birthday, the size of its vocabulary explodes. The child acquires approximately 21 words in the eight months following the appearance of its first word, but from the 18th to the 24th month it acquires approximately 250 new words (Smith, 1926). How quickly the young child changes from a nonverbal organism to one capable of carrying on quite sophisticated conversation!

Vocabulary composition

Although the child's beginning vocabulary includes nearly all the parts of speech, pronouns, verbs, and nouns account for nearly one half of its total vocabulary (Young, 1941). Normative studies of speech and language have favored the longitudinal method. For example, Przetacznikowa (1972) studied the speech of ten Polish children over varying lengths of time in order to describe when the parts of speech make their appearance and to assess the parental factors that are related to the child's early language behavior.

Among these children, nouns were the part of speech most commonly used by two-year-olds, although, as in all aspects of language behavior, there were marked individual differences. The nouns most commonly used were names of familiar persons (21.4 percent). Other noun types used, in the order of their frequency, were: names of animals (15.9 percent); names of foods and drinks (13.3 percent); names of body parts, clothing, and common objects (each 7 percent); and names of toys, household furnishings, and objects outside the home (2–4 percent each). During the preschool years, abstract nouns, such as those associated with form, color, weight, measurement, time, and social relationship gradually increased in frequency. Przetacznikowa found, as Young (1941) had earlier, that two-year-olds use very few adjectives. However, during the preschool years, adjectives of "value judgments" (ugly, pretty, good, bad) increase in frequency, as do adjectives describing sensations, such as those associated with color, form, temperature, size, and weight.

Articulation

Every caregiver knows that the speech of young children is hard to understand. Young children simply do not speak clearly. With practice, caregivers develop an understanding of the meaning of different sounds and of the semantic range of the same sound. Nevertheless, articulation difficulties sometimes create quite a chore for caregivers, as they make repeated attempts to determine just what the young child is trying to communicate. The results of one study suggest a marked improvement in articulation from roughly 14 months to 24 months. In this experiment Liiamina (1960) asked children to identify objects in response to the question "What is this?" The 14-month-old not only articulates poorly (only 2.8 percent of the responses were judged to be well articulated), but is also likely not to respond at all (only 39.9 percent of the experimenter's requests were answered).

Holophrastic speech

The toddler's one-word sentences often convey considerably more information than is contained in the word itself. For example, *"daddy"* may at various times mean: *"Where is daddy?" "There's my daddy,"* or *"Daddy help me."* The utterance *"(m)ilk!"* may mean *"I want a drink of milk."* Such one-word utterances have been called *holophrastic speech*. By some as yet unexplained process, parents can decipher the messages contained in holophrastic speech with amazing accuracy. No doubt, prior correct and incorrect interpretations provide the base from which parents determine the meaning of these one-word sentences. The really intriguing questions are, Does the young child "know" that different inflections and intonations of the same word convey different meanings, and if so, how does the child know?

Telegraphic speech

When young children are asked to repeat an adult sentence or when they spontaneously emit a sentence, they typically omit low-information words and include only nouns, verbs, or other high-information words. Such sentences have been called *telegraphic speech* because of their obvious similarity to telegrams (Brown & Fraser, 1963). Telegraphic speech has been cited as one of the possible universal characteristics of language development (Slobin, 1971). Thus, in response to the parent's "Now I must go to the store," the young child may say "Me go store." Several explanations have been advanced to account for telegraphic speech, including the suggestion that the young child's vocabulary is too limited and its memory span is too short for successful imitation of adult sentences. Moreover, during receptive language development, children probably construct some cognitive rule that guides them to high-information words. Whereas the young child's early sentences are telegraphic, in responding to such utterances, adults frequently expand the telegraphic sentence to its adult form. It is not clear how such expansions influence early language development.

Pivots and opens   Early studies of language behavior suggested that the young child's telegraphic speech was composed of two basic word categories, *pivot* and *open* words (Braine, 1963). It was hypothesized that pivot and open words differed in their frequency of occurrence and in their rate of development. The pivot category included a relatively small number of frequently used words. The open category included many more words, all of which occurred less frequently than did pivot words. New pivot words were added more slowly than new open words. Examples of pivot words included *my, see, that, it, hi, allgone,* and *big* (Braine, 1963; Brown & Bellugi, 1964). Examples of open words included *mommy, daddy, shoe, cup* and *baby.*

Now this was an exciting hypothesis for it suggested that one could discover the full range of early sentence construction by analyzing samples of children's speech. Moreover, by finding which words serve as pivots and which as opens, one could infer the linguistic systems used to construct two- and three-word sentences. Unfortunately, a recent detailed analysis suggests that this area of research may be a blind alley (Brown, 1973). In fact, pivot and open words seem to be used so interchangably that efforts to place words into these neat, dichotomous categories are almost doomed to be swamped by the exceptions to the rule.

Tags

Many of the preschool child's sentences have little questions attached to them (Brown & Hanlon, 1970). *"I a good girl, huh, daddy?" "It's a nice picture, isn't it?"* What do these questions mean? Brown (1973) suggests that they represent the child's request for *confirmation.* The child apparently expects the listener to confirm the proposition, and when parental responses to tag questions were studied, "Yes" and "That's right" were found to be the most frequent responses (Brown & Hanlon, 1970).

How many tags do young children use? How do children learn to use them? The answer to the first question is probably several hundred. Consider the following, and then generate some of your own, perhaps the ones you use most frequently: "didn't I?" "right, daddy?" "isn't it?" "does she?" Remember that a tag must be at the end of a sentence and must imply a request for confirmation.

The answer to the second question is that we don't know. Grammatically, tags represent rather complex and sophisticated linguistic structures. Moreover, since the right tag must be affixed to the right sentence, it is hard to imagine that tag-sentence combinations are memorized or learned in any sense of what the term *learning* implies. Thus, the child (and the adult) must use some cognitive process or grammatical rule to combine sentences and tags. Just what rules should be used, however, has not been discovered. In any event, tagging seems to begin sometime between three and five years of age, with linguistically less complex forms appearing ("Okay?") before linguistically more complex forms ("Isn't it?") (Brown & Hanlon, 1970).

Universal stages of language development

Is language development the same for all human beings, regardless of the specific language spoken? Amidst all the diversity, is there an invariant sequence that accurately describes language development? Roger Brown (1973) believes that there is, though his five-stage sequence currently describes only the sequence for American English, its potential for universality looks promising. According to Brown, the stages are organized sequentially, are not tied to specific ages, and are not completely independent. Each successive stage adds to the previous stage, and children's language can reflect operations at various stages. However, a child just constructing the linguistic operations essential for Stage I will not have Stage II language. The stages are named to reflect those aspects of language being focused on by the child—Stage I: Basic semantic and grammatical role; Stage II: The modulation of meaning; Stage III: Modalities of the simple sentence; Stage IV: Embedding one simple sentence with another; Stage V: The conjunction of one simple sentence with another (Brown & Herrnstein, 1975).

Stages I and II have been the most systematically studied, and Brown (1973) summarizes this work in the first of what promises to be a sequence of scholarly volumes exploring both the universality and the diversity of language development. Stage I deals with the semantic (meaning) and syntactic (word order) features of first sentences and is concerned largely with telegraphic speech. Stage II deals with the organization of 14 grammatical morphemes in American English, such as those associated with past tense, possession, and pluralization. Whether or not other languages have 14 morphemes is unimportant. (In fact, in many languages the number of morphemes far exceeds 14.) What is important is that the morphemes regulating expressive meaning, assumed to be a finite class, become organized and used during Stage II. The key to the stage sequence is its invariant order of development.

As Brown points out, it may be difficult to find universality beyond Stage I. Nevertheless studies of language development involving over 30 languages are currently being conducted. As results from these studies become available, Brown and others will be provided with evidence regarding the universality of Stages II through V. In any event, Brown's contribution is important even if Stages I through V apply only to English.

Learning to talk

MacNamara (1972) suggests that infants first determine the intended meaning of adult utterances and then use this information to analyze the relationship between meaning and language. In other words, semantics develops before syntax. MacNamara's hypothesis rests on the assumption that the cognitive ability to decipher meaningfulness develops before the ability to combine words according to the rules of grammar. Surely even toddlers at the level of holophrastic speech respond appropriately to rather complex directions, such as "Katherine! Close that door and let my pots and pans alone." Language comprehension not only develops prior to language production but seems to predict certain aspects of language production (Nelson, 1973). Toddlers who show early language comprehension are the "best" talkers at later ages.

Nelson's study of language development reflects the contemporary emphasis on the infant as an active, organizing, information processing organism—an organism that constructs cognitive models and acts on the basis of those models. Although Nelson places great emphasis on the infant as an active information processing organism, she does not suggest that all language learning depends on processes occurring inside the child's head. The language and rearing environment is equally important. Nelson was concerned specifically with maternal influences on children's speech. She concluded that the first words the child speaks are directly related to the cognitive models of the world constructed by the child during the pre-linguistic period. Words, then, mirror the relative importance of things, interpersonal relations, and actions in the child's experiential world. Some children talk most about the things in their environment. Nelson labeled this type of word orientation *Referential*. Some children talk most about other persons or about themselves. Such children were said to have an *Expressive* word orientation. During the second year of life, children with a referential orientation showed more rapid vocabulary growth and had larger overall vocabularies than did children with an expressive orientation. Nelson went on to identify a variety of word orientations, the most beneficial of which was *Match-Referential-Acceptance*. This pattern occurred frequently but not exclusively among mothers of firstborn female children. Mother's speech corresponded well with her toddler's cognitive expectancies. Her vocabulary emphasized the labeling of objects and actions, and she generally accepted and encouraged her child's initial attempts to speak. On the other hand, the *Mismatch-Expressive-Rejection* pattern was associated with slow speech development. Here, maternal speech did not match the child's cognitive models. Mother tended to ignore her toddler's attempts to articulate words and ideas, and she generally tried to control her child's early language. Words tended to be oriented toward persons. Surprisingly, Nelson concluded that explicit attempts to apply contingent or differential reinforcement slowed down language acquisition.

Although many contemporary theorists think that language comprehension is one aspect of or is at least highly related to cognitive development, the specific cognitive processes used by the toddler to infer meaning are not known. In any event, this rather remarkable ability of the toddler provides an excellent focal issue around which one can organize the study of cognitive and linguistic processes during early development. On the practical side, the fact that comprehension precedes production is reason enough to encourage parents to maintain a rich verbal environment and to support their children's initial attempts to communicate verbally rather than gesturally.

Language competence

The comprehension and production of language are the first two general events marking the linguistic stage of vocal behavior. The third is language competence, or the knowledge of the grammatical rules used to form correct multiword sentences. All the evidence indicates that the toddler does not know the rules of phonology, semantics, and syntax, but that by five to eight years of age these rules are almost totally mastered.

Nonetheless, it is obvious that phonology, semantics, and syntax have their developmental origins in the first two years of life. In fact, if such theorists as MacNamara and Nelson are correct in their assessment of early language, then we could justifiably conclude that the child begins to organize a semantic system sometime prior to the production of its first meaningful word and that it begins to organize a syntactic system sometime prior to its production of sentences.

The child's formation of tenses and plurals not only gives parents many amusing moments (for example, such overgeneralizations as "my foots" or "I hitted it") but also indicates that young children begin to understand the rules for correct grammatical constructions long before any formal effort is made to teach those rules systematically. Apparently, speaking according to rules requires no learning as learning is traditionally conceptualized.

Much of our knowledge of the grammatical rules of language, such as those associated with tense formation and pluralization, stems directly from the work of Brown and his associates. In a frequently cited experiment (Brown & Berko, 1960), four- to seven-year-old children were presented with pictures of nonsense objects and asked a series of questions designed to evaluate their understanding of pluralization. One of the objects was a line drawing called a "wug." The experimenter was required to present each picture, ask a question, and record the child's response. For example, the experimenter would say, "This is a wug. Here is another one. There are two ? ." Although children of all ages made errors, even the youngest children often gave the correct plural form. Errors decreased with age. These and many similar experiments have given clear evidence that many children "know" the rules for pluralization as early as age three. Surely few other equally complex developmental phenomena show such early mastery.

Paternal influences on language development

We have repeatedly referred to studies of maternal influences on the young child's vocal and language behavior. Particularly noteworthy were the laboratory studies illustrating the power of contingent social reinforcement for modifying infant vocal behavior and the studies examining mother-child language interactions in the natural setting of the home. Whether conducted in the laboratory, in an institution of some kind, or at home, all these studies implicitly assumed that mother is the primary agent influencing the child's language development.

In 1965 John Nash published a review of the literature on paternal influences on the child's development. His review amounted to an exposé of our lack of systematic knowledge concerning the father as caregiver. In the few short years following its publication, research directly assessing the father's caregiving role has mushroomed.

The interview technique has been used to assess the father's role in general child rearing. Using this technique, Pederson and Robson (1969) obtained child-rearing participation ratings on 45 fathers of firstborn male and female infants. Although the study suffers because it solicited ratings from mothers rather than directly from fathers, the results provide much food for thought. Forty of the 45 wives reported that their husbands spent some time in caregiving. The fathers were seen as establishing early emotional involvement with their infants and as expressing more concern for the well-being of female infants than of male infants. The fathers spent an average of eight hours a week in play activities, with slightly more than 33 percent receiving the highest score on a rating of roughhouse play. Even though the fathers averaged only 26 hours a week at home during the baby's waking hours, 75 percent of the wives reported that their babies had a clear attachment to their fathers. These wives perceived their husbands as "nurturant, active, patient, and emotionally invested in rearing."

Given the possibility that fathers may be more involved with general child rearing than is traditionally believed, what might this mean for such specific behaviors as language? The scanty evidence that bears on this question suggests that infants are not often exposed to direct verbal interaction with their fathers. Two studies, both of which tape-recorded natural language behavior in the home, offer evidence to support this conclusion.

In the first study the language environment of two 12-month-old infants was recorded (Friedlander, Cyrulic, & Davis, 1971). Even this small sample disclosed individual differences. In one of the two homes radio and television broadcasts accounted for 70 percent of the child's language environment, while in the other home they accounted for 25 percent of the language environment. Seventy percent of the adult utterances in both homes came from mother, 25 percent from father, and 5 percent from nonfamilial visitors in the home. Most of the adult utterances were either imitations of infant vocalizations or questions posed to the infant.

The second study focused exclusively on the father's verbal interactions with infants (Rebelsky & Hanks, 1971). In this study a 24-hour tape recording was made every two weeks over the first three months of life. Seven father-son and three father-daughter pairs were studied. The mean daily total of fa-ther-to-child vocalizations was an astounding 37.7 seconds (yes, seconds). Fathers tended to verbalize more to their daughters at the second and fourth postnatal weeks, but by the third month they verbalized more to their sons. Over the first three months, there was an overall *decrease* in the vocalizations directed to both sexes, although the effect was strongest for vocalizations directed to daughters. This pattern of vocal behavior differs from that of maternal vocal behavior over the same age span. Mothers gradually *increased* their vocalizations (for both sexes) over the first three months. At three weeks mothers of male infants vocalized more, but by three months mothers of female infants vocalized more (Moss, 1967). It has been suggested that these data may reflect the emergent organization of mother-daughter and father-son dyadic social pairings as early as the third month of life (Fitzgerald, in press).

These studies are certainly no basis for firm conclusions regarding the long-term implications of father-infant verbal interaction. In fact, the studies pose an interesting paradox. If fathers spend an average of eight hours a week playing with their children, but only talk to them about 40 seconds a day, one wonders what kinds of games they play. Only silent ones? Clearly, this inconsistency must be clarified in future research.

RECEPTIVE LANGUAGE

As the infant's waking hours increase during the latter part of the first year, so too does its overall exposure to the conversations of parents, sib-lings, visitors in the home, and persons encountered outside the home. Ob-viously the infant and toddler spend much more time listening to speech than they spend producing it.

Listening is the *receptive* component of language, and speaking is the ex-pressive component. No one has studied receptive language more intensely than Bernard Friedlander. Using a cleverly constructed apparatus which at-taches to the infant's crib or playpen, Friedlander is able to obtain con-tinuous records of the infant's spontaneous discrimination of auditory stimuli (Friedlander, 1968, 1970). For example, one switch on the apparatus may activate a recording of mother's voice, while another may activate a recording of a female stranger's voice. Daily recording of the amount of time the infant activates one switch or the other reflects the baby's preference for one or the other stimuli. This apparatus could also be used to study such other variables as message redundancy, vocabulary, and voice intonation.

Friedlander (1970) has been especially critical of language theorists who neglect receptive language. He argues that a complete understanding of language development is not possible without intensive study of the processes the listening infant uses to decode and encode the grammatical characteristics of adult speech. His research has led him to conclude that the receptive and expressive aspects of speech differ in at least two important ways: *control* and *convergence-divergence*. Since the listener's task is one of accommodating the information contained in the speaker's message, his only opportunity for control comes when it is time to indicate that the message has or has not been understood. The speaker, on the other hand, has nearly complete control of what is said, how it is said, and when it is said.

Friedlander poses an interesting question concerning early parent-child language interactions. Suppose that during these interactions mother becomes increasingly aware of her child's ability to understand adult communications. As a result, she may adapt her conversational level to match her child's comprehension level and thereby strengthen the communication bond. One might also expect to find that fathers speak less to their young children because they are less cognizant of their children's comprehension level and therefore less skilled at adjusting their speech to that level. A vicious circle develops. Father does not think the child understands him (and indeed the child may not) so he does not freely engage the child in conversations. Further study of parent-toddler communication interactions is needed to determine whether or not these notions are correct. Nevertheless, at the intuitive level it makes sense that when a young child cannot understand parental communications, the general pattern of parent-child interaction is adversely affected.

Friedlander's second important distinction between receptive and expressive language concerns the degree to which speaking and listening reflect *convergent* or *divergent processes*. He suggests that listening is primarily a convergent process, whereas speaking is primarily a divergent process. Recall from the previous chapter Guilford's distinction between open, flexible divergent thinking and closed, restrictive convergent thinking. In Friedlander's analogous distinction, the listener is limited to processing the information contained in the message, whereas the speaker has nearly unlimited freedom to construct any sort of message and to move the pattern of communication in a number of different directions.

Control and convergence-divergence are not the only dimensions along which listening and speaking can be contrasted. Nevertheless, they are the first important psychological distinctions that have been made between speakers and listeners. Friedlander's empirical and theoretical emphasis on receptive language holds promise for an ultimate understanding of how the listening infant organizes early linguistic systems and subsequently becomes a speaker who follows the rules of phonology, syntax, and semantics. As is indicated in Table 8–2, the multiplicity of factors that might influence receptive language development illustrates well that at present we have more questions than answers regarding early language acquisition.

THE VERBAL REGULATION OF BEHAVIOR

Thus far, our discussion has emphasized the influence of other persons on the young child's language. However, language behavior is not restricted to conversations with others; we also talk to ourselves. When do we use language for self-communication? We use language for this purpose when we think (covertly or overtly), solve problems, or attempt to regulate our behavior.

Whereas, so far as we know, most adult self-communication is silent, much of the young child's self-communication is vocal. This self-communication is most frequently referred to as *egocentric speech*, and it is, of course, one aspect of the egocentric thought discussed in the previous chapter with regard to Piaget's theory of cognitive development. Egocentric speech can be observed in practically any three- or four-year-old child who talks continually while engaged in play, giving directions and/or commenting on various aspects of that play. In such instances, the child does not seem to be directing the communications to anyone except itself.

The noted Russian psychologist Vygotsky (1962) suggested that the function of egocentric speech is to direct or regulate behavior. Following Vygotsky's theory, Luria (1961) devised a method for studying the regulatory function of speech. The child is given a balloonlike bulb to squeeze, and the experimenter attempts to get the child to stop squeezing. When 18-month to two-year-old children were told to stop, they kept right on squeezing. Commands to stop were effective with three- and four-year-olds, but not nearly as

TABLE 8–2
Receptive language development in infancy: Processes and variables

A. Psychological domains and processes	b. Maturation
1. Pattern recognition	(1) Structural
a. Process: Signal shaping (stimulus	(2) Biochemical
selection, rejection, filtration,	(3) Neurophysiological
transformation)—from acoustics	c. Intelligence
to perception	d. Sex
b. Materials	2. Signal/message
(1) Acoustical-verbal segments	a. Acoustical properties
(2) Speech stream	b. Speaker identity
2. Induction and elaboration of	c. Linguistic properties
rule systems	(1) Intonation
a. Phonological, referential, and	(2) Rate and order
grammatical categories	(3) Vocabulary
b. Emergence of communication	(4) Complexity
competence	(5) Redundancy
c. Whole/part, part/whole infer-	(6) Novelty/familiarity
ences	d. Repetition
d. Toward "linguistic autonomy"	e. Concurrent visual and tactile
(decreased reliance on gesture,	cues
intonation, context, and other	f. Adaptive significance
supplementary cues)	3. Family/social
3. Psychodynamics	a. Birth order, siblings
a. Ego	b. Family size
b. Affect	c. Affective tone
c. Social interaction	d. "Infant inclusion"
d. Motivation	e. Contingency awareness
e. Anxiety and assurance	f. Patterns & routines (stable versus
	irregular)
B. Dimensions of variability	g. Model stability/diversity
1. Infant	4. Developmental stages: terra
a. System integrity	incognita (categories not specified)

Source: From B. Z. Friedlander, "Receptive language development in infancy: Issues and problems," *Merrill-Palmer Quarterly*, 1970, *16*, 7–51. With permission of the author and the Merrill-Palmer Institute.

effective as telling themselves to stop. In general, the rhythmic pattern of the command was a more influential regulator than the actual meaning of the command. Thus, preschoolers given commands in the pattern "stop-stop" squeezed the bulb in rhythm with the patterned commands. By four or five years of age, adult commands were effective inhibitors of bulb squeeze-ing. Although this task involves only the inhibition of behavior it probably closely parallels what happens when parents attempt to teach their small children the meaning of *no* or *don't touch.* The toddler's initial orienting response to the spoken command "no" habituates all too rapidly!

Not all parental commands are intended to inhibit behavior: many are given in an effort to induce action. Often parents give both types of com-mands in sequence: "Steven, stop crying and pick up your toys." Luria (1961) has used the bulb-squeezing task to study activation-inhibition aspects of verbal regulation. The child is instructed to squeeze the bulb when a stimulus light is on (activation) and not to squeeze it when the stimulus light is off or when a different colored light comes on (inhibition). Children only 2½ years of age were able to comply with the activation instructions. But as in the case cited above, children under the age of five had great difficulty cognizing the inhibition instructions.

Strommen (1973) has adapted an old children's game, Simon Says, to study even more complex aspects of the verbal regulation of behavior. Ac-cording to Strommen, playing Simon Says is more difficult than Luria's bulb-squeezing task. First, in Simon Says each instruction given to the child is in fact an instruction to respond. The only difference between the activation and inhibition instructions is that for activation the instructions begin with the words "Simon says. . . ." Second, Simon Says requires a different motor response on each trial, whereas in Luria's task the child's response is the same throughout. Third, the activation signal and one part of the instructions for responding are verbal, requiring the child to make a more difficult dis-crimination.

Strommen played the Simon Says game with children in preschool, kinder-garten, and the first and third grades. The results indicated that children of all age levels had little difficulty with activation trials. In inhibition trials preschoolers made the most errors, followed in very tidy order by kin-dergarteners, first graders, and third graders. At all age levels, girls made fewer errors than boys. Strommen suggests that the sex difference may reflect the more rapid cortical maturation of girls and their general superiority in verbal skills. However, she cautions against drawing hasty conclusions, since other verbal regulation studies have not reported sex differences.

What tentative conclusions may be drawn regarding the child's ability to activate or inhibit behavior in response to verbal instructions? There is clear evidence to suggest that even toddlers can respond appropriately when adults give them verbal instructions that are designed to activate their be-havior. On the other hand, it is equally clear that children under five can inhibit behavior only with considerable difficulty. But if young children can verbalize the inhibition command, response inhibition is facilitated. In other words, the very young child seems to be more responsive to self-admonitions than to the admonitions of others.

INDIVIDUAL DIFFERENCES IN LANGUAGE DEVELOPMENT

In most popular child-rearing books, the data on language acquisition are usually presented as normative developmental milestones. When does baby say its first word, attend to human voices, name objects, or combine words into sentences? Table 8–3 lists 25 such normative milestones. Although these data are extremely useful and important for understanding the sequence of language development and for assessing deviations from the norm, they may be a source of great discomfort for many parents. "What is wrong with my child? She says only 5 words when according to the book she should be saying 22." The important information glossed over by normative data is the marked individual variation in the ages at which children reach the various levels of development. If a child's behavior does not measure up to the norm, it does not necessarily follow that the child is retarded or deficient. The normal range of behavior is a very wide range indeed. On the other hand, it does have limits. Thus, when parents become concerned because their child is not performing within the normal range, they should consult a professional rather than rely exclusively on popular child-rearing texts.

Many investigators have studied individual differences in language behavior, too many, in fact, to permit more than a composite overview of several of the more widely documented differences. For thorough reviews, consult Harris (in press) and Maccoby and Jacklin (1974). Here we will briefly summarize differences attributable to sex, family size, multiple births, socioeconomic class, bilingualism, and institutionalization.

TABLE 8–3
Normative ages at which 25 selected language milestones are achieved

Age (months)	Milestone achieved	Age (months)	Milestone achieved
1	Differential cries	9	Vocalizes bye-bye
1½–2	Emits several vocalizations	11	Imitates syllables
2	Attends to speaking voice	12	Two words or more
3	Cooing (babbling)	11–15	Understands simple commands
4	Localizes a speaking voice		
4	Vocalizes in self-initiated play	15	First imitative word
		16–20	Understands prohibitions
5	Vocalizes eagerness	17–22	Names objects
5	Vocalizes displeasure	17–18	Asks with words
6	"Talks" to a person	18	Points to facial features
6–7	Vocalizes satisfaction	20	Names two objects
7	Vocalizes ma or da	21	Joins two words in speech
8	Vocalizes recognition	23	First phrase
9	Listens to familiar words		

Source: Adapted from D. McCarthy, "Language development in children," in L. Carmichael (Ed.), *Manual of child psychology*, 2d ed. (New York: Wiley, 1954) with permission of John Wiley & Sons, Inc.

Sex differences

Many investigators have found that girls surpass boys in nearly all aspects of language behavior, including the length of utterances, comprehension of speech, articulation, the number of words spoken, the number of different words spoken, amount of speech, and sentence complexity. On the other hand, boys talk faster and have more speech disorders than girls. Bear in mind that in many instances the very nature of individual differences has produced conflicting results. Moreover, very little is known about the long-term stability of these differences. In some cases, early sex differences seem to be reflections of the female's faster rate of development. For example, Smith (1926) found that at ages two and three, girls had larger vocabularies than boys and that the difference had disappeared by four years of age.

Family size

Only children, especially girls, show accelerated language development. Most theorists assume that this can be attributed to the high degree of adult contact enjoyed by only children. Surprisingly, however, there appear to be no substantive differences as a function of ordinal position. That is, the language behavior of firstborn children does not differ consistently from that of second- or third-born children. More than likely, *density* (the spacing of births) is one important determinant of whether ordinal position correlates with language performance. If children are closely spaced, parents may find it difficult to distribute their attention equitably. One might expect the children receiving the least adult attention to show the slowest language development.

With regard to multiple births, the evidence is much more consistent. Multiple birth shows an almost linear relationship to the rate of language development, with twins being slower than singletons, triplets slower than twins, and so on. However, one should not conclude that multiple birth in itself is the cause of slow language development. It is difficult for parents to give as much attention to each of two or three infants of identical age as to only one infant.

Socioeconomic class

Language skills are consistently higher in members of upper-class families than for members of lower-class families. Investigators have found that upper-class children excel over lower-class children in articulation, sentence length, the use of different parts of speech, and amount of speech. It is difficult to pinpoint the precise causes for these differences, although they are probably related to such factors as the relative use of physical versus verbal forms of discipline, the acceptability of verbal versus physical modes of expressing aggression, the educational materials available in the home and the resources utilized outside the home, and the amount of time parents interact with children. Clearly, research in this area should move in the direction of specifying the variables producing class differences in language behavior rather than merely continuing to demonstrate a rather consistent finding.

Bilingualism

Because of the steady stream of immigrants to the United States, American educators have had to grapple with the problems of bilingual children for many years. Early studies indicated that children from bilingual homes suffered marked language retardation as compared with children from monolingual homes. However, the plain truth is that many bilingual children have no difficulty whatsoever in mastering two languages. Obviously, it is not the simple presence of two languages that adversely affects the learning of either.

Smith's studies provide the most definitive information yet obtained on the effects of bilingualism (see Smith & Kasdin, 1961). Very generally, these studies demonstrated differences between bilingual and monolingual children in various aspects of speech, although bilingualism per se did not retard the development of speech. Moreover, Smith concluded that when children received their language instruction from different sources, interference was minimized. For example, in a culture in which Spanish is the native language the child might learn Spanish from father and English from mother. If bilingualism per se does not dictate language retardation, what other factors might covary with bilingualism to suppress language development? Smith's studies may hold one answer to this complex problem. Comparing the vocabulary growth of bilingual and monolingual children, Smith (1949) found that only the brightest bilingual children were able to match the vocabulary size of monolingual children. Perhaps bright children have sufficient cognitive facilities to master two labels for each object and two grammatical structures, whereas less bright children are cognitively overwhelmed by the demands of learning two languages.

Institutionalization

The effects of institutional care on language development can be summarized rather neatly—institutionalization retards language development. Most studies in this area report language retardation and/or speech defects in 50 percent or more of the subjects studied. What cannot be summarized so neatly are the answers to such questions as these: How long must the child be institutionalized for language retardation to occur? Is institutionally produced language retardation reversible, or is the retardation permanent? Is institutionalization itself responsible for language retardation, or does the quality of the institution have an important bearing on the results? Obviously, not all institutionalized children show language retardation. What factors permit some institutionalized children to be more successful than others? Despite voluminous research on the effects of institutionalization, there are no definitive answers to any of these questions. Suffice it to say that poor institutional care is extremely detrimental to language development.

SUMMARY

Despite the fact that research has touched upon nearly every major aspect of language development, many questions remain unanswered. Although various cognitive models have been advanced, it is not yet known how the infant processes language information. Study of the infant as listener and of parent-infant communication patterns is beginning to provide useful information concerning the infant's transition from the prelinguistic period of language development to the linguistic period.

Any successful theory of language acquisition must take both biological and environmental determinants into account. Language is an epigenetic constructive process. The infant develops cognitive structures which are utilized to decode and encode structural properties of adult language. How these cognitive structures are constructed and how they in turn are used by the infant is not yet fully understood. However, suggestions that they represent innate capacities rather than epigenetically constructed processes seem unwarranted. Although reinforcement contributes to the acquisition of language and perhaps to the development of higher-order cognitive abstractions, reinforcement theory alone cannot account for all language acquisition. This is particularly true of linguistic competence.

It is a well-documented truism that parents influence language development. It may be that maternal influences are greater than paternal influences. However, we must be cautious about drawing conclusions until considerably more is known about the father's role as caregiver in general and as a stimulant for language development in particular.

On the whole, children seem to acquire concrete nouns and action verbs before they acquire other parts of speech. Nevertheless, there are individual differences in early vocabulary growth which appear to be related to individual differences in maternal-infant communication patterns. Children whose language is dominated and controlled by their mothers tend to have less advanced language skills than do children whose mothers adapt their speech to their children's cognitive level and encourage their children to speak.

General factors that have been associated with slow language development include multiple birth, ordinal position, bilingualism, institutionalization, the sex of the child, and social class. None of these factors can be viewed as exclusive causative determinants of slow language development. For example, many bilingual children have no difficulty in mastering two languages simultaneously.

SUGGESTED ADDITIONAL READING

Brown, R.   *A first language: The early stages.* Cambridge, Mass.: Harvard University Press, 1973.

Gardner, R. A., & Gardner, B. T.   Teaching sign language to a chimpanzee, *Science,* 1969, *165,* 664–672.

Harris, L. J.   Sex differences in the growth and use of language. In E. Donelson & J. Gullahorn (Eds.), *Women: A Psychological Perspective.* New York: Wiley, in press (1977).

Lenneberg, E. H., & Lenneberg, E. (Eds.).   *Foundations of Language Development.* Vols. 1 and 2. New York: Academic Press, 1975.

BOX 9–1
Study questions

How do infants and toddlers contribute to the socialization process?

What adaptive function does the attachment of infant to caregiver serve?

What is a social behavior?

If you were a baby, whom would you prefer: mother, father, or stranger?

What causes babies to laugh?

When do infants recognize their mothers?

Do all babies like to be cuddled? Do all caregivers like to cuddle babies?

What are infants afraid of?

What factors influence the exploratory behavior of infants and toddlers?

What do fathers think about their newborn infants, and what role do they play as caregivers?

When do young children know their correct gender?

When do young children become aware of sex-role stereotypes?

9

SOCIALIZATION: ORGANIZATION OF SOCIAL BEHAVIOR

Much of the historical literature concerning parent-child interaction has rested on the assumption that one could easily understand the child's social behavior and personality development by studying parental patterns of child rearing. The historical model was one of the *unidirectional* flow of influence from parent to child. Perhaps because of the residual influence of John Watson's radical behaviorism, little attention was paid to the possibility that the infant might play an active and influential role in determining the quality and/or quantity of caregiving it received. If the problem of understanding socialization were one of specifying the parental antecedents of the infant's social and personality development a major portion of the problem might have already been solved. There is a vast literature demonstrating various parental influences on the social behavior of the child. However, the problem is the much more difficult one of understanding the complex interactions of at least two active agents during socialization. Indeed, socialization is well pictured as a dialectical process in which each new level of development requires both parent and child to restructure their behavioral reactions to each other.

RECIPROCAL SOCIALIZATION

Richard Bell (1968) was one of the first authors to point out the fallacy of the unidirectional flow model of socialization. He suggested that productive study of socialization is possible only if one accepts the premise that parent and child mutually influence the process. Reviewing the evidence supportive

207

of congenital differences among children, particularly in assertiveness and person orientation, Bell concluded that these differences could elicit different patterns of maternal caregiving. Children high in person orientation tend to be more attentive to their mothers and to reinforce maternal attempts to engage them in social interactions. Children low in person orientation tend to elicit less nurturance and to receive more physical punishment from caregivers. Evidence of trait stability from the newborn period, when environmental influences are still at a minimum, provides further support for the view that the newborn is less of a tabula rasa than had been previously supposed (Thomas, Chess, & Birch, 1968).

Rheingold (1968) has offered four propositions related to early socialization that give perspective to the interactive nature of the process. Three of the propositions address the infant's role in socialization, and one addresses the parents' role. (1) From the moment of birth the infant is a social organism. The infant is a member of a social dyad (infant-caregiver) and is born into a family which is itself part of a larger social unit. (2) The infant behaves socially. That is, the infant's behavior can elicit, maintain, or modify the behavior of others. (3) The infant socializes others. Often, the caregiver's daily routine is substantially modified to meet the infant's demands (to change a soiled diaper, to have a midnight feeding). These three propositions, however, do not mean that Rheingold is proposing a unidirectional model of socialization from infant to parent. Quite the contrary, as can be seen from the final proposition. (4) It is obviously the caregiver who provides the infant with an environment, with comfort and security, and with reinforcing information concerning the appropriateness of the infant's behavior. It is the caregiver who ultimately decides whether the baby's diaper will be changed or the midnight feeding will be forthcoming.

One important aspect of reciprocity is the degree to which the caregiver is aware of and responsive to the infant's signaled needs. One longitudinal investigation of mother-child interaction indicated that affectionate, happy, smiling toddlers had mothers with similar personality characteristics (Clarke-Stewart, 1973). Presumably, mother and infant had a smoothly flowing relationship satisfying to both. In another study, high-stimulation mothers were aware of their infants' needs, engaged them in nonroutine caregiving play, and provided rich auditory and tactile stimulation (Brody & Axelrad, 1971). Low-stimulation mothers restricted their interactions to routine caregiving chores and provided little sensory or social stimulation beyond that required for such chores. High maternal stimulation was related to high infant responsiveness, whereas low maternal stimulation was related to low infant responsiveness.

The fact that caregiver-infant interaction is not always equal does not contradict its reciprocal nature (Bell, 1974). Indeed, current studies of early social interaction clearly illustrate that the infant both influences and is influenced by parental behavior. That is, the infant both behaves socially and socializes others.

Attachment-dependence: Detachment-independence

The functional or adaptive significance of reciprocal socialization appears to be that of assisting the establishment of a special relationship between parent and child. Historically, this relationship was called *dependency;* more recently, it has been called *attachment.* Recall our discussion in Chapter 1 of the theoretical influences on developmental psychology. There we noted that social learning theorists set out to determine the behavioral components of dependency and to specify the critical child-rearing variables responsible for the child's dependence on its caregivers. This research led to a definition of dependency in terms of physical contact and behaviors related to seeking help, attention, or approval. Clearly, the implication was that the child is dependent on the parent, not the parent on the child. Psychological dependency was thought to be a learned outgrowth of the infant's physiological dependence on its caregivers. Recognizing that prolonged dependence must give way to greater autonomy and independence, social learning research explored parental techniques for encouraging or even demanding independence from their children. Once again, the emphasis was on parental influences on the child.

The concept of attachment implies something more than dependence. It implies a reciprocal social-emotional bond between infant and caregiver. But the character of the attachment relationship must change during the various stages of development. The infant and caregiver must detach themselves: they must change the nature of the social-emotional bond that is formed in infancy and early childhood. Attachment is not reducible to a specific behavior or set of behaviors. It is a construct much like "organization," "adaptation," "intelligence," or, for that matter, "learning." Conceptually, attachment is a social-emotional bond, an aspect of adaptation, which functions to assure survival of the species (Bowlby, 1969). Detachment, then, is a breaking away from this bond, or at least a change in its nature.

Without question, John Bowlby (1969) has offered the most comprehensive theoretical analysis of the concept of attachment. Bowlby cites five adaptive biobehavioral systems which are thought to prompt and solidify the social-emotional bond between infants and their caregivers. These biobehavioral systems are *crying, smiling, sucking, clinging,* and *following.* According to Bowlby, these systems provide for reciprocal interaction between infant and caregiver and form the behavioral substrate from which attachment is constructed. A sixth behavioral system, *mutual gaze* (eye-to-eye contact), has also been suggested (Robson, 1967).

The fact is that dependency and attachment, as well as independence and detachment, are difficult terms to distinguish. Operationally, the terms are defined by essentially the same behaviors. Maccoby and Masters offer one solution to the problem. Combining the operational ingredients of the two terms they define dependency *and* attachment as a class of behavior "that maintains contact of varying degrees of closeness between a child and one or more other individuals and elicits a reciprocal attentive and nurturant behavior from these individuals" (Maccoby & Masters, 1970, p. 75). This definition of dependency-attachment is consistent with our concept of socialization in its emphasis on the reciprocal nature of the process and on the child's active role in the process.

Throughout this chapter we will use the term *attachment,* primarily because we believe that for infancy and early childhood it implies a reciprocal social-emotional relationship that is not implicit in the concept of dependency. Moreover, we will focus our discussion of the organization of social behavior on several of the behavioral systems that are thought to regulate the emergence of the attachment relationship.

THE ORGANIZATION OF SOCIAL BEHAVIOR

Mutual gaze

The affective character of mutual gaze is difficult to describe. The subjective picture is one of caregiver and infant staring at each other and obviously enjoying the experience. Sometimes mutual gazes last for unusually long periods of time, far in excess of typical adult gaze durations. Not all mutual gazes are positive, however, for example a caregiver and young child may glare at each other following some misdeed committed by the child.

Mutual gaze emerges sometime between the third and the sixth postnatal week, just prior to the appearance of the first social smile. Apparently, mother and infant are equally skilled at initiating and terminating mutual gaze; however, about 94 percent of the time the infant initiates and/or terminates the interaction (Stern, 1974).

Studies with human adults (Kendon, 1967) indicate that gaze behavior has four important functions for their social interaction and communication: *cognitive* (encoding stimulus information); *monitoring* (using visual regard to check the listener's attentiveness, reactivity, and the like); *regulative* (eliciting or inhibiting the listener's responsivity); and *expressive* (indicating interest or a lack of interest). Stern offers a similar analysis of caregiver-infant mutual gaze but adds the interesting idea that mutual gaze may be the immediate forerunner of social play. Social play is viewed as an effort to maintain an optimal level of arousal throughout an ongoing pleasurable interaction. Play such as peekaboo and pat-a-cake obviously involves mutual gaze. Toddlers seem to derive great joy from "looking the other way" in response to a parent's "Where's my little Katherine?" only to squeal with delight when mutual gaze is reinstated. On a more cognitive level, Stern suggests that mutual gaze may be the mechanism regulating the formation of the infant's schema of human facial expressions.

What happens to the organization of social behavior when mutual gaze is not available as a regulator of caregiver-infant interaction? When this occurs, do caregivers and infants use other means for organizing the attach-

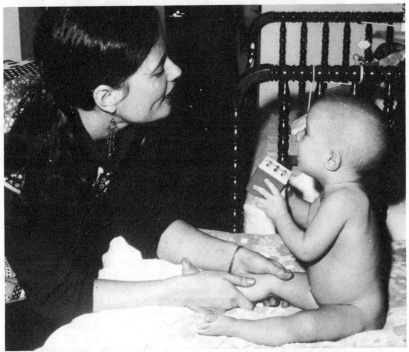

Photograph courtesy Paul Rochlen

FIGURE 9–1 Throughout the centuries writers have attempted to capture the essence of eye-to-eye contact. Cervantes once described the eyes as "silent tongues of love." Lord Byron wrote, "And oh, that eye was in itself a soul." Psychologists too are interested in eye contact as it relates to the regulation of adult social interactions and of the attachment between caregiver and infant.

ment relationship? Apparently they do. Mothers of blind infants have difficulty interpreting their infants' facial expressions (Fraiberg, 1974) primarily because facial emotional expressions are not well differentiated in blind infants. Sighted infants have a rich repertoire of facial expressions, many of which reflect adult emotions, such as delight or happiness, sobriety or attentiveness, anguish or distress, and boredom. Recall that sighted infants carry the major responsibility for initiating and terminating mutual gaze. Obviously, the blind infant can neither use visual behavior to initiate or terminate an interaction nor use vision to gain feedback from adult facial expressions.

Nevertheless, Fraiberg found that the general sequence of attachment was the same for blind and sighted infants, although somewhat delayed for blind infants. Apparently, blind infants make use of other sensory modalities, especially auditory and tactile modalities, to organize early social relations. Mothers also compensate for their infants' visual deficit by providing extra

FIGURE 9–2 Babies show many different facial expressions. These babies are participating in an experiment designed to study the development of facial expressions in relation to events in the environment. One might guess that these babies are

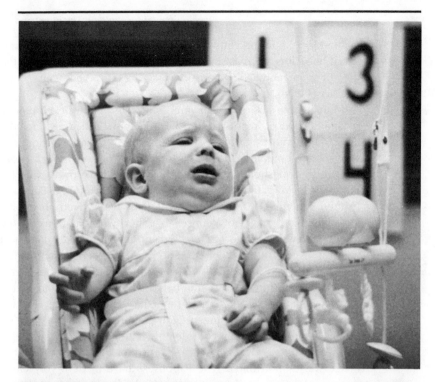

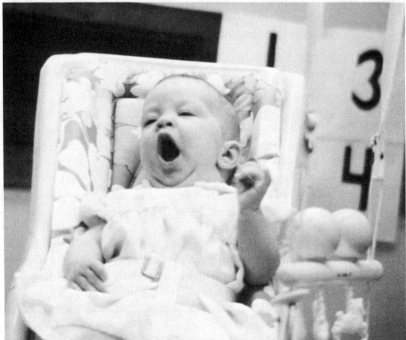

Photographs courtesy Suzanne Siemering

showing (a) delight or happiness, (b) sobriety or attentiveness, (c) anguish or fret-fulness, and (d) boredom or fatigue.

tactile-kinesthetic and auditory stimulation to convey affectivity and to elicit social behaviors, such as smiling. Still, blind infants do not develop the degree of spontaneity characteristic of facial expressiveness in sighted infants (Fraiberg, 1974).

Mutual gaze also plays an important role in the development of self-recognition. Most infant-toddler developmental schedules include an item "reaction to mirror image" to assess the child's social behavior as well as its self-recognition. When does self-recognition occur? There is no clear answer to this question, although the Papouseks have devised a clever technique for investigating its early development (Papousek & Papousek, 1974). In their experiment, five-month-old infants were given an opportunity to view television images of themselves under two conditions. In one condition the television image was a tape recording of the baby made prior to the viewing session. In the other condition the baby viewed an image televised "live." The taped images allowed for mutual gaze, but there was no contingent relationship between the behavior of the image and that of the infant viewing the image. Conversely, the activity of the live image was obviously completely contingent with that of the infant being televised. Although some infants spent considerably long periods of time gazing at their televised live image, an overall preference for the noncontingent videotape image was demonstrated. The Papouseks have made a very clever use of instrumentation to study an aspect of early development, and we can look forward to gaining new information on the development of self-recognition as their research continues.

Smiling

The baby's first smiles are elicited by either exogenous stimulation (auditory, tactile, olfactory, visual) or unspecified endogenous stimulation. Despite widespread belief, there is little evidence to link "gas pains" with newborn smiling. The smiles of newborns appear to be nonsocial, but since they represent the facial configurations which will later be called "social" smiles we should be cautious about referring to them as reflexive.

In any event, we can be certain that social smiling appears shortly after mutual gaze is established, or sometime between the second week and the second month of life for most babies. Initially, smiles are given out indiscriminately—baby smiles as generously to strangers as to familiar caregivers. From the fourth month through the first year, smiling becomes increasingly selective. Now baby reserves the bulk of its smiles for familiar caregivers and is much less likely to smile at strangers.

Ahrens' (1954) classic study suggests that smiling is elicited by facial configurations that include the eyes at a minimum. Gradually, more and more facial details are necessary until, at about the fifth to the seventh month, smiling is most easily elicited by the whole facial configuration. In addition to facial characteristics and familiarity, dimensionality gains increasing importance as an aspect of the natural stimuli for eliciting smiling. The young infant may smile at a human face whether it is a two-dimensional photo-graph or a three-dimensional live face. However, the six- to seven-month-old shows a marked preference for the live face. Throughout the second and third years, smiling gradually becomes indiscriminate again.

The initial control mechanisms regulating smiling are biological. Con-genitally blind infants and sighted infants show the same onset of early smiling behavior. However, since visual feedback is not available to blind infants, their smiles are usually less expressive and somewhat disorganized. That the blind infant's smile does not disappear completely suggests that visual feedback is neither a necessary nor a sufficient condition for smiling. As we have already noted, mothers give their blind infants more tactile-kinesthetic and auditory stimulation in order to elicit smiling and to facili-tate the development of affect.

Although the initial control mechanisms for smiling may be biological, much of its organization is dependent upon reinforcement. Brackbill (1958) demonstrated the operant conditioning of smiling in 3½- to 4½-month-old infants. Reinforcement consisted of smiling back at baby, speaking softly, and picking up baby. Baby was then jostled, patted, and talked to for 30 seconds. This complex procedure does not allow one to specify the effec-tiveness of specific aspects of reinforcement. Do babies need to be talked to, smiled at, patted, jostled, and jiggled in order to reinforce their smiling behavior? Apparently not. Brossard and DeCarie (1968) suggest that the kinesthetic component of complex social reinforcement may be extremely important. They compared the relative effectiveness of visual, auditory, tactile, and kinesthetic stimuli, singly and in combinations, for reinforcing infant smiling. The only significant difference they observed when compar-ing the time required for each group to reach criterion was that between the least effective reinforcer (tactile) and the most effective reinforcer (visual and kinesthetic—smiling and picking up the baby). They also found that in-fants whose reinforcement involved some kind of kinesthetic stimulation conditioned faster than the other infants.

Brossard and DeCarie's infants were institution-reared, whereas those studied by Brackbill were home-reared. Therefore, we do not know whether handling is an equally potent reinforcer for home-reared and institution-reared infants. However, it is clear that kinesthetic stimulation in the form of handling is a powerful component of social reinforcement for modifying infant smiling.

Laughter   Many theorists have offered analyses of laughter; however, few empirical studies of laughter have been conducted. Some authors suggest that laughter is a response made to relieve tension. Others suggest that laughing is used to make fun of others, reflects a response to incongruity or surprise, or represents simple playfulness. Ambrose (1963) suggested that laughter, like mutual gaze, is used in a regulatory way to sustain or terminate social interactions. Recently, Sroufe and Wunsch (1972) reported a detailed analysis of situations which elicit laughter from 4 months to 12 months of life. Their results indicate that social and tactile stimuli are most effective with 4-month-olds, whereas social and visual stimuli are most effective with 12-month-olds. Nevertheless, throughout the first year of life many different stimulus situations involving many different sensory modalities are associated with laughter.

Early studies with older children reported that the laughter of two-year-olds was most often related to motion or to socially incongruous situations (Kenderine, 1931). For three-year-olds, socially incongruous situations were most likely to produce laughter. Laughter elicited by motion can often be observed when toddlers and preschoolers are spinning round and round or are being tossed into the air by a familiar caregiver. Daddy creeping about the floor barking like a dog can be equally laughter provoking. Recently, Sherman (1975) reported a joyous, exuberant group reaction which he called *group glee*. Children from 2½ to 5 years of age were observed in a preschool setting for 596 lesson periods. Group glee was defined as a positive, affective state involving at least 50 percent of the group. Behaviorally,

Photograph courtesy Paul Rochlen

FIGURE 9–3 What makes young children laugh?

group glee was indicated by vigorous laughter, chantlike or random screaming, and increased physical activity, such as hand clapping and jumping up
and down. Sherman found that group glee usually lasted four to nine seconds and was most likely to occur in groups with both boys and girls consisting of about seven–nine children in all. Smaller groups of only one sex
were suggested as least likely to produce much group glee. In most instances, group glee did not disrupt the lesson. When it did disrupt the lesson,
the teacher had in most instances failed to provide a nicely flowing organized program.

Physical contact

In their study of the development of social attachments, Schaffer and
Emerson (1964a) observed that infants seemed to have different preferred
modes of physical contact. In a subsequent study, they identified two groups
of infants on the basis of the type of handling interaction they seemed to
prefer (Schaffer & Emerson, 1964b). *Cuddly* infants responded positively and
consistently to maternal attempts to snuggle and cuddle and actively sought
close contact interactions. *Noncuddly* infants were characterized by their
active resistence to close physical contact.

Mothers were also differentiated into two groups on the basis of their
desire to handle their infants; that is, some mothers were *handlers* and others
were *nonhandlers*. How does a cuddly infant react to a nonhandling mother?
The infant actively seeks cuddling from other members of the family and
through persistent effort generally receives such support. How does a
handling mother react to a noncuddling infant? Schaffer and Emerson suggest that in such instances the mother modifies her behavior to meet the
demands of her infant. Several authors, including Bowlby, have suggested
that contact with the mother has special significance for the social and
emotional development of the child. The research we have reviewed concerning the interaction of mothers and blind infants certainly supports the
view that contact or handling is an important aspect of early social
interaction.

Social pacification   In our earlier discussion of pacification (see Chapter
3), we noted that continuous, monotonous stimulation from any sensory
modality has a pacifying effect on young infants. This conclusion was based
on laboratory demonstrations of the pacifying effectiveness of nonsocial
physical stimulation and involved newborns for the most part. What about
social stimulation and a more natural interaction between mother and infant? Is social pacification as effective as or more effective than nonsocial
pacification?

To investigate this question, Davidson (1973) first rated mothers and
their 9- to 12-week-old infants according to the frequency of close physical
contact during an interview. High-contact infants spent most of their time
in close physical contact with mother during the interview. Mothers reported that these babies also seemed to need a lot of snuggling at home.

Low-contact infants were only minimally interested in close snuggling during the interview or at home. These two groups, selected from an initially much larger sample, were observed under two nonsocial pacification conditions (swaddled and unswaddled) and two social pacification conditions (mother and stranger). Neither the mothers nor the stranger were aware that handling or contact preference were being investigated.

Davidson found that low-contact infants protested the motor restraint of swaddling more vigorously, cried longer, and took more time to fall asleep than did high-contact infants. In general, the low-contact infants' reaction to swaddling supports Schaffer and Emerson's suggestion that non-cuddlers dislike restriction of movement and close contact. Davidson adds to this suggestion the idea that low-contact infants may have a greater need for stimulus variation than do high-contact infants. Both mother and stranger seemed to be aware of this need, for they gave low-contact infants more frequent and more active handling (bouncing, jostling, fast rocking) than they gave high-contact infants. However, comparison of the behavior of mother and stranger disclosed an interesting difference in their reaction to the babies. The stranger was more likely to handle low-contact infants during quiet periods. Perhaps the mothers had already learned to avoid their low-contact infants during such periods. On the other hand, the stranger's persistent handling of low-contact infants independent of their state may have produced some side effects. For example, low-contact infants smiled, vocalized, and initiated visual regard more to stranger than to mother. High-contact infants vocalized more to mother but showed no difference in smiling to mother and stranger. Obviously, we cannot conclude that the stranger's extra handling of low-contact infants caused greater social responsiveness, but a strong relationship is certainly evident.

Pacification has been interpreted as a passive process involving subcortical neural structures (Brackbill, 1971). Continuous exogenous stimulation of a generally moderate intensity quiets baby without baby's active participation. Davidson's study suggests that the passive model may be only part of the story, and that the model may be restricted to the newborn period. As long as exogenous stimulation is capable of distracting baby from endogenous stimulation, the passive model may hold. As baby becomes a more active information processing organism—when the amount of exogenous stimulation is not adequate to counterbalance endogenous stimulation—a more active model may be required. This seems likely for the low-contact infant, and it may also be true for older infants and toddlers or even, for that matter, adults. Consider, for example, a situation in which the radio is turned on to pacify a three-year-old at bedtime only to have the child ask that the channel be changed so that a different type of music is playing.

Strangers, strange places, and separation

Fear   Knowledge of the things that cause fear reactions in older children is based primarily on data obtained by asking children "What are the things to be afraid of?" Using this self-report technique, Maurer (1965) found that the fears of kindergarten and first-grade children most frequently involved animals, people, darkness, spooks, and machines. Changes in the subject matter of fears occur during middle childhood. At that time, fears related to animals, darkness, and spooks decline, while those related to people, natural hazards, and machines increase.

Obviously, we cannot rely on verbal self-report techniques to gain knowledge about the fears of infants and toddlers. Nor, for that matter, can we be certain that the observed emotion we think is fear is not some more general distress reaction. Nevertheless, most investigators do assume some continuity between early distress reactions, such as crying, freezing, or hiding, and such later fear behaviors as running away, crying, or trembling.

Infants and toddlers become distressed or show fear in a variety of situations. In one study, infants and toddlers were placed on a visual cliff; put into the presence of a stranger, a masked adult, or a mechanical object; or stimulated with a loud noise (Scarr & Salapatek, 1970). Although the main purpose of the study was to investigate emotional behavior, various aspects of cognitive and motor behavior were also observed. The results suggested that fear reactions make their first appearance during the second half of the first year of life, reach their peak during the second year, and stabilize or decline thereafter (see Figure 9–4).

About half of the seven- to nine-month-old infants showed fear of depth when placed on the visual cliff. By 13–18 months, however, distress reactions were observed in all infants when they were placed on the cliff. The infants' behavior on the cliff provided a prime example of the interrelations of the motor, visual, and emotional systems. Infants who had not yet begun to creep were not distressed when placed on the cliff, suggesting that the organization of depth perception and emotional distress are in part dependent upon the development of self-locomotion.

Generally negative infants who had low response thresholds and poor rhythmicity and adaptability were more likely to show fear in all experimental situations. Cuddlers were less afraid of the jack-in-the-box, the dog, and the visual cliff, suggesting to the investigators that there may be a relationship between the amount of handling an infant receives and its ability to deal with fear-inducing situations. In other words, infants who receive adequate handling may be more secure when placed in novel situations. Finally, there was no evidence of a direct link between object permanence and fear of strangers.

Although studies such as Scarr and Salapatek's provide important information regarding the stability and generality of fear reactions in both social and nonsocial settings, the most extensively investigated aspect of fear in infancy is that involving fear of strangers. However, before one can fear a stranger, one must be able to recognize differences between familiar and unfamiliar persons. Consequently, before we consider stranger fear, we will consider a prior developmental step, the discrimination of mother from stranger.

Subjects showing any fear (in percent)

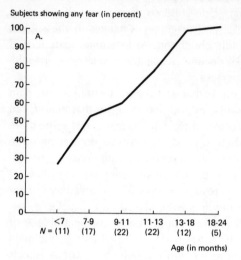

Subjects showing any fear (in percent)

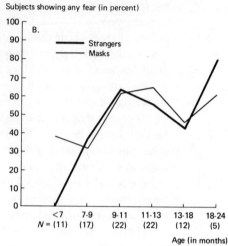

Subjects showing any fear (in percent)

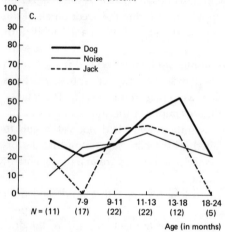

Source: Adapted and reprinted from S. Scarr and P. Salapatek, "Patterns of fear development during infancy," *Merrill-Palmer Quarterly,* 1970, *16*, 53–90. With permission of the authors and the Merrill-Palmer Institute.

FIGURE 9–4a. The percentage of infants showing fear of the visual cliff at various ages. **9–4b.** The percentage of infants showing fear of strangers and masks at various ages. **9–4c.** The percentage of infants showing fear of the jack-in-the-box, the mechanical dog, and the loud noise at various ages.

The discrimination of mother from stranger   The development of attachment presupposes that the infant can perceptually discriminate its primary caregiver (usually its mother) from other adults. Since the infant spends so much time with its mother, it should not be surprising that mother gradually becomes a very familiar object.

Psychiatric, clinical, and developmental theory has assumed that infants acquire the ability to perceptually discriminate familiar from unfamiliar human faces between the fourth and the sixth month of life. The appearance of selective smiling and of differential emotional responsivity to familiar and unfamiliar adults is often offered as evidence of baby's ability to discriminate mother from stranger. However, selective smiling and selective emotional responsivity are emotional behaviors that may reflect a level of behavior organization more sophisticated than that implied by perceptual discrimination. In other words, it seems reasonable that baby must first learn to perceptually discriminate familiar from unfamiliar before emotional differentiation is possible.

Recent studies clearly indicate that by four months of age infants have already discriminated mother from stranger. In one experiment, one-, two-, and four-month-old infants were presented with two-dimensional television videotape pictures of their mother, a stranger, and three geometric designs (Fitzgerald, 1968). One-month-old infants showed greater responsivity to mother than to stranger, as measured by the amount of pupillary dilation elicited by the pictures. However, the magnitude of the difference in the response level to mother and stranger, though large, was not statistically significant. Two-month-old infants showed no difference in their responsivity, but the stranger received significantly larger responses from four-

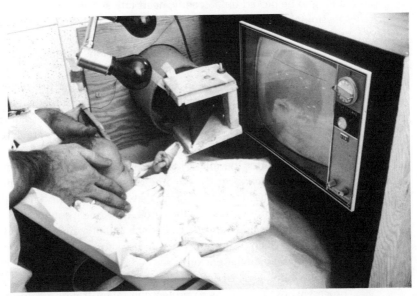

Source: Brackbill, Y. & Fitzgerald, H. E. Development of the sensory analyzers during infancy. In L. P. Lipsitt & H. W. Reese (Eds.) *Advances in child development and behavior.* New York: Academic Press, Inc., 1969. With permission of Academic Press, Inc.

FIGURE 9–5 An infant is gazing at the television picture of his mother as an experimenter photographs his pupillary reactions to this stimulus.

month-olds than did the mother. This suggests that by four months of age
mother may be such a familiar stimulus that, given the choice, baby reacts
more to the novel stranger than to its mother.

There is conflicting evidence regarding mother-stranger discrimination
at younger ages. Carpenter and her associates (Carpenter, 1972; Carpenter,
Tecce, Stechler, & Friedman, 1970) reported successful discrimination of
mother from stranger by infants from two weeks to seven weeks of age.
However, Laub and McCluskey (1975) found that ten-week-old infants were
unable to discriminate mother from stranger on the basis of visual stimulation alone. When mother's voice was combined with her face and stranger's
voice with her face, successful discrimination did occur. Since ten-week-
old infants can discriminate mother's voice from stranger's voice (Boyd,
1975), the safest conclusion is that mother-stranger discrimination occurs
sometime during the first three months of life. Whether infants less than
one-month-old can discriminate mother from stranger remains an open
question.

Stranger fear When baby comes into contact with a stranger, the
stranger often receives one or more negative reactions rather than a hoped-
for positive reaction. Although this is especially true if baby is between 6
and 12 months old, negative reactions to strangers can be observed well into
the toddler and preschool years. Such negative reactions may include any
of the following: crying with or without tears, gaze aversion, hiding the face,
fretful facial expressions, getting close to or hiding behind the caregiver, and
asking to be picked up. Recently, heart rate acceleration has been used as a
physiological index of stranger fear (Waters, Matas, & Sroufe, 1975). When
an approaching stranger was about to pick up the baby, a marked heart rate
acceleration occurred along with gaze aversion. Neither behavior was observed when mother picked up the baby.

Many attempts have been made to account for the development of
stranger fear. In the psychoanalytic tradition, stranger fear is tied to the fear
of being separated from a love object, usually the mother (Spitz, 1950). In
the learning tradition, cognitive and perceptual processes are thought to play
an important role. For example, Schaffer (1971) suggests that stranger fear
emerges only after the infant has achieved the ability to recognize stimuli
as known and unknown. Through perceptual learning, the infant first gains
the ability to discriminate objects, that is, it comes to know that mother
and stranger differ in the way they look, feel, smell, sound, and so on. Then
a response selection process guides the infant's approach and avoidance
tendencies, which in turn provide the basis for emotional discrimination of
familiar and unfamiliar persons.

In the ethological tradition stranger fear is thought to reflect an adaptive
process whose purpose is to protect the infant from predators and thus to
assure its survival. Working within this tradition, Bronson (1971) suggests
that stranger fear is but one aspect of a more general "wariness of visual
novelty." During roughly the first half-year of life, unpatterned or disor-

ganized visual stimulation tends to distress infants. During these early months, infants are most effectively pacified by maternal contact. Later in infancy and early in toddlerhood, novel visual stimuli evoke distress reactions, but now only mother's visual presence is required to give the infant sufficient security to deal with the novel stimulation. Wariness to visual novelty is overcome when the young child is able to deal competently with visual stimulation when mother is absent.

Investigators continue to argue the relative merits of these theoretical accounts of stranger fear. However, the fact is that all of these theories offer a more or less reasonable explanation of the behavior. What none of them adequately explain is why so many infants never show fear of strangers.

The universality of stranger fear   Until recently, stranger fear was regarded as a universal characteristic of human social and personality development. In reality, not all infants react negatively when confronted by strangers. Indeed, one can legitimately ask why an infant should ever show stranger fear when in most instances strangers have only the most positive intentions toward the infant (Rheingold & Eckerman, 1973).

The following generalizations, based on two recent critical reviews of the literature (Gouin-DeCarie and Associates, 1974; Rheingold & Eckerman, 1973), summarize the current status of stranger fear research.

1. Stranger fear is not a universal characteristic of infancy; some infants react negatively to strangers; others do not.
2. Stranger fear usually first appears between the 6th and the 13th month, peaking at 12½ months.
3. Stranger fear appears earlier and more intensely in females than in males, but occurs more frequently in males than in females.
4. Stranger fear occurs earlier in firstborn infants than in later-born infants.
5. Adult males elicit stronger and more frequent negative reactions in infants than do adult females.
6. From ten months of age, stranger fear is more readily elicited by physical contact or nearness to stranger than by the mere visual presence of stranger.
7. Stranger fear is strongest when infant and mother are separated, although it also occurs when infant and mother are in close contact.
8. The greater the contact with strangers during early infancy, the more delayed is the onset of stranger fear.

While there is more evidence to support some of these conclusions than others, the complexity of stranger fear is evident. At minimum, whether or not an infant will show stranger fear seems to depend on the infant's age, sex, birth order, previous contact with strangers, on the physical proximity of mother and/or stranger, and on the sex of the stranger. Undoubtedly, other factors influencing the occurrence of stranger fear will be uncovered as research continues.

BOX 9–2
Conditioned emotional responses

Many years ago, Watson and Rayner (1920) pointed out the important role that learning plays in the development of fear, or what they termed *conditioned emotional responses*. Watson and Rayner knew that loud noise and loss of support would elicit distress reactions in infants, and that these reactions were at best minimally dependent upon prior learning experiences. What they wished to find out was whether such stimuli as loud noises provided a base from which other fears could be learned.

The baby in their experiment, Albert B., was the son of a wet nurse in a hospital for invalid children. When Albert was nine months old, he was presented in sequence with a variety of stimuli in order to establish a baseline of emotional behavior. Albert proved to be a very placid baby. Watson and Rayner reported that not even the slightest distress reaction was observed when Albert was confronted with a white rat, a rabbit, a dog, a monkey, a bearded adult, cotton, wool, or a burning newspaper. However, when a steel bar behind Albert was struck with a hammer, a pronounced startle reaction was elicited. After several hammer blows, Albert's startle reaction became a "sudden crying fit." (Although Watson and Rayner were concerned about the ethics of this experiment, their decision was to continue. Today, ethical considerations would dictate the opposite decision.)

When Albert was 11 months 3 days old, the learning experiment began. A white rat was presented to Albert, who was free to touch the rat, crawl away, or make any other response. When Albert reached out to touch the rat, bang went the hammer on the bar. One more trial was given. Seven days later, Albert returned to the laboratory. On the first trial only the rat was presented. Albert did not attempt to touch it, although when given blocks to play with, he promptly picked them up. On the next three trials, presentation of the rat was reinforced by striking the bar with the hammer. On the fifth trial, the rat was once again presented without reinforcement. Albert's response was to whimper and turn away from the rat. Clearly, a learned distress or fear was taking shape. After two more reinforced trials the rat was again presented alone. Albert's reaction is best described in Watson and Rayner's own words. "The instant the rat was shown the baby began to cry. Almost instantly he turned sharply to the left, fell over on left side, raised himself on all fours and began to crawl away so rapidly that he was caught with difficulty before reaching the edge of the table" (Watson & Rayner, 1920, p. 167). During the next two months, generalization of the conditioned emotional response was studied. Objects such as a rabbit, a fur coat, a dog, a Santa Claus beard, and even Watson himself elicited strong negative reactions from Albert. Unfortunately, but perhaps understandably, Albert and his mother stopped coming to the laboratory, and Watson was unable to locate them. Consequently, the learned fear was never experimentally extinguished. Assuming that Albert's mother did not continue the conditioning at home, the conditioned emotional response probably decayed with time. However, if you know someone in his late 50s who is afraid of white furry things. . . .

The stability of stranger fear   Stranger fear is not a universal characteristic of infancy, and its presence or absence is determined by a complex set of factors. What remains to be examined is the stability of the behavior. In other words, can we predict anything about the infant's later social behavior if we know whether or not it shows stranger fear?

On the whole, the answer to this question is no. For most children fear of strangers tends to decline steadily between the ages of two and three, while positive reactions to strangers steadily increase. Most two-year-olds readily smile at and speak to strangers when mother is present, although many toddlers are shy and reserved in the presence of strangers when mother is absent. Strangers fare much better with three-year-olds even when mother is absent. For example, most three-year-olds readily adapt to the nursery school setting. In fact, in parent-cooperative nursery schools social shyness and withdrawal from group activities often reach a peak when the child's mother or father is serving as teacher's aide. Even when toddlers and preschool children are "shy" with strangers, however, one must be careful not to confuse flirtation or play behavior with fear of strangers.

One problem in determining the stability of stranger fear concerns the number of times that an infant is observed interacting with strangers. In most experiments, observations have been made on one day only. But, like adults, infants and toddlers have their good and bad days. Thus, the infant's reaction to a stranger on one day may or may not give an accurate indication of how the same infant will react to strangers on another day.

This point is supported by one of the few empirical studies of the stability of infants' reaction to strangers (Shaffran & Gouin-Decarie, 1973). In this study, 8-, 10-, and 13-month-old infants were visited in their homes on three separate occasions over a 12-day span. Only 17 percent of the infants consistently responded negatively to the stranger, providing further evidence that stranger fear is not a universal norm of infancy. Children who responded positively on the first visit tended to react in a similar fashion on subsequent visits. Infants who responded negatively on the first visit were equally likely to respond negatively or positively on subsequent visits. However, the strongest evidence for stable responses to strangers came from 8- and 10-month-old-boys who responded positively!

Other investigators have reported stable stranger fear behavior in male infants, although it generally involves negative responses (see Bronson, 1968). The early onset of stranger fear in male infants was correlated with shyness and social withdrawal during the preschool and early childhood years. Bronson has argued that boys are more vulnerable to psychological stress than are girls, just as they are more vulnerable to biological stress. His hypothesis has merit and may apply to situations other than those involving stranger fear. For example, negative reactions to being separated from a caregiver are more frequently observed in male toddlers than in female toddlers (Tennes & Lample, 1964). Maccoby and Jacklin (1971) observed toddlers playing in a room with mother present. While the children were playing, a loud noise was sounded. Both the female and the male toddlers were startled when the sound was presented, but the male toddlers took considerably longer to recover their composure and continue to explore and play.

Strangers, strange places, and separation   The child's reaction to strangers in the research laboratory may or may not coincide with its reactions to strangers in the more familiar setting of the home. In the research laboratory the infant may be a "stranger in a strange land." The problem created by the laboratory setting is one of determining whether the infant's reaction to an unfamiliar person in an unfamiliar setting is equivalent to the infant's reaction to an unfamiliar person in a familiar setting. There is reason to suspect that infants do not react similarly in both settings. For example, in their laboratory study, Scarr and Salapatek observed stranger fear in about 60 percent of 9–11-month-olds and nearly 80 percent of 18–24-month-olds. However, in studies conducted in the infant's home with mother present, Shaffran and Gouin-DeCarie observed stranger fear in only 17 percent of 8-, 10-, and 13-month-old infants.

Perhaps a more basic question is, How do infants react in familiar and unfamiliar situations when mother is present, but a stranger is not? The detachment process begins at least as early as when the infant can first crawl away from caregiver. During the remaining years of infancy and early childhood, the amount of time the child spends separated from its caregiver gradually increases. Yet, the same three-year-old who plays several rooms removed from mother at home or runs off in the midst of strangers at the grocery store, may refuse to enter the doctor's office or the research laboratory or even to ride to nursery school in a neighbor's car.

The degree to which mother is aware of her infant's needs may be one factor regulating early exploratory behavior. Ainsworth and her associates studied mothers and their one-year-old infants (Ainsworth, Bell, & Strayton, 1971). The mothers were rated on a continuum of sensitivity to their infants' needs. The ratings were then related to infant exploratory behavior both at home and in strange situations. Three levels of sensitivity were identified. *Sensitive mothers* were available to their infants, cooperative, and accepting. At home, their infants used them as a secure base from which to launch exploration of the environment. When placed in a strange situation, the infants' initial exploratory behavior matched their exploratory behavior at home. Gradually, however, there was an increase in the amount of time they spent close to mother. Most infants of sensitive mothers became upset when separated from their mothers.

Inconsistent mothers sometimes showed sensitivity to the needs of their infants, and sometimes they did not. These mothers often interfered in the infants' activities and often ignored their infants' requests. As you might guess, the infants of inconsistent mothers were themselves inconsistent in their use of mother as a secure base. When in the strange situation, they used mother as a base initially. Ultimately, however, these infants spent significantly more time away from their mothers while exploring the novel environment than did the infants of sensitive mothers.

Insensitive mothers showed little concern for baby's needs, and tended to be high in rejection and low in offering close physical contact. Their infants showed little concern when separated from them, and when mother and infant were reunited, the infant expressed more interest in the environment than it did in mother.

Children's exploration of unfamiliar settings is related not only to maternal sensitivity but also to the objects contained in the setting and mother's position relative to those objects. Rheingold and Eckerman (1970) designed a clever study to observe developmental changes in the distance that young children will move away from their mothers. The setting was an L-shaped lawn. Mother was instructed to remain seated but to respond to her child otherwise. Observers stationed in the house recorded the distance the child traveled from mother during a 15-minute observation period. The distance increased at each age level. One-year-olds traveled an average of 6.9 meters; two-year-olds, 15.1 meters; three-year-olds, 17.3 meters; and four-year-olds, 20.6 meters. This study used an unfamiliar setting appreciably more naturalistic than the typical research laboratory. However, mothers reported that at home their children traveled even greater distances. Casual observations of preschool children and even of toddlers playing in their own neighborhoods indicate that for the most part children play in the vicinity of their own homes. Nevertheless, it is not uncommon for them to roam several blocks away, while incidentally, not always knowing how to get back.

Rheingold and Eckerman also studied the effects of environmental content on exploratory behavior. In one experiment, mother and toddler were placed in a small room connected to a much larger adjoining room. Toddlers were allowed to come and go as they pleased from one room to another, but mother remained seated in the small room. For one half of the toddlers a toy was placed in the large room; for the other half the large room was empty. No toddler showed distress when leaving mother to explore the large room. Toddlers in both groups spent an equal amount of time in the large room. However, toddlers with the toy present brought the toy into the small room and spent nearly half of the session playing with it. Toddlers for whom a toy was not present passed the bulk of their time in close proximity to mother. In another experiment the effect of one toy versus three toys was studied. Toddlers with three toys roamed farther away from mother and spent more time away from her than did toddlers for whom only one toy was available. Throughout all the experiments, toddlers were never observed to be upset or fretful when returning to mother. In fact, only pleasant reunions occurred.

How often young children return to close proximity with mother in strange situations may be related to where mother is seated or where she is looking. Children 18- to 30 months-old were allowed to explore a strange environment with toys present (Carr, Dabbs, & Carr, 1975). Mother's position relative to the toys varied. In one condition mother was seated facing the toys; in another condition mother was seated facing away from the toys; and in the third condition mother was seated behind a partition and was not visible from the part of the room in which the toys were located. When mother was seated facing the toys, the children spent 94 percent of their time playing with the toys. In the other two conditions, the children played with the toys only 50 percent of the time. In most instances, when the children left the toys, it was to position themselves in mother's visual field. The authors felt that the children were attempting to at least set up the possibility that mutual gaze could be established. When mother's position decreased the possibility for visual contact, the children increased their verbal contacts with mother and their proximity-seeking behavior.

Thus, when mother and child are in an unfamiliar setting *with no stranger present,* the child shows a readiness to explore, a readiness which appears to be strengthened if the environment contains interesting objects. The child's exploratory behavior is constrained by such factors as maternal sensitivity, the presence of strangers, and the ease with which the child can establish eye-to-eye contact with mother. The amount of prior experience with novel situations also influences exploratory behavior (Maccoby & Feldman, 1972). Nursery school children who had already shown evidence of generalized attachment made the most rapid adjustment to the school situation. However, merely having multiple caregivers is not the same as having frequent exposure to strangers. For example, even children reared by multiple caregivers in group settings, as in the Israeli Kibbutz, show stranger fear and separation anxiety as well as attachment to their parents (Maccoby & Feldman, 1972).

PATERNAL ATTACHMENT

Thus far we have been discussing the attachment-detachment process as if mother were the child's only caregiver. Obviously, she is not. We have already noted instances of paternal influences on the child, specifically in terms of verbal and cognitive development. Fathers are caregivers, and they influence the child's development through direct interaction, as models, or indirectly via interactions with their wives. The quality of the husband's relationship with his wife may affect the quality of her relationship with their children. If the husband shows little interest either in his wife as a person or in her daily activities (including her caregiving activities), she may come to regard the children as intruders in their relationship. Conversely, if a wife shows little interest in her husband's activities or regards his attempts to become involved in caregiving as intrusions into her "special" domain, he too may come to regard their children as intruders (Bartemeier, 1953).

Fathers are caregivers, but the fact remains that in our culture women continue to carry the major responsibility for rearing children, especially infants and young children. The father's traditional role has been that of provider, his caregiving responsibilities overemphasizing the punative aspects of child rearing (Nash, 1965). When father's job takes him out of the home for substantial periods of time, his role as caregiver may disappear altogether. However, in the family-owned small business or on the farm, fathers and their children—especially fathers and sons—frequently work together, thereby increasing father's opportunities to blend his provider and caregiver roles. But even in these circumstances, father is unlikely to carry much responsibility for the care of infants and toddlers.

Some authors have argued that fathers in primitive societies should be more influential caregivers than fathers in technologically developed societies. Barry and Paxson's (1971) survey of 186 societies revealed a most interesting set of variables influencing the father's caregiving role. In general, the father's role during infancy is important in societies where:

1. The line of descent is bilateral or matrilineal rather than patrilineal.
2. Monogamy or limited polygyny is practiced.
3. A high god does not rule.
4. Males are not circumcised.
5. Games of physical skill rather than games of strategy are played.
6. Birds or small animals, rather than large game, are hunted.
7. Animal husbandry is nonexistent or unimportant.
8. Land transport is by humans rather than by pack animals.
9. Adolescent males are not segregated.
10. The training of children in responsibility and obedience is relatively lenient.

Analogous data are not available for Western cultures as a whole or for our own culture specifically. Nevertheless, there is some evidence relevant to two aspects of father's caregiving. The first involves father-infant attachment; the second involves the father's perception of his role as caregiver, including his views of appropriate behavior for his children.

Engrossment and attachment

Although only a few studies have been concerned with infant-father attachment, these are consistent in indicating that the attachment process binds father and infant in much the same way that it binds mother and infant. In a most interesting study, Greenberg and Morris (1974) investigated the effects of the first newborn on the father's *engrossment*—or sense of absorption, preoccupation, and interest—in the newborn. Most fathers were happy with the sex of their newborn, could not distinguish their baby's cry from that of others, and expressed a desire to share the responsibility of raising the baby. Characteristics of engrossment included:

1. *Visual awareness*—fathers enjoyed looking at their newborn.
2. *Tactile awareness*—fathers desired and derived pleasure from tactile contact.
3. *Awareness of distinctive characteristics*—fathers were aware of their newborn's individual characteristics and more often than not felt that the newborn resembled them.
4. *Infant perceived as perfect*—despite the rather ungainly appearance of most newborns.

5. *Focus of attention on infant*—fathers felt drawn to the infant, especially to its face.
6. *Feelings of extreme elation*—fathers described themselves as "stunned, stoned, drunk, dazed, off-the-ground, full of energy, feeling ten feet tall, feeling different, abnormal, taken away, taken out of yourself" (p. 524).
7. *Increased sense of self-esteem*—fathers took pride in their fatherhood.

The infant's behavior contributed to the strength of the father's engrossment. Many fathers were astonished when observing their infants' motor behavior, reflexes, eye movements, and orienting responses to the sound of their voices.

The studies of infant-father attachment parallel those of infant-mother attachment; that is, they investigate infants' reactions to strangers and separation, as well as infants' exploratory behavior in father presence or absence. Many of these studies do differ in one important respect from infant-mother studies in that fathers, strangers, *and* mothers are involved. Through such studies one can directly assess the relative degree of attachment between the infant and each of its caregivers.

In one study, infants with fathers described as high in family interaction showed less fear of strangers than did infants with fathers rated low in family interaction (Spelke, Zelazo, Kagan, & Kotelchuck, 1973). Using the separation method, Lester and his associates studied infants and parents in the United States and Guatemala (Lester, Kotelchuck, Spelke, Sellers, & Klein, 1974). Consistent with other reports, this study showed infant separation protest to be most intense between 12 and 18 months. Infants protested separation from mother or father, although their protest reactions were most intense when they were separated from mother. Guatemalan infants showed less protest to separation from father and in general showed separation protest to either parent's absence earlier than did American infants.

In another study (Cohen & Campos, 1974) the potency of father, mother, and stranger as elicitors of attachment behavior in 10-, 13-, and 16-month-old infants was examined. The measures of attachment included proximity seeking, distress vocalizations, and mutual gaze. At all age levels, fathers were superior to strangers but inferior to mothers, as elicitors of attachment. When infants were given a choice between mother and father, they went to mother twice as often as they went to father. However, when only father was present infants spent more time in close proximity to him than they spent in close proximity to mother when only she was present. This suggests that mother is a more secure base for encouraging exploration than is father, a conclusion supported by the fact that infants maintained more visual contact with strangers when in the presence of their mothers. Nevertheless, some infants did show stronger attachment to their fathers than to their mothers.

Father as caregiver

Despite the relative neglect among child psychologists of father as caregiver, few could seriously doubt that he plays an influential role in child rearing. But whether fathers are participants or participant observers in child rearing, they clearly perceive themselves as important. Fathers report that they discipline, teach words to, answer questions, and play with children under six. During their children's elementary years, fathers see their role as one of providing guidance in economic, social, and educational status (Gardner, 1943). Since Gardner's study was conducted nearly 35 years ago, one wonders how fathers' perceptions have changed since then, especially in light of the contemporary emphasis on fathers as caregivers and mothers as providers.

Tasch (1952) interviewed fathers from various economic, social, racial, and religious backgrounds. She identified several father-rearing patterns which she labeled "doing for" infants and toddlers and "clearing the hurdle" in school and with peers. Generally, fathers were more involved in routine daily chores and safety provisions with girls, and in motor activities with boys. In any event, the main point of Tasch's study is that fathers were involved in daily routine care of their sons and daughters and perceived themsleves as important participants in all their children's activities.

Aeberle (1952) hypothesized that what fathers expect of their children together with their attitudes toward child rearing would be a composite of their overall personality makeup as well as their occupational role. Fathers of upper- and lower-middle-class children in nursery school were interviewed. Although fathers felt that their occupational role had little relevance for their role as caregiver, they did expect their sons to complete a college education and obtain a "middle-class" job. For daughters, college and a career were seen as desirable but not crucial. Half of the fathers interviewed rejected outright a career for their daughters. Academic careers for sons were also rejected, because such careers were identified with weakness and femininity. Fathers expected their sons to be obedient, aggressive, and athletic and to assume responsibility, take initiative, and perform well academically. They expected their daughters to be nice, sweet, concerned, pretty, and affectionate. More contemporary research in this area is essential if we wish to know whether efforts to undo male and female role stereotypes are having an effect.

That fathers expected their sons to be aggressive and their daughters to be affectionate is not surprising, considering the time-honored stereotype that boys are aggressive and competitive and girls are dependent and nurturant. Certainly by the time children are three years old they have internalized stereotypes concerning gender roles (Thompson, 1975). Moreover, parents seem to purchase toys for their children which facilitate sex role stereotypes (Rheingold & Cook, 1975). In the latter study, the investigators analyzed the contents of middle-class children's bedrooms for the types of toys they contained. The children ranged in age from one month to almost six years. The boys' toys reflected such nondomestic matters as sports, the military, automobiles, and animals. The girls' toys, however, emphasized domestic activities—keeping house and taking care of children. Obviously, environmental factors play an important role in sex role stereotyping.

The evidence supporting environmental explanations of differences in aggression and dependency is less clear-cut. When one looks at aggression and dependency cross-culturally, sex differences appear to be fairly stable, suggesting a biological influence, at least for male aggression (see Maccoby & Jacklin, 1974). The six cultures studied by Whiting and Edwards (1973) also seem to strengthen the case for biological determinants of sex differences in aggression. However, when Whiting and Edwards examined individual cultures they found convincing support for the importance of socialization practices as determinants of aggressiveness.

Some studies suggest that within our own culture mothers tend to reward aggressive behavior in boys but not in girls (Hatfield, Ferguson, & Alpert, 1967). Moreover, evidence from infant-toddler day-care projects in which efforts are made to minimize sex role stereotyping provides an interesting parallel to that noted above. In one study, girls were rated as more autonomous, belligerent, irritable, hyperactive, and less passive than a comparison group of home-reared girls who presumably were more exclusively influenced by parental socialization practices (Fowler, 1972).

SUMMARY

The infant is a social organism—it socializes and is socialized by others. Viewing socialization as a reciprocal parent-child affair has been one of the most refreshing recent advances in developmental psychology, for it has directed attention to the infant and young child as active agents in the organization of social behavior.

The efforts to differentiate dependency from attachment have been clearest at the theoretical level. In general, dependency has been associated with a one-way view of the socialization process and has emphasized the specific social behaviors acquired by the child. Attachment, on the other hand, posits a reciprocal emotional bond between infant and caregiver as well as social behavior. Operationally, the specific social interactions studied under the dependency and attachment labels are identical.

Empirical study of the organization of social behavior has focused on such behaviors as mutual gaze, smiling, physical contact, proximity seeking, and reactions to strangers, separation, and strange situations. Research has emphasized the nature of mother-child interaction, although there is also much contemporary interest in father-child interaction. Evidence suggests that infants form social-emotional bonds with both their mothers and their fathers, though these are not necessarily equal in strength. Both fathers and mothers seem to contribute to the emergence of sex role stereotypes, and in some instances sex role behaviors clearly indicate an organism-environment interaction, most notably in the case of aggression.

Attachment-dependency provides a foundation for the infant's basic trust in the world and in caregivers, and detachment-independence encourages autonomy and initiative. The desired product of these processes is a school-aged child who has acquired the skills necessary to deal effectively with the environment. Our emphasis in this chapter has been on the organization of social behavior in infants and young children reared at home. One might hypothesize that the infant and young child would develop differently if rearing occurred in settings other than the home. To some extent this is true, and to some extent it is not. In the next chapter we will consider the organization of social behavior in group care settings which either replace the home or provide for supplementary care outside the home, as well as continue our discussion of home influences. Our focus in the next chapter, however, will be the development of the child's ability to deal with its environment effectively and competently.

SUGGESTED ADDITIONAL READING

Bowlby, J. *Attachment.* New York: Basic Books, 1969.

Lynn, D. B. *The father: His role in child development.* Belmont, Calif.: Brooks/Cole, 1974.

Maccoby, E. E., & Jacklin, C. N. *The psychology of sex differences.* Stanford, Calif.: Stanford University Press, 1974.

Schaffer, H. R. *The growth of sociability.* Baltimore: Penguin Books, 1971.

BOX 10–1
Study questions

What is competent behavior?

How do babies develop trust in the environment and in persons?

How does play facilitate the development of competence?

How do parental attitudes and child-rearing practices influence the development of children's competence?

What is missing from permissive child rearing that makes it ineffective for developing highly competent children?

When is the young child ready for school?

How do maternal deprivation, maternal employment, institutionalization, and paternal deprivation influence the development of young children?

Why should developmental approaches to educational enrichment be more successful than remedial approaches?

Who is the "new" school-age child?

What are the effects of day care on children less than two years old?

10

SOCIALIZATION: COMPETENCE AND CAREGIVING

The first years of human life are exciting ones. In four years the human being progresses from a small reflexive organism to one whose behavior is so complex in comparison as to stagger the imagination. During the early years of development the human being becomes capable of sensory exploration, upright locomotion, verbal communication, learning and thinking. In short, during the first four years of life the human being becomes capable of active and effective involvement with the environment.

Over the years various theorists have attempted to capture the flavor of the motive which impels the human being toward increasingly skillful interaction with the environment. Such processes as "instinct to mastery" (Hendrick, 1942) and "autonomous ego functions" (Hartmann, 1958) have been proposed. Today, however, *competence* is receiving wide acceptance as the concept which best expresses the motivational force that binds all the organizational processes affecting the child's interaction with the environment.

COMPETENCE

The idea of competence motivation was first proposed by Robert White (1959). White used the term in its biological sense, in much the same way that Bowlby uses the term *attachment*. In this sense, competence is an intrinsic characteristic of the organism, a motivational force underlying adaptation to the environment. In order to assess attachment it was necessary to refer to specific behaviors which were thought to reflect the more general process. Similarly, in order to assess competence we must identify behaviors which give substance to the inferred process. Defining competence in terms of skills, abilities, knowledge, and values makes it possible to assess degrees of competence. We can say that a child is more or less competent relative to some specific skill. But more important, we can study the factors which influence the development of competent behavior so that factors detrimental to its development can be countered. Are certain patterns of caregiving or certain caregiving settings better than others for producing highly competent children? Do mothers and fathers share equally in fostering competent behavior in their children? How do cognitive and emotional factors influence the emergence of competent behavior? These are some of the questions that will be explored in this chapter.

Competent behavior

What is competent behavior? Answers to this question usually refer to skills and abilities which enable the child to deal with the social and nonso-

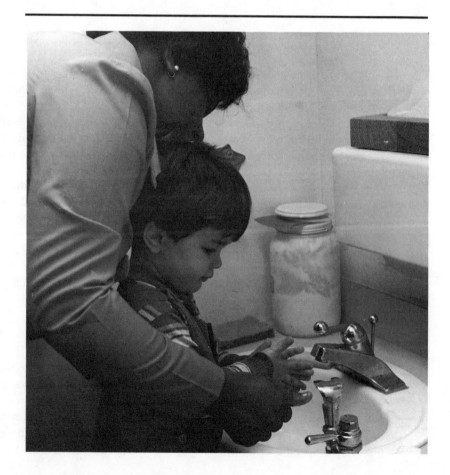

Photographs courtesy Paul Rochlen

FIGURE 10–1 Competence skills emerge from the child's interaction with environment, both socially and nonsocially. Young children can be encouraged to become self-sufficient (a) as well as to engage in cognitive activities (b) within the context of social interaction.

cial environment effectively and efficiently. In a project sponsored by the Appalachia Educational Laboratory a national panel of child development specialists was asked to evaluate behaviors thought to reflect competence (Trout, 1975). The starting point for this project was the question, What should a six-year-old child know how to do? The answer was structured as a series of abilities. For example, the specialists agreed that a six-year-old child should be able to express feelings, count, articulate, measure, sort, label, use nonverbal cues, control large muscles, persist in actions, get attention, and so on. In one study of competence, Burton White and his associates developed the following criteria for assessing social and nonsocial competence (White & Watts, 1973).

A. *Social abilities*
  1. To elicit and maintain attention of adults in socially acceptable ways.
  2. To use adults as resources.
  3. To express both affection and hostility to adults.
  4. To lead and follow peers.
  5. To express both affection and hostility to peers.
  6. To compete with peers.
  7. To praise oneself and/or show pride in one's accomplishments.
  8. To involve oneself in adult role-playing behaviors or to otherwise express the desire to grow up.

B. *Nonsocial abilities*
  1. Linguistic competence—extensive use of expressive language.
  2. Intellectual competence.
     a. Ability to sense dissonance or note discrepancies.
     b. Ability to anticipate consequences.
     c. Ability to deal with abstractions.
     d. Ability to take perspective of another.
     e. Ability to make interesting associations.
  3. Executive competence.
     a. Ability to plan and carry out multiple activities.
     b. Ability to use resources effectively.

The clearest theme common to such efforts to define competence is that it cannot be defined by any single skill or ability. To be sure, proficiency in any given area of competence requires the individual to acquire the requisite skills, abilities, and values which give structure to that area of competence (Gale & Pol, 1975). At each step along the way, however, the emergent level of competence cannot be explained by a simple addition of the skills necessary to achieve that level. Competence emerges from the interrelationships of its component parts, yet is not reducible to those parts.

Although efforts have been made to define competence skills comprehensively, cognitive skills have received the most attention from researchers and educational practitioners. In addition, many investigators have become increasingly concerned with the emotional aspects of competence and with the interrelationship of social-emotional and cognitive areas of competence.

Emotional aspects of competence

Erik Erikson (1950) has described eight stages of human social-emotional development. During each stage the individual is confronted with a conflict which must be resolved before movement to the next stage is possible (see Table 10–1). The first three of Erikson's stages encompass the years of infancy and early childhood. In the first year of life, the infant must resolve the conflict between *trust and mistrust.* If the infant has been well cared for, loved, and made to feel secure, a sense of trust in the world as safe and people as dependable emerges. Conversely, if the infant has been poorly cared for, a sense of doubt or mistrust develops.

During the toddler years the child is faced with a conflict between *autonomy and doubt.* The child emerges from this stage either with a feeling of competence and pride in accomplishment or with a feeling of doubt in his or her ability to handle new situations. In the third stage, *initiative versus guilt,* the preschool-aged child actively initiates new behaviors. If the child's attempts to deal effectively with the environment are successful, the child develops a sense of initiative. If the child's attempts at self-initiated behavior are disparaged, a sense of shame and guilt emerges.

Although the conflict at one stage must be resolved before the next stage can be mastered, the stages are not mutually exclusive. For example, the crucial feature of the third stage concerns the child's perceived outcome of his or her attempts at self-initiated behavior. But self-initiated behavior begins early in infancy. Thus, although Erikson's stages may be viewed as critical periods in emotional development, events at any given stage are dependent upon both the past and the present accomplishments of the child. It is conceivable that an infant could develop a strong attachment relationship and gain a high degree of trust in the world and in caregivers, but during the toddler years repeatedly have efforts to achieve autonomy and independence suppressed by otherwise loving parents. One must remember that restrictive or overprotective caregivers are not necessarily any less loving of their children. Nevertheless, it does appear that parental attitudes toward their children and parental patterns of child rearing influence the child's ability to deal effectively with the environment.

TABLE 10–1
The stages of psychosocial development according to Erik Erikson

Stage	Approximate age span	Conflict
I	Infancy	Trust versus mistrust
II	Toddlerhood	Autonomy versus doubt
III	Preschool	Initiative versus guilt
IV	Middle childhood	Industry versus inferiority
V	Adolescence	Identity versus role diffusion
VI	Young adulthood	Intimacy versus isolation
VII	Middle age	Generativity versus stagnation
VIII	Maturity	Integrity versus despair

Parental attitudes

Studies of parental attitudes toward their children generally take one of the following forms: (1) parental reports of their children's behavior are correlated with the children's actual behavior; (2) children's reports of their parents' behavior are correlated with their parents actual behavior; (3) parents and children are studied independently; or (4) parent-child interaction is observed naturalistically or manipulated in the laboratory. Correlational techniques tend to be used in analyzing the data obtained from such studies, with the possible exception of laboratory studies. Since any one study may produce literally hundreds of correlations, conceptual models have been developed to facilitate the organization and presentation of the complex relationships generally found in these studies.

One investigator has proposed three major factors or dimensions along which one can order the relationships among parental behaviors as rated by children (Schaefer, 1965). How were these dimensions derived? Schaefer developed a scale to evaluate 26 categories of parent behavior, such as strictness, punishment, irritability, autonomy, sharing, and emotional support. Each category contained ten items which children rated relative to whether their parents were "Like" or "Not Like" the item description. Then a score was obtained for each category and analyzed to determine whether there were any relationships among the categories that would suggest general patterns of parent behavior. Three general patterns emerged: *acceptance-rejection; autonomy-control; lax control–firm control.* Then Schaefer looked to the specific items which made up these general categories. For example, this analysis indicated that an accepting parent is rated "Like" by children on items which reflect devotion to child rearing, interest in the child's school activities and games, acceptance and trust of the child, nurturance, and a loving home environment. A rejecting parent is rated "Like" on items which reflect little interest in the child's activities, excessive use of verbal punishment and ridicule, and general hostility and aggression. How did these ratings correlate with the children's actual behavior? The accepting parents tended to have children who were inquisitive, independent, capable of assuming responsibility, and low in antisocial aggression. In short, the accepting parents tended to have children who were high in social competence skills. The rejecting parents tended to have children who were dependent, hostile, high in antisocial aggression, or withdrawn and submissive. In short, children who were low in social competence.

Obviously, few parents fall neatly into discrete accepting or rejecting categories. Parenting is a bit more complicated than that. To one degree or another, all parents control the behavior of their children. Some parents use rigid control techniques with their children, while others are lax and sometimes haphazard in their control. In short, Schaefer's model suggests that most parent behavior can be accounted for by three general patterns, and how parents are rated within each of the three categories will determine the overall child-rearing climate as perceived by the child. One can then observe the child's behavior and relate it to the child-rearing climate.

Patterns of child rearing

Over the years many patterns of child rearing have been identified and, at one time or another, recommended as the optimal child-rearing climate. During the 1950s and 1960s child-rearing experts favored democratic and permissive climates, while discouraging authoritarian and laissez-faire climates. In particular, the warm permissive home emphasizing love-oriented disciplinary techniques was advocated as the ideal setting in which to rear children. Today, permissiveness still ranks high as an "ideal" pattern of child rearing. However, it may not be the ideal climate for promoting the development of competence.

What permissiveness seems to lack is a sufficient amount of parental control over the child's behavior (Baumrind, 1966, 1971). *Permissive* parents tend to be accepting and nonpunitive, expect children to participate in decision making, and use reason to accomplish their child-rearing goals. However, they are inconsistent in the application of discipline and lax in rule enforcement. At the other extreme, *authoritarian* parents are controlling and punitive, value obedience, and set absolute standards for their children's behavior. In the middle of the road are *authoritative* parents who are very similar to permissive parents but different from them in the extent to which they play a controlling or directive role in the regulation of their children's behavior (see Table 10–2).

TABLE 10–2
Familial climate and parental control dimensions

Parents' control dimensions	Familial climate		
	Permissive	Authoritarian	Authoritative
1. Disciplinary style: punitive	Low	Variable	Low
2. Disciplinary technique: withdrawal of love	Variable	Variable	Low
3. Use reason and encourage verbal give and take	High	Low	High
4. Enforce demands for socially desirable behavior in home	Low	High	Moderate
5. Restrict autonomy	Low	High	Moderate
6. Power assertion	Low	High	Moderate
7. Rule enforcement	Low	High	High

Source: Adapted from material in D. Baumrind, "Effects of authoritative parental control on child behavior," *Child Development*, 1966, *37*, 887–907. With permission of the author and The Society for Research in Child Development, Inc. © 1966, all rights reserved.

The various child-rearing climates summarized thus far are more complicated than they appear at first glance, because both parents may not fall in the same category, and because child-rearing climates may change. For example, one parent may be authoritarian while the other is permissive, or both may be authoritative with a firstborn child but permissive with laterborn children, or both may be permissive with their male children and authoritative with their female children. Now, perhaps, you can appreciate the complex relationships that must be dealt with in studies which attempt to isolate significant parental influences on the child's behavior.

Nevertheless, important advances have been made in our understanding of the relationship between parental rearing climates and children's behavior. In one study (Baumrind, 1966), nursery school children were rated on self-control, approach-avoidance tendencies, buoyancy versus dysphoria (hostility, anxiousness, unhappiness), self-reliance (independence, realism, skill in getting help), and peer affiliation (ability to express warmth to others).

Confident children were high in social competence; dysphoric children were socially withdrawn and generally low in social competence. Immature children were high in dependence and low in self-control. Baumrind then compared the three child behavior patterns to the three adult behavior patterns noted above. Confident children tended to have authoritative parents; immature children, permissive parents; and dysphoric children, authoritarian parents.

An important difference between permissive and authoritative parents appears to be the degree to which authoritative parents do exercise control over their children's behavior. But what kind of control is it? It is certainly not control in the restrictive sense. Restrictive parents tend to dominate their children, provide no explanations for limits, and interfere even in the child's fantasy play. This type of control is negatively related to the development of competence. On the other hand, parents who exercise control by providing information to the child about feelings and object reality, give explanations for the limits set on the child's behavior, and enforce the rules of the household, tend to have children who score high in social competence (Liberman, 1970).

Competent children and competent caregivers

In a previously mentioned study of mother-child interaction, optimal maternal caregiving was associated with high competence and low fretfulness in children (Clarke-Stewart, 1973). High competence was related, not to the amount of caregiving received, but to the quality of caregiving. Happy, loving mothers tended to have affectionate, happy children. Conversely, maternal restrictiveness was related to low child involvement, activity, and exploration.

Direct studies of competence in children and caregivers provide support for the relationships suggested in studies of parental attitudes and parental child-rearing climates. Burton White and his associates at the Harvard Preschool Project found that mothers of highly competent children were low in restrictiveness and high in language stimulation (White & Watts, 1973). Mothers of high-competence children scored high in enjoyment of children and awareness of the importance of the early years of development; were less concerned about maintaining an orderly, immaculate home; and permitted toddlers to take greater risks while exploring the environment. In contrast, mothers of low-competence children were high in restrictiveness and low in language stimulation. Low-competence children received the bulk of their verbal stimulation from television rather than from their caregivers.

White and his associates identified children representing the extremes of competence and then studied the younger siblings of these children. The children were studied over a two-year period, with one group beginning at age one and a second group beginning at age two. Compared to children with low-competence older siblings, children with high-competence older siblings were more skilled at making use of adults as resources and in gaining adult attention in socially approved ways, more effective in expressing pride in their accomplishments and in themselves, and more competent in their use of language skills. Low-competence children were especially difficult to deal with from the time marking the emergence of negativism in the second year of life through the remainder of the study.

White and his associates suggest that the toddler years represent a critical period for the organization of competence. It is during the toddler years that mother (and father) either support and encourage their child's striving for autonomy and independence or restrict and perhaps suppress their child's autonomous and self-initiated efforts to deal effectively with the environment.

Competence, play, and peer interaction

During the toddler and preschool years, many of the child's attempts to gain effective control of the environment and autonomy occur in the context of social interaction with peers. Play facilitates the development of competence and autonomy and helps the child to achieve a balance between independence and dependence. Play stimulates cognitive growth through active involvement with the environment and provides one example of learning by doing. Moreover, play facilitates language competence. Through play, children are stimulated to use language to solve problems, ask questions, share experiences, and direct activities. In short, play can be one of the major ways in which children experiment with social relations and develop social skills.

Play and peer interaction   During the years from two to five, peer social interaction diversifies and true mutual give and take begins to develop. First friendships are made, cooperative play increases, and first peer groups are formed. One often-cited study (Parten, 1932) suggested that there were six different levels of play and peer interaction: *unoccupied* (the child is not occupied in any specific task); *solitary* (the child plays alone); *onlooker*, (the child watches other children playing but does not participate); *parallel* (children play alongside one another but not with each other); *associative* (children interact, take turns, and share materials); and *cooperative* (children work together to achieve commonly held goals).

From a different perspective, that of Piaget, the perceptual-motor activities of the sensorimotor period represent the infant's first attempts at play. Examples include finger staring, mouthing objects, and banging blocks—often against tables or windows—as well as repetitive behaviors, such as "hitting a string to watch it swing." Toward the end of the sensorimotor period, much of the child's play is exploratory or inventive, whereas much of the preoperational child's play is make-believe or symbolic. The emphasis is decidedly on play as a cognitive activity of the child. Other investigators, emphasize the emotional as well as the cognitive aspects of play. Sutton-

Smith (1971) notes that the imitative play of caregiver and infant often results in peals of laughter from both.

In any event, most of the infant's and toddler's play is solitary. For many years child psychologists and early childhood education specialists interpreted solitary play as a sign of social immaturity in kindergarteners and older children. It was generally conceded that solitary play was important for role playing, acting out, and make-believe. However, children who played apart from the group were often judged to be socially immature, and those with rich imaginations and much fantasy play were often thought to be too far removed from reality. Although such judgments may be true for any particular child, it does not follow that solitary play is itself a sign of immaturity. In fact, just the opposite may be true.

When the play behavior of kindergarten children is observed during free-play time, most of the solitary play seems to be goal directed, involving such activities as putting puzzles together, doing arts and crafts work, building with blocks, reading, and role playing (Moore, Evertson, & Brophy, 1974). Such activities are indicative of mature behavior in that they are functionally appropriate to the school setting, aid the child in establishing role identity, and satisfy the need for occasional "private time."

True social play probably does not begin until after the toddler has acquired the concept of objects as existing independent of self. Early in the toddler period, children tend to treat one another as obstacles to direct access to play materials, and much of toddler peer interaction involves struggling over the possession of desired objects (Maudry & Nekula, 1939). Possessiveness remains high throughout the preschool years. Two- and three-year-old children often seem to perceive toys as extensions of the self rather than as existing independent of the self. The toddler may be as reluctant to share a favorite toy as he or she is to share a "security blanket."

Characteristics of objects and infant play   What characteristics make toys most attractive to infants? This is a question which undoubtedly stimulates toy companies to fund extensive market research. Developmental psychologists are also interested in the question because of the implications the answers may have for our understanding of attentional processes and exploratory activities during infancy. Infants and young children seem to be attracted to toys that are compatible with their cognitive abilities but sufficiently complex to be challenging. Easily manipulated toys that have a potential for making sound seem to be especially attractive to older infants (McCall, 1974). Battery-operated toys and toys considerably beyond the child's cognitive capabilities are soon forgotten or are played with in ways not intended by the manufacturer. For example, the three-year-old may decide that the battery sockets on the new doll or dump truck are better used as an oven for making mud pies.

No toy, however novel or compelling, can hold an infant's attention for very long. Moreover, when only a few toys are available, infants may quickly direct their seemingly limitless energy and insatiable desires to explore other aspects of the environment.

Photograph courtesy Paul Rochlen

FIGURE 10–2   Peer interaction in the day-care setting. The caregiver plays a non-directive role, allowing children to develop spontaneous and self-initiated interactions.

Competence, preschool, and peer interaction

Going to school marks a significant change in the socialization of the child. It marks the occasion when the child is for the first time exposed systematically to socializers other than family members, neighborhood adults, and peers. For many children, however, the playground, sandlot, street, or housing project is the environment in which the first social interactions of this kind occur. Unfortunately, less is known about peer interaction in such settings than is known of peer interaction in the preschool setting.

School readiness   When is the child ready for school? Six-year-olds are legally required to attend school. But are they ready? Most first-grade teachers would probably be able to cite numerous instances of six-year-olds who were not ready for school. *School readiness* usually refers to whether or not the child has reached a level of social, emotional, physical, and cognitive competence sufficient to indicate that he or she is capable of successful adjustment to school. The legal age criterion fails to take into account many factors which may affect the child's potential for successful school adjustment. For example, chronological age does not take into account maturational differences between boys and girls or individual differences in motivation to learn, level of competence, early or late maturation, and preschool experience. All of these factors may influence readiness for school.

Value of preschool Preschool education has not always been designed with the needs of children in mind. In fact, until recently, preschools were designed primarily to meet the needs of adults. Initially, preschools were developed as teaching centers for child care training (Hodges & Spicker, 1967). During the depression of the 1930s, preschools were used to meet teachers' employment needs, and in the 1940s and 1950s preschools were developed to provide a place for working mothers to leave their children during working hours. Hodges and Spicker suggest that preschools shifted from adult needs to children's needs as a spin-off of the intensified interest in education sparked by the Soviet launching of the first sputnik. Consequently, the preschool as a medium for enhancing the young child's cognitive, intellectual, social, and emotional needs has a comparatively short history.

Today, parents place their children in preschool for a variety of reasons, including the need for quality supplemental care while the parents are at work and the parents' desire to enhance the child's contacts with peers. However, many parents place their children in preschool on the assumption that as a result of attending preschool their children will be better prepared for kindergarten and elementary school. How justified is this assumption? Does preschool give children a better preparation for later schooling? There is no simple answer to these questions. Perhaps the most general conclusion is that preschool best facilitates the development of cognitive and social competence when it supplements rather than replaces qualitative experiences in other settings (Sears & Dowley, 1963). In fact, there is little evidence to suggest that otherwise advantaged children derive any unique benefits from preschool. For otherwise disadvantaged children, however, preschool may play an important role in the development of competence. (We will return to this point later.)

Most children adjust to the preschool setting with little or no difficulty. However, many children have mixed feelings about the whole affair. On the one hand, they may be excited and eager to discover just what it is that older neighborhood children or older siblings do when they go to school. On the other hand, they may be hesitant to leave the security, comfort, and familiarity of their home environment—a hesitancy that usually reaches its peak as mother says good-bye and prepares to leave her child alone to cope with the novel preschool setting.

Preschool can serve many functions for the young child. The preschool provides a relatively organized and controlled environment in which young children can gain respect for the rights of others, can learn to accomplish tasks in cooperation with others, and can develop a sense of personal competence for dealing with the environment. Obviously, the young child could also learn these things on the sandlot, playground, or street. Perhaps the key advantage of preschool, then, is that it provides an environment in which the opportunities to develop social and nonsocial competence skills can be maximized. A competent preschool teacher can help the child expand its range of interests and to learn socially acceptable ways of expressing negative feelings toward others by strengthening the child's self-understanding as well as its understanding and acceptance of others.

In nearly all cultures, one of the major nonacademic responsibilities given to or assumed by the schools is that of transmitting cultural values, standards, and rules of conduct. Our own culture is a blend of persons from various ethnic, racial, religious, and socioeconomic backgrounds. But until recently, the cultural model espoused by the school was based on a mythical conception of the white middle-class child. It has been estimated that as recently as the 1960s, during any one year more than 6 million black children were reading elementary school textbooks which contained few, if any, photographs of black children and still fewer references to nonwhite persons who had made outstanding contributions to American culture. Obviously, exposure to such educational materials can hardly be expected to strengthen the child's self-concept or encourage the child's development of competence. Racism in textbooks is, of course, only one aspect of the conditions which breed humiliation, loss of self-esteem, poor academic achievement, and low competence skills.

The preschool could play an important role in eliminating the destructive forces of prejudice. By bringing together children and parents from various ethnic, racial, and socioeconomic backgrounds, the preschool could be effective in countering other socializing elements in society which directly or indirectly act to perpetuate dehumanizing prejudicial attitudes toward specific groups of people.

Peer interaction   The preschool is an excellent natural laboratory for studying many facets of early peer interaction. Studies of peer interaction in preschool settings have focused on such behaviors as playmate selection, racial awareness, aggression, competitiveness and quarreling. In one study of the factors that influence *playmate selection,* both black and white boys and girls were asked to express their choice of desired playmate (Helgerson, 1943). Children were presented with pairs of photographs and asked to select which member of the pair they would prefer to play with. Photographs of white and black boys and girls were presented in various paired combinations. Sex of playmate was the most important determinant of playmate preference, although for both racial groups, preferences for playmates of the same race increased with age.

There is limited evidence to suggest that playing with a same-sex peer facilitates girls' social competence (Langlois, Gottfried, & Seay, 1973). Three- and five-year-old girls showed more advanced social competence skills when playing with other girls. However, three-year-old boys were more socially mature when paired with girls, suggesting that the girls' more mature social competence influenced boys to behave more competently. Changing partners seemed to enhance social competence in all three-year-olds, independent of the sex of the new or the old partner. This was not the case for five-year-olds. For them, increased social behavior occurred when the new playmate was of the same sex as the previous playmate, whether or not the previous playmate was of the same sex as the child.

Most preschool peer interactions are positive. Young children do seek attention and praise from their peers in constructive ways. In many instances, young children gain more from peer interaction than from interactions with adults. In one study, infants and toddlers were observed in a novel setting in which each child's mother as well as an unfamiliar mother and her child were present (Eckerman, Whatley, & Kutz, 1975). Social play showed a steady increase over the three age groups (10–12 months, 16–18 months, 22–24 months), with the increase accounted for by more play with peers than with mother. Direct interaction with mother peaked at 16–18 months, whereas interactions with the unfamiliar female adult rarely occurred.

The most frequent behaviors used by peers to establish contact with one another were vocalizations and smiles. Peer interactions involved taking toys, struggling over toys, and coordinating activities with toys. Nevertheless, taking and struggling accounted for less than half of peer interactions. In most instances, peer interactions were positive.

Toddlers engage in relatively little *competitive behavior,* but by the end of early childhood nearly all children compete in one situation or another. Active physical *aggression* steadily increases until about age five, when children begin to use more socially mature ways to express their aggressiveness and vent their frustrations. At all age levels, boys tend to be more physically and verbally aggressive than do girls.

Quarrels are more frequent among children who are friends than among casual acquaintances or strangers (Green, 1933). The frequency of quarreling decreases during the preschool years, but the intensity and severity of quarrels tend to increase. Fortunately, young children do not hold grudges for very long. Children who seem to be mortal enemies in the morning may be the most congenial of friends in the afternoon.

EDUCATIONAL ENRICHMENT

During the past decade intensive efforts were made to enhance social and nonsocial competence skills among lower class children. As a result, thousands of children were enrolled in preschool programs, the most famous of which was Head Start. Research projects showed that remedial approaches to educational enrichment, such as Head Start, did produce increments in such things as IQ but that the gains were all too often lost after children entered public school. The declines in IQ gave critics of educational enrichment programs all the justification they needed to decry such programs as an enormous waste of national resources. By some strange logic, these protectors of the national treasury did not seem to consider the nation's children as a vital resource. Others argued that the basic failure of Head Start was in providing too little educational enrichment too late in the child's development. According to this line of reasoning, one of the basic flaws in preschool intervention was adopting a remedial rather than a developmental model for intervention.

Developmental intervention

A basic assumption of remedial intervention is that a limited short-term experience can compensate for deficiencies acquired during prior years of development. In contrast, *developmental intervention* assumes that whatever level of competence is attained by the four-year-old is dependent upon the previous four years of accumulated experience. Thus, developmental approaches to educational intervention emphasize starting at as young an age as possible and continuing into the school-age period, if not beyond. Developmental intervention also tends to emphasize the whole child, rather than focus exclusively on one aspect of development at the expense of other equally important aspects. Recently, developmental approaches have extended the breadth of intervention to include caregivers as well as children.

One of the most promising developmental intervention programs is that conducted by Heber and his associates in Milwaukee, Wisconsin (Heber and Garber, 1975). In a preliminary survey it was found that nearly 80 percent of children who scored below 80 on IQ tests had mothers whose IQ scores were also below 80. This similarity between the child's and the mother's IQ did not begin to appear until the child was about two years of age, providing support for suggestions that the first two years of life may be critical for the organization of competence skills.

Forty mothers scoring below IQ 75 and their infants were then selected for the study. Mother-infant dyads were assigned to an experimental condition and control condition. The control children received no intervention but were tested at intervals corresponding to the assessment regimen used for the experimental children.

Intervention for children in the experimental group began at an average age of three months and continued to six years of age. The intervention was intense. These children were involved in the enrichment program all day, every day of the year. During the first two years, the program focused on social-emotional, cognitive-language, and perceptual-motor stimulation. The program was derived from the items on the Cattell Infant Test. During the preschool years the enrichment program concentrated on perceptual-motor skills, reading, mathematics, problem solving, language, and social-emotional skills. A 1:1 ratio of teacher to child was maintained throughout infancy; from 12 to 15 months the ratio was 1:2; and from about 18 months on, the experimental children were placed in homogeneous age groups with three teachers per group. Nearly every comparison made between the experimental children and the control children was in favor of the experimental group, with the most dramatic differences occurring in IQ. After six years of enrichment, the experimental children scored substantially above the average IQ category, whereas the control children showed the characteristic decline so often observed in disadvantaged children toward the end of early childhood.

Maternal competence training

Maternal competence training is an outgrowth of a concept of home-based developmental intervention which recognizes that the family is a powerful educational force in society. In the Milwaukee project, mothers received educational enrichment in the form of reading and arithmetic skill improvement as well as vocational training which included homemaking skills, nutrition, and child care. The idea behind the project was that the enhancement of maternal competence will lead to the enhancement of children's competence through mother-child interaction.

Several projects have been developed to teach competency skills to mothers. These have resulted in IQ gains in children similar to those found in the Milwaukee project, even with far less intensive daily enrichment. In one project, mothers attended a two-hour meeting each week. Here toddlers with parents as teachers obtained IQ scores averaging 16 points higher than those obtained by toddlers in a control condition (Karnes, Teska, Hodgins, & Badger, 1970). The Ypsilanti-Carnegie Infant Education Project (Weikert & Lambie, 1970) has been equally successful. In this project, teachers from the local schools visited the homes of disadvantaged preschool children, teaching a curriculum that emphasized manipulative activities, dramatic play, perceptual discrimination, classification, and language skills. In Schaefer's (1972) program the tutors were college students who visited the child's home for one hour each day, five days a week, over a 21-month period. The children who received tutoring averaged 17 IQ points higher than did the children in a control condition.

The collective impact of these and other studies is to suggest that parent-centered enrichment is as effective as child-centered enrichment in improving the competency skills of young children. These studies also suggest that parent-centered enrichment may have more lasting effects. Moreover, the home training of parents and children is certainly far less expensive than child-centered enrichment programs conducted in day-care centers (Schaefer, 1972).

One parent-training project currently in progress at the Houston Parent-Child Development Center has made a concerted effort to bring fathers into the enrichment program (Johnson, 1975). This program serves low-income Mexican-American families and includes home training. Several times throughout the year the whole family gathers together for weekend workshops. The objectives of the weekend retreats are to strengthen the family unit and to have fathers become directly involved in parent effectiveness training, a tactic rarely taken in educational enrichment programs.

Home-based developmental intervention is consistent with the theoretical models we have discussed previously. The essential ingredients involve the establishment of a basic trust between parent and child through reciprocal attachment. Parents are then trained to maximize the development of their children's competence skills. As the children acquire interests, motivation, and competence, they function more effectively as autonomous persons (Schaefer, 1970).

THE NEW SCHOOL-AGE CHILD

No matter how successful parent education programs ultimately prove to be, their success will not offset the increasing demand for group-care facilities for young children. In 1964, 19 percent of employed mothers had children less than three years of age: by 1967, there were over 2 million part-time or full-time working mothers in the United States; and it has been estimated that by 1980 there will be over 6 million working mothers with children under five years of age. If we add to this total the children of poor families, handicapped children, and children whose mothers are themselves ill or handicapped—not to mention the children of college students—we would probably arrive at a figure of close to 10 million potential users of day-care facilities. A significant portion of those children will be less than two years old, suggesting that the infant and toddler are on the threshold of becoming America's new school-age child.

The implications of massive day care are staggering not only in terms of the financial resources that would be required but also in terms of the potential effects on traditional family-centered patterns of child rearing. Psychologists, politicians, specialists in early childhood education and parents differ among themselves, often heatedly, in their positions on infant-toddler day care. For every argument in support of day care there is a counter-argument, and there are few uncontestable facts on either side. Indeed, some long-standing "facts" concerning infants and their caregivers no longer seem as clear-cut as they did just a decade ago. For example, there is no consistent empirical evidence that multiple caregiving, maternal employment, or institutional group care are necessarily detrimental to the wholesome development of infants and toddlers.

Separation from parents

Separation from parents is a daily event for children of all age levels during early childhood. Putting baby down for a nap, going to the grocery store or to work, going out for dinner or to a party, are all events which separate parents from children. With the exception of parental employment, the effects of everyday separations on the child's behavior have not been studied, and there are no particularly compelling reasons to do so. However, everyday separations probably have an overall beneficial influence on the young child, encouraging autonomy, independence, and the development of social competence. This is not to say that toddlers and preschoolers will always accept their parents' departure. In fact, as parents are about to leave it is quite common for the toddler to make a tearful last effort to get them to stay. Wise parents, having secured the services of a competent baby-sitter, will give their child a pleasant kiss and leave. Reinforcing the child's protest by giving in and staying home only serves to intensify protest when the next occasion arises.

There are separations, however, which can have profoundly disruptive influences on the young child's development. These include the prolonged separations associated with death, divorce, desertion by one parent, or the loss of both parents, as in institutionalization. Until recently, the study of the effects of prolonged separation on the child's development has focused on maternal separation involving the institutionalization of illegitimate children. This research raised the basic question, What are the consequences of prolonged maternal deprivation on the child's development? To some extent, the hesitancy of American parents to rush into massive group day care for infants and toddlers is traceable to the belief that group care is detrimental to normal growth and development. This belief is rooted in studies of institutionally reared infants which long ago pointed out the dangers of *poor* institutional care and deprivation from significant caregivers.

Maternal deprivation   Without question, long-term deprivation retards the organization of social competence. Institutionalized children have been found to have deficits in social, linguistic, cognitive, and motoric skills and in the ability to control their behavior. Prolonged exposure to poor institutional care is associated with apathy, despair, and a pronounced deficit in social responsiveness. Moreover, the effects of institutionalization are strongest if the infant is institutionalized during the period when attachment to significant caregivers normally occurs.

Typical explanations for the detrimental influences of institutionalization emphasize loss of the mother as the significant determinant of psychological deprivation in the child. One prominent theorist has described two psychopathological conditions associated with institutionalization (Spitz, 1965). *Anaclitic depression* involves separation from the mother for periods ranging from three to five months. Symptoms of anaclitic depression include weepiness, sleep disturbances, susceptibility to respiratory ailments, a decline in social responsiveness, and increasing developmental retardation. When such infants are reunited with their mothers, the symptoms of anaclitic depression disappear, and there appear to be no long-term holdover effects. A key feature of this clinical disorder is that the infant must have established an attachment bond with its mother prior to separation. Thus, Spitz argues, the principal etiological cause of anaclitic depression is loss of the loved object. If institutionalization persists beyond five months, anaclitic depression becomes transformed into *hospitalism,* a pervasive emotional deprivation syndrome. Hospitalism in its extreme form is associated with marked psychopathology (Spitz, 1965), and in such instances the longer institutionalization persists, the more irreversible is the damage.

Given the pattern of behavior thus far described, it is perfectly clear why parents and professionals alike would view group day care of infants and toddlers with disdain. However, many infants reared in institutions do not show symptoms even remotely approximating those described by Spitz. In fact, in one of Spitz's own studies, only 19 of 123 children showed clear-cut symptoms of anaclitic depression (Spitz, 1965, p. 269). Might it be that characteristics of institutional settings completely independent of the loss of mother adversely influence the development of some children reared in such settings? Indeed it might!

If we view the maternal deprivation literature as a whole it appears that factors other than the loss of mother are important determinants of the developmental retardation associated with institutionalization. Poor institutional settings disturb the quality of the infant's sensory-perceptual interaction with the environment. To be sure, infants reared in institutions may not suffer from a quantitative lack of sensory-perceptual stimulation. However, what they may lack are opportunities for contingency learning, that is, qualitative experiences with the environment. Thus, infants reared in poor institutions may have few opportunities to develop a sense that their behavior influences events in the environment.

Whether or not conditions are ripe for such learning is directly related to the availability of caregivers and to the quality of the caregiving interaction. It is well documented that poor institutions are inadequately staffed, so that caregivers generally have little time for all but the routine caregiving chores associated with feeding and cleansing infants. Even during these interactions a caregiver responsible for 8, 10, or 15 infants simply has no time (or energy) to make the interaction a qualitative one. Thus, developmental retardation and anaclitic depression or hospitalism seem to be due not to loss of mother but to inadequate *mothering,* where mothering refers to caregiving. This is an important point because perhaps the greatest error of theorists who equate institutionalization with maternal deprivation is that they fail to recognize that institutionalization also involves paternal deprivation. In any event, the infant reared in a poor institutional setting has few opportunities to develop competency skills in the context of social interactions with primary caregivers.

Maternal employment Given the literature which suggests that prolonged maternal (caregiver) deprivation during the first two years of the child's life is detrimental to normal growth and development, it is legitimate to ask whether the maternal separation associated with going to work is in any way comparable to maternal deprivation.

Working mothers provide different role models for their children than do nonworking mothers. For example, the daughters of working mothers tend to be more independent and more achievement oriented than do the daughters of nonworking mothers. Both the sons and the daughters of working mothers tend to assume greater responsibility for household chores and develop more positive attitudes toward maternal employment than do the children of nonworking mothers. In addition, the husbands of working wives tend to become more involved with routine household tasks and with caregiving than do husbands whose wives do not work.

One key determinant of the effects of maternal employment on her children's behavior is the degree to which mother is satisfied with her work and with the alternative child care arrangements available for her children. In fact, there is some indication that mothers who are satisfied with their way of life, including their work, are more competent mothers than are mothers who neither work nor are satisfied with their way of life (see Hoffman, 1974).

Unfortunately, the effects of maternal employment on infant and toddler behavior has not received much research attention. This may be due to the greater availability of child care facilities for children beyond the age of two. Working mothers with children under two comprise the smallest proportion of working mothers with children under five. Moreover, mothers of children under two who do work probably utilize home-based child care, thus reducing their availability for research. There is no way to estimate how many mothers with children less than two years of age would seek employment if high-quality day-care facilities were available. We suspect that the number would be considerable.

Paternal deprivation   The most accurate summary statement that can be made at present regarding the effects of paternal deprivation on infants and toddlers must be that we simply do not know what they are. Certainly, fathers do seem to be engrossed in their newborns, and they do establish reciprocal attachments with their infants.

However, there are sound reasons for hypothesizing that father absence during the first five years of life will affect the child's psychological development. For example, nearly every theory of development gives father a central part in the sex role identification of his children, although this part is thought to be most important during the middle childhood years. Studies of father absence during middle childhood have produced some general findings. Although father absence can affect the development of boys and girls, it seems to have greater effects on boys than on girls. Many studies have suggested that boys reared in father-absent homes tend to be less masculine than do boys reared in father-present homes. Hetherington and Deur (1972) suggest that father absence may lead to high rates of aggressive behavior in boys as they attempt to maintain a masculine identification in the absence of the appropriate sex role model. However, the effects of father absence may depend, in part, on how mother reacts to husband absence. Evidence from many cultures suggests that father absence is associated with maternal rejection of the children and with increased hostility and aggression toward the sons. Since boys tend to be more aggressive than girls even in father-present homes, their even greater aggressiveness in father-absent homes may reflect the boys' modeling of heightened maternal aggression rather than father absence.

How long must father be gone before his absence will have a negative influence on the development of his children? Again, studies directly relevant to the behavior of infants and toddlers are unavailable. However, several studies suggest that father absence during this period may have an adverse effect on children's cognitive development. For example, father-absent boys tend to perform more poorly on quantitative tests than do father-present boys (Herzog & Sudea, 1970). Decreasing the opportunities for interaction with father also seems to interfere with the development of quantitative skills in girls. Girls whose fathers worked the night shift when the girls were from one to nine years old tended to score lower on quantitative tests than did girls whose fathers did not work the night shift during those years (Landy, Rosenberg, & Sutton-Smith, 1969). Presumably, fathers who work at night sleep during the day and have less overall interaction with their children. However, we do not know what specific aspects of the father's interaction with his children may affect the children's competence in quantitative skills.

Intensive study of the father's caregiving role during infancy and early childhood must be encouraged. With increasing frequency, divorce courts are awarding fathers the custody of their children, single men are being allowed to adopt children, and wives are deserting their families. Moreover, in many intact families parental roles are changing as more couples attempt to achieve a balance in their responsibilities as caregivers and as providers. Both single-parent families and families with working mothers are potential consumers of high-quality supplemental child care. However, need for day care alone is not sufficient to justify its existence. Considering the literature which has pointed out the potential hazards of institutionalization, parents must have assurance that group day care represents *quality* care for their children rather than custodial care.

Infant-toddler day care

Infant day-care programs exist in nearly every European country and can now be found in Canada and the United States. The most systematically developed educational curriculum for children under three years of age is that used in the Soviet Union (see Chauncey, 1969). In the Soviet Union the day-care nursery is viewed as an extension of the home, with both parents and the nursery staff sharing the responsibilities for socializing the child. This relationship between family and nursery reflects the view of the prominent Soviet educator A. S. Makarenko that the family is the primary socialist collective (Bronfenbrenner, 1962). As a socialist collective, the family derives its authority from the state and has shared responsibilities with other socialist collectives, including the nursery. Thus, parents and nursery staff share the task of rearing the Soviet citizens of the future (Bronfenbrenner, 1962).

The day-care nursery's curriculum for infants emphasizes sensory, motor, linguistic, and cognitive development and at later ages, moral development, social competence, and mastery of personal skills, such as those involved in dressing, eating, and hygiene. Peer interaction begins early. Specially built playpens capable of housing five infants are used to foster early social interaction and represent what may best be described as the first peer social collective. Head nurses are well trained; the nursery atmosphere reflects tender, loving care; and each caregiver is responsible for only a few infants. Of unique interest are strengthening programs which are thought to enhance the child's natural resistance to disease.

BOX 10–2
Soviet strengthening programs for infant day care

From the age of one month, infants take air baths. At first, the baths are two minutes long but gradually they are lengthened to 10–15 minutes, for one-year-old infants, and to 30 minutes for three-year-old infants. The temperature of the room where the air baths are taken is 71.6° F. for infants under one year and from 64.4° to 68° F. for those between one and three years. During the summer, air baths are taken in the garden in the shade at the above temperatures. Air baths are never given directly after meals nor on an empty stomach. The infant having an air bath is quite naked, and should not necessarily be lying down, but may play quiet games.

They also sleep outdoors in the daytime at all seasons. In winter the infants sleep in special sleeping bags, if the temperature outdoors is not lower than 14° F. At lower daytime temperatures or in a strong wind they sleep indoors with the windows open.

The water strengthening treatment is both local and general. Local water strengthening means a daily sponging or douche of the feet with cool water once or twice a day, beginning at age one month. The temperature of the water is gradually decreased to that of tap water. This type of strengthening is [believed to be] a good prophylaxis for infants against colds, rheumatic illnesses, and aggravation of all chronic diseases connected with chilling.

A general water treatment for infants from six to twelve months of age is general sponging. At first, the temperature of the water is 96.8° F.; every two or three days it is lowered by 1.8°F. until it reaches 77° F. After the age of one year, infants receive showers instead of general sponging. The temperature of the water is also gradually lowered every two or three days by 1.8° F.— from 86° to 77° F. In the summer time showers are taken out of doors.

Before receiving sun baths the infants are carefully examined. If there are no contraindications, they are given sun baths from the age of six to twelve months at an air temperature of from 71.6° F. to 73.4° F. The sun baths are about two minutes long. Their duration is increased very gradually to 14 minutes, for the younger infants, and to 30 minutes for infants up to three years.

Source: Reprinted from Y. Brackbill, "Research and clinical work with children," in R. A. Bauer (Ed.), *Some views on Soviet psychology* (Washington, D.C.: American Psychological Association, 1962), pp. 101–103, with permission of the author and the American Psychological Association, Inc. Copyright, 1962.

With some exceptions, day-care programs in East Germany, Hungary, and Czechoslovakia are similar to those in the Soviet Union, although observers tend to rate them as providing somewhat less than quality care (Meers & Marans, 1968; Wagner & Wagner, 1971). Day-care centers in Yugoslavia have bright, cheerful atmospheres, are well equipped and staffed, and provide high-quality care. At present, there is no central control or common curriculum for Yugoslavia's day-care centers.

A day-care program that is successful in some cultures may or may not be successful in other cultures. For example, Czechoslovakia's centrally controlled curriculum which requires the child and the family to fit into the nursery program would probably not be acceptable in Denmark. There, day-care programs are developed to fit the needs of children and their families, local control and parental involvement are emphasized, and less importance is attached to orderliness (Wagner & Wagner, 1971). In the United States, as in Denmark, no single, inflexible curriculum for infant-toddler day care is likely to find broad appeal.

Certainly, the single inflexible curriculum has not evolved at the preschool level or, for that matter, at any other educational level. In fact, if American education has any single characteristic feature it is the lack of unified national educational objectives and an almost blind faith that the only reasonable curriculum is one that is constantly in a state of flux. Consequently, some advocates of structured preschool curriculum programs have argued that the traditional well-equipped and well-run American preschool and the newer infant-toddler day-care centers do not function as educational settings but rather as settings for custodial care (Bereiter, 1972).

Preschool programs which advocate a specific educational model are available in the United States. Examples include preschools that follow the methods of Maria Montessori and those that use the more recently developed structured curriculum of Bereiter and Engelmann. The Montessori Method is a skill-oriented approach to early childhood education which emphasizes sensory training, motor control, and language competence. Characteristic features of the Montessori Method are that the child must have freedom to select activities and exercise creativity while at the same time learning practical skills (see Evans, 1971). The teacher's role is directive in many respects resembling that of Baumrind's authoritative parent.

The Bereiter-Engelmann Method provides a highly structured preschool curriculum with specific behavioral objectives (see Evans, 1971). The program focuses on language, arithmetic, and reading competence skills, and derives its theoretical substance from general learning theory. Thus, the program emphasizes immediate feedback, transfer of training, and learning through repetition. Behavioral objectives are regarded as important because they clarify what the learner must learn and what the teacher must teach.

Although the Montessori and Bereiter-Engelmann methods encourage teachers to find new uses for materials, these methods constrain teachers' deviations from the prescribed curriculum model. In the traditional preschool the only constraints on teachers are those imposed by the limits of the teachers' creativity, imagination, and training in early childhood education. Some children seem to do best with structured programs, whereas others seem to thrive on unstructured programs, although a recent comparative-longitudinal study of four preschool programs (Montessori, Bereiter-Engelmann, DARCEE, and Traditional) suggests that structured programs may produce more long-term cognitive benefits, at least for lower-class black male children (Miller & Dyer, 1975). On the other hand, "non-cognitive" competencies, such as curiosity, persistence, and achievement motivation, showed greater stability over the three-year study than did "cognitive" competencies, with the more structured preschool programs.

Photograph courtesy Paul Rochlen

FIGURE 10–3 Infant-toddler day-care programming must be flexible enough to allow for spontaneous play between caregiver and children.

For infants and toddlers, curriculum programs similar to those of Montessori and Bereiter-Engelmann do not exist. Most infant day-care programs are an eclectic blend of cognitive-developmental theory, usually of the Piagetian variety, Eriksonian psychosocial theory, and general learning theory. The curricula of different child care centers give different emphases to the three traditions. Whatever specific theoretical model or models guide a particular program, all high-quality infant-toddler day care must provide an atmosphere in which the infant can learn to trust its environment and the persons with whom it interacts. In other words, quality-care programming must reflect aspects of all the psychobiological systems so often referred to throughout this volume.

Since each psychobiological system is in an emergent stage during the first four years of life, as well as becoming increasingly interdependent with other psychobiological systems, the burden of curriculum planning for infants and toddlers is an especially heavy one. How much of the curriculum should be devoted to specific educational programs, and how much of the curriculum should the child be left free to self-initiate? There are no simple answers. Introducing programs out of proper sequence may be as disruptive to behavior organization as not introducing them at all. For example, in one preschool program children were taught categorization skills before they were trained in object characteristics (Sigel, 1972). With this sequence, object characteristic training interfered with categorization skill learning. When the sequence was reversed, object characteristic training facilitated categorization skill learning. The sequence of learning experiences was an important determinant of the child's ability to perform. Although the dictum that any child can be taught anything at any time is not true, we are far from a complete knowledge of the constraints placed on the child's ability to profit from specific experiences. Additional problems in day-care curriculum planning may be brought about by the nature of the particular day-care center. How does one provide consistent programming for drop-in centers or for children who attend day-care centers only a few half-days each week?

The idea of sequence is fundamental to stage theories of development and to the concept of critical periods. Are there critical periods when children are optimally prepared to benefit from specific environmental experiences? Is the first year of life a critical period for the development of basic trust, and is the second year critical for the development of competence? There is evidence for affirmative answers to each of these questions, but the evidence is far from complete. Perhaps for the present, infant-toddler day-care programs should attempt to match as closely as possible the model of the competent home as exemplified in White's studies of competent mothers. Perhaps specific structured sequential learning environments should be avoided in favor of more spontaneous naturalistic settings. While there are no incontestable answers to many crucial problems, there is an expanding literature which suggests that high-quality infant-toddler day care can be a reality.

Effects of infant-toddler day care   Research comparing infants reared in demonstration day-care projects with home-reared controls supports the contention that quality care can be provided in group settings. In fact, when differences do appear the general trend is for infants and toddlers reared in day-care projects to achieve higher levels of performance than do home-reared controls. Several studies have reported that the cognitive, linguistic, and social competence skills of day-care infants and toddlers are more advanced than those of home-reared controls (Robinson & Robinson, 1971; Fowler, 1972; Lally, 1973; Honig & Brill, 1970; Keister, 1970). Moreover, although day-care infants establish more generalized attach-

Photograph courtesy Paul Rochlen

FIGURE 10–4 Moments to remember: Taking a quiet break from the routine of the day care center program.

ments, their primary attachment is to their mother (Caldwell, Wright, Honig & Tannenbaum, 1970). Day-care mothers, on the other hand, tend to be somewhat less permissive than do home mothers. The study by Caldwell et al. found no significant differences between day-care–reared and home-reared children in their relationships with other children. However, other investigators have reported that day-care–reared toddlers are less attentive to peers than are home-reared toddlers (Kagan, Kearsley & Zelazo, 1975).

Thus far, the results of studies comparing day-care–reared infants and toddlers to home-reared controls are encouraging. However, many potential problem areas associated with infant-toddler day care have yet to be systematically studied (Stevenson & Fitzgerald, 1972). Will day care change parental attitudes toward their child-rearing responsibilities? Is day care appropriate for all infants? How much time should infants spend in a day-care setting? How might parents be effectively involved in the day-care program?

Perhaps the basic problem, however, is the cost of infant-toddler day care. Infant day care is expensive! Estimates of the annual cost of day care for each infant range from $2,000 to $3,000 or more, pricing significant numbers of potential consumers out of the market. Obviously, the massive implementation of infant-toddler day care would require a substantial infusion of government funds. It remains to be seen whether our society will judge it worthwhile to make this financial investment to protect our most vital natural resource—our children—and to assure high-quality care for the new school-age child.

SUMMARY

Infancy and early childhood is a time for skill acquisition. It is a time from which the child emerges either with an inner feeling that he or she is able to deal effectively with the events and persons in the environment or, conversely, with a feeling that little control over the environment is possible. The specific skills and behavior patterns which reflect the child's mastery of the environment are referred to collectively as competence skills. Competence skills include both social and nonsocial skills, but in either case are the foundation upon which social behavior is constructed.

The development of a sense of trust in one's environment and in one's significant caregivers provides an optimal foundation for the development of competence. Parents who are loving, supportive, and accepting, who allow children to participate in decision making, and who expect children to obey household rules, create a climate which enhances the development of competence. Many aspects of social competence are learned through peer interaction. Play and peer involvement provide many opportunities for children to solve problems, ask questions, share experiences, and direct activities. Although a good deal of early play is solitary, such play is usually goal-directed and often rich in fantasy and creative expression. During the toddler and preschool years children develop the social skills essential for cooperative play and effective social give-and-take with peers and adults. Many preschools facilitate the learning of skills by providing children with a controlled environment in which they can test their developing competencies. In preschools, teachers and peers help children to learn respect for others and to achieve desired goals through cooperation. Preschools can help children to learn self-control, sharing, and concern for others, all of which are effective competence skills. Moreover, preschools can provide children from diverse ethnic and racial backgrounds with living and learning experiences that can be an important means of countering the destructive and dehumanizing forces of prejudice.

For one reason or another, many children are reared in environments which inhibit the development of trust, inner-directedness and competence. Educational enrichment programs based on the concept of developmental intervention and involving both children and parents have been successful in enhancing competence. Today many changes in our society are stimulating increased demand for supplementary child care. So great is the potential demand for these services that the infant and toddler may well be the new school-age child. Demonstration projects have provided some evidence to suggest that infants and toddlers who attend day-care centers do not experience developmental lag or suffer from the effects of maternal absence, maternal employment, father absence, or group care. In fact, quite the opposite seems to be the case. Nevertheless, many important issues regarding the day care of infants and toddlers have yet to be systematically studied. In all likelihood, the supplementary child care of the future will consist of some blend of day care, home care, and increased father involvement in routine caregiving. In the final analysis, the important question will be whether supplementary child care provides the opportunity for all children and their parents to have happy, productive, satisfying, and meaningful lives.

SUGGESTED ADDITIONAL READING

Provence, S. *Guide for the care of infants in groups.* New York: Child Welfare League of America, Inc., 1967.

Stevenson, M. B., & Fitzgerald, H. E. "Standards for infant day care in the United States and Canada," *Child Care Quarterly,* 1971, *1,* 89–110.

White, B. L., & Watts, J. C. *Experience and environment: Major influences on the development of the young child.* Englewood Cliffs, N.J.: Prentice-Hall, 1973.

GLOSSARY

Adaptation Changing behavior appropriately to meet social and nonsocial environmental demands.

Affect A synonym for emotion.

Aggression Inflicting harm on a person or an object. Some definitions require that the act be intentional; others do not.

Amniotic fluid A "salty" solution that fills the amniotic sac and protects the embryo and fetus from mechanical injury.

Anticipatory grief An emotional state that develops in parents when separated from their prematurely born infant. They "anticipate" that the infant will die. This interferes with the subsequent development of the attachment relationship.

Associationism A theory which maintains that the contents of consciousness reflect the associative links formed between ideas. Stimulus-response associations are thought to be particularly important.

Attachment The social-emotional bond between infants and caregivers. Separating oneself from the attached object is referred to as *detachment*.

Attention The ability to focus on specific features of available stimulation while inhibiting one's reaction to distracting or irrelevant stimulation.

Biological rhythms Regular, repeating patterns of activity of various lengths or cycles.

Biological vulnerability The degree to which the developing organism is detrimentally influenced by environmental or biological stress. Can produce damage (morbidity) or death (mortality).

Brain waves   The activity of the brain recorded electronically by the use of electrodes placed on the scalp. Recordings of brain waves are called electroencephalograms.

Centration   Focusing on one aspect of a stimulus or problem and failing to incorporate other aspects. In a sense, looking at one part while failing to see the whole.

Chromosomes   Threadlike substances in the cell nucleus on which genes (alleles) are located.

Classical conditioning   The Pavlovian procedure for studying the formation of stimulus-stimulus and stimulus-response associations.

Cognitive styles   Concept categories used to relate objects. Three cognitive styles have been identified: descriptive, relational-contextual, and categorical-inferential.

Competence   In the biological sense, an intrinsic motivational force. Operationally, the specific skills and abilities that enable efficient and effective interaction with the environment.

Conscience   The internalization of rules (moral standards) of conduct.

Contingent   A relationship involving a dependency: to say that *A* is contingent upon *B* implies that *B* must occur before *A* can.

Correlation   The relationship between variables. Expressed numerically, the degree to which variables deviate from a perfect relationship.

Critical period   A time when the organization of behavior is most easily influenced positively or negatively by environmental events.

Cross-sectional study   A research procedure in which groups of subjects are observed at different periods in time so that differences relating their ages may be described. Yields information regarding *age differences*.

Cytoplasm   The substance of a cell exclusive of the nucleus.

Dependency   Being reliant on someone else to have one's needs gratified. As self-initiated and autonomous behavior emerges, the organism becomes increasingly *independent* and capable of self-gratification.

Developmental psychology   The subarea of psychology concerned with changes in the organization of behavioral systems throughout the life span.

Dominant gene   A gene that will be expressed in the phenotype of an organism whenever it is paired with a recessive gene or another dominant gene.

Dyad   A social unit consisting of two persons.

Endogenous stimulation   Stimulation arising inside the body.

Entrainment   The regulation of a biological rhythm by an external stimulus.

Epigenesis   The principle of development which asserts that organization is a constructive process in which each new level of organization represents a reorganization of prior levels.

Exogenous stimulation   Stimulation arising in the external environment.

Expressive language   The ability to communicate through spoken language.

Extinction   A gradual reduction in the strength or frequency of a learned behavior due to the withdrawal of reinforcement.

Gametogenesis   A process which results in the production of sperm (spermatogenesis) and ova (oogenesis), the reproductive cells.

Genetic epistemology   Literally, the biology of knowledge. Piaget's designation for his theory of cognitive development.

Genotype   The inferred genetic makeup of the individual.

Habituation   A decrease in the strength of the orienting reaction upon repeated presentations of the same stimulus.

Histogenesis   The formation and development of the tissues of the body.

Holophrase   A single word which represents a more complex linguistic utterance. A "one-word sentence."

Homeostasis   Stability. The regulatory process which enables the organism to maintain a degree of stability or equilibrium. Usually applied to physiological and biochemical processes.

Identification   Behaving like a model and adopting the values, attitudes, and beliefs of the model.

Intelligence   Various definitions including: (a) some innate capacity, (b) specific abilities, (c) a test score, and (d) the effectiveness with which the organism adapts to its environment.

Invariant   Unchanging. An invariant stage sequence is a sequence which always occurs in the same order.

Lateralization   The idea that each hemisphere of the brain is especially adapted for certain functions: for example, the left hemisphere for language and the right hemisphere for spatiotemporal processing.

Learning   Relatively permanent changes in behavior as a function of adapting to the environment. The changes must not be due to fatigue, drugs, altered stages of consciousness, and so on.

Level of arousal   The organism's overall level of functioning—ranging from deep sleep to screaming rage—at any given moment in time.

Longitudinal study   A research procedure in which the same individuals are studied over time and changes in their behavior are observed.

Maturation   Changes in behavior that cannot be accounted for by learning as it is traditionally defined. From the psychobiological perspective, however, maturation is not considered to be completely independent of experience.

Mechanistic   A view of the organism as analogous to a machine. Posits that the whole is no more than the sum of its parts.

Meiosis   Cell division in which pairs of chromosomes separate and the nucleus divides, leaving only one member of each pair in each new germ cell (sperm or ovum).

Mitosis   Cell division in which chromosomes split and separate, producing two identical new cells.

Morphogenesis   The differentiation of cells and tissues which establishes the form and structure of the various organs and parts of the body.

Motion parallax   A monocular visual cue which results from movement of the head or eye.

Object concept   The concept of objects as independent entities apart from the self (subject). When one "knows" that objects not directly available to sensory perception exist, *object permanence* is said to develop.

Obstetrical medications   Drugs used to reduce or eliminate the pain associated with labor and delivery.

Ontogenesis   The individual's interaction with the environment during development. Individual adaptation.

Operant conditioning   The Skinnerian form of learning. Occurs when spontaneous behavior is followed by reinforcement.

Organismic   The view of the organism as a living system, as a whole which is not reducible to its component parts.

Organization   The degree to which the parts of a system are interdependent.

Orienting reaction (response, reflex)   The organism's initial response to a stimulus change. Consists of physiological and behavioral components which are not necessarily positively related.

Ovulation   The release of the ovum from the ovary. Usually occurs about midway through the menstrual cycle.

Pacification   Reducing the arousal level of social or nonsocial external stimulation. Pacification due to constant, monotonous, slightly intense nonsocial stimulation has been termed the "continuous stimulation effect" (Brackbill).

Parturition   The birth process, including labor, delivery, and afterbirth.

Perceptual constancy   The perceptual compensation by means of which objects retain constant properties despite changes in their appearance, as for example, in size, shape, or color.

Perceptual systems   James Gibson's term for the basic modes of external attention. These include the basic sensory apparatus and the more central perceptual processes.

Phylogenesis   The origin and evolution of a species: Species adaptation.

Prelinguistic vocalizations   Vocal behaviors prior to the development of linguistic speech. Include crying, babbling, lallation, echolalia.

Pseudoconditioning   General sensitization of the organism resulting from the presentation of an unconditional stimulus (UCS). The UCS causes an unconditional response (UCR) to occur after presentation of any stimulus. This response may appear to be the same as a conditional response (CR), but it is not time-locked or contingent on the occurrence of a conditional stimulus (CS).

Psychobiology The view which asserts that behavioral organization is most comprehensively understood by considering the biological and psychological determinants of behavior as reciprocally influential.

Psychosexual theory Freud's theory of personality development, which posits five stages: oral, anal, phallic, latency, and genital.

Receptive language The ability to understand spoken language.

Replication Repeating an experiment precisely as it was conducted previously.

Representational competence The ability to deal effectively with symbolic representations of objects.

Retinal disparity A binocular visual cue that retinal images of an object are out of line with each other.

Schema An internal (mental) representation of an event.

Scheme Actions or operations used to transform objects.

Sex role A set of expectations for a person's behavior and characteristics that is based on that person's sex. An ascribed role rather than an achieved role.

Socialization The process whereby one's attitudes, beliefs, values, and behaviors are influenced by others.

Social learning theory A theory of development which asserts that all behavior is learned. Emphasizes the importance of observational learning, imitation, and reinforcement.

Stranger fear Wariness or "fear" of unfamiliar persons. Typically, this appears during the second half of the first year of life and peaks in intensity around the end of the first year. It is not observed in all children, and its appearance is affected by a variety of setting variables.

System A set of organized and interdependent entities which function as a whole.

Tags Questions attached to the end of a sentence which request a confirmation of the statement.

Threshold The level of stimulation intensity which will elicit a response at least 50 percent of the time it is presented.

Variable An event. *Independent* variables are the events that the experimenter observes, manipulates, or controls in order to assess their effects on dependent variables. *Dependent* variables vary systematically with independent variables and are the events used to measure the effects of the experimental manipulation.

Weanling diarrhea Caused by nutritionally inadequate diets following the termination of breast feeding. Occurs in underdeveloped cultures.

REFERENCES

Aeberle, D. F. Middle class fathers: Occupational role and attitude toward children. *American Journal of Orthopsychiatry,* 1952, *22,* 366–378.

Ahrens, R. Beitrag zur Entwicklung des Physiognomie- und Mimikerkenness. (Contribution on the development of physiognomy and mimicry recognition.) *Z. Exp. Angew. Psychol.,* 1954, *2,* 412–454, 599–633.

Ainsworth, M. D. S., & Bell, S. M. Some contemporary patterns of mother-infant interaction in the feeding situation. In A. Ambrose (Ed.), *Stimulation in early infancy.* New York: Academic Press, 1969.

Ainsworth, M. D. S.; Bell, S. M. V.; & Strayton, D. J. Individual differences in strange-situation behavior of one-year-olds. In H. R. Schaffer (Ed.), *The origins of human social relations.* New York: Academic Press, 1971.

Allen, F. R., Jr., & Dimond, L. K. Prevention of kernicterus: Management of erythroblastosis fetalis according to current knowledge. *Journal of the American Medical Association,* 1954, *155,* 1209–1213.

Altman, J. *Organic foundations of animal behavior.* New York: Holt, Rinehart & Winston, 1966.

Ambrose, J. A. The concept of a critical period for the development of social responsiveness. In B. M. Foss (Ed.), *Determinants of infant behavior.* Vol. 2. London: Methuen, 1963.

Andre-Thomas, Chesni, Y., & St. Anne-Dargassies, S. *The neurological examination of the infant.* London: Medical Advisory Committee of the National Spastics Society, 1960.

Antonov, A. N. Children born during the siege of Leningrad in 1942. *Journal of Pediatrics,* 1947, *30,* 250–259.

Aronson, E., & Rosenbloom, S. Space perception in early infancy: Perception within a common auditory-visual space. *Science,* 1971, *172,* 1161–1163.

Aschoff, J. (Ed.). *Circadian clocks.* Amsterdam: North-Holland, 1965.

Ball, W., & Tronick, E. Infant responses to impending collision: Optical and real. *Science,* 1971, *171,* 818–820.

Bandura, A., & Walters, R. H. *Social learning and personality development.* New York: Holt, Rinehart & Winston, 1963.

Barnes, A. C. *Intra-uterine development.* Philadelphia: Lea & Febiger, 1968.

Barry, H. A., & Paxson, C. M. Infancy and early childhood: Cross-cultural codes. 2. *Ethnology,* 1971, *10,* 466–509.

Bartemeier, L. The contribution of the father to the mental health of the family. *American Journal of Psychiatry,* 1953, *110,* 277–280.

Bartley, S. H. *Principles of perception.* New York: Harper & Row, 1969.

Baumrind, D. Effects of authoritative parental control in child behavior. *Child Development,* 1966, *37,* 887–907.

Baumrind, D. Current patterns of parental authority. *Developmental Psychology Monographs,* 1971, *4*(1), 1–103.

Bayley, N. Comparisons of mental and motor test scores for ages 1–15 months by sex, birth order, race, geographical location, and education of parents. *Child Development,* 1965, *36,* 379–411.

Bayley, N. & Schaefer, E. S. Correlations of maternal and child behavior with the development of mental abilities: Data from the Berkeley Growth Study. *Monographs of the Society for Research in Child Development,* 1964, *29,* Serial No. 97.

Beckwith, L. Relationships between attributes of mothers and their infants' IQ scores. *Child Development,* 1971, *42,* 1083–1097.

Bell, R. Q. A reinterpretation of the direction of effects in studies of socialization. *Psychological Review,* 1968, *75,* 81–95.

Bell, R. Q. Contributions of human infants to caregiving and social interaction. In M. Lewis & L. A. Rosenblum (Eds.), *The effect of the infant on its caregiver.* New York: Wiley-Interscience, 1974.

Bell, R. Q., & Costello, N. S. Three tests for sex differences in tactile sensitivity in the newborn. *Biologia Neonatorum,* 1964, *7*(6), 335–347.

Bell, S. M., & Ainsworth, M. D. S. Infant crying and maternal responsiveness. *Child Development,* 1972, *43,* 1171–1190.

Bereiter, C. An academic preschool for disadvantaged children: Conclusions from evaluation. In J. C. Stanley (Ed.), *Preschool programs for the disadvantaged.* Baltimore: Johns Hopkins University Press, 1972.

Berger, R. J. Oculomotor control: A possible function of REM sleep. *Psychological Review,* 1969, *76,* 144–164.

Bergman, T.; Haith, M. M.; & Mann, L. Development of eye contact and facial scanning in infants. Paper presented at the meeting of the Society for Research in Child Development, Minneapolis, April 1971.

Biber, B. *Children's drawings: From lines to pictures.* New York: Bureau of Educational Experiments, 1934.

Bijou, S. W., & Baer, D. M. *Child development I: A systematic and empirical theory.* New York: Appleton-Century-Crofts, 1961.

Bower, T. G. R. The visual world of infants. *Scientific American,* 1966, *215,* 80–92.

Bowes, W. A., Jr. Obstetrical medication and infant outcome: A review of the literature. In W. A. Bowes, Jr., Y. Brackbill, E. Conway, & A. Steinschneider, The effects of obstetrical medication on fetus and infant, *Monographs of the Society for Research in Child Development,* 1970, *35,* Serial No. 137.

Bowlby, J. *Attachment.* New York: Basic Books, 1969.

Boyd, E. F. Visual fixation and voice discrimination in 2-month-old infants. In F. D. Horowitz (Ed.), Visual attention, auditory stimulation, and language discrimination in young infants. *Monographs of the Society for Research in Child Development,* 1975, *39,* Serial No. 158.

Brackbill, Y. Extinction of the smiling response in infants as a function of reinforcement schedule. *Child Development,* 1958, *29,* 115–124.

Brackbill, Y. Research and clinical work with children. In R. A. Bauer (Ed.), *Some views of Soviet psychology.* Washington, D.C.: American Psychological Association, 1962.

Brackbill, Y. A national disgrace. *Contemporary Psychology,* 1969, *14,* 373–374.

Brackbill, Y. The cumulative effects of continuous stimulation on arousal level in infants. *Child Development,* 1970, *42,* 17–26.

Brackbill, Y. The role of the cortex in orienting: Orienting reflex in an anencephalic human infant. *Developmental Psychology,* 1971, *5,* 195–201.

Brackbill, Y. Continuous stimulation reduces arousal level: Stability of the effect over time. *Child Development,* 1973, *44,* 43–46.

Brackbill, Y. Continuous stimulation and arousal level in infancy: Effects of stimulus intensity and stress. *Child Development.* 1975, *46,* 364–369.

Brackbill, Y.; Adams, G.; Crowell, D. H.; & Gray, M. L. Arousal level in neonates and preschool children under continuous auditory stimulation. *Journal of Experimental Child Psychology,* 1966, *4,* 178–188.

Brackbill, Y.; Douthitt, T. C.; & West, H. Neonatal posture: Psychophysiological effects. *Journal of Pediatrics,* 1973, *82,* 82–84.

Brackbill, Y., & Fitzgerald, H. E. Development of the sensory analyzers during infancy. In L. P. Lipsitt & H. W. Reese (Eds.), *Advances in child development and behavior.* Vol. 4. New York: Academic Press, 1969.

Brackbill, Y., & Fitzgerald, H. E. Stereotype temporal conditioning in infants. *Psychophysiology,* 1972, *9,* 569–577.

Brackbill, Y.; Fitzgerald, H. E.; & Lintz, L. M. A developmental study of classical conditioning. *Monographs of the Society for Research in Child Development,* 1967, *38,* Serial No. 116.

Brackbill, Y., & Kappy, M. S. Delay of reinforcement and retention. *Journal of Comparative and Physiological Psychology,* 1962, *55,* 14–18.

Braine, M. D. S. The ontogeny of English phrase structure: The first phase. *Language,* 1963, *39,* 1–13.

Brennan, W. M.; Ames, E. W.; & Moore, R. W. Age differences in infants' attention to patterns of different complexities. *Science,* 1966, *151,* 354–356.

Brody, S., & Axelrad, S. Maternal stimulation and the social responsiveness of infants. In H. R. Schaffer (Ed.), *The origins of human social relations.* New York: Academic Press, 1971.

Bronfenbrenner, U. Soviet methods of character education: Some implications for research. *American Psychologist,* 1962, *17,* 550–564.

Bronshtein, A. I.; Antonova, T. G.; Kamenetskaya, A. G.; Luppova, N. N.; & Sytova, V. A. On the development of the functions of analyzers in infants and some animals at the early stage of ontogenesis. In *Problems of Education of Physiological Functions.* U.S.S.R.: Academy of Science, 1958.

Bronson, G. The hierarchical organization of the CNS: Implications for learning processes and critical periods in early development. *Behavioral Science,* 1965, *10,* 7–25.

Bronson, G. The development of fear in man and other animals. *Child Development,* 1968, *39,* 409–431.

Bronson, W. C. The growth of competence: Issues of conceptualization and measurement. In H. R. Schaffer (Ed.), *The origins of human social relations.* New York: Academic Press, 1971.

Brossard, L. M., & DeCarie, T. C. Comparative reinforcing effects of eight stimulations on the smiling response in infants. *Journal of Child Psychology and Psychiatry and Allied Disciplines,* 1968, *9,* 51–59.

Brown, R. *A first language: The early stages.* Cambridge, Mass.: Harvard University Press, 1973.

Brown, R., & Bellugi, U. Three processes in the child's acquisition of syntax. *Harvard Educational Review,* 1964, *34,* 133–151.

Brown, R., & Berko, J. Word association and the acquisition of grammar. *Child Development,* 1960, *31,* 1–14.

Brown, R., & Fraser, C. The acquisition of syntax. In C. N. Cofer & B. S. Musgrave (Eds.), *Verbal behavior and learning: Problems and processes.* New York: McGraw-Hill, 1963.

Brown, R., & Hanlon, C. Derivational complexity and order of acquisition in child speech. In J. R. Hayes (Ed.), *Cognition and the development of language.* New York: Wiley, 1970.

Brown, R., & Herrnstein, R. J. *Psychology.* Boston: Little, Brown, 1975.

Bruner, J. S. The course of cognitive growth. *American Psychologist,* 1964, *19,* 1–15.

Bruner, J. S. *The process of education.* Cambridge, Mass.: Harvard University Press, 1960.

Caldwell, B. M.; Wright, C. M.; Honig, A. S.; & Tannenbaum, J. Infant day care and attachment. *American Journal of Orthopsychiatry,* 1970, *40,* 397–412.

Campbell, D. Adaptations to the environment by the newborn child. *Canadian Psychologist,* 1968, *9,* 467–473.

Campbell, D. T., & Stanley, J. C. *Experimental and quasi-experimental designs for research.* Chicago: Rand McNally, 1963.

Canestrini, S. Über das Sinnesleben des Neugeborenen. (Sensations of the neonate.) *Monogr. a. d. Gestamtgeb. d. Neur. u. Psychiat.,* No. 5. Berlin: Springer, 1913.

Caron, A.; Caron, R.; Caldwell, R.; & Weiss, S. Infant perception of the structural properties of the face. *Developmental Psychology,* 1973, *9,* 385–399.

Carpenter, G. C. Attention to moving and stationary faces in early infancy. Paper presented at the meeting of the British Psychological Society, Nottingham, April 1972.

Carpenter, G. C.; Tecce, J. J.; Stechler, G.; & Friedman, S. Differential visual behavior to human and humanoid faces in early infancy. *Merrill-Palmer Quarterly,* 1970, *16,* 91–108.

Carr, S. J.; Dabbs, J. M., Jr.; & Carr, T. S. Mother-infant attachment: The importance of the mother's visual field. *Child Development,* 1975, *46,* 331–338.

Casler, L. The effects of extra tactile stimulation on a group of institutionalized infants. *Genetic Psychology Monographs,* 1965, *71,* 137–175.

Catz, S. C., & Giacorca, G. P. Drugs and breast milk. *Pediatric Clinics of North America,* 1972, *19,* 151–166.

Chase, H. P., & Martin, H. P. Undernutrition and child development. *New England Journal of Medicine,* 1970, *282,* 933–939.

Chauncey, H. (Ed.). *Soviet preschool education.* Vol. 1.: *Program of instruction.* Princeton, N.J.: Educational Testing Service, 1969.

Chomsky, N. A. *Aspects of the theory of syntax.* Cambridge, Mass.: MIT Press, 1965.

Chukovsky, K. *From two to five.* (Miriam Morton, Ed. & Trans.) Berkeley: University of California Press, 1963.

Chun, R. W. M.; Pawsat, R.; & Forster, F. M. Sound localization in infancy. *Journal of Nervous and Mental Disease,* 1960, *130,* 472–476.

Clark, M. Kwashiorkor. *East African Medical Journal,* 1951, *28,* 299–336.

Clarke-Stewart, K. A. Interaction between mothers and their young children: Characteristics and consequences. *Monographs of the Society for Research in Child Development,* 1973, *38,* Serial No. 153.

Cobb, K.; Goodwin, R.; & Saelens, E. Spontaneous hand positions of newborn infants. *Journal of Genetic Psychology,* 1966, *108,* 225–237.

Cohen, A. I. Hand preference and developmental status of infants. *Journal of Genetic Psychology,* 1966, *108,* 337–345.

Cohen, L. J., & Campos, J. J. Father, mother, and stranger as elicitors of attachment behaviors in infancy. *Developmental Psychology,* 1974, *10,* 146–154.

Condon, W. S., & Ogston, W. D. Sound film analysis of normal and pathological behavior patterns. *Journal of Nervous and Mental Disease,* 1966, *143,* 338–347.

Condon, W. S., & Sander, L. W. Synchrony demonstrated between movements of the neonate and adult speech. *Child Development,* 1974, *45,* 456–462.

Conway, E., & Brackbill, Y. Delivery medication and infant outcome: An empirical study. In W. A. Bowes, Jr., Y. Brackbill, E. Conway, & A. Steinschneider, The effects of obstetrical medication on fetus and infant. *Monographs of the Society for Research in Child Development,* 1970, *35,* Serial No. 137.

Corner, G. W. *Ourselves unborn: An embryologist's essay on man.* New Haven: Yale University Press, 1944.

Crano, W. D., & Brewer, M. B. *Principles of research in social psychology.* New York: McGraw-Hill, 1973.

Crano, W. D.; Kenny, D. A.; & Campbell, D. T.

Does intelligence cause achievement? A cross-lagged panel analysis. *Journal of Educational Psychology, 1972, 63,* 258–275.

Cratty, B. J. *Perceptual and motor development in infants and children.* New York: Macmillan, 1970.

Cravioto, J., & Robles, B. Evolution of adaptive and motor behavior during rehabilitation from kwashiorkor. *American Journal of Orthopsychiatry,* 1965, *35,* 449–464.

Crowell, D. H.; Jones, R. H.; Kapuniai, L. E.; & Nakagawa, J. K. Unilateral cortical activity in newborn humans: An early index of cerebral dominance. *Science,* 1973, *180,* 205–207.

Davids, A., & Rosengren, W. R. Social stability and psychological adjustment during pregnancy. *Psychosomatic Medicine,* 1962, *24,* 579–583.

Davidson, N. H. Pacification in infants as a function of the agent and preference for tactile stimulation. Unpublished doctoral dissertation, Michigan State University, East Lansing, 1973.

Davidson, N. H., & Fitzgerald, H. E. Recency and summation effects of frustrative nonreward in children. *Journal of Experimental Child Psychology,* 1970, *10,* 16–27.

Dennis, W. A description and classification of the responses of the newborn infant. *Psychological Bulletin,* 1934, *31,* 5–22.

Denny, M. R., & Ratner, S. C. *Comparative psychology.* Homewood, Ill.: Dorsey Press, 1970.

Denny-Brown, D. The general principles of motor integration. In J. Field (Ed.), *Handbook of physiology.* Vol. 2, section 1: *Neurophysiology.* Washington, D.C.: American Physiological Society, 1960.

Dobbing, J. Undernutrition and the developing brain. In W. Himwich (Ed.), *Developmental neurobiology.* Springfield, Ill.: Charles C Thomas, 1970.

Doman, R. J.; Spitz, E. B.; Zucman, E.; Delacato, C. H.; & Doman, G. Children with brain injuries: Neurological organization in terms of mobility. *Journal of the American Medical Association,* 1960, *174,* 257–262.

Douglas, J. W., & Bloomfield, J. M. *Children under five.* London: George Allen & Unwin, 1958.

Dreyfus-Brisac, C. The bioelectric development of the nervous system during early life. In F. Falkner (Ed.), *Human development.* Philadelphia: Saunders, 1966.

Drillien, C. M. *The growth and development of the prematurely born infant.* Edinburgh: E. & S. Livingstone, 1964.

Drillien, C. M. Intellectual sequelae of "fetal malnutrition." In. H. A. Waisman & G. Kerr (Eds.), *Fetal growth and development.* New York: McGraw-Hill, 1970.

Dubowitz, L. M. S.; Dubowitz, V.; & Goldberg, C. Clinical assessment of gestational age in the newborn infant. *Journal of Pediatrics,* 1970, *77,* 1–10.

Eckerman, C. O.; Whatley, J. L.; & Kutz, S. L. Growth of social play with peers during the second year of life. *Developmental Psychology,* 1975, *11,* 42–49.

Eimas, P. D.; Siqueland, E. R.; Jusczyk, P.; & Vigorito, J. Speech perception in infants. *Science,* 1971, *171,* 303–306.

Eisenberg, R. B.; Coursin, D. B.; & Rupp, N. R. Habituation to an acoustic pattern as an index of differences among human neonates. *Journal of Auditory Research,* 1966, *6,* 239–248.

Elkind, D. Cognition in infancy and early childhood. In Y. Brackbill (Ed.), *Infancy and early childhood.* New York: Free Press, 1967.

Emde, R. N.; Harmon, R. J.; Metcalf, D.; Koenig, K. L.; & Wagonfeld, S. Stress and neonatal sleep. *Psychosomatic Medicine.* 1971, *33,* 491–497.

Erikson, E. H. *Childhood and society.* New York: Norton, 1950.

Evans, E. D. *Contemporary influences in early childhood education.* New York: Holt, Rinehart & Winston, 1971.

Ferreira, A. J. *Prenatal environment.* Springfield, Ill.: Charles C Thomas, 1969.

Fitzgerald, H. E. Autonomic pupillary reflex activity during early infancy and its relation to social and nonsocial visual stimuli. *Journal of Experimental Child Psychology,* 1968, *6,* 470–482.

Fitzgerald, H. E. Infants and caregivers: Sex differences as determinants of socialization. In E. Donelson & J. Gullahorn (Eds.), *Women: A psychological perspective.* New York: Wiley, in press.

Fitzgerald, H. E., & Brackbill, Y. Organizacija draz-odgovor, stanje i mogucnost uslovaljavanja u ranom detinjstru. (Stimulus-response organization, state, and conditionability during early infancy.) *Psihologija,* 1974, *7,* 46–57.

Fitzgerald, H. E., & Brackbill, Y. Classical conditioning in infancy: Development and constraints. *Psychological Bulletin,* 1976, *83,* 353–376.

Fitzgerald, H. E., & Porges, S. W. A decade of infant conditioning and learning research. *Merrill-Palmer Quarterly,* 1971, *17,* 79–117.

Forgus, R. H. *Perception.* New York: McGraw-Hill, 1966.

Fowler, W. A developmental learning approach to infant care in a group setting. *Merrill-Palmer Quarterly,* 1972, *18,* 145–175.

Fraiberg, S. Parallel and divergent patterns in blind and sighted infants. *Psychoanalytic Study of the Child,* 1968, *23,* 264–300.

Fraiberg, S. Blind infants and their mothers: An examination of the sign system. In M. Lewis & L. A. Rosenblum (Eds.), *The effect of the infant on its caregiver.* New York: Wiley-Interscience, 1974.

Freedman, D. A.; Fox-Kolenda, B. J.; Margileth, D. A.; & Miller, D. H. The development of the use of sound as a guide to affective and cognitive behavior—a two-phase process. *Child Development,* 1969, *40,* 1099–1105.

Friedlander, B. Z. The effect of speaker identity, voice inflection, vocabulary, and message redundancy on infants' selection of vocal reinforcement. *Journal of Experimental Child Psychology,* 1968, *6,* 443–459.

Friedlander, B. Z. Receptive language development in infancy: issues and problems. *Merrill-Palmer Quarterly,* 1970, *16,* 7–52.

Friedlander, B. Z.; Cyrulic, A.; & Davis, B. Time-sampling analyses of infants' natural language environments in the home. Paper presented at the meeting of the Society for Research in Child Development, Minneapolis, April 1971.

Gale, L. E., & Pol, G. Competence: A definition and conceptual scheme. *Educational Technology,* 1975, June, 19–25.

Gallagher, J. J., & Bradley, R. H. Early identification of developmental difficulties, *Seventy-First Yearbook of the National Society for the Study of Education.* Chicago: University of Chicago Press, 1972.

Gardner, L. P. A survey of the attitudes and activities of fathers. *Journal of Genetic Psychology,* 1943, *63,* 15–53.

Gardner, R. A., & Gardner, B. T. Teaching sign language to a chimpanzee. *Science,* 1969, *165,* 664–672.

Gesell, A. The ontogenesis of behavior. In L. Carmichael (Ed.), *Manual of child psychology.* New York: Wiley, 1954.

Gesell, A., & Amatruda, C. S. *The embryology of behavior: The beginnings of the human mind.* New York: Harper & Row, 1945.

Gibson, E. J., & Walk, R. D. The "visual cliff." *Scientific American,* 1960, *202,* 64–71.

Gibson, J. *The senses considered as perceptual systems.* Boston: Houghton Mifflin, 1966.

Golden, M., & Birns, B. Social class, intelligence, and cognitive style in infancy. *Child Development,* 1971, *42,* 2114–2116.

Golden, M.; Birns, B.; Bridger, W.; & Moss, A. Social-class differentiation in cognitive development among black preschool children. *Child Development,* 1971, *42,* 37–45.

Gomez, F.; Ramos-Galvan, R.; Frenk, S.; Cravioto Muñoz, J.; Chavez, R.; & Vasquez, J. Mortality in second and third degree malnutrition. *Journal of Tropical Medicine,* 1956, Sept., 77–83.

Gouin-DeCarie, T., and Associates. *The infant's reaction to strangers.* New York: International Universities Press, 1974.

Graham, F. K., & Jackson, J. C. Arousal systems and infant heart rate responses. In H. W. Reese & L. P. Lipsitt (Eds.), *Advances in child development and behavior.* Vol. 5. New York: Academic Press, 1970.

Green, E. H. Friendships and quarrels among preschool children. *Child Development,* 1933, *4,* 237–252.

Greenberg, D. J. Accelerating visual complexity levels in the human infant. *Child Development,* 1971, *42,* 905–918.

Greenberg, M., & Morris, N. Engrossment:

The newborn's impact upon the father. *American Journal of Orthopsychiatry,* 1974, *44,* 520–531.

Gruenwald, P. Fetal malnutrition. In H. A. Waisman & G. R. Kerr (Eds.), *Fetal growth and development.* New York: McGraw-Hill, 1970.

Guilford, J. P. Intelligence: 1965 model. *American psychologist,* 1966, *21,* 20–26.

Guthrie, H. A. Infant feeding practices—a predisposing factor in hypertension? *American Journal of Clinical Nutrition,* 1968, *21,* 863–867.

Harfouche, J. K. The importance of breast feeding. *Journal of Tropical Pediatrics,* 1970, 135–175.

Harlow, H. F. *Learning to love.* San Francisco: Albion, 1970.

Harris, L. J. Neurophysiological factors in spatial development. Paper presented at the Society for Research in Child Development symposium on "Children's spatial development: Different research orientations," Philadelphia, March 1973.

Harris, L. J. Sex differences in the growth and use of language. In E. Donelson & J. Gullahorn (Eds.), *Women: A psychological perspective.* New York: Wiley, in press.

Hartmann, H. *Ego psychology and the problem of adaptation.* (D. Rappaport, trans.) New York: International Universities Press, 1958.

Hatfield, J. S.; Ferguson, L. R.; & Alpert, R. Mother-child interaction and the socialization process. *Child Development,* 1967, *38,* 365–414.

Hayes, K. J., & Hayes, C. Imitation in a home raised chimpanzee. *Journal of Comparative and Physiological Psychology,* 1952, *45,* 450–459.

Hebb, D. O. *A textbook of psychology.* Philadelphia: Saunders, 1966.

Heber, R., & Garber, H. The Milwaukee project: A study of the use of family intervention to prevent cultural-familial mental retardation. In B. Z. Friedlander, B. M. Sterritt, & G. E. Kirk (Eds.), *Exceptional infant.* Vol. 3: *Assessment and intervention.* New York: Brunner/Mazel, 1975.

Helgerson, E. The relative significance of race and sex and facial expression in choice of playmate by the preschool child. *Journal of Negro Education,* 1943, *12,* 617–622.

Hendrick, I. Instinct and the ego during infancy. *Psychoanalytic Quarterly,* 1942, *11,* 33–58.

Herrick, C. J. *The evolution of human nature.* Austin: University of Texas Press, 1956.

Hershenson, M. Visual discrimination in the human newborn. *Journal of Comparative and Physiological Psychology,* 1964, *58,* 270–276.

Herzog, E., & Sudea, C. E. *Boys in fatherless families.* Washington, D.C.: United States Department of Health, Education, and Welfare, Office of Child Development, Children's Bureau, 1970.

Hetherington, E. M., & Deur, J. The effects of father absence on child development. In W. W. Hartup (Ed.), *The young child: Reviews of research.* Vol. 2. Washington, D.C.: National Association for the Education of Young Children, 1972.

Himwich, H. E. *Brain metabolism and cerebral disorders.* Baltimore: Williams & Wilkins, 1951.

Hodges, W. L., & Spicker, H. H. The effects of preschool experiences on culturally deprived children. In W. W. Hartup & N. L. Smothergill (Eds.), *The young child: Reviews of research.* Washington, D.C.: National Association for the Education of Young Children, 1967.

Hoffman, L. W. Effects of maternal employment on the child: A review of research. *Developmental Psychology,* 1974, *10,* 204–228.

Honig, A. S., & Brill, S. A comparative analysis of the Piagetian development of twelve-month-old disadvantaged infants in an enrichment center with others not in such a center. Paper presented at the meeting of the American Psychological Association, Miami, September, 1970.

Honzik, M. P.; Hutchings, J. J.; & Burnip, S. R. Birth record assessments and test performance at eight months. *American Journal of Diseases of Childhood,* 1965, *109,* 416–426.

Hooper, F. H. Cognitive assessment across the life-span: Methodological implications of the organismic approach. In J. R. Nesselroade & H. W. Reese (Eds.), *Life-span developmental psychology: Methodological issues,* New York: Academic Press, 1973.

Horn, J. L. Intelligence—why it grows and why it declines. *Trans-action,* 1967, *4,* 23–31.

Horn, J. L. Organization of abilities and the development of intelligence. *Psychological Review,* 1968, *75,* 242–259.

Hull, C. L., & Hull, B. I. Parallel learning curves of an infant in vocabulary and in voluntary control of the bladder. *Pedogogical Seminary,* 1919, *26,* 272–283.

Hurlock, E. B. *Child development.* 4th ed. New York: McGraw-Hill, 1964.

Ingram, E., & Fitzgerald, H. E. Individual differences in infant orienting and autonomic conditioning. *Developmental Psychobiology,* 1974, *7,* 359–367.

Irwin, O. C. Effects of strong light on the body activity of newborns. *Journal of Comparative Psychology,* 1941, *32,* 233–236.

Jeffrey, W. E., & Cohen, L. B. Effect of spatial separation of stimulus, response, and reinforcement in selective learning in children. *Journal of Experimental Psychology,* 1964, *67,* 577–580.

Jensen, A. R. How much can we boost IQ and scholastic achievement? *Harvard Educational Review,* 1969, *39,* 1–123.

Jensen, K. Differential reactions to taste and temperature stimuli in newborn infants. *Genetic Psychology Monographs,* 1932, *12,* 361–479.

Johnson, D. L. The development of a program for parent-child education among Mexican-Americans in Texas. In B. Z. Friedlander, G. M. Sterritt, & G. E. Kirk (Eds.), *Exceptional infant* Vol. 3: *Assessment and intervention.* New York: Brunner/Mazel, 1975.

Kagan, J. On the need for relativism. *American Psychologist,* 1967, *22,* 131–142.

Kagan, J. Attention and psychological change in the young child. *Science,* 1970, *170,* 826–832.

Kagan, J.; Kearsley, R. B.; & Zelazo, P. R. The emergence of initial apprehension to unfamiliar peers. In M. Lewis & L. Rosen-

blum (Eds.), *Peer relations and friendship.* New York: Wiley, 1975.

Kagan, J., & Moss, H. A. *Birth to maturity: A study in psychological development.* New York: Wiley, 1962.

Karnes, M. B.; Teska, J. A.; Hodgins, A. S.; & Badger, E. D. Educational intervention at home by mothers of disadvantaged infants. *Child Development,* 1970, *41,* 925–936.

Kasatkin, N. I. First conditioned reflexes and the beginning of the learning process in the human infant. In G. Newton & A. H. Riesen (Eds.), *Advances in psychobiology.* New York: Wiley-Interscience, 1972.

Keister, M. E. A demonstration project: Group care of infants and toddlers. Final report submitted to the Children's Bureau, Office of Child Development, United States Department of Health, Education, and Welfare, 1970.

Kellogg, S., & O'Dell, S. *Analyzing children's art.* Palo Alto, Calif.: National Press Books, 1969.

Kellogg, W. N. Communication and language in the home-raised chimpanzee. *Science,* 1968, *162,* 423–427.

Kenderdine, M. Laughter in the pre-school child. *Child Development,* 1931, *2,* 228–230.

Kendler, H. H., & Kendler, T. S. Developmental changes in discrimination learning. *Human Development,* 1970, *13,* 75–89.

Kendon, A. Some functions of gaze-aversion in social interaction. *Acta Psychologica,* 1967, *26,* 22–63.

Kessen, W., & Mandler, G. Anxiety, pain, and the inhibition of distress. *Psychological Review,* 1961, *68,* 396–404.

King, W. L., & Seegmiller, B. Performance of 14- to 22-month-old black firstborn male infants on two tests of cognitive development: The Bayley Scales and the Infant Psychological Development Scale. *Developmental Psychology,* 1973, *8,* 317–326.

Koch, J. Conditioned orienting reactions to persons and things in 2–5 month-old infants. *Human Development,* 1968, *11,* 81–91. (a)

Koch, J. The change of conditioned orientation reactions in 5-month-old infants through phase shift of partial biorhythms. *Human Development,* 1968, *11,* 124–137. (b)

Kodera, T. L. Cognitive classical conditioning mechanisms in infant exploratory behavior. Unpublished doctoral dissertation, Michigan State University, East Lansing, 1975.

Krachkovskaia, M. B. Reflex change in the leukocyte count of newborn infants in relation to food intake. *Pavlov Journal of Higher Nervous Activity,* 1959, *9,* 193–199.

Kron, R. E.; Stein, M.; & Goddard, K. E. Newborn sucking behavior affected by obstetric sedation. *Pediatrics,* 1966, *37,* 1012–1016.

Kulka, A., Fry, C.; & Goldstein, F. J. Kinesthetic needs in infancy. *American Journal of Orthopsychiatry,* 1960, *30,* 562–571.

Lakin, M. Personality factors in mothers of excessively crying (colicky) infants. *Monographs of the Society for Research in Child Development,* 1957, *22,* No. 1.

Lally, R. J. The family development research program: A program for prenatal, infant, and early childhood enrichment. College for Human Development, Syracuse University, 1973.

Landy, F.; Rosenberg, B. G.; & Sutton-Smith, B. The effect of limited father absence on cognitive development. *Child Development,* 1969, *40,* 941–944.

Langlois, J. H.; Gottfried, N. W.; & Seay, B. The influence of sex of peer on the social behavior of preschool children. *Developmental Psychology,* 1973, *8,* 93–98.

Latif, I. The physiological basis of linguistic development and the ontogeny of meaning. 1, 2. *Psychological Review,* 1934, *41,* 55–85, 153–176.

Laub, K. W., & McCluskey, K. A. Visual discrimination of social stimuli with and without auditory cues. In F. D. Horowitz (Ed.), Visual attention, auditory stimulation, and language discrimination in young infants. *Monographs of the Society for Research in Child Development,* 1975, *39,* Serial No. 158.

Lee, L. D. Concept utilization in young children. *Child Development,* 1965, *36,* 221–227.

Lenneberg, E. H. *Biological foundations of language.* New York: Wiley, 1967.

Lenneberg, E. H. On explaining language. *Science,* 1969, *164,* 635–643.

Lenneberg, E. H.; Rebelsky, F. C.; & Nichols, I. A. The vocalizations of infants born to deaf and to hearing parents. *Human Development,* 1965, *8,* 23–37.

Lester, B. M. Cardiac habituation of the orienting response to an auditory signal in infants of varying nutritional status. *Developmental Psychology,* 1975, *11,* 432–442.

Lester, B. M. The consequences of infantile malnutrition. In H. E. Fitzgerald & J. P. McKinney (Eds.), *Developmental psychology: Studies in human development.* Rev. ed. Homewood, Ill.: Dorsey Press, 1977.

Lester, B. M.; Kotelchuck, M.; Spelke, E.; Sellers, M. J.; & Klein, R. E. Separation protest in Guatemalan infants: Cross-cultural and cognitive findings. *Developmental Psychology,* 1974, *10,* 79–85.

Levine, M. I. A modern concept of breast feeding. *Journal of Pediatrics,* 1951, *38,* 472–475.

Levinson, B., & Reese, H. W. Patterns of discrimination learning set in preschool children, fifth-graders, college freshmen, and the aged. *Monographs of the Society for Research in Child Development,* 1967, *32,* Serial No. 115.

Lewis, M. Individual differences in the measurement of early cognitive growth. In J. Hellmuth (Ed.), *Exceptional infant.* Vol. 2: *Studies in abnormality.* New York: Brunner/Mazel, 1971.

Lewis, M., & Goldberg, S. Perceptual-cognitive development in infancy: A generalized expectancy model as a function of the mother-infant interaction. *Merrill-Palmer Quarterly,* 1969, *15,* 81–100.

Liberman, A. M. The grammars of speech and language. *Cognitive Psychology,* 1970, *1,* 301–323.

Lieberman, M. Early development stress and later behavior. *Science,* 1963, *141,* 824.

Liiamina, G. M. Mechanisms by which children master pronunciation during the second and third year. Third Macy Conference on the Central Nervous System and Behavior, Princeton, New Jersey, 1960.

Lindemann, E. Symptomatology and management of acute grief. In H. J. Parad (Ed.), *Crisis intervention: Selected readings*. New York: Family Service Association of America, 1965.

Lintz, L. M.; Fitzgerald, H. E.; & Brackbill, Y. Conditioning the eyeblink response to sound in infants. *Psychonomic Science*, 1967, *7*, 405–406.

Lipsitt, L. P.; Engen, T.; & Kaye, H. Developmental changes in olfactory threshold of the neonate. *Child Development*, 1963, *34*, 371–376.

Little, A. H. Eyelid conditioning in the human infant as a function of the interstimulus interval. Paper presented at the biennial meeting of the Society for Research in Child Development, Minneapolis, 1971.

Luria, A. R. *The role of speech in the regulation of normal and abnormal behavior*. London: Pergamon Press, 1961.

Maccoby, E. E., & Feldman, S.S. Mother-attachment and stranger reactions in the 3rd year of life. *Monographs of the Society for Research in Child Development*, 1972, *37*, Serial No. 146.

Maccoby, E. E., & Jacklin, C. N. Sex differences and their implications for sex roles. Paper presented at the annual meeting of the American Psychological Association, Washington, D.C., 1971.

Maccoby, E. E., & Jacklin, C. N. *The psychology of sex differences*. Stanford, Calif.: Stanford University Press, 1974.

Maccoby, E. E., & Masters, J. C. Attachment and dependency. In P. H. Mussen (Ed.), *Carmichael's manual of child psychology*. Vol. 2. New York: Wiley, 1970.

MacNamara, J. Cognitive basis of language learning in infants. *Psychological Review*, 1972, *79*, 1–13.

Makeyeva, O. *Prevention of maternal and infant disease*. Moscow: Foreign Language Publishing House, 1959.

Marquis, D. P. Learning in the neonate: The modification of behavior under three feeding schedules. *Journal of Experimental Psychology*, 1941, *29*, 263–282.

Mata, L. J.; Fernandez, R.; & Urrntia, J. J. Diarrheal disease in a cohort of Guatemalan village children observed from birth to age 2 years. *Tropical Geographic Medicine*, 1967, *19*, 247.

Maudry, M., & Nekula, M. Social relations between children of the same age during the first two years of life. *Journal of Genetic Psychology*, 1939, *54*, 193–215.

Maurer, A. What children fear. *Journal of Genetic Psychology*, 1965, *106*, 265–277.

McCall, R. B. Attention in the infant: Avenue to the study of cognitive development. In D. Walcher & D. L. Peters (Eds.), *Early childhood: The development of self-regulatory mechanisms*. New York: Academic Press, 1971.

McCall, R. B. Exploratory manipulation and play in the human infant. *Monographs of Society for Research in Child Development*, 1974, *39*, Serial No. 155.

McCarthy, D. Language development in children. In L. Carmichael (Ed.), *Manual of child psychology*. 2d ed. New York: Wiley, 1954.

McGraw, M. B. *The neuromuscular maturation of the human infant*. New York: Hafner, 1946.

McNeill, D. The development of language. In P. H. Mussen (Ed.), *Carmichael's manual of child psychology*. Vol. 1. New York: Wiley, 1970.

Meers, D. R., & Marans, A. E. Group care of infants in other countries. In Dittmann, L. L. (Ed.), *Early child care*. New York: Atherton Press, 1968.

Meredith, H. V. Body weight at birth of viable human infants: A worldwide comparative treatise. *Human Biology*, 1970, *42*, 217–264.

Mestyan, G., & Varga, F. Chemical thermoregulation of full-term and premature newborn infants. *Journal of Pediatrics*, 1960, *56*, 623–629.

Miller, L. B., & Dyer, J. L. Four preschool programs: Their dimensions and effects. *Monographs of the Society for Research in Child Development*, 1975, *40*, Serial No. 162.

Miller, W. S. A study of operant conditioning under delayed reinforcement in early infancy. *Monographs of the Society for*

Research in Child Development, 1972, *37,* Serial No. 147.

Miller, W. S., & Schaffer, H. R.   The influence of spatially displaced feedback on infant operant conditioning. *Journal of Experimental Child Psychology,* 1972, *14,* 442–453.

Miller, W. S., & Schaffer, H. R.   Visual-manipulative response strategies in infant operant conditioning with spatially displaced feedback. *British Journal of Psychology,* in press.

Moffitt, A.   Consonant cue perception by twenty- to twenty-four-week-old infants. *Child Development,* 1971, *42,* 717–731.

Moore, N. V.; Evertson, C. M.; & Brophy, J. E. Solitary play: Some functional considerations. *Developmental Psychology,* 1974, *10,* 830–834.

Moss, H. A.   Sex, age, and state as determinants of mother-infant interactions. *Merrill-Palmer Quarterly,* 1967, *13,* 19–36.

Naeye, R. L.   Structural correlates of fetal undernutrition. In H. A. Waisman & G. R. Kerr (Eds.). *Fetal growth and development.* New York: McGraw-Hill, 1970.

Naito, T., & Lipsitt, L. P.   Two attempts to condition eyelid responses in human infants. *Journal of Experimental Child Psychology,* 1969, *8,* 263–270.

Nash, J.   The father in contemporary culture and current psychological literature. *Child Development,* 1965, *36,* 261–297.

Neel, J. A.   The effect of exposure to the atomic bomb on pregnancy termination in Hiroshima and Nagasaki: Preliminary report. *Science,* 1953, *118,* 537–541.

Neisser, U.   *Cognitive psychology.* New York: Appleton-Century-Crofts, 1967.

Nelson, K.   Structure and strategy in learning to talk. *Monographs of the Society for Research in Child Development,* 1973, *37,* Serial No. 149.

Newton, N.   Psychologic differences between breast and bottle feeding. *American Journal of Clinical Nutrition,* 1971, *99,* 993–1004.

Olson, G. M.   An information processing analysis of visual memory and habituation in infants. In T. J. Tighe & R. N. Leaton (Eds.), *Habituation: Perspectives from child development, animal behav-*

ior, and neurophysiology. Hillsdale, N.J.: Lawrence Erlbaum Associates, 1976.

Overton, W. F., & Reese, H. W.   Models of development: Methodological implications. In J. R. Nesselroade & H. W. Reese (Eds.), *Life-span developmental psychology: Methodological issues.* New York: Academic Press, 1973.

Papousek, H.   Conditioned head rotation reflexes in infants in the first months of life. *Acta Paediatrica,* 1961, *50,* 565–576.

Papousek, H., & Papousek, M.   Mirror image and self recognition in young human infants. 1. A new method of experimental analysis. *Developmental Psychobiology,* 1974, *7,* 149–157.

Parten, M. B.   Social participation among pre-school children. *Journal of Abnormal and Social Psychology,* 1932, *27,* 243–269.

Pavlov, I. P.   *Conditional reflexes.* London: Oxford University Press, 1927.

Pederson, D. R., & Vrugt, D. T.   The influence of amplitude and frequency of vestibular stimulation on the activity of two-month-old infants. *Child Development,* 1973, *44,* 122–128.

Pederson, F. A., & Robson, K. S.   Father participation in infancy. *American Journal of Orthopsychiatry,* 1969, *39,* 466–472.

Piaget, J.   *The origins of intelligence in children.* New York: International Universities Press, 1952.

Piaget, J.   *Six psychological studies.* New York: Random House, 1967.

Piaget, J.   *The mechanisms of perception.* New York: Basic Books, 1969.

Piaget, J.   Piaget's theory. In P. Mussen (Ed.), *Carmichael's manual of child psychology.* Vol. 1. New York: Wiley, 1970.

Pratt, K. C.; Nelson, A. K.; & Sun, K. H.   *The behavior of the newborn infant.* Columbus: Ohio State University Press, 1930.

Premack, D.   Language in chimpanzee? *Science,* 1971, *172,* 808–822.

Przetacznikowa, M.   A study in the use of the longitudinal method for investigating the verbal behavior of children of preschool age. In F. J. Monks, W. W. Hartup, & J. de Wit (Eds.), *Determinants of behavioral development.* New York: Academic Press, 1972.

Rabin, A. I. Motivation for parenthood. *Journal of Projective Techniques and Personality Assessment,* 1965, *29,* 405–411.

Radin, N. Observed paternal behaviors as antecedents of intellectual functioning in young boys. *Developmental Psychology,* 1973, *8,* 369–376.

Ramey, C. T., & Ourth, L. L. Delayed reinforcement and vocalization rates of infants. *Child Development,* 1971, *42,* 291–297.

Ranson, S. W., & Clark, S. L. *The anatomy of the nervous system: Its development and function.* Philadelphia: Saunders, 1959.

Rebelsky, F. G., & Hanks, C. Fathers' verbal interaction with infants in the first three months of life. *Child Development,* 1971, *42,* 63–68.

Reese, H. W., & Overton, W. F. Models of development and theories of development. In L. R. Goulet & P. B. Baltes (Eds.), *Life-span developmental psychology.* New York: Academic Press, 1970.

Rheingold, H. L. The social and socializing infant. In D. A. Goslin (Ed.), *Handbook of socialization: Theory and research.* Chicago: Rand McNally, 1968.

Rheingold, H. L., & Cook, K. V. The contents of boys' and girls' rooms as an index of parents' behavior. *Child Development,* 1975, *46,* 459–463.

Rheingold, H. L., & Eckerman, C. O. The infant separates himself from his mother. *Science,* 1970, *168,* 78–83.

Rheingold, H. L., & Eckerman, C. O. Fear of the stranger: A critical examination. In H. W. Reese (Ed.), *Advances in child development and behavior.* New York: Academic Press, 1973.

Rheingold, H. L.; Gewirtz, J. L.; & Ross, H. W. Social conditioning of vocalizations in infants. *Journal of Comparative and Physiological Psychology,* 1959, *52,* 68–73.

Rhodes, P. Sex of fetus in antepartum hemorrhage. *Lancet,* 1965, *2,* 718–719.

Richards, M. P. M., & Bernal, J. F. Social interactions in the first days of life. In H. R. Schaffer (Ed.), *The origins of human social relations.* New York: Academic Press, 1971.

Roberts, P. Foreword. In G. Wilson (Ed), *A linguistics reader.* New York: Harper & Row, 1967.

Robinson, H. B., & Robinson, N. M. Longitudinal development of very young children in a comprehensive day care program: The first two years. *Child Development,* 1971, *42,* 1673–1684.

Robson, K. S. The role of eye-to-eye contact in maternal-infant attachment. *Journal of Child Psychology and Psychiatry,* 1967, *8,* 13–25.

Roffwarg, H. P.; Muzio, J. N.; & Dement, W. C. Ontogenetic development of the human sleep-dream cycle. *Science,* 1966, *152,* 604–619.

Rosenzweig, M. R. Effects of environment on development of brain and of behavior. In E. Tobach, L. R. Aronson, & E. Shaw (Eds.), *The biopsychology of development.* New York: Academic Press, 1971.

Rotter, J. B. *Social learning and clinical psychology.* Englewood Cliffs, N.J.: Prentice-Hall, 1954.

Rotter, J. B. Generalized expectancies for internal versus external control of reinforcement. *Psychological Monographs,* 1966, *80,* 1–28.

Routh, D. K. Conditioning of vocal response differentiation in infants. *Developmental Psychology,* 1969, *1,* 219–226.

Rovee, C. K. Psychophysical scaling of olfactory response to the aliphatic alcohols in human neonates. *Journal of Experimental Child Psychology,* 1969, *7,* 245–254.

Rovee, C. K. Olfactory cross-adaptation and facilitation in human neonates. *Journal of Experimental Child Psychology,* 1972, *13,* 368–381.

Rovee, C. K.; Cohen, R. Y.; & Shlapack, W. Life span stability in olfactory sensitivity. *Developmental Psychology,* 1975, *11,* 311–318.

Saayman, G.; Ames, E. W.; & Moffett, A. Response to novelty as an indicator of visual discrimination in the human infant. *Journal of Experimental Child Psychology,* 1964, *1,* 189–198.

Salk, L. The role of the heart beat in the relations between mother and infant. *Scientific American,* 1973, *228,* 24–29.

Sander, L. Regulation and organization in

the early infant-caretaker system. In R. J. Robinson (Ed.), *Brain and early behavior.* New York: Academic Press, 1969.

Scarr, S., & Salapatek, P.   Patterns of fear development during infancy. *Merrill-Palmer Quarterly,* 1970, *16,* 53–90.

Scarr-Salapatek, S.   Race, social class, and IQ. *Science,* 1971, *174,* 1285–1295.

Schaefer, E. S.   A configurational analysis of children's reports of parent behavior. *Journal of Consulting Psychology,* 1965, *29,* 552–557.

Schaefer, E. S.   Need for early and continuing education. In V. H. Denenberg (Ed.), *Education of the infant and young child.* New York: Academic Press, 1970.

Schaefer, E. S.   Parents as educators: Evidence from cross-sectional, longitudinal and intervention research. *Young Children,* 1972, *27,* 227–239.

Schaffer, H. R.   Objective observations of personality development in early infancy. *British Journal of Medical Psychology,* 1958, *31,* 174–183.

Schaffer, H. R.   *The growth of sociability.* Baltimore: Penguin Books, 1971.

Schaffer, H. R., & Emerson, P. E.   The development of social attachments in infancy. *Monographs of the Society for Research in Child Development,* 1964, *29,* Serial No. 94. (a)

Schaffer, H. R., & Emerson, P. E.   Patterns of response to physical contact in early human development. *Journal of Child Psychology and Psychiatry,* 1964, *5,* 1–13. (b)

Schaffer, H. R., & Parry, M. H.   Perceptual-motor behavior in infancy as a function of age and stimulus familiarity. *British Journal of Psychology,* 1969, *60,* 1–9.

Schaffer, H. R., & Parry, M. H.   The effects of short-term familiarization on infants' perceptual-motor coordination in a simultaneous discrimination situation. *British Journal of Psychology,* 1970, *61,* 559–569.

Schaie, K. W.   A general model for the study of developmental problems. *Psychological Bulletin,* 1965, *64,* 92–107.

Schwartz, A.; Rosenberg, D.; & Brackbill, Y.   An analysis of the components of social reinforcement of infant vocalizations. *Psychonomic Science,* 1970, *20,* 323–325.

Scott, J. P.   *Early experience and the organization of behavior.* Belmont, Calif.: Brooks/Cole, 1968.

Scott, J. P.; Stewart, J. M.; & De Ghett, V. J.   Critical periods in the organization of systems. *Developmental Psychobiology,* 1974, *7,* 489–513.

Sears, P. S., & Dowley, E. M.   Research on teaching in the nursery school. In N. L. Gage (Ed.), *Handbook of research on teaching.* Skokie, Ill.: Rand McNally, 1963.

Sears, R. R., Dollard, J., et al.   *Frustration and aggression.* New Haven: Yale University Press, 1941.

Sears, R. R.; Maccoby, E. E.; & Levin, H.   *Patterns of child rearing.* New York: Harper & Row, 1957.

Shaffran, K., & Gouin-DeCarie, T.   Short term stability of infants' responses to strangers. Paper presented at the meeting of the Society for Research in Child Development, Philadelphia, March 1973.

Sherman, L. W.   An ecological study of glee in small groups of preschool· children. *Child Development,* 1975, *46,* 53–61.

Shipiro, H.   The development of walking in a child. *Journal of Genetic Psychology,* 1962, *100,* 221–226.

Shirley, M. M.   *The first two years: A study of twenty-five babies.* Vol. 1: *Postural and locomotor development.* Institute of Child Welfare Monograph, Series No. 6. Minneapolis: University of Minnesota Press, 1931.

Sigel, I. E.   Developmental trends in the abstraction ability of children. *Child Development,* 1953, *24,* 131–144.

Sigel, I. E.   The distancing hypothesis: A causal hypothesis for the acquisition of representational thought. In M. R. Jones (Ed.), *The effects of early experience.* Miami, Fla.: University of Miami Press, 1970.

Sigel, I. E.   The distancing hypothesis revisited: An elaboration of a neo-Piagetian view of the development of representational thought. In M. E. Meyer (Ed.), *Cognitive learning.* Bellingham: Western Washington State College Press, 1972.

Sigel, I. E., & McBane, B.   Cognitive competence and level of symbolization among five-year-old children. In J. Hellmuth (Ed.), *Disadvantaged child.* Vol 1. New York: Brunner/Mazel, 1967.

Simner, M. L. Newborn's response to the cry of another infant. *Developmental Psychology*, 1971, *5*, 136–150.

Simpson, G. G. *The meaning of evolution.* New Haven: Yale University Press, 1949.

Siqueland, E. Reinforcement patterns and extinction in human newborns. *Journal of Experimental Child Psychology*, 1968. *6*, 431–442.

Skinner, B. F. *The behavior of organisms.* New York: Appleton-Century-Crofts, 1938.

Slobin, D. I. Developmental psycholinguistics. In W. O. Dingwall (Ed.), *A survey of linguistic science.* College Park, Md.: William Orr Dingwall, Linguistics Program, University of Maryland, 1971.

Smith, M. E. An investigation of the development of the sentence and the extent of vocabulary in young children. *University of Iowa Studies in Child Welfare*, 1926, *3*, No. 5.

Smith, M. E. Measurement of vocabularies of young bilingual children in both of the languages used. *Journal of Genetic Psychology*, 1949, *74*, 305–310.

Smith, M. E., & Kasdin, L. M. Progress in the use of English after 20 years by children of Filipino and Japanese ancestry in Hawaii. *Journal of Genetic Psychology*, 1961, *99*, 129–138.

Sokolov, Ye. N. *Perception and the conditioned reflex.* New York: Macmillan, 1963.

Sontag, L. W. Maternal anxiety during pregnancy and fetal behavior. *Report on the 26th Ross Pediatric Research Conference*, 1957.

Sontag, L. W., & Richards, T. W. Studies of fetal behavior. 1. Fetal HR as a behavior indicator. *Monographs of the Society for Research in Child Development*, 1938, *3*, Serial No. 5.

Spears, W. C. Assessment of visual preference and discrimination in the four-month-old infant. *Journal of Comparative and Physiological Psychology*, 1964, *57*, 381–386.

Spears, W. C., & Hohle, R. H. Sensory and perceptual processes in infants. In Y. Brackbill (Ed.) *Infancy and early childhood.* New York: Free Press, 1967.

Spelke, E.; Zelazo, P.; Kagan, J.; & Kotelchuck, M. Father interaction and separation protest. *Developmental Psychology*, 1973, *9*, 83–90.

Sperry, R. W. Mechanisms of neural maturation. In S. S. Stevens (Ed.), *Handbook of experimental psychology.* New York: Wiley, 1951.

Spitz, R. A. Anxiety in infancy: A study of its manifestations in the first year of life. *International Journal of Psychoanalysis*, 1950, *31*, 132–143.

Spitz, R. A. *The first year of life.* New York: International Universities Press, 1965.

Sroufe, L. A., & Wunsch, J. P. The development of laughter in the first year of life. *Child Development*, 1972, *43*, 1326–1344.

Staats, A. W.; Brewer, B. A.; & Gross, M. C. Learning and cognitive development: Representative samples, cumulative-hierarchical learning, and experimental longitudinal methods. *Monographs of the Society for Research in Child Development*, 1970, *35*, Serial No. 141.

Stechler, G. Newborn attention as affected by medication during labor. *Science*, 1964, *144*, 315–317.

Stephen, M. W., & Delys, P. A locus of control measure for preschool children. *Developmental Psychology*, 1973, *9*, 55–65.

Stern, D. N. Mother and infant at play: The dyadic interaction involving facial, vocal, and gaze behaviors. In M. Lewis & L. A. Rosenblum (Eds.), *The effect of the infant on its caregiver.* New York: Wiley-Interscience, 1974.

Stevenson, M. B., & Fitzgerald, H. E. Standards for day care in the United States and Canada. *Child Care Quarterly*, 1972, *1*, 89–111.

Stevenson. R. E. *The fetus and newly born infant.* St. Louis: Mosby, 1973.

Stoch, M. B., & Smythe, P. M. Undernutrition during infancy, subsequent brain growth and intellectual development. In A. E. Scrimshaw & J. E. Gordon (Eds.), *Mal-*

nutrition, learning, and behavior. Cambridge, Mass.: MIT Press, 1968.

Stokoe, W. C.; Casterline, D.; & Croneberg, C. C. A dictionary of American Sign Language. Washington, D.C.: Gallaudet College Press, 1965.

Stott, L. H., & Ball, R. S. Infant and preschool mental tests: Review and evaluation. Monographs of the Society for Research in Child Development, 1965, 30, Serial No. 101.

Strommen, E. A. Verbal self-regulation in a children's game: Impulsive errors on Simon Says. Child Development, 1973, 44, 849–853.

Sutton-Smith, B. Children at play. Natural History, December, 1971.

Sutton-Smith, B.; Rosenberg, B. G.; & Landy, F. Father-absence effects on families of different sibling compositions. Child Development, 1968, 39, 1213–1221.

Taft, L. T., & Cohen, H. J. Neonatal and infant reflexology. In J. Hellmuth (Ed.), Exceptional infant. Vol. 1: The normal infant. New York: Brunner/Mazel, 1967.

Tasch, R. J. The role of the father in the family. Journal of Experimental Education. 1952, 20, 319–361.

Taussig, H. B. The thalidomide syndrome. Scientific American, 1962, 207, 29–35.

Tennes, K. H., & Lample, E. E. Stranger and separation anxiety in infancy. Journal of Nervous and Mental Disease, 1964, 139, 247–254.

Thomas, A.; Chess, S.; & Birch, H. G. Temperament and behavior disorders in children. New York: New York University Press, 1968.

Thompson, S. K. Gender labels and early sex role development. Child Development, 1975, 46, 339–347.

Trout, G., Jr. A competency base for curriculum development in preschool education. Vols. 1–4. Charleston, W.V.: Appalachia Educational Laboratory, 1975.

Turkewitz, G.; Gordon, E. W.; & Birch, H. G. Head turning in the human neonate: Spontaneous patterns. Journal of Genetic Psychology, 1965, 107, 143–158.

Uzgiris, I. C. Patterns of vocal and gestural imitation in infants. In F. J. Monks, W. W. Hartup, & J. DeWitt (Eds.), Determinants of behavioral development. New York: Academic Press, 1972.

Vygotsky, L. S. Thought and language. Cambridge, Mass.: MIT Press, 1962.

Wagner, M. G., & Wagner, M. M. Day care programs in Denmark and Czechoslovakia. In E. H. Grotberg (Ed.), Day care: Resources for decisions. Washington, D.C.: United States Public Health Service, Office of Economic Opportunity, 1971.

Warner, F. The children: How to study them. London: Hodgson, 1887.

Wasz-Hockert, O.; Partanen, T.; Vuorenkoski, V.; Valanne, E.; & Michelson, K. Effect of training on ability to differentiate preverbal vocalizations. Developmental Medicine and Child Neurology, 1964, 6, 393–396.

Waters, E.; Matas, L.; & Sroufe, L. A. Infants' reactions to an approaching stranger: Description, validation and functional significance of wariness. Child Development. 1975, 46, 348–356.

Watson, J. B. Psychological care of infant and child. New York: Norton, 1928.

Watson, J. B., & Rayner, R. Conditioned emotional reactions. Journal of Experimental Psychology, 1920, 3, 1–14.

Watson, J. S. Memory and "contingency analysis" in infant learning. Merrill-Palmer Quarterly, 1967, 13, 55–76.

Weikart, D. P., & Lambie, D. Z. Early enrichment in infants. In V. H. Denenberg (Ed.), Education of the infant and young child. New York: Academic Press, 1970.

Weiner, B. From each according to his abilities: The role of effort in a moral society. Human Development, 1973, 16, 53–60.

Weisberg, P. Social and nonsocial conditioning of infant vocalizations. Child Development, 1963, 34, 377–388.

Weisberg, P., & Fink, E. Fixed ratio and extinction performance of infants in their second year of life. Journal of the Experimental Analysis of Behavior, 1966, 9, 105–109.

Weisberg, P., & Tragakis, C. J. Analysis of DRL behavior in young children. Psychological Reports, 1967, 21, 709–715.

Werner, E. E.; Honzik, M. P.; & Smith, R. S. Prediction of intelligence and achievement at 10 years from twenty months prediatric and psychological examinations. *Child Development*, 1968, *39*, 1063—1075.

Werner, H. *Comparative psychology of mental development.* New York: Interternational Universities Press, 1948.

Wertheimer, M. Psychomotor coordination of auditory and visual space at birth. *Science*, 1961, *134*, 1823.

White, B. L.; Watts, J. C.; et al. *Experience and environment.* Vol. 1. Englewood Cliffs, N.J.: Prentice-Hall, 1973.

White, R. W. Ego and reality in psychoanalytic theory: A proposal regarding independent ego energies. *Psychological Issues.* Vol. 3. New York: International Universities Press, 1963.

White, S. H. Evidence for a hierarchical arrangement of learning processes. In L. P. Lipsitt & C. C. Spiker (Eds.), *Advances in child development and behavior.* Vol. 2. New York: Academic Press, 1965.

Whiting, B., & Edwards, C. P. A cross-cultural analysis of sex differences in the behavior of children aged three through eleven. *Journal of Social Psychology*, 1973, *91*, 188–201.

Whiting, J. W. M., & Child, I. L. *Child training and personality.* New Haven: Yale University Press, 1953.

Wiener, G.; Rider, R. V.; Oppel, W. C.; Fischer, L. K.; & Harper, P. A. Correlates of low birth weight: Psychological status at six to seven years of age. *Pediatrics*, 1965, *35*, 434–444.

Willerman, L.; Broman, S. H.; & Fielder, M. Infant development, preschool IQ, and social class. *Child Development*, 1970, *41*, 69–77.

Winick, M. & Rosso, P. The effect of early severe malnutrition in cellular growth of human brain. *Pediatric Research*, 1963, *3*, 181–184.

Wolff, P. H. The causes, controls, and organization of behavior in the neonate. *Psychological Issues.* New York: International Universities Press, 1966.

Wolff, P. H. The role of biological rhythms in early psychological development. *Bulletin of the Menninger Clinic*, 1967, *31*, 197–218.

Wolff, P. H. Stereotypic behavior and development. *Canadian Psychologist*, 1968, *9*, 474–485.

World Health Organization. Public health aspects of low birth weight. *Technical Report Series*, 1961, No. 217.

Yamazaki, J. N.; Wright, S. W.; & Wright, P. M. Outcome of pregnancy in women exposed to atomic blast in Nagasaki. *American Journal of Diseases of Children*, 1954, *87*, 448–463.

Young, F. M. An analysis of certain variables in a developmental study of language. *Genetic Psychology Monographs*, 1941, *23*, 3–141.

Zaporozhets, A. V. The development of perception in the preschool child. In P. Mussen (Ed.), European research in child development. *Monographs of the Society for Research in Child Development*, 1965, *30*, Serial No. 100.

Zeaman, D., & House, B. J. The role of attention in retardate discrimination learning. In N. R. Ellis (Ed.), *Handbook of mental deficiency.* New York: McGraw-Hill, 1963.

Zelazo, P. R.; Zelazo, N. A.; & Kolb, S. "Walking" in the newborn. *Science*, 1972, *176*, 314–315.

Ziai, M.; Janeway, C. A.; & Cooke, R. E. (Eds.). *Pediatrics*, Boston: Little, Brown, 1969.

INDEXES

INDEXES

AUTHOR INDEX

SUBJECT INDEX

293

*This book has been set in 9 and 8 point Optima,
leaded 2 points. Part numbers and titles are in 24
point (large) Optima. Chapter numbers are in 54
point Weiss Series I and chapter titles are in 24 point
(small) Optima. The size of the type page is 26 by
47½ picas.*